STUDIES IN WELSH HISTORY

Editors

RALPH A. GRIFFITHS   CHRIS WILLIAMS
ERYN M. WHITE

21

WAR AND SOCIETY IN MEDIEVAL WALES, 633–1283

WAR AND SOCIETY IN MEDIEVAL WALES, 633–1283

WELSH MILITARY INSTITUTIONS

by

SEAN DAVIES

UNIVERSITY OF WALES PRESS

© Sean Davies, 2004

Reprinted 2014, 2022, 2023, 2025

All rights reserved. No part of this book may be reproduced in any material form (including photocopying or storing it in any medium by electronic means and whether or not transiently or incidentally to some other use of this publication) without the written permission of the copyright owner. Applications for the copyright owner's written permission to reproduce any part of this publication should be addressed to the University of Wales Press, 10 Columbus Walk, Brigantine Place, Cardiff CF10 4UP.

www.uwp.co.uk

British Library CIP Data
A catalogue record for this book is available from the British Library

ISBN 978-1-78316-139-3

eISBN 978-1-78316-142-3

The right of Sean Davies to be identified as author of this work has been asserted by him in accordance with sections 77 and 79 of the Copyright, Designs and Patents Act 1988.

Printed and bound by CPI Group (UK) Ltd, Croydon, CR0 4YY

EDITORS' FOREWORD

Since the Second World War, Welsh history has attracted considerable scholarly attention and enjoyed a vigorous popularity. Not only have the approaches, both traditional and new, to the study of history in general been successfully applied to Wales's past, but the number of scholars engaged in this enterprise has multiplied during these years. These advances have been especially marked in the University of Wales.

In order to make more widely available the conclusions of recent research, much of it of limited accessibility in postgraduate dissertations and theses, in 1977 the History and Law Committee of the Board of Celtic Studies inaugurated a new series of monographs, *Studies in Welsh History*. It was anticipated that many of the volumes would originate in research conducted in the University of Wales or under the auspices of the Board of Celtic Studies. But the series does not exclude significant contributions made by researchers in other universities and elsewhere. Its primary aim is to serve historical scholarship and to encourage the study of Welsh history. Each volume so far published has fulfilled that aim in ample measure, and it is a pleasure to welcome the most recent addition to the list.

CONTENTS

EDITORS' FOREWORD	v
ACKNOWLEDGEMENTS	ix
ABBREVIATIONS	x
MAP OF MEDIEVAL WALES	xiv

	INTRODUCTION	1
I	THE *TEULU*	14
II	THE *LLU*	50
III	CAMPAIGN STRATEGY AND TACTICS	85
IV	EQUIPMENT AND TACTICAL DISPOSITIONS	143
V	FORTIFICATIONS	190
VI	CONDUCT IN WARFARE	218
	CONCLUSION	259

BIBLIOGRAPHY	264
INDEX	277

ACKNOWLEDGEMENTS

To begin at the beginning, my undying love and gratitude for the genesis of this work must go to my parents, Jim and Monica, and my brother, Mike. Without their support in all areas of my life I could never have completed an undergraduate degree, much less a Ph.D. Peter Williams – the finest teacher anyone could wish for – first awakened my taste for history at Bishop Hedley High School, Merthyr Tydfil. At the University of Wales Swansea, the teaching and guidance of Ifor Rowlands and Professor John France were invaluable. They set me on the course for this study, and their insight and expertise have been inspiring. I would like to thank the History Department of Cardiff University for providing the funding and backing to allow me to take my studies into a Ph.D. Since then the attention and scholarship of my tutors – Professor Gwynfor Jones and Dr Kari Maund – have been vital in giving the work focus and direction. The interest shown by Professor Ralph Griffiths in publishing this book was both flattering and inspiring, and his probing analysis of the drafts always offered fresh insights. Finally, I would like to thank Ruth Dennis-Jones and all the staff at the University of Wales Press for their exertions in hammering my text into something fit for publication.

Sean Davies

ABBREVIATIONS

AC	*Annales Cambriae*
Age	R. R. Davies, *The Age of Conquest, Wales 1063–1415* (Oxford, 1991)
ANS	*Anglo Norman Studies*
ANW	M. J. Strickland (ed.), *Anglo-Norman Warfare* (Woodbridge, 1992)
AP	I. Williams (ed.), *Armes Prydein o Lyfr Taliesin* (Cardiff, 1955), Eng. vers. R. Bromwich, (Dublin, 1972)
Arch. Camb.	*Archaeologia Cambrensis*
ASC	*The Anglo-Saxon Chronicle*, ed. and trans. D. Whitelock (London, 1961). All given dates follow this edition
Asser	Asser, *Life of King Alfred*, in S. Keynes and M. Lapidge (ed. and trans.), *Alfred the Great* (Harmondsworth, 1983)
BBCS	*Bulletin of the Board of Celtic Studies*
Bede	*Bede's Ecclesiastical History of the English People*, ed. and trans. B. Colgrave and R. A. B. Mynors (Oxford, 1969)
Beginnings	I. Williams, *The Beginnings of Welsh Poetry*, ed. R. Bromwich (2nd edn, Cardiff, 1980)
BIHR	*Bulletin of the Institute of Historical Research*
BM	*Breuddwyd Maxen*, ed. I. Williams (3rd edn, Bangor, 1928)
BR	*Breudwyt Ronabwy*, ed. G. Melville Richards (Cardiff, 1948)
Bren.	*Brenhinedd y Saesson or The Kings of the Saxons*, ed. and trans. T. Jones (Cardiff, 1971). All year references are to the amended dates given by Jones
Brut (Pen. 20)	*Brut y Tywysogyon or The Chronicle of the Princes, Peniarth MS. 20 Version*, ed. and trans. T. Jones (Cardiff, 1952). All year references are to the amended dates given by Jones
Brut (RBH)	*Brut y Tywysogyon or The Chronicle of the Princes, Red Book of Hergest Version*, ed. and trans. T. Jones (Cardiff, 1955). All year references are to the amended dates given by Jones
CaO	*Culhwch ac Olwen*, ed. R. Bromwich and D. Simon Evans (Cardiff, 1992)
CBT	R. G. Gruffydd (ed.), *Cyfres Beirdd y Tywysogyon*, 7 vols (Cardiff, 1991–6). The modern Welsh renderings are quoted

ABBREVIATIONS

Chrons.	Howlett, R. (ed.), *Chronicles of the Reigns of Stephen, Henry II, and Richard I*, 4 vols (Rolls Series, London, 1884–9)
CMCS	*Cambrian / Cambridge Medieval Celtic Studies*
Conquest	Gerald of Wales, *Expugnatio Hibernica / The Conquest of Ireland*, ed. and trans. A. B. Scott and F. X. Martin (Dublin, 1978)
CT	I. Williams (ed.), *Canu Taliesin* (Cardiff, 1960)
CW	T. Jones (ed.), '*Cronica de Wallia* and other documents from Exeter Cathedral Library Ms. 3514', *BBCS*, 12 (1946–8), 27–44
Defences	G. R. J. Jones, 'The defences of Gwynedd in the thirteenth century', *TCHS*, 30 (1969), 29–43
Description	Gerald of Wales, *The Description of Wales*, ed. and trans. L. Thorpe, (Harmondsworth, 1978)
Dulliau	A. D. Carr, 'Dulliau rhyfel yr Arglwydd Rhys', in N. A. Jones and H. Pryce (eds.), *Yr Arglwydd Rhys* (Cardiff, 1996), pp. 76–93
Earliest	J. P. Clancy, *The Earliest Welsh Poetry* (London, 1970)
EHR	*English Historical Review*
FH	*Flores Historiarum*, ed. H. R. Luard, 3 vols (Rolls Series, London, 1890)
GC	K. L. Maund (ed.), *Gruffudd ap Cynan: A Collaborative Biography* (Woodbridge, 1996)
Gildas	Gildas, *The Ruin of Britain and Other Works*, ed. and trans. M. Winterbottom (London, 1978)
Gododdin	Aneirin, *Y Gododdin*, ed. and trans. A. O. H. Jarman (Llandysul, 1988)
Gruffudd ap Cynan	*A Mediaeval Prince of Wales: The Life of Gruffudd ap Cynan*, ed. and trans. D. Simon Evans (Llanerch, 1990)
GS	*Gesta Stephani*, ed. and trans. K. R. Potter and R. H. C. Davis (2nd edn, Oxford, 1976)
Handlist	K. L. Maund, *Handlist of the Acts of Native Welsh Rulers, 1132–1283* (Cardiff, 1996)
HB	*Historia Brittonum*, in J. Morris (ed. and trans.), *Nennius: British History and the Welsh Annals* (London, 1980)
HH	Henry of Huntingdon, *Historia Anglorum*, ed. and trans. D. Greenway (Oxford, 1996)
Horse	Sioned Davies and N. A. Jones (eds.), *The Horse in Celtic Culture: Medieval Welsh Perspectives* (Cardiff, 1997)
HW	J. E. Lloyd, *A History of Wales from the Earliest Times to the Edwardian Conquest*, 2 vols (3rd edn, London, 1939)
Journey	Gerald of Wales, *The Journey through Wales*, ed. and trans. L. Thorpe (Harmondsworth, 1978)

JW	*The Chronicle of John of Worcester*, ed. R. R. Darlington and P. McGurk, trans. J. Bray and P. McGurk, 3 vols (Oxford, 1995–). All given dates follow this edition
Law	D. Jenkins (ed. and trans.), *The Law of Hywel Dda* (Llandysul, 1986)
LG	J. B. Smith, *Llywelyn ap Gruffudd, Prince of Wales* (Cardiff, 1998)
Life of King Edward	*The Life of King Edward (who rests at Westminster, attributed to a monk of Saint Bertin)*, ed. and trans. F. Barlow (2nd edn, Oxford, 1992)
LL	J. G. Evans (ed.), *The Text of the Book of Llan Dâv* (Oxford, 1893)
Lludd	*Cyfranc Lludd a Llevelys*, ed. I. Williams (2nd edn, Bangor, 1932)
Mabinogi	*The Mabinogion*, ed. and trans. J. Gantz (Harmondsworth, 1976)
Map	Walter Map, *De Nugis Curialium / Courtiers' Trifles*, ed. and trans. M. R. James, C. N. L. Brooke and R. A. B. Mynors (Oxford, 1983)
Meilyr	J. E. Caerwyn Williams, 'Meilyr Brydydd and Gruffudd ap Cynan', in *GC*, pp. 165–86
Military	G. R. J. Jones, 'The military geography of Gwynedd in the thirteenth century' (unpublished MA thesis, University of Wales Aberystwyth, 1949)
MP	*Mattoei Parisiensis, Monachi Sancti Albani, Chronica Majora*, ed. H. R. Luard, 7 vols (Rolls Series, London, 1872–83)
MP (T)	*Matthew Paris' English History*, ed. and trans. J. A. Giles, 3 vols (London, 1852–4)
NLWJ	*National Library of Wales Journal*
OV	Orderic Vitalis, *Historia Ecclesiastica*, ed. and trans. M. Chibnall, 6 vols (Oxford, 1969–80)
Owein	*'Owein' or 'Chwedyl Iarlles y Ffynnawn'*, ed. R. L. Thomson (Dublin, 1968)
P&P	*Past and Present*
PBA	*Proceedings of the British Academy*
PK	I. Williams (ed.), *Pedeir Keinc y Mabinogi* (Cardiff, 1930)
PR	*Pipe Roll*
RH	*Magistri Rogeri de Houedene*, ed. W. Stubbs, 4 vols (Rolls Series, London, 1868–71)
RH (T)	*The Annals of Roger de Hoveden*, ed. and trans. H. T. Riley, 2 vols (London, 1853)
RW	Roger of Wendover, *Flores Historiarum*, ed. H. G. Hewlett, 3 vols (Rolls Series, London, 1886–9)

ABBREVIATIONS

RW (T)	Roger of Wendover, *Flowers of History*, ed. and trans. J. A. Giles, 2 vols (London, 1849)
Saga	J. Rowland, *Early Welsh Saga Poetry* (Cambridge, 1990)
Stanzas	T. Jones, 'The Black Book of Carmarthen *Stanzas of the Graves*', *PBA*, 53 (1967), 97–137
TCHS	*Transactions of the Caernarvonshire Historical Society*
THSC	*Transactions of the Honourable Society of Cymmrodorion*
TRHS	*Transactions of the Royal Historical Society*
Triads	*Trioedd Ynys Prydein / The Welsh Triads*, ed. and trans. R. Bromwich (2nd edn, Cardiff, 1978)
TWNFC	*Transactions of the Woolhope Naturalists Field Club*
Vegetius	Vegetius, *De Re Militari*, ed. C. Lang (Leipzig, 1885), trans. in T. R. Phillips, *The Roots of Strategy* (London, 1943)
Vitae	A. W. Wade-Evans (ed. and trans.), *Vitae Sanctorum Britanniae et Genealogiae* (Cardiff, 1944)
Welsh Poems	G. Williams, *Welsh Poems, Sixth Century to 1600* (London, 1973)
Welsh Verse	T. Conran, *Welsh Verse* (2nd edn, Southampton, 1986)
WHR	*Welsh History Review*
WM	William of Malmesbury, *Gesta Regum Anglorum / The History of the English Kings*, ed. and trans. R. A. B. Mynors, R. M. Thomson and M. Winterbottom (Oxford, 1998)
WN	William of Newburgh, *The History of England*, in *English Historical Documents II*, ed. D. C. Douglas (London, 1968)
WVIE	G. Jones, *The Oxford Book of Welsh Verse in English* (Oxford, 1983)
WW	J. France, *Western Warfare in the Age of the Crusades, 1000–1300* (London, 1999)

Map of Medieval Wales

INTRODUCTION

Dominant perceptions of Wales in the Middle Ages still tend to be formed from the accessible descriptions of Gerald of Wales. With regard to warfare, we may picture a poor and simple – yet proud and ferocious – people, heroically defending their homeland in the face of invasion from the powerful neighbouring English state. In Gerald's words, 'not only the leaders but the entire nation are trained for war. Sound the trumpet for battle and the peasant will rush from his plough to pick up his weapons as quickly as the courtier from the court.'[1] This image suited the Welsh of later generations, who were happy to stress the uniqueness of their land and the heroics of their forebears. It also suited the conquerors of Wales, who could be seen as the bringers of 'civilization'.

Developments in Welsh historiography have advanced our knowledge of the country in the Middle Ages. There has been a movement away from the view of medieval Wales as a nation of free, footloose pastoralists who acknowledged no social superiors and avoided fixed settlements.[2] Studies include Wales in the mainstream of historical development in post-Roman Europe, discrediting earlier views of the country which portrayed it as different, even unique.[3] This more realistic approach to Welsh history has yet to be applied to military history; a picture still holds true of poor, free Welsh warriors drawn from the entire community who defended their homeland with ferocity but little professional skill. In this respect Welsh historiography has not kept pace with studies of military history elsewhere in Europe that see medieval armies and commanders as pragmatic, professional and skilled. Whilst allowing for differences given the

[1] Gerald of Wales, *The Journey through Wales/The Description of Wales*, ed. and trans. L. Thorpe (Harmondsworth 1978): *Description*, I, 8, p. 233.
[2] For this view of Wales, see F. Seebohm, *The Tribal System in Wales* (2nd edn, London, 1904).
[3] See, for example, K. R. Dark, *Civitas to Kingdom: British Political Continuity, 300–800* (Leicester, 1984); W. Davies, *Wales in the Early Middle Ages* (Leicester, 1982); R. R. Davies, *The Age of Conquest: Wales, 1063–1415* (Oxford, 1991).

nature, economy, geography and topography of the country, it can be seen that Welsh military developments from the end of Roman rule to the Edwardian Conquest generally corresponded with those seen in the rest of western Europe. A critical approach should also be taken to the suggestion that warfare in Wales was more brutal and 'barbaric' than elsewhere, with atrocities a commonplace phenomenon.

This study takes a thematic rather than chronological approach to Welsh military institutions, examining the social structure that put forces in the field and the actions of the troops on campaign. The organization of Welsh troops is considered through an analysis of the essential household force (the *teulu*), and the expanded army (the *llu*). Strategy, tactics and equipment in the field are considered, with a chapter dedicated to fortifications. The study closes with an examination of Welsh conduct in warfare and of whether accusations of 'barbarism' directed at them are justified. The chronology of the work takes Wales's history from the earliest post-Roman developments to the conquest of the principality of Gwynedd in 1283. The wars of conquest are well known and are not studied in depth here; rather, they are placed in the context of previous engagements between the Welsh and their enemies from England. The geographical scale of the study diminishes with the advances of the Anglo-Saxons and Anglo-Normans into Welsh territory. Welsh troops in the service of these external peoples are considered in the context of what they can tell us about military forces under independent Welsh command. The study does not generally go beyond the destruction of the independent principality of Gwynedd in 1283, although there are references to later developments, notably the Glyndŵr revolt.

Sources

Previous perceptions of the Welsh at war must be largely accounted for by the attitude of Anglo-French writers from the twelfth century, the earliest period from which we start to get extensive, accessible, written works on Wales. Anglo-French writers of the period either saw or, more probably, desired to portray Wales as different from the other lands of Latin

Christendom. W. R. Jones has described how dominant civilizations have always tended to regard their less developed neighbours with 'condescension, suspicion, scorn and dread'.[4] In the early Middle Ages such judgements were reserved for Christendom's pagan attackers, but Jones has shown that by the twelfth century, as the pagan attacks ceased, this definition was breaking down. The revival of learning led to the reapplication of the classical definition of a barbarian: ferocious, belligerent and cruel. Rather than being directed at pagans, such definitions were applied to those societies on the fringes of Europe left behind in the great economic growth and social changes sweeping the continent. The Scandinavians, Slavs, Magyars, Scots, Irish and, of course, the Welsh lived in poorer societies, societies with fewer trappings of civility: pastoral rather than urban economies, less economic and technological sophistication, differing religious and cultural practices and with less scope for the fine arts. Commentators tended to generalize and standardize their view of the barbarian, and this applied to their opinions of the barbarian at war.

GERALD OF WALES

Gerald of Wales (1145/6–1223) is our most influential source on Welsh military organization.[5] Although Gerald was born in Wales, the Anglo-Normans in lowland Wales identified with continental Europe. Gerald himself was an intellectual humanist with European perceptions. He had studied and taught at the schools of Paris and was a popular and voluminous Latin writer; he had served as a courtier to the first three Angevin kings, worked as an administrator in the Angevin Empire and as a cleric and Church reformer, and he had travelled widely, including four visits to the court of Innocent III at Rome. It is

---

[4] W. R. Jones, 'The image of the barbarian in medieval Europe', *Comparative Studies in Society and History*, 13 (1971), 376–407; 'England against the Celtic fringe: a study in cultural stereotypes', *Journal of World History*, 13 (1971), 155–71; J. Gillingham, *The English in the Twelfth Century* (Woodbridge, 2000); J. France, *Western Warfare in the Age of the Crusades, 1000–1300* (London, 1999); M. J. Strickland, *War and Chivalry: The Conduct and Perception of War in England and Normandy, 1066–1217* (Cambridge, 1996).

[5] For a full discussion of Gerald's influence, see my 'Anglo-Welsh warfare and the works of Gerald of Wales' (unpublished MA thesis, University of Wales Swansea, 1996). See also R. Bartlett, *Gerald of Wales, 1146–1223* (Oxford 1982), ch. 6.

important to consider Gerald's scholastic background. He was a student in the schools of Paris at the height of the twelfth-century renaissance and his career bears comparison with that of contemporary literary figures like Walter Map and Peter of Blois. Gerald admitted that he wanted literary fame, so it may be understood that in his Irish and Welsh works he painted a broad picture to show his knowledge and skill to an educated European audience.[6]

The renaissance's emphasis on the revival of the classics is seen throughout Gerald's writing. He filled his work with *exempla* to emphasize moral or theological points. Gerald's most original contributions were his ethnographic studies. He revived and developed this form of writing, but the inspiration came from the classics. The most obvious example of Gerald's classical and scholastic education is to be seen in his continual use of the thesis/anti-thesis form in the *Descriptio Cambriae*. This work is divided into two books, the first outlining the praiseworthy points of the Welsh, the second their faults. The form is also apparent in chapters 9 and 10 of Book II, where Gerald gave his advice on how the Welsh could be conquered and how they could best defend themselves. The *Descriptio* is often taken at face value, but the scholastic method is artificial, a device for Gerald to show off his ability to argue both sides of a case impartially. His thesis portrays the Welsh as pure, unspoilt examples of humanity, whilst his anti-thesis shows them as barbarous beasts. The truth lies somewhere between and it must always be asked whether Gerald was exaggerating the differences from mainstream Europe to make an impact on his audience.

Gerald provides one of the most influential passages relating to the Welsh at war in the *Descriptio Cambriae*:

> In war the Welsh are very ferocious when battle is first joined. They shout, glower fiercely at the enemy, and fill the air with fearsome clamour, making a high-pitched screech with their long trumpets. From their first fierce and headlong assault, and the shower of javelins which they hurl, they seem most formidable opponents. If the enemy resists manfully and they are repulsed, they are immediately thrown into confusion. With further resistance they turn their backs, making no attempt at a

---

[6] H. Pryce, 'In search of a medieval society: Deheubarth in the writings of Gerald of Wales', *WHR*, 13 (1986–7), 265–81 (p. 280).

counter-attack, but seeking safety in flight. As the poet knew only too well, this is disastrous on the battlefield . . . Their sole idea of tactics is either to pursue their opponents, or else to run away from them. They are lightly armed and they rely more on their agility than on brute strength. It follows that they cannot meet the enemy on equal terms, or fight violently for very long, or strive hand-to-hand for victory . . . Although beaten today and shamefully put to flight with much slaughter, tomorrow they march out again, no whit dejected by their defeat and their losses. They may not shine in open combat and in fixed formation, but they harass their enemy by their ambushes and their night attacks. In a single battle they are easily beaten, but they are difficult to conquer in a long war, for they are not troubled by hunger or cold, fighting does not seem to tire them, they do not lose heart when things go wrong, and after one defeat they are ready to fight again and to face once more the hazards of war.[7]

The Welsh were portrayed as noble savages; the distinct, hierarchical structure in Welsh society was ignored as they were pictured as a race of equal freemen living a primitive life.[8]

Gerald also gives the single most influential passage relating to the strategy, tactics, equipment and conduct in war of Welsh forces in the Middle Ages in the *Descriptio Cambriae*. Purporting to describe the differences between 'French' troops and those Anglo-Normans used to fighting according to 'Welsh rules', Gerald wrote:

They [the 'French'] are used to fighting on the level, whereas here the terrain is rough; their battles take place in the open fields, but here the country is heavily wooded; with them the army is a honourable profession but with us it is a matter of dire necessity; their victories are won by stubborn resistance, ours by constant movement; they take prisoners, we cut off their heads; they ransom their captives but we massacre them. When troops fight in flat open country, heavy complicated armour, made partly out of cloth and partly out of iron, offers good protection and certainly looks smart; but in a marshy or thickly-wooded terrain, where footsoldiers have the advantage over cavalry, light armour is far better. Against men who wear no armour at all and where the battle is almost always won or lost at the first onslaught, light protection is much more

---

[7] *Description*, II, 3, pp. 259–60.
[8] For a similar, though independent, reaction to Gerald's view of warfare in Ireland, see M. T. Flanagan, 'Irish and Anglo-Norman warfare in twelfth-century Ireland', in T. Bartlett and K. Jeffery (eds), *A Military History of Ireland* (Cambridge, 1996), pp. 52–75.

suitable. When the enemy is retreating at full speed through narrow defiles and up mountain-sides, the pursuers must be able to move quickly: they need to be protected, but their armour should be very light. If they have high curved saddles and wear heavy complicated equipment, mounting their horses and dismounting will be a great problem, and they will never be able to advance on foot. Against men who are heavily armed, fighting on the flat where victory is won by main force, and relying upon brute strength and the sheer mass of iron which they wear, I have no doubt at all that you must pit armour against armour and weight against weight . . . Against an army so mobile and lightly armed as the Welsh, who always prefer to do battle on rough terrain, you need troops with little equipment and who are used to the same sort of warfare.[9]

This passage has useful points, but it has been overused, taken out of context and considered universally applicable to Welsh troops in any situation. It was repeated, almost verbatim, from the *Expugnatio Hibernica*. In both works Gerald was anxious to protect the conquests made by the Anglo-Normans from Wales, his kinsmen and friends, against the encroachments of the Angevin kings; consequently he was keen to exaggerate any perceived differences in order to stress that only his people knew how to handle the Welsh. Furthermore, the passage occurs in the second book of the *Descriptio Cambriae* where Gerald is presenting his assessment of the unworthy characteristics of the Welsh. Claims to accuracy are undermined later when Gerald produces a limited synthesis; he says that the 'French' need to adopt Welsh fighting methods to conquer the country, but then criticizes the native ability of the Welsh and says that, in order for them best to defend themselves, they should adopt 'French' arms and tactics![10]

Sources from England and France

A study of the native sources, combined with appropriate use of other works, reveals that Wales from post-Roman times to 1283 was developing along lines more akin to the rest of Europe than is generally acknowledged. Certain major English and French sources present valuable information on Wales.

[9] *Description*, II, 8, p. 268.
[10] *Description*, II, 10, p. 273.

Bede, writing in Northumbria in the early eighth century, sought in his *Ecclesiastical History* to tell the story of the conversion of the English people to Christianity. An underlying criticism of the native British people runs throughout his work for their perceived failure to share the faith with the Anglo-Saxons; the Britons were seen as heretics, people who were feeble in war and spiteful in peace. Bede's treatment of the Welsh mostly dealt with events from the seventh century, and the tone he adopted was a continuation of the criticism of the British writer Gildas.

The Anglo-Saxon Chronicle generally takes little interest in Wales, but does provide some useful, if biased, references. The quality and reliability varies greatly and appropriate entries need to be treated on an individual basis. Of most relevance are the sections of the chronicle used and expanded by John of Worcester. His work was composed at Worcester in the first half of the twelfth century. John's main sources were Bede and the Anglo-Saxon Chronicle, but he used other, lost works and added localized interest, knowledge and understanding of the Welsh border. From 1066 there are increasing divergences from the Anglo-Saxon Chronicle, with information of particular value for the early twelfth century.

Walter Map was a contemporary of Gerald of Wales whose training and career followed a similar pattern. He was probably a Welshman who lived and worked in Herefordshire, serving Bishop Gilbert Foliot and Henry II and eventually rising to the position of archdeacon of Oxford. His humorous writings contain exaggerations and need to be taken with a pinch of salt, but the works contain collections of folk tales and anecdotes about the Welsh, some of which are based on native sources. Geoffrey of Monmouth (d. 1155) was another man of the March, the son of a Breton settler who made his home on the Welsh border. Geoffrey spent most of his life in England where he mixed in ecclesiastical and aristocratic circles. His best-known works, *The History of the Kings of Britain* (*c.*1136) and *The Life of Merlin* (*c.*1150), combine mythology, prophecy and romance and were written to please his court audience. Geoffrey had access to some Welsh sources, written and oral, which are now lost, but these were liberally mixed with his own imagination.

Orderic Vitalis was born near Shrewsbury in 1075 and spent his first ten years in the Welsh March. In 1085 he moved to the monastery of Saint-Evroult in Normandy where he compiled the thirteen books of his epic *Historia Ecclesiastica*. Orderic retained his interest in the Anglo-Norman lords on the Welsh frontier and provided valuable information on the likes of Robert of Rhuddlan. Amongst the many other works from England and France that touch on Wales, some of those utilized are William of Malmesbury, Henry of Huntingdon, John of Hexham, the *Gesta Stephani*, William Newburgh, Roger of Howden, Roger of Wendover and Matthew Paris. All tend to share the common view of the Welsh as outsiders, but in certain instances there are notable exceptions.

NATIVE SOURCES

Gildas was a churchman from northern Britain who is thought to have been schooled in south Wales. He provides us with the only narrative history of fifth-century Britain, meaning that his opinions have had a disproportionate influence on later historians. His work, written *c*.540, is a fierce denunciation of the churchmen and rulers of his day. It is important to remember that Gildas was not trying to write history, as the narrative section provides only a brief introduction to a religious work. Gildas's writing harks back to the golden days of Roman rule. His version of the end of Roman Britain was copied by Bede, whose *Ecclesiastical History* was well known and respected throughout the Middle Ages, and consequently Gildas's conclusions, taken out of their proper context, are reflected in the treatment of the Welsh by other medieval writers. Gildas wrote that 'it became a mocking proverb far and wide that the British are cowardly in war and faithless in peace'.[11] Maximus' expedition to Rome was said to have completely drained Britain of its manpower and military might:

> After that Britain was despoiled of her whole army, her military resources, her governors, brutal as they were, and her sturdy youth, who had followed in the tyrant's footsteps, never to return home. Quite ignorant of

[11] Gildas, p. 18.

the ways of war, she groaned aghast for many years, trodden under foot first by two exceedingly savage overseas nations, the Scots from the north-west and the Picts from the north.[12]

Unable to face their enemies, the Britons are said to have made three separate appeals for Roman help. The Romans tried to encourage them to defend themselves, but: 'It was always true of this people (as it is now) that it was weak in beating off the weapons of the enemy but strong in putting up with civil war and the burden of sin.'[13] Such conclusions were intended to shame the Britons of Gildas's day, but later writers seized the arguments to relate Welsh problems to failings of morality and character. Gerald of Wales even connected the supposed fourth-century expedition of Maximus to the military problems faced by thirteenth-century Welsh rulers!

Historia Brittonum is a confused and erratic collection of sources from early medieval Britain. It was compiled by an anonymous early ninth-century author, a synchronizing historian who was faced with the problem of a lack of sources for earlier centuries. He tried to make sense of, and harmonize, the limited and un-reliable information he had to hand. Care must be exercised in using the work as the early sources have been tampered with.

Most surviving saints' lives were first composed in Latin in the twelfth century, when the authors were determined to assert and defend the antiquity and rights of the native Welsh Church in the face of reforming Anglo-Norman clerics. Whilst much of the evidence is difficult to date, some ancient material survives, notably in the *Life of St Cadog* (probably composed in the late eleventh century). A number of the lives have charters appended to support claims made in the stories. *Liber Landavensis* was com-piled in the 1120s when Norman clerics at Llandaff adapted traditions from ancient Welsh monastic centres in the form of saints' lives, charters, papal bulls and relics, in order to support the claims of their struggling diocese. The book contains the lives of the three (supposed) founding bishops and saints of the see, and 158 charters claiming to be dated from the sixth to the end of the eleventh century. There are many problems with the

[12] Ibid., p. 21.
[13] Ibid., p. 24.

dating and reliability of the material, but there is early information there and the book establishes the fact that a charter tradition existed in different monastic centres in south Wales before the coming of the Normans. *Liber Landavenis* can also help to reveal the expected behaviour of Welsh lords and churchmen and gives examples of their conduct on campaign.

The *Triads* were developed as a method of cataloguing and recalling a variety of information, including legal precedents, bardic grammar, moral lessons and proverbs. They were an index to a body of orally preserved narrative, formed for the benefit of those whose professional duty was to deliver and hand on such knowledge. Such triple groupings are common in all early Celtic records and the surviving literature is just part of a much larger body of work.

Surviving poetry provides some of our earliest evidence for the period in question. The recent work of the University of Wales Centre for Advanced Welsh and Celtic Studies has been followed for dates and context. As a style point, references to Welsh poetry are given in English and Welsh unless a reliable, critical English translation is available; in the latter case, only the English version is given. Possibly the most valuable source on the military tactics of the Britons in the earliest period of this study is the *Gododdin*. The work survives in the thirteenth-century Book of Aneirin, but the traditional belief is that its author composed the poem towards the end of the sixth century in memory of a mid-sixth-century battle. The work was preserved by oral tradition and earlier written copies that are now lost. The overall historical reliability of the *Gododdin* has been questioned, but it is of value in describing the actions of warriors in battle. The poem was sung throughout the ages in the military households of kings, and whilst it seeks to glorify the British warriors as heroes, its description of warfare should be considered as largely within the bounds of what was believable and possible. Other early poetry echoes descriptions of warfare in the *Gododdin*. When such works are used as sources for Welsh warfare, it must be remembered that the verses depicted what the audience wanted to hear, gave few actual details and offered only a limited, noble view of combat; the most striking neglect is the absence of references to infantry. As such works were sung throughout the medieval period to celebrate contemporary warfare, they should not be discounted. They accord with what we know of warfare from other sources and the tactic of using light cavalry in alliance with the (unmentioned) infantry would be effective in the rugged conditions that prevailed throughout much of Wales.

Culhwch and Olwen and the *Four Branches of the Mabinogi* (comprising the prose tales *Pwyll, Branwen, Manawydan* and *Math*) are a collection of stories from Gwynedd, Dyfed and Gwent which were brought together in one narrative, probably some time between the late eleventh and early twelfth century. *Culhwch and Olwen* is perhaps of most value to this study. It is believed to have been composed in something like its present form towards the end of the eleventh century, but it preserves much earlier traditions and the atmosphere seems a reflection of Wales in the early Middle Ages. The *Four Branches of the Mabinogi*, though later than *Culhwch and Olwen*, are likely to contain information relating to the pre-Norman period. In contrast, the later romance tales (including *The Dream of Maxen, Lludd and Llefelys, The Dream of Rhonabwy, Owein, Peredur* and *Gereint*) were composed in their present form some time in the thirteenth century and contain influences from European literary styles and fashions. In certain instances they can be useful in outlining changes in Welsh military fashions and practices. Extracts from Gantz's translations of the prose tales have been used, giving Welsh terminology where appropriate and including references to the Welsh editions.

The Welsh chronicles are all ultimately based on a set of Latin annals of the usual monastic pattern. The surviving Latin texts show us the annals at different stages of composition under different political influences, and all are earlier than the surviving Welsh chronicles. Including the *Cronica de Wallia*, there are four surviving versions of *Annales Cambriae*. The earliest text ends in 954 when we lose the original scribe. Until *c.*770 the annals take information from Ireland, Scotland, Strathclyde and England, but from that date they assume the character of a chronicle kept in Wales, almost certainly at St Davids. The coverage is haphazard, with periods of activity followed by long lacunae. Two of the later texts, both from the thirteenth century, are closely related until 1202 when they diverge. They have a strong English interest from the 1090s, reflecting the diversities of Anglo-Welsh society. The *Cronica de Wallia* is another thirteenth-century text, beginning its coverage in 1190 and telling the story of Welsh Wales, particularly the lands ruled by the Lord Rhys and his descendants. From 1190 to 1248 the text is the closest we can get to the Latin original of the *Brutiau* before those texts became conflated with supplementary material. For the period 1231–46, the text shows signs of being a Strata Florida document, after which point it is thought to have moved to Whitland. Until 1263 the annal speaks with the voice of independent Wales and revels in the glories of Llywelyn ap Gruffudd's early successes.

The Latin original of the *Brutiau* was compiled towards the end of the thirteenth century by a Cistercian monk in Wales. Its chronicle sources had moved from St Davids *c.*1100 and by the late twelfth century the work was a Strata Florida document, with information added from the other Cistercian houses of Wales. There are no extant copies of the Latin original, nor any indication that one survived the dissolution of the monasteries, although traces can be found in *Annales Cambriae* and *Cronica de Wallia*. Three distinct versions of the *Brutiau* have emerged in Welsh translation from the Latin original: the *Red Book of Hergest*, *Peniarth MS 20* and *Brenhinedd y Saesson*. The three, probably produced in different Welsh monastic houses, are independent translations of the same original until 1197, from which point *Brenhinedd y Saesson* depends entirely on the other two. The translations from the Latin can be very unreliable, especially in *Brenhinedd y Saesson*. *Peniarth MS 20* is the most complete of our texts, but is not always the most reliable. The *Brutiau* provide much fuller accounts than *Annales Cambriae*, revealing that the compiler had other sources to hand. Much of the material would seem to be based on records made soon after the events described. Coverage depends on the interests of the author and his sources, implying that regional and personal preferences colour much of our information.

Gruffudd ap Cynan is the only extant biography of a Welsh king. Just one copy of the text remains, which is in Welsh rather than the lost Latin original. The work comes from a similar tradition to the praise poetry sung to Welsh leaders and was probably written by an ecclesiastic and diplomat close to the centre of power in Gwynedd. There has been controversy over whether the work should be dated to soon after Gruffudd's death in 1135, or to a date around 1200 when it would have been used to promote the value of legitimate kingship to support the Venedotian regime; the weight of opinion and evidence would seem to support the latter conclusion.[14]

There are forty surviving manuscripts of the Welsh laws dating from the time when they were still in force in the country.[15] Only two of these manuscripts are identical, but none of them is entirely different from the others. The manuscripts were the working books of lawyers where they recorded information that they found useful, the usual form being to have an orderly collection of tractates and a tail of miscellaneous items. The books collected the customary laws that governed Wales and were dispensed in local assemblies and arbitrations. The earliest surviving written texts date from the early thirteenth century, but there is a much older tradition of common legal concepts and procedures. The texts claim that codification and standardization date to the reign of Hywel Dda in the early tenth century, but this cannot be proven. All the surviving codes have material from the centuries after Hywel's reign, but lawyers were reluctant to abandon obsolete laws so that archaic information survives. We see a progressive encroachment of royal power in the later texts, especially in those associated with Gwynedd.

---

[14] For further reading, see K. L Maund (ed.), *Gruffudd ap Cynan: A Collaborative Biography* (Bury St Edmunds, 1996).
[15] See D. Jenkins, 'Excursus: the lawbooks and their relation', in T. M. Charles-Edwards, M. E. Owen and P. Russell (eds), *The Welsh King and his Court* (Cardiff, 2000), pp. 10–14.

I
THE *TEULU*

The predominantly military household surrounding a Welsh lord has received little scholarly attention, although it was one of the key Welsh institutions throughout the Middle Ages.[1] This neglect limits our understanding of native Wales, since the study of a lord surrounded by his military following who together formed a military elite has been set in its social, political and military contexts in many parts of medieval Europe. Such studies have considered a variety of models, from the bands of tribal chiefs who overwhelmed the Roman Empire in the fifth century to the chivalric households of lords in the fifteenth century, yet all of them shared certain characteristics. These households allowed a leader to stay in touch with his greatest men, to keep an eye on them and to forge bonds of friendship, trust, loyalty, affection and mutual dependability, all vital in an age when personalities dominated government and a leader needed to make his will felt in distant provinces. The ability to retain and display a great household was a visible sign of a lord's power, to his lesser subjects, to members of the household and to outside powers. The prestige given was a prop to the lord's social position and the strength displayed was a deterrent to any challenger.

Numerous writers have stressed the significance of the household in Europe since Tacitus' account of the German chiefs and their *comitatus*. The Merovingian kings who rose above their rival Frankish dynasties and came to dominate Gaul after the fall of Rome based their military system on the band of loyal men surrounding the king and known as *antrustiones* or *pueri*. Each noble had his band of *antrustiones* who would come under their overlord to serve in a greater army when the king required. These

---

[1] For many years the fullest treatment was found in *HW*, I, pp. 316–17. The deficiency has begun to be addressed with S. S. Evans's *The Lords of Battle: Image and Reality in the 'Comitatus' in Dark-Age Britain* (Woodbridge, 1997); A. D. Carr, '*Teulu* and *penteulu*', in T. M. Charles-Edwards, M. E. Owen and P. Russell (eds), *The Welsh King and his Court* (Cardiff, 2000), pp. 63–81.

men had to be respected and appeased with booty and land and they could influence the policy of a king.[2] Studies of Anglo-Saxon warfare agree, in varying measure, that the household was the most significant element in the organization and conduct of war. Abels stressed its key role, demonstrating how a lord's men were duty-bound to support him even if he were to rebel unjustly against the king, and he concluded that, at least in the earlier Anglo-Saxon period, the individual warbands of each lord would combine to form the king's host.[3] Hollister laid more stress on the institution of the *fyrd*, but he too recognized that the household represented the military elite of any Anglo-Saxon force, as demonstrated at Maldon.[4] In a study of the housecarls of eleventh-century English kings, Hooper emphasized that, although they were a highly trained, well-motivated and equipped force, in this they differed little from previous or contemporary households; they were in no way unique.[5]

In the Anglo-Norman period, households in Europe changed and developed, but their importance did not decrease. J. O. Prestwich stressed the importance of the household to the Anglo-Norman state.[6] It was a permanent, sizeable force that could be rapidly expanded in war, enforce the king's will in distant regions and, when centralized, provide leadership to a larger army. Members of the household varied in social rank, from the mightiest nobles in the realm to young knights of humble background. Levels of royal patronage also varied; men served for food and lodging, money retainers, booty and land, but possibly most significant was the hope of their lord's favour and the future rewards this might bring. William Marshal, for example, went from being the penniless younger son of a minor noble to regent of England.[7] Morillo stressed the importance of the household to the Anglo-Norman military system.[8] It gave a professional, disciplined core to their armies; Morillo cites the example of

---

[2] See B. S. Bachrach, *Merovingian Military Organisation* (Minneapolis, 1972).
[3] R. P. Abels, *Lordship and Military Obligation in Anglo-Saxon England* (London, 1988).
[4] C. W. Hollister, *Anglo-Saxon Military Institutions* (Oxford, 1962), p. 11. See also F. Barlow, *Edward the Confessor* (London, 1989), p. 170; S. C. Hawkes (ed.), *Weapons and Warfare in Anglo-Saxon England* (Oxford, 1989), p. 3.
[5] N. Hooper, 'The housecarls in England in the eleventh century', in *ANW*, pp. 1–15.
[6] J. O. Prestwich, 'War and finance in the Anglo-Norman state', *TRHS*, 4 (1954), 19–43; 'The military household of the Norman kings', *EHR*, 96 (1981), 1–37.
[7] D. Crouch, *William Marshal* (London, 1990).
[8] S. Morillo, *Warfare under the Anglo-Norman Kings, 1066–1135* (Woodbridge, 1994).

Bourgthéroulde (1124), but other battles like Tinchebrai (1106) and the Standard (1138) are equally valid. The household was important in the mustering of larger armies because it provided professional leadership within a larger unit and had superior arms and armour. In stressing the importance of the royal household, it is important to note, however, that each lord had his own retinue, as did lords in those states bordering Anglo-Norman lands. Though effective, the household of the Anglo-Norman kings was hardly unique; such retinues were common, established and successful institutions throughout Europe and similar models can be seen in different cultures worldwide.

The pioneering work of G. R. J. Jones provides information on the social organization in Wales that supported, and was exploited by, the *teulu*.[9] Jones's research helped produce the picture of a society dominated by an aristocratic, military elite, supported by the labour of bondmen working the land. The legal model that Jones used as the basis of his work is too rigid and unrealistic, but it provides a framework of social organization. The laws outline an ideal *cantref* (hundred) of two commotes, each containing twelve *maenolydd* (manors) of four *trefi* (townships). Two other *trefi* in each commote were reserved for the king's use, meaning that each *cantref* contained 100 *trefi*. Of the twelve *maenolydd* of a commote, four were worked by the king's bondmen, one was used to support the king's chancellor, another the king's reeve. The remaining six were owned by the free notables (W. *uchelwyr*, L. *optimates*) of Welsh society. Welsh kings exploited their domains whilst on *cylch* (circuit) with their households, the renders taking the form of food and shelter and, in the later period, commuted renders. Such a model would be comprehensible throughout Europe in the Middle Ages; we see a servile majority tied to the land, performing labour service to support the noble minority. The king or prince held a dominant position but needed to pay attention to the demands of his powerful nobility.

[9] See in particular G. R. J. Jones, 'The tribal system in Wales: a re-assessment in the light of settlement studies', *WHR*, 1 (1960–3), 111–32; 'The distribution of bond settlements in north-west Wales', *WHR*, 2 (1964–5), 19–36; 'Post Roman Wales', in H. P. R. Finberg (ed.), *The Agrarian History of England and Wales*, I, ii (Cambridge, 1972), pp. 281–382; 'Multiple estates and early settlement', in P. H. Sawyer (ed.), *Medieval Settlement* (London, 1976), pp. 15–40.

Despite the problems involved in using the thirteenth-century law texts as evidence for an earlier age, the social organization described is supported by evidence from marginal notes in the ninth-century Lichfield Gospels and, as has been suggested, its acceptance brings Wales into line with the rest of post-Roman Europe. Moreover, all the other evidence available supports the picture of a hierarchical society dominated by the king and his *teulu*. Whilst Jones's argument for the widespread survival of multiple estates can be questioned, the existence of small, nucleated settlements (*trefi*) throughout Wales, used as administrative units by lords and exploited on their *cylch*, is beyond dispute.[10] K. R. Dark contended that the polities of Britain emerging in the fifth and sixth centuries derived from Roman *civitates* which were themselves based on pre-Roman, Iron Age kingdoms.[11] The general argument is supported by evidence of continuity from the Roman period observed in Cornwall and recorded following the Anglo-Saxon conquest there.[12]

The earliest leaders of post-Roman Britain rose to prominence as commanders of military bands from power bases in their own localities. In the west, it is possible that there was significant continuity from the pre-Roman past as the *teulu* appears to emerge as an ancient but effective form of social organization. A pre-Norman view of post-Roman Britain saw the figure of Arthur as the 'leader of the Britons in battle' (L. *Dux erat bellorum*).[13] This accords with the view of Arthur and his contemporaries in the lives of Welsh saints; although the earliest of these survive only in twelfth-century form, it is possible that they reflect traditions dating back to the fifth and sixth centuries. The leaders of the day are depicted, surrounded by their military households, indulging in raids against the lands of rival leaders and travelling the country demanding board and lodging from the religious establishments of the saints. Gildas painted a similar picture of the 'tyrants' of his day who, he claimed, plundered, terrorized,

---

[10] See T. M. Charles-Edwards, 'Early medieval kingship in the British Isles', in S. Bassett (ed.), *The Origins of Anglo-Saxon Kingdoms* (Leicester, 1989), pp. 28–39; D. Longley, 'The royal courts of the Welsh princes of Gwynedd, AD 400–1283', in N. Edwards (ed.), *Landscape and Settlement in Medieval Wales* (Oxford, 1997), pp. 41–54; J. K. Knight, 'Welsh fortifications of the first millenium AD', *Château Gaillard*, 16 (1992), 277–84.

[11] K. R. Dark, *Civitas*, pp. 135–6.

[12] Ibid., pp. 155–7.

[13] *HB*, p. 35.

sinned, lied, waged unjust civil wars and rewarded thieves as their companions: 'they despise the harmless and humble, but exalt to the stars, so far as they can, their military companions, bloody, proud and murderous men, adulterers and enemies of God'.[14] He singled out the greatest *dux*, Maelgwn Gwynedd, for particular condemnation; Gildas deplored the court where Maelgwn sat surrounded by warriors and lauded by bards for his bravery and military skill.[15] Maelgwn and his retainers are also criticized in a number of the lives of Welsh saints.[16]

The emergence of the *duces* as military leaders, soon to be labelled kings, mirrors the situation in fifth-century Gaul. There, some of the greatest senatorial aristocrats had been excluded from the centre of imperial power. Their wealth and private military forces remained, however, and they tended to retreat to their estates where they were able to dominate the regions as the most significant powers. Examples include St Germanus of Auxerre and the family of Gregory of Tours. Such leaders dominated Gaul when the Franks entered the area and it was the success of Clovis and his successors in manipulating these powers that facilitated the rise of the Merovingians.[17]

Terminology

Latin terms to be discussed are simple and in accord with usage elsewhere in Europe. The Latin word for household, *familia*, is used to describe a Welsh king's following in lives of Welsh saints, *Annales Cambriae*, *Liber Landavensis* and Walter Map. The *Brutiau* almost universally translate *familia* from the Latin chronicles as *teulu* and it seems likely that *familia* was the word used in the lost original Latin *Life of Gruffudd ap Cynan*. Sometimes the sources describe a lord's military followers as his *satellites*, *milites* or *tirones*; this is common in European sources and easily comprehensible.

Descriptions of the household in Welsh are more varied. By far the most common usage is *teulu* and this can be taken directly

---

[14] Gildas, p. 29.
[15] Ibid., pp. 32–4.
[16] *Vitae*, pp. 11–15, 73–5, 137–9, 247–9, 257–9.
[17] See Bachrach, *Merovingian*, pp. 15–17.

as *familia*, but there are a number of variations in terminology. The earliest of these is *gosgordd*. This is usually translated as retinue and Bromwich suggested that it may represent a force larger than the *teulu*.[18] This is supported by the Welsh laws:

> The king is entitled to have in his company thirty-six persons on horseback, to wit, the twenty-four officers and the twelve guests, besides his bodyguard [W. *teulu*] and his goodmen and his servants and his musicians and his needy ones; that is called the king's retinue [W. *gosgordd*].[19]

This *gosgordd* includes domestic elements, though, and when the term is used in a purely military context it is more difficult to separate from the *teulu*. The *Gododdin* always refers to the *gosgordd*, rather than the *teulu*, of Mynyddog Mwynfawr, and the fact that this was an inflated household recruited for a special expedition may have led Bromwich to her conclusion.[20] *Teulu* is used three times in the *Gododdin*, twice when apparently referring to the opposing Anglo-Saxons and once when dealing with one of Mynyddog's men, Tudfwlch;[21] in the latter example, the *teulu* may be seen as a subdivision of the larger force. Further confusion arises in the *Gododdin*, however, for it is unclear whether the *gosgordd* represents the entire force present or if it merely supplied the leadership within a larger host. A variety of terms is used for 'host' or 'army' and these should be differentiated from the *gosgordd*. Such separation is seen in the ninth-century poem *The Praise of Tenby*, which states, 'there was a retinue in the court, and a host besides [W. *Bu goscor a bu kerd yn eil mehyn*]'.[22]

If it is possible to separate the *gosgordd* from the *teulu* in the way Bromwich suggests for the *Gododdin*, such distinctions disappear in later sources. In the *Triads* there is little to choose between the 'Three Faithful Warbands [W. *teulu*]' of Britain and the 'Three Noble Retinues [W. *gosgordd*]';[23] both have references to forces

---

[18] *Triads*, pp. 65–6.
[19] *Law*, p. 6.
[20] For discussion of the use of the *Gododdin* as a source, see J. Rowland, 'Warfare and horses in the *Gododdin* and the problem of Catraeth', *CMCS*, 30 (1995), 13–40.
[21] *Gododdin*, pp. 8, 40, 64.
[22] *Beginnings*, p. 163.
[23] *Triads*, pp. 57–8, 65–6.

that fought at Arfderydd and each band is said to have contained 2,100 men. It should be noted that one of the 'Three Faithless *Teulu*' was said to be that of Gwrgi and Peredur at Arfderydd;[24] these were the sons of Eliffer Gosgorddfawr ('Eliffer of the Great Retinue') and it may be speculated that they were leading a detachment of his *gosgordd*. Other than this, there seems little distinction to be drawn between the use of *gosgordd* and *teulu* and in any case any problem is eased in later sources because the term *gosgordd* tends to fall out of fashion.

The other term regularly associated with *teulu* is *nifer*. It is a word rarely found in early texts but one that grows in popularity. Its only appearance in the *Triads* is in a late addition concerning Arthur which has clear post-Galfridian influences.[25] *Nifer*, which in modern Welsh is translated as 'number', is less specific than other terms and is used in a variety of contexts. The example from the *Triads* refers to Arthur's army or host. In the *Canu Heledd* cycle of poems, dating from the mid to late ninth century but purporting to tell a seventh-century story, the orator bemoans Cynddylan's Hall because it is left 'without a lord, without a *nifer*, without defence'.[26] Rowland translates *nifer* as 'host', but in the following lines, which seem simply to repeat the previous message for dramatic effect, we are told that the hall has been left 'without a fire, without a *teulu* [translated as "household troop"]'. The terms *teulu* and *nifer* seem interchangeable in the tale of *Pwyll* from the *Mabinogi*. In the dispute between Pwyll and Gwawl, the *nifer* and *teulu* of the leaders are referred to, but there is no way to distinguish the two.[27] In the same tale, however, Pwyll climbs the mound of Arberth with his *nifer* and Gwawl is captured with his entire *nifer*;[28] both examples seem to refer to the entire courtly household surrounding the lords rather than the militarized *teulu*. This would also appear to be the appropriate translation in *Culhwch*, where the eponymous hero enters Arthur's court and greets the assembled 'company' (W. *nifer*) and 'troops' (W. *catbritogya*) and in further examples from *Branwen*

---

[24] Ibid., p. 61.
[25] Ibid., p. 133.
[26] *Saga*, p. 485.
[27] *Mabinogi*, p. 56; *PK*, p. 14. See also when Pwyll returns to his land after a year's absence and is delighted to greet his 'company [W. *nifer*] and troops [W. *teulu*]'; *Mabinogi*, p. 50; *PK*, p. 6.
[28] *Mabinogi*, pp. 52, 57; *PK*, pp. 8, 16.

and *Manawydan*.²⁹ In *Culhwch*, the army assembled by Arthur to hunt Twrch Trwyth is called both a *nifer* and a *llu* and at one point Arthur's *teulu* detaches itself from the larger force to tackle the beast.³⁰

The term *nifer* is used twice in *Gruffudd ap Cynan*. The first occasion is after the battle of Gwaed Erw when the victorious Gruffudd and his *nifer* pursued his enemy Trahaearn;³¹ this could refer to the entire force which had fought the engagement, but in the post-battle confusion it is likely that a smaller, disciplined household force close to Gruffudd would be used for the pursuit. The second use is when Gruffudd was lured into a trap by the earls of Shrewsbury and Chester.³² It is said that he was captured along with his *nifer*, which would again imply a household troop. This *nifer* contained foreign mercenaries, each of whom had his right thumb cut off by the Normans. It is possible that Gruffudd, seeking to establish himself in Wales from a power base in Ireland, relied excessively on foreign soldiers rather than Welshmen and for this reason his personal bodyguard is not identified as a *teulu*.

The *Brutiau* are capricious in their use of the term *nifer*. In 1109, Owain ap Cadwgan of Powys is said to have taken a *nifer* (translated by Thomas Jones as 'a small number') of about fourteen men to abduct Nest from Cenarth Bychan.³³ These would have been Owain's closest companions, probably the younger members of the royal household, who stole away secretly from Cadwgan's court late at night. If they were a detachment of Cadwgan's *teulu*, their number is too small for them to represent the entire complement of his following. In the same year, in *Brut (Pen. 20)*, *nifer* is used to describe a small group sent by Uchdryd ab Edwin as messengers. It is similarly used in 1223 for a small detachment of the main host (W. *llu*) of William Marshal (II). To confuse matters, however, in 1109 the *Red Book of Hergest* version of the *Brutiau* uses *nifer* to describe a large host mustered by four Welsh princes and called in *Brut (Pen. 20)* a *llu*.

---

[29] *Mabinogi*, pp. 139, 67–9, 86–7; *CaO*, p. 6; *PK*, pp. 29–32, 52.
[30] *Mabinogi*, pp. 169–71; *CaO*, pp. 36–8. The great army led to Ireland in *Branwen* is called a *nifer*: *Mabinogi*, p. 74; *PK*, p. 38.
[31] *Gruffudd ap Cynan*, p. 61.
[32] Ibid., p. 69.
[33] *Brut (Pen.20)*, s.a. 1109.

In 1116 the force led by Gruffudd ap Rhys is called a *nifer*.³⁴ This was presumably a significant troop that grew as his rising gained momentum. As in the case of Gruffudd ap Cynan, Gruffudd ap Rhys was a landless prince trying to recover his inheritance. He drew support from disaffected groups in society, men from diverse regions (possibly including Ireland) hoping to win a fortune and who, therefore, dissociated themselves from the usual bonds of society and lordship. This could again explain the reluctance to use the name *teulu*.³⁵ The final use of the term meriting discussion is seen in *Brenhinedd y Saesson* for 1066. The various armies referred to in this year are all labelled *lluoedd*, but we are told that, at Hastings, Harold was slain with all his *nifer*.³⁶ This could mean his entire force, but it seems likely to refer to the slaying of Harold and his housecarls.

The term *tylwyth* as a description of the household is rare and presents none of the problems posed by *gosgordd* and *nifer*. It is used occasionally in poetry, once in *Branwen*,³⁷ and once in *Gruffudd ap Cynan*,³⁸ and in each case it could easily be substituted by *teulu*.

Size of the *Teulu*

Estimating the size of any force in an age before government records of pay and recruitment is a notoriously difficult task. Sources regularly underestimate or overestimate the numbers on opposing sides to praise the deeds of their heroes or patrons. Even if a writer intended to give an accurate number, it proved difficult to perform a reliable head-count. This problem is eased when dealing with the *teulu* as the numbers were, in general, quite small. There are few unambiguous references to numbers, though, and it is impossible to indicate a standard size for a *teulu*; numbers varied greatly according to the power, needs and

---

³⁴ Ibid., s.a. 1116.
³⁵ R. S. Babcock, 'Imbeciles and Normans: the *ynfydion* of Gruffudd ap Rhys reconsidered', *The Haskins Society Journal*, 4 (1992), 1–8.
³⁶ *Bren.*, s.a. 1066.
³⁷ *Mabinogi*, p. 78; *PK*, p. 43.
³⁸ *Gruffudd ap Cynan*, p. 65.

personality of a lord and the size and geography of his land.[39] The potential for variation is enormous.

To look at contemporary armies in Wales's neighbouring lands, forces formed from the combined households of lords and kings, Hawkes suggests an early Anglo-Saxon army size of 80–200 men;[40] Hines numbers continental Saxon armies of the early Middle Ages at around 250 men;[41] the laws of Ine of Wessex state that a raiding party of over thirty-six was an army and in 786 Cyneheard nearly captured a kingdom with eighty-five men.[42] Early Irish literature claimed that twenty men were 'ready for a raid' and 100 'ready for battle'.[43]

When considering the numbers in a Welsh king's *teulu*, the assumption has been that its 'traditional size' was 300 men. This is based on Sir Ifor Williams's analysis of the *Gododdin*, which cannot be relied on; Mynyddog's *gosgordd*, which in the poem is numbered at either 300 or 363 of whom eighty-six are named, did not represent a standard *teulu*. The *Gododdin* may commemorate a battle fought by the men of Gododdin and certain allies, but the many heroes recorded from distant lands are added for the literary effect of portraying 'all Britain' united against the Saxons. The number 300 reflects the fascination with the mystical number three seen repeatedly in poetry and literature.[44] A figure of 300 would be too small for an army that had drawn together all the nobles mentioned along with their military followings, but, equally, if 300 merely represents the leaders then the force would be unbelievably large; if we accept the figures, we might as well accept the 100,000 said to be ranged against

---

[39] It is difficult to know how powerful a lord needed to be to have a *teulu*. Literary references to the likes of Belyn of Llŷn and Gronw the Radiant of Penllyn could suggest that a *cantref* was seen as the minimum holding expected of the lord of a *teulu*, but we lack evidence to substantiate this, or to give it time-scale (and we must remember that we cannot fix the chronological establishment of the *cantref* as an administrative unit). Organization is unlikely to have been rigid and individual cases probably reflected great variation.

[40] Hawkes, *Weapons*, p. 3.

[41] J. Hines, 'The military context of the *Adventus Saxonum*: some continental evidence', in ibid., pp. 25–48.

[42] L. Alcock, *Economy, Society and War among the Britons and Saxons* (Cardiff, 1987), pp. 232, 300–1. S. S. Evans argues that none of the kingdoms of fifth- and sixth-century Britain could raise a force of 1,000 men, that several hundred was the maximum and that a British *comitatus* was of a similar size to its Anglo-Saxon equivalent: S. S. Evans, *Lords*, pp. 26–7.

[43] H. E. Davidson, 'The training of warriors', in Hawkes, *Weapons*, pp. 11–23.

[44] See, for example, *HB*, p. 32; *Beginnings*, p. 27; *Earliest Welsh Poetry*, p. 142; *Vitae*, pp. 27, 77; *Brut (Pen. 20)*, s.a. 1210.

them! The influence of the *Gododdin* adversely affects other comments in literature about the size of the *teulu*, which are unrealistic multiplications of the 300 in the *Gododdin*.⁴⁵

Given estimations of army sizes in Wales's neighbouring lands in the early post-Roman period, the number 300 for a standard *teulu* seems much too high. There are many other references to numbers but, as has been suggested, finding a standard is nearly impossible. Great chronological leaps are made in the evidence discussed below, but the intention is merely to indicate the numbers which might surround a lord. To begin with some of the lower figures, Peryf ap Cedifor's twelfth-century lament on the killing of Hywel ab Owain Gwynedd refers to seven warriors fighting together;⁴⁶ yet this could refer to a select fighting group within the *teulu* and not the entire force. In 1109 Owain ap Cadwgan took a *nifer* of around fourteen men to abduct Nest, but again this may only be a detachment of his father's *teulu*.⁴⁷ Gerald of Wales tells the story of the military followers of Owain Gwynedd's youngest son Rhodri who were defeated in a skirmish by a local band of robbers, but we cannot be sure that they were part of a *teulu* and Gerald can hardly be trusted, particularly as the tale was designed to castigate the young men for refusing to take the Cross.⁴⁸ The *Life of St Tatheus* pictures King Caradog of Gwent visiting the saint's court accompanied by twenty-four *milites*, but this was not his entire retinue.⁴⁹ Similarly, the *subregulus* Paulentus of Glamorgan visited St Cadog with twelve 'picked soldiers'.⁵⁰ At Irfon Bridge in 1282, eighteen 'notable men' fell with Llywelyn ap Gruffudd.⁵¹ These were presumably members of his *teulu*, but it is unlikely that they represented more than a small detachment of the following of such a prince.

A larger body of evidence hints that the *teulu* of a Welsh prince could number around fifty men. The *Anglo-Saxon Chronicle* states that, at the battle of Chester, Brocmail of Powys failed to fight and defend the monks entrusted to his care but fled the field with

---

⁴⁵ *Triads*, pp. 57–61; the *teuluoedd* mentioned are each said to number 2,100 men. This in turn influences the numbers said to leave with each of the 'Three Levies of Britain' – 21,000 men: ibid., pp. 75–8.
⁴⁶ *Welsh Verse*, p. 148; *CBT*, II, 19.1–2.
⁴⁷ *Brut (Pen. 20)*, s.a. 1109.
⁴⁸ *Journey*, II, 7, p. 186.
⁴⁹ *Vitae*, p. 275.
⁵⁰ Ibid., p. 43.
⁵¹ *LG*, p. 565, n. 185.

his fifty men.⁵² The Welsh laws claim that a king's *gosgordd* consisted of thirty-six men besides his *teulu* and domestic servants.⁵³ In the *Life of St Cadog*, the members of Paulentus' household out on a hunting trip under Illtud were said to number fifty.⁵⁴ In 916, Æthelflaed, the 'Lady of the Mercians', sent a force against the king of Brycheiniog's court (W. *llys*) at Llangors, where thirty-three of his men were captured.⁵⁵ At the battle of Mynydd Carn (1081), Trahaearn ap Caradog was killed along with twenty-five of his *teulu* after an unspecified number of other members of his *teulu* had already been killed in the front row of his force.⁵⁶

Some references suggest an even larger *teulu* for the greater Welsh nobles of literature and history. In the *Mabinogi*, the *nifer* and *teulu* of Pwyll, lord of Dyfed, numbered ninety-nine (or 100 including Pwyll himself).⁵⁷ *Gruffudd ap Cynan* refers to its hero losing fifty-two of his 'knights' and *teulu* in an attack and suggests that this was not his entire force, and it later describes him gathering 160 men to attack the Normans in Gwynedd, though these are not called his *teulu*.⁵⁸ The most significant reference is to Gruffudd ap Llywelyn, said to have lost about 140 men from his *teulu* in 1047; despite this, he remained strong enough to take revenge on the men of Ystrad Tywi who had committed the outrage.⁵⁹ This suggests that Gruffudd's *teulu* numbered well over 140, even though in 1047 he was not at the height of his power. Gruffudd ap Llywelyn is exceptional: he came to dominate all Wales and even threaten the stability of the English state. He had more wealth to support such a *teulu* than any other Welsh ruler in the Middle Ages. He had more sources of patronage, more offices to fill, more land to distribute and more booty from his raids. It is to be expected that his *teulu* would be larger than that of any previous Welsh ruler, but even so it may be suspected that the numbers he lost from his *teulu* in 1047 have been exaggerated

---

⁵² *ASC*, s.a. 604.
⁵³ *Law*, p. 6.
⁵⁴ *Vitae*, p. 63.
⁵⁵ *ASC*, s.a. 916; it should be noted that these may have been domestic staff who were captured along with the king's wife. The king seems to have been absent, possibly with his *teulu*.
⁵⁶ *Gruffudd ap Cynan*, p. 68.
⁵⁷ *Mabinogi*, p. 56; *PK*, p. 16.
⁵⁸ *Gruffudd ap Cynan*, pp. 62, 71.
⁵⁹ *Brut (Pen. 20)*, s.a. 1047.

or confused.⁶⁰ The numbers retained by the princes of thirteenth-century Gwynedd were significant, but references to *teulu* numbers are scarce. Llywelyn ap Gruffudd took provender for 500 men from the lands of Basingwerk Abbey when he went to Penllyn to hunt each year, but this was for his entire court rather than just the *teulu*.⁶¹

Although the sources are difficult to use, a force of around fifty seems to be a reasonable estimate. Given the reservations expressed earlier, this number cannot be defended strenuously or applied universally. It must be remembered that all these sources refer to princes and kings of significant power, the greater nobility on the Welsh political scene. As each lesser lord also had his military followers, numbers in the company of such men would drop to a handful, though at this level *teulu* may not be the appropriate terminology.

Composition

A wide social range could be included in the military household of a leader in medieval Europe, from the greatest nobles to men of meagre means dependent on their master for food and lodging. The Welsh laws make allowance for the old, middle and young parts of the *teulu*, suggesting men of varying ages and means.⁶² The sons of free men aged from fourteen to twenty-one were retained at court and trained in arms, but the *teulu* could also include the leading nobles of the realm. In his examination of the Anglo-Saxon household, Abels found that the nobles did not have an exclusive monopoly in war, and some of the lower classes were allowed in the warband.⁶³ War was, however, the profession of the nobles, their love, their sport and their reason for being. Membership of the *teulu* would probably have been denied to the unfree bondmen of Welsh society. Although the

---

[60] *HW*, II, p. 361, says that the loss of 140 men shattered Gruffudd's power in the south for eight years, allowing the rise of Gruffudd ap Rhydderch, but this interpretation of events in south Wales can be questioned: T. M. Davies, 'Gruffudd ap Llywelyn, King of Wales', *WHR*, 21 (2002), 207–48, 220.

[61] D. Stephenson, *The Governance of Gwynedd* (Cardiff, 1984), p. 5.

[62] *Law*, p. 11; *Journey*, II, 7, p. 186, refers to 'youths' in the military following of Rhodri ab Owain.

[63] Abels, *Lordship*, pp. 36–7.

quality of horses, arms and armour might vary according to the means of each member of the *teulu*, each man was part of a mounted military elite set apart in appearance, position and prestige from the rank and file of society.

Crouch contended that 'the *teulu* had little aristocratic cachet, it was very much a mixed bag; that of Gruffudd ap Cynan of Gwynedd had a large Irish contingent, the *teulu* of Glamorgan in the eleventh century contained Normans.'[64] This statement is open to question, both in terms of idealized *teuluoedd* seen in literature and those we can trace in the historical record. In the *Gododdin*, the named members of Mynyddog's *gosgordd* are aristocratic and the poem is largely devoted to singling out individual members and singing their praises. *Branwen* pictures King Brân of Britain in court with the greatest nobles of the land 'as ought to surround a king'.[65] Stories from the lives of Welsh saints make it clear that military service in the royal household was considered appropriate even for those of most distinguished birth. St Gwynllyw was said to be the son of King Glywysyet; 'his youthful age matured in royal military service [L. *regali militia*]'.[66] Bicanus, the father of St Illtud, came from a noble line and during his exile (in either Brittany or Ireland) he served in a military retinue, maintaining a position of honour and marrying a noble woman.[67] Illtud, the product of this marriage, returned to Britain where he approached King Paulentus of Glamorgan:

> The king, perceiving that he was a court soldier and honourable, retained him with much affection, loving him before all of his household and rewarding him bounteously. So he remained with very great honour until he merited to be chosen to preside over the royal household.[68]

Not all members of the *teulu* had royal blood. Iestyn ap Gwrgant was a follower of King Caradog of Glamorgan in the eleventh century, holding much of west Glamorgan from him. Crouch speculates that Iestyn was the man powerful enough to stop the advance of Robert fitz Hamo in the 1090s at the River

---

[64] D. Crouch, *The Image of Aristocracy in Britain, 1000–1300* (London, 1992), p. 160.
[65] *Mabinogi*, p. 67; *PK*, p. 29.
[66] *Vitae*, p. 173.
[67] Ibid., p. 195.
[68] Ibid., p.197.

Ogmore, following the collapse of Glamorgan after Caradog's death in 1081.[69] Caradog ap Rhiwallon, a noble (L. *comes*) deemed powerful enough by a twelfth-century scribe to have made his own reparation grant of land to Llandaff, was a member of the *comitatus* of King Meurig ab Hywel of Glamorgan.[70] The Llancarfan charters record that Guengarth, a foster-son of King Morgan, was a member of the king's *teulu*.[71]

Another non-royal noble in military service is found in the *Life of St Wenefred*: 'In the days, therefore, wherein Cadfan was reigning over the province of Gwynedd, a certain strenuous soldier [L. *miles*], the possessor of at least three vills [L. *villarum*], Teuyth son of Eylud by name, was abiding in Tegeingl.'[72] His only child was a daughter, Wenefred, who wanted to devote herself to God. Teuyth wished to entrust her to the holy man Beuno, who requested Teuyth's estate in exchange, but for this Teuyth needed the king's permission. Cadfan agreed to grant one of the three vills as he did not wish to alienate the other land 'from the common use of the province'; this land had to return to the king's hands where it could be used as a source of patronage for his *teulu* and to support his military presence.

The Welsh laws have information on non-royal *teulu* members: 'The worth of an innate *bonheddig* is three kine and three score kine; his *sarhaed* is three kine and three score pence. If he is a man of the *teulu* his worth will be four kine and four score kine; his *sarhaed* is four kine and four score pence.'[73] Individuals from the *bonheddig* or 'gentry' class were accepted into the *teulu* and had their social position raised as a result of this privilege. There was also a body of 'squires' in Welsh society, men associated with the *teulu*, possibly as junior members. Crouch noted that Welsh words like *daryanogyon* (the shield bearers who attended *uchelwyr*) signified the equivalent of Anglo-Saxon offices and were pre-Norman in character.[74] This is supported by the poem *Claf*

---

[69] D. Crouch, 'The slow death of kingship in Glamorgan, 1067–1158', *Morgannwg*, 29 (1985), 20–41. Iestyn's lands were partitioned following his death *c*.1127–30, and his sons were threatened by the advance of Henry I and his 'new men'; but in Stephen's reign the family recovered and remained a significant force.

[70] *LL*, pp. 260–61. Caradog's prominence is further revealed in a later charter of Gruffudd ap Llywelyn. He is third on the witness list, following Gruffudd himself and the king's son Maredudd: ibid., p.270.

[71] *Vitae*, p. 131.
[72] Ibid., pp. 289–91.
[73] *Law*, p. 131.
[74] Crouch, *Image*, p. 165.

Abercuawg, dating from around the tenth century: 'The leper was a squire [W. *mackwy*]; he was a bold warrior in the court of a king.'[75] The term *mackwy* was borrowed from Ireland and is difficult to translate, but represents a 'page' or 'young squire' during the early stage of his career at a lord's court.[76] It is possible that the strongest and most military able from the lowest, unfree classes of society could be recruited when young to make up any shortfall in a lord's retinue and that they could rise through distinguished service, but we have no evidence to substantiate such an idea.

The final group to consider in the make-up of the *teulu* is the alien element, drawn possibly from far afield to join a lord's household. Such a man might be a low-status waged warrior or an honoured noble in an alien court; if the term 'mercenary' is to be applied, it is as well to remember the distinctions in status that are possible. Hostages are likely to have been taken from other *teuluoedd* by a successful lord in order to enforce his will, and such men would have their status respected. Lords were anxious to attract the best military talents into their retinues. The *Juvencus Englynion*, the earliest surviving Welsh manuscript poetry dating from the late eighth or early ninth century, relates: 'My *teulu* is not overly big – I and my *ffranc* around our cauldron.'[77] Rowland translates *ffranc* here as freedman. In a section from the tenth-century poem *Caranfael* in the *Canu Heledd* cycle, Rowland translates thus: 'When Caranfael wore the battle cloak of Cynddylan and shook his ash spear / The Frank [W. *ffranc*] did not get peace from his lips.'[78] In this example, *ffranc* is taken to mean 'the enemy', the Anglo-Saxons who, on their entry into Britain, were identified by the natives as 'Franks'.[79] Both translations are debatable and Sir Ifor Williams suggested that in both poems the translation 'foreign mercenary' is applicable. Thus, in the first poem the leader laments the loss of his entire *teulu* so that he is left only with the company of its one survivor, his foreign mercenary. The second poem can be understood as praising

---

[75] *Saga*, p. 499.
[76] *LL*, pp. 271–2, records the presence of a 'young man', Einion, in the *teulu* of Iestyn ap Gwrgant (Iestyn was his uncle).
[77] *Saga*, p. 510.
[78] Ibid., p. 492.
[79] For a discussion of the secondary literature on this point, see J. Rowland, 'Old Welsh *franc*: an Old English borrowing?', *CMCS*, 26 (1993), 21–5.

Caranfael for not allowing his soldiers to remain idle but instead driving them on to heroic deeds.

In these examples the alien members of the *teulu* are held in low esteem, but this treatment was not universal. In the *Gododdin*, Mynyddog drew warriors from far afield and these outsiders are honoured in the poem. A line in the *Llywarch Hen* cycle of poems suggests that Maen Wyn, one of Llywarch's noble sons, had served Maelgwn Gwynedd as steward (W. *maer*),[80] and a certain Owain Môn ('of Anglesey') can be traced in the *teulu* of Gwallawg of Elmet.[81] In the poem *The Drinking Horn*, two outsiders perform with honour in the *teulu* of Owain Cyfeiliog:

> Gwrol [oedd y] dewrion [o] wŷr Mochnant o wlad Powys
> A ffyrnigrwydd ymladd ynddynt ill dau[82]

> (Proud is Mochannwys's lord in Powys
> Hearing of how the two of them fought).[83]

It was Welsh custom for a lord to send his son to the court of another ruler to receive his early training and education, and the young man's relations with his foster-father could become close; perhaps this is the position in the above poem.[84] The cases of the exiles St Illtud and his father, both of whom were highly valued by their royal employers, have been considered. Perhaps in such cases a lord enjoyed basking in the reflected glory of having men of noble stock serving in his retinue. It may have been a lord's duty to provide a foster-son with arms and a horse when he reached adulthood; in *Pwyll*, Teirnon Trwchiant, king of Gwent, raised Pwyll's son Pryderi and gave him a fine colt before he left his home.[85]

Crouch considered that the presence of Irish and Normans in eleventh-century Welsh *teuluoedd* diminished their 'aristocratic

---

[80] *Saga*, p. 471.
[81] *CT*, XI, p. 14.
[82] *CBT*, II, 14.89–90.
[83] *Earliest*, p. 126.
[84] Compare Hywel ab Owain Gwynedd's close relations with his foster brothers, the sons of Cedifor.
[85] *Mabinogi*, p. 63; *PK*, p. 25. Teirnon himself is said to have once been Pwyll's man; perhaps we are supposed to imagine that he was fostered out as a member of Pwyll's *teulu* in his youth.

cachet' and hence their social impact. However, the examples he cites need examination. Gruffudd ap Cynan was a landless adventurer seeking to win a kingdom in Wales. He was raised in Ireland and found his main military support there and thus it is hardly surprising to find Irishmen in his military following. It is likely that many of his Irish followers had noble backgrounds, but this meant little to the Welsh of Gwynedd and the reluctance to use the term *teulu* has been suggested. Gruffudd also had Welshmen in his household and in one passage the elements of his following are carefully distinguished: 'Then his Danes [W. *Daynysseit*], the men of his household [W. *guyr y dy*] and his own warband [W. *tylwyth*] were angered, because they were not getting what they were accustomed to, as had been promised them.'[86] Whilst it is likely that some Irish were included in his inner household, the majority of the foreigners are labelled 'his Danes'. Following the capture of Gruffudd and his *nifer* by Hugh of Chester, the source again isolates Gruffudd's 'foreign mercenaries' as a distinct entity.[87] An account of Gruffudd's raiding in south Wales in the *Life of St Gwynllyw* separates the activities of Gruffudd and his closest companions from the 'pirates' (presumably from Ireland) in his fleet who rampaged out of control.[88]

Crouch's claim that Caradog ap Gruffudd employed Normans in his *teulu* has less to substantiate it. Caradog used the Normans as allies against his Welsh enemies, certainly in 1072 and 1081, and possibly on other occasions.[89] However, there is no evidence to suggest that Caradog accepted Normans into his *teulu*. If any were so employed, their number is likely to have been small and there is no indication that they threatened the character of Caradog's court, household or kingdom.

When foreigners were employed in a *teulu*, they did not overwhelm its traditional, native, highly stratified structure. The *teulu* was a keystone of Welsh society and membership was a privilege essential to members of the military aristocracy. Welsh leaders seem to have used fewer mercenaries from the latter half of the twelfth century onwards, as the Anglo-Norman activity in

---

[86] *Gruffudd ap Cynan*, p. 65.
[87] Ibid., p. 69.
[88] *Vitae*, p. 185.
[89] See *Brut (Pen. 20)*, s.a. 1072; *Gruffudd ap Cynan*, p. 66.

Ireland cut off this source of hired help and their lack of resources meant that they could not compete for such troops against the demands of the marcher lords or lords from England. This may have contributed to the reluctance to accept outsiders into the *teulu* at a time when households elsewhere in Europe were seeing increasing moves towards waged service.

THE *PENTEULU*

The prestigious position of head of the lord's household (W. *penteulu*) was coveted by the greatest members of the nobility. It may be expected that the duty of the *penteulu* was to lead his lord's forces into battle whilst his master remained at court, but such a role as a back-room general was foreign to leaders of the day. War leadership was an essential part of kingship throughout the Middle Ages as lords were expected to be vigorous and to lead their nobility to glory and booty. Dafydd Benfras's description of Llywelyn ap Gruffudd in the thirteenth century is appropriate to leaders throughout the period of study: 'When he goes to battle he does not hide himself.'[90] A lord who relinquished his war leadership before he established his martial credentials risked losing the respect, trust and loyalty of his men and was in danger of being removed by a more active kinsman. To kill the opposing lord in battle, or force him to flee the field, would usually end the encounter and signal victory. An exceptional case was noted in the *Triads*, and the heroics of the forces involved led them to be labelled as one of the 'Three Faithful Warbands of Britain': 'The *teulu* of Gwenddolau son of Ceidiaw at Arfderydd, who continued the battle for a fortnight and a month after their lord was slain'.[91] There were times when a lord did not lead his *teulu* – due to age, illness, or other commitments – and on these occasions leadership presumably passed to the

---

[90] N. Bosco, 'Dafydd Benfras and his Red Book poems', *Studia Celtica*, 22 (1987), 49–117 (p. 102).
[91] *Triads*, p. 59.

penteulu.⁹² In the *Gododdin*, Mynyddog Mwynfawr was responsible for gathering the force sent to Catraeth, but he took no part in the expedition. It could be speculated that he was a senior king whose reputation encouraged the response to his call but whose age meant that his campaigning days were over. Math, lord of Gwynedd, could not accompany his *teulu* on its *cylch* for the rather extraordinary reason that he could only move his feet from a virgin's lap when waging war!⁹³ In his absence, his nephews led the *teulu*. The *Life of St Cadog* describes a *teulu*, that of the regulus Paulentus of Glamorgan, on an outing led by the *penteulu* (St) Illtud, described as *princeps militie*.⁹⁴ In 1215 Llywelyn ap Iorwerth gathered a coalition of the princes of Wales. The *Brutiau* present a list of the lords present before concluding with the words 'and the *teulu* of Madog ap Gruffudd Maelor'.⁹⁵ Madog is the exception in not leading his forces and, as his age does not preclude him, perhaps we can assume ill health. To employ a *penteulu* reflected honour on the lord, indicating a *teulu* of considerable size and importance. In the *Canu Heledd* cycle of poems, Heledd praises her four 'lordly brothers' each of whom had a *penteulu*.⁹⁶

The office of *penteulu* was reserved for the higher nobility within a leader's following. The laws state that: 'When the *penteulu* dies, the king is entitled to his horse and his arms and his dog and his hawks, in lieu of his *ebediw* (death duty), since there is no right to any *ebediw* from a king's member, except his harness.'⁹⁷ Jenkins notes that by the thirteenth century the *ebediw* of ordinary men had been commuted, but because of the close relation between a *penteulu* and his lord, payment in kind continued. Crouch wrote of the status of the *penteulu*: '[he] was one of the king's chief ministers,

---

⁹² In 1157, Owain Gwynedd entrusted detachments of his forces to his sons Dafydd, Cynan and Hywel; see below, p. 73. In 1263, when Llywelyn ap Gruffudd and Dafydd were in Gwynedd, Llywelyn had a large army in the south led by his *distain*, Goronwy ab Ednyfed: see Smith, *LG*, p. 151. Gerald of Wales says that Gwenllian, wife of Gruffudd ap Rhys, led an army against their Marcher enemies in 1136. This was when Gruffudd was in north Wales — presumably with his *teulu* — trying to win support for his rising and suggests that battle was forced by the Marchers, making Gwenllian's role an emergency measure; *Journey*, I, 9, p. 137.
⁹³ *Mabinogi*, p. 99; *PK*, p. 67. In *Culhwch and Olwen*, Arthur's men tell him not to accompany the *llu* on some errands because the duties are too petty; *Mabinogi*, p. 163; *CaO*, p. 31.
⁹⁴ *Vitae*, p. 63.
⁹⁵ *Brut (Pen. 20)*, s.a. 1215.
⁹⁶ *Saga*, p. 493.
⁹⁷ *Law*, p. 11.

preferably a kinsman, never one of his suspect gentry.'[98] This implies that the greater men were only chosen because the king could trust them, but such men posed the greatest threat to a leader's position. The evidence suggests that the higher nobility were chosen as *penteulu* because it was a prestigious office that social sensibilities allowed only them to fill. The laws reflect the position of honour accorded the *penteulu*; he is first among the king's officers and receives a favourable position in the hall with many privileges. It is further stated in the *Iorwerth* redaction:

> It is right for the *penteulu* to be the king's son or nephew, or a man so high that he can be made *penteulu*. It is not right that an *uchelwr* should be *penteulu*; the reason it is not right is that the captain's status depends on the king, and that of no *uchelwr* does so.[99]

The sensitivity involved in his appointment can be glimpsed in the *Triads*. The proud nobles in the *teulu* disliked being led by anyone but their lord and we are told of the 'Three Battle Horsemen of Arthur's Court': 'they would never endure a *penteulu* over them.'[100]

Evidence for the elevated social position of those chosen as *penteulu* is found in the prose tales and in traditions concerning the saints of Wales. The inactive Math chose his nephews to lead his *teulu* and in the *The Dream of Rhonabwy* Madog ap Maredudd of Powys asked his brother Iorwerth to become his *penteulu*.[101] This was intended as compensation to Iorwerth because Madog was ruling all of Powys and, although the offer was refused, it was a genuine attempt at conciliation. In the lives of the Welsh saints, the authors were trying to stress the nobility of their subjects and their families; they chose to do this by portraying them in the position of *penteulu*. St Illtud led the household of King Paulentus of Glamorgan, St Cybi's father was *princeps militie* for a king in Cornwall and the military term *dux cohortis* was used to describe St Padarn's duty as leader of a band of monks.[102]

---

[98] Crouch, *Image*, p. 160.
[99] *Law*, p. 8; other versions differ from the *Iorwerth* redaction, naming the king's son or nephew as appropriate *penteulu* but not excluding *uchelwyr*.
[100] *Triads*, p. 31.
[101] *Mabinogi*, p. 178; *BR*, p. 1. In *Owein*, the eponymous hero is named *penteulu* to Arthur: *Mabinogi*, p. 216; *Owein*, p. 30.
[102] *Vitae*, pp. 63, 197, 235, 275.

Support for these literary passages is found in chronicle references of the twelfth and thirteenth centuries. Rhys ap Gruffudd's nephew Einion ab Anarawd, the son of Rhys's eldest brother, was his *penteulu*;[103] Carr contends that two of Rhys's sons, Morgan and Cynwrig, served as *penteulu* to their brothers Gruffudd and Maelgwn;[104] Dafydd ap Gruffudd of Gwynedd was *penteulu* to his brother Owain and may later have served Llywelyn ap Gruffudd in this position.[105]

Thirteenth-century evidence reveals that the administrative office of *distain* had (or had come to acquire) a military role similar to that of the *penteulu*. Ednyfed Fychan, a prominent *uchelwr*, held this position under Llywelyn ap Iorwerth and, in the prince's absence, was sent on expeditions at the head of Llywelyn's forces.[106] It has been suggested that the office of *distain* had supplanted that of *penteulu* as the princes were anxious to take military power from the hands of their close kin and potential rivals.[107] There does not seem to be enough evidence to support this theory and it is more likely that the increasing power and widespread interests of the princes created a demand for more subordinate military officers.[108]

In addition to the prestige enjoyed by the *penteulu*, the laws list numerous privileges accorded to the office-holder. He was to be lodged in the largest house in the *tref* and the king was to provide horses, arms, fodder, horseshoes and nails for him. In a later addition in the law texts, the *penteulu* was entitled to three pounds annually from the king as his bounty (W. *rhaith*), twenty pence from every pound paid to the king in judicial cases concerning land and twenty-four pence from every man of the *teulu* in 'the first year he rides'.[109] Further privileges included a song from the *bardd teulu* whenever he requested it, free medical treatment from

---

[103] *Brut (Pen. 20)*, s.a. 1164.
[104] A. D. Carr, 'Dulliau rhyfel yr Arglwydd Rhys,' in N.A. Jones and H. Pryce (eds), *Yr Arglwydd Rhys* (Cardiff, 1996), pp. 76–93 (pp. 77–8); *Teulu and penteulu*, p. 78.
[105] *CW*, s.a. 1255.
[106] For discussion of Ednyfed's role in 1263, see A. D. Carr, 'The last and weakest of his line: Dafydd ap Gruffydd, the last Prince of Wales,' *WHR*, 19 (1999), 375–99, p. 395.
[107] T. Jones-Pierce, 'The age of the Princes', in J. B. Smith (ed.), *Medieval Welsh Society* (Cardiff, 1972), pp. 19–38.
[108] Jones-Pierce's claims are rejected by D. Stephenson in *Governance*, pp. 15–17. Stephenson argues that administrative officers were flexible and able to perform a variety of duties. However, J. B. Smith agrees with Jones-Pierce and says that the *distain* took the military role of the *penteulu* just as he took the judicial role of the *ynad llys*: *LG*, p. 204.
[109] *Law*, pp. 9, 92.

the physician (W. *meddyg*) of the *teulu*, a due-collecting *cylch* around the king's townlands after Christmas,[110] and shares of the booty won by the *teulu* on campaign.[111]

In return for these concessions, the laws demanded specific duties from the *penteulu*. He was to accompany the king at all times and be ready to do his bidding, only leaving his side when performing an errand for the king.[112] His main duty seems to have been to maintain discipline and harmonious relations within the *teulu* to ensure its effectiveness:

> If any man of the *teulu* goes away from the king by reason of anger, it is right for him [the *penteulu*] to invite him to his meal, and to reconcile him with the king . . . the *teulu* is not entitled to give away their clothing without the leave of the *penteulu*. It is right for him to go before them everywhere, and that they should do nothing save with his counsel.[113]

The *penteulu* was responsible for the mechanics of mustering and organizing the *teulu* for a given campaign, raid or errand:

> His lodging is the largest house in the townland and the most central, and with him those he wishes of the *teulu*, with the others surrounding him so that it shall be convenient for him to find them at need . . . When the *teulu* must go on a raid, or on some other errand, it is right for him to choose those whom he wants to send, and he is not entitled to be refused.[114]

The *teulu* formed the core of a Welsh leader's military power, but when a greater force was required this core played a key role in gathering and leading it. It may be suggested that in a large muster each member of the *teulu* would have some responsibility for gathering troops.[115] Possibly the junior members would be used as messengers to the localities, able to ride there quickly and

---

[110] It may be of significance that Harold Godwinesson attacked Gruffudd ap Llywelyn after Christmas (1062) when, according to the law texts, the *teulu* was away from its lord on a *cylch* of his townships under the *penteulu* (*Law*, p. 11); Gruffudd seems to have been unable to muster a significant force at this time.
[111] *Law*, pp. 10–11.
[112] Ibid., p. 11.
[113] Ibid., pp. 9–10.
[114] Ibid.
[115] In *Branwen*, Brân was at court when he heard of his sister's mistreatment in Ireland. He 'immediately began to muster the island', suggesting that messengers were sent from his court to gather 'the full complement of 154 districts': *Mabinogi*, p. 74; *PK*, p. 38.

with power to enforce their leader's will. The *Brutiau* show us the system in action in 1110. The fugitives Cadwgan ap Bleddyn and his son Owain entered the land of Uchdryd ab Edwin:

> And when the sons of Uchdryd and their *teulu*, whom Uchdryd had left defending their land, heard that they sent to Meirionnydd to bid everyone assemble together to drive them out of their land. And the men of Meirionnydd gathered to the sons of Uchdryd.[116]

THE *TEULU* AND ITS LORD

Without the presence and support of a *teulu*, effective rule would have been impossible for a lord. Its importance is made clear in the laws: 'The three indispensables of a king are his priest, for blessing the food and singing mass; the court justice, for resolving doubtful things; and his *teulu*, for his necessities.'[117] The *teulu* protected the king from his enemies. It ensured his social position, both by giving him the physical force to rule as part of a military elite and by providing him with the prestige and trappings of nobility.

A great household allowed a king to express his superiority over other nobles. Walter Map tells the story of an argument between two Welsh kings during which each tried to prove his strength by boasting about the size of his household.[118] Similar pride may be seen in the description of the household of St Gwynllyw: 'The largeness of his household could not be certified at a fixed number, they could not be quartered in royal courts and houses, but tents were wont to be set up on the open ground to quarter them.'[119] The *teulu* established a lord's position over other nobles at a more practical level, that of attacking, raiding and coercing his neighbours. In Walter Map's story the kings boast that their extensive households mean that they can raid anyone, seize booty and return home without their enemies daring to challenge them. Raiding was a common feature of Welsh life that dominated warfare and provided a means of

---

[116] *Brut (Pen. 20)*, s.a. 1110.
[117] *Law*, p. 39; see also p. 11.
[118] Map, pp. 153–5.
[119] *Vitae*, p. 173.

exerting political pressure. A leader needed a powerful *teulu* to establish his position as a war leader, which was essential to retain the loyalty of his men and to win additional political hegemony.

Before a lord could consider attacking his rivals, he needed to defend his own land effectively. Early in his career, Gruffudd ap Cynan encountered resistance to his attempts to consolidate his position in Gwynedd. The nobles of the land turned on him and in a surprise attack killed fifty-two of his 'knights' and his *teulu* (W. *varchogyon Gruffud a'e deulu*).[120] This loss delighted Gruffudd's rival Trahaearn, who gathered a force, raided Gruffudd's land and was able to drive him to Ireland. In 1110 Uchdryd ab Edwin left his sons and their *teulu* in his land to organize its defence and they attempted to counter the moves of Owain and Cadwgan of Powys.[121]

The importance of the *teulu* as a bodyguard was seen at the battle of Pwllgwdig (1078): 'the whole *teulu* of Rhys [ab Owain] fell, and he himself fled like a wounded frightened stag through the thorns and briars before the hounds. And at the close of that year Caradog ap Gruffudd slew Rhys and Hywel, his brother.'[122] Court poetry lauds a *teulu* that remained faithful to its lord. In the *Lament for Llywelyn ap Gruffudd*:

> Pob teulu, teilwng oedd iddaw,
> Pob cedwyr, cedwynt adanaw[123]
>
> (All retainers were true to his trust,
> All warriors were his defenders.)[124]

Teulu members were expected to stand by their lord to the last and do everything in their power to protect him. Gruffudd ap Cynan was saved after the battle of Bron-yr-erw turned against him when a member of his *teulu* dragged him from the heat of the action to his ship.[125] Gruffudd got his revenge at the battle of Mynydd Carn, where his rival Trahaearn was killed, but only

---

[120] *Gruffudd ap Cynan*, p. 62.
[121] *Brut (Pen. 20)*, s.a. 1110.
[122] Ibid., s.a. 1078.
[123] *CBT*, VII, 36.77–8.
[124] *Beginnings*, p. 33.
[125] *Gruffudd ap Cynan*, p. 63.

after twenty-five of Trahaearn's *teulu* had been cut down around their lord and other *teulu* members had been killed in the front line of battle.[126]

When the *llu* had been gathered, the military professionalism of the *teulu* was utilized to maximize the potential of the less experienced troops by placing *teulu* members as subordinate commanders. The existence of such an officer corps from the *teulu* is suggested by a number of literary passages. The *Triads* refer to the 'Three Battle Diademed [W. *Taleithyavc*] Men of Britain', leaders in battle distinguished by torques worn on their heads, the equivalent of the heroes wearing *cae* who fought in the van in the *Gododdin*.[127] Archaeological evidence suggests that such torques had not been worn in Britain since pre-Roman times, but references to them indicate that battle leaders were distinguished in some way. Taliesin described the members of Urien of Rheged's *teulu* with their torques around their heads,[128] and Cynddelw Brydydd Mawr refers to a 'golden torqued gold throng'.[129]

Given the effectiveness of the *teulu* as a military force, it is not surprising to find Welsh leaders using it at times for what could be described as special force operations. The *Brutiau* record the use of *teuluoedd* in night manoeuvres and attacks.[130] They were effective in siege operations, their successful assaults on castles being described in the *Brutiau*.[131]

It was considered right for a *teulu* to remain true to its immediate overlord, even if he was in the wrong or in rebellion against a higher overlord, and if necessary to follow him into exile.[132] Abels considered this a duty of the households of Anglo-Saxon lords,[133] and it seems equally true in Wales. In the

---

[126] Ibid., p. 68. It is recorded that eighteen 'notable men' were killed with Llywelyn ap Gruffudd at Irfon Bridge in 1282 and it is assumed that these were members of his *teulu*: *LG*, p. 565, n.185.

[127] *Triads*, p. 37; see also p. 167, 'The Three Fettered Warbands [W. *Hualhogeon Deulu*] of Britain'.

[128] *Earliest*, p. 27; *CT*, V, 5.

[129] *Earliest*, p. 143; *CBT*, III, 8.23 (W. 'Yn fintai wych o ryfelwyr yn gwisgo torchau aur').

[130] *Brut (Pen. 20)*, s.a. 1113, 1210; for more discussion, see below, pp. 40–2.

[131] *Brut (Pen. 20)*, s.a. 1116, 1146, 1158, 1193, 1260; *Brut (RBH)*, s.a. 1096, 1202; for more discussion, see below, pp. 207–17.

[132] One of the 'Three Faithful Warbands' was that of Cadwallon, said to have followed their lord into exile in Ireland for seven years: *Triads*, p. 57.

[133] Abels, *Lordship*, p. 17.

Gododdin, Mynyddog sent his *gosgordd* on a hopeless quest, a suicide mission, yet the greatest praise is lavished on every man for not fleeing the situation but fighting to the bitter end and 'earning their mead'. In the *Llywarch Hen* poems, Llywarch's son Gwên promised to fight heroically at the ford of the Llawen and only withdraw when prudent or necessary. Llywarch goads his son into fighting to the last, even when it would be senseless to continue. Gwên is then praised (and mourned) for following such foolish orders and getting killed.[134] Generally, a retainer was not expected to fight to the death in a hopeless cause, but he should have been prepared to die in his lord's place and he had a duty to avenge his lord's death.[135] Such idealized expectations were seen in Anglo-Saxon military households, even if the principles were not always reflected in practice.[136]

The *Triads* describe the 'Three Faithless Warbands of Britain'.[137] Two of these were *teuluoedd* which abandoned their lords during, or on the eve of, battles, thus earning themselves everlasting infamy. The other example is even more revealing: 'The *teulu* of Goronwy the Radiant of (Penllyn), who refused to receive the poisoned spear from Lleu Skilful-Hand on behalf of their lord, at the Stone of Goronwy at the head of the Cynfal'. The prose tale which this triad was designed to herald has survived. In the tale of *Math*, Goronwy plotted to murder Lleu and succeeded in injuring him by throwing a spear at him. After his recovery, Lleu demanded revenge by being allowed to throw a spear at Goronwy, who consequently appealed: 'Nobles, troops, foster-brothers, will any of you take the blow in my stead?'[138] We may find their refusal to accept certain death in order to save their treacherous, dishonourable lord understandable, but the Welsh literary tradition castigates them and considers it their duty to have died in Goronwy's place.

---

[134] *Saga*, pp. 14–20.
[135] In 1188 Gerald of Wales met a retainer of Owain Fychan ap Madog. Owain had been murdered in the previous year and the man refused to take the Cross until '. . . with this spear which I hold in my hand I have first avenged my master's death': *Journey*, II, 12, p. 201.
[136] R. Woolf, 'The ideal of men dying with their lord in the *Germania* and in *The Battle of Maldon*', *Anglo-Saxon England*, 5 (1976), 63–81; S.D. White, 'Kinship and lordship in early medieval England: the story of Sigeberht, Cynewulf and Cyneheard', *Viator*, 20 (1989), 1–18; S. Fanning, 'Tacitus, Beowulf and the comitatus', *The Haskins Society Journal*, 9 (1997), 17–38.
[137] *Triads*, p. 61.
[138] *Mabinogi*, p. 116; *PK*, pp. 91–2.

Given this duty ethic expected of *teulu* members, the institution can be considered to have had a disruptive influence on Welsh society. Wendy Davies contends that any aristocrat with a military following could establish himself in Wales in the eleventh century, even if his genealogical claims were weak.[139] In the twelfth and thirteenth centuries the Welsh political scene was thrown into chaos by the influx of Anglo-Normans. Political violence ruled the day and we see feuds between the Welsh ruling classes, with various royal lines seeking to establish themselves. Again we see the *teulu* at the forefront of this action and the *Brutiau* present examples of *teuluoedd* ambushing, capturing and murdering political rivals.[140] They were motivated by duty to their lord and the promise of reward if their man were to win additional land and wealth.

In discussing the duty of a *teulu* to its lord, it is important to remember the influence which it wielded over his actions. He was obliged to lead his men on successful military expeditions, to satisfy their martial lust and to win booty and land with which to reward them. Pwyll was praised by his nobles for his rule in the previous year: 'never have you distributed your goods more freely, never was your discernment so marked.'[141] Following his revolt against the English in 1256, Llywelyn ap Gruffudd was praised because he kept 'naught for himself but only fame and honour'.[142] The twelfth-century poem *Breintiau Gwyr Powys* is concerned to protect the fighting men's entitlement to plunder.[143] A lord had a duty to at least consider the advice of his leading men. The king's nobles forced Pwyll to punish and put aside his beloved wife Rhiannon because she seemed unable to bear a son who would lead the kingdom to future success.[144] Similarly, the nobles of St Cadog's father, Gwynllyw, a notable

---

[139] W. Davies, *Patterns of Power in Early Wales* (Oxford, 1990), p. 80. Although they cannot be entirely trusted, the Llandaff charters describe the *familia* of Welsh rulers at the centre of any mischief, performing unlawful killings, attacking the church and breaking sanctuary.

[140] *Brut (Pen. 20)*, s.a. 1111, 1113, 1139, 1143, 1197, 1204.

[141] *Mabinogi*, p. 51; *PK*, p. 8. Compare Arthur's speech in *Culhwch and Olwen*: 'We are noble men so long as others come to us, and the more gifts we distribute, the greater will be our reputation and fame and glory': *Mabinogi*, p. 139; *CaO*, pp. 5–6.

[142] *Brut (Pen. 20)*, s.a. 1256.

[143] T. M. Charles-Edwards and N. A. Jones, '*Breintiau Gwŷr Powys*: The liberties of the men of Powys', in Charles-Edwards, Owen and Russell (eds), *The Welsh King and his Court*, pp. 191–223.

[144] *Mabinogi*, pp. 59–60; *PK*, pp. 18–19.

military leader, complained when his religious son abstained from 'feasting, playing dice and other activities of the household': 'What means this religion of our son? We were expecting the increase of the kingdom from him, who by his preaching destroys our household. Let us force him to warfare, because he knows better than us how to rule the people.'[145]

If a Welsh leader lost the trust, confidence and belief of his men the result could be disastrous. In an early attempt to win power in Gwynedd, Gruffudd ap Cynan denied his household and mercenary troops the plundering to which they felt they were entitled.[146] He was lucky in that they merely ignored him and ravaged Anglesey before forcibly returning Gruffudd to Ireland. In other cases the leader was killed, the most famous recipient of this treatment being Gruffudd ap Llywelyn. Following Harold's campaign of 1063 and a year spent hiding in the wastelands of Wales, Gruffudd's men lost faith in their king; they killed him and delivered his head to Harold.

Motivation for *teulu* members ranged from the most practical and everyday reasons to social and psychological factors specific to Welsh society of the day. At the most basic level a lord provided his followers with board and lodging. In medieval society this raised a man from being a producer to a consumer, elevating him to the aristocracy which disdained working the land for a living.[147] A recurring phrase in Welsh poetry was that a man should do his duty to his lord and thereby 'earn his mead'.[148]

> Since a lord has gone into Rhodwydd Iwerydd,
> Oh *teulu* do not flee.
> After mead do not wish for disgrace.[149]

As one of the favourite images of the bards, the phrase 'earning your mead' came to have a greater symbolism than its basic

---

[145] *Vitae*, p. 35.
[146] *Gruffudd ap Cynan*, p. 65.
[147] In *Pwyll*, after receiving a mortal blow, Hafgan's main concern was to tell his men, 'I can no longer maintain you.' Consequently, they became the men of the victor, Pwyll: *Mabinogi*, p. 50; *PK*, p. 6.
[148] The most famous references are in the *Gododdin*, and later poetry consciously imitates this work. The phrase is unlikely to have been coined in the *Gododdin*, however; the 'earning of mead' is an ancient notion with parallels in other cultures and societies.
[149] *Saga*, p. 503.

reading suggests, but a man's duty to earn his victuals always remained.[150] A retainer also expected a lord's social leadership through the provision of entertainment, feasting and song at court. In all these aspects of court life a lord was expected to participate; in *The Dream of Maxen*, the *teulu* of the love-struck emperor begin to slander their lord for no longer feasting, drinking mead from golden cups, or listening to songs and entertainment with them.[151] The laws make special provision for the office of the *bardd teulu*, a man whose duty was both to fight with the *teulu* and to entertain them in the hall afterwards.[152]

A lord was obliged to provide his men with suitable clothing. Members of the *teulu* needed the permission of the *penteulu* before giving away their clothes, showing that they ultimately belonged to the king.[153] The quality of a man's clothes reflected on the dignity of his lord. Prydydd y Moch's poem *In Praise of Llywelyn ap Iorwerth* glorified the prince by describing his 'red-robed retainers'.[154] Llywelyn ap Gruffudd gained appreciation from the people of Gwynedd for his generosity to his men in distributing robes at Christmas.[155] To wear the clothes given by a great lord reflected honour on the warrior; in *Canu Heledd*, Caranfael is said to have worn the battle cloak of Cynddylan.[156] Equally, a lord could be condemned for cladding his followers in inappropriate attire. On his journey through north Wales, Gerald of Wales met Maredudd ap Cynan, who was embarrassed by the old cloak worn by one of his men.[157]

When referring to clothing it is likely that the provision of weapons by a lord was included. This would raise a man into the

---

[150] Survivals of the notion can be seen in the households of the Anglo-Norman kings. At Bourgthéroulde (1124), Henry I's household troops are urged to fight a superior enemy force as otherwise '. . . we shall never again be entitled to eat the king's bread': OV, VI, 12, pp. 349–53. In later official records of men retained on money fiefs in England, the term used is *uictus* ('sustenance'); the ancient requirement of food and lodging still retained a significance.
[151] *Mabinogi*, pp. 121–2; *BM*, p. 4.
[152] See D. Jenkins, 'The *Bardd Teulu* and the *Pencerdd*', in Charles-Edwards, Owen and Russell (eds), *The Welsh King and his Court*, pp. 142–66.
[153] *Law*, p. 10.
[154] *CBT*, V, 20.34. Madog ap Maredudd was similarly praised by Cynddelw Brydydd Mawr: ibid., III, 7.16.
[155] L. B. Smith, 'The *Gravamina* of the community of Gwynedd against Llywelyn ap Gruffudd', *BBCS*, 31 (1984), 158–76 (clause 95).
[156] *Saga*, p. 510.
[157] *Journey*, II, 5, p. 182.

military elite and the practice is suggested by the duty of the *penteulu* to arrange for the return of his horse and arms to the king after his death.[158] A generous lord could win glory by his gifts. Witness Gwalchmai ap Meilyr's poem *To Owain Gwynedd*:

> Fe roddodd i mi o'i ysbail heb atal
> Feirch cadarn eu cnawd, anrhydeddus o rodd.
> Ac yn awr adwaen i ar unwaith [yr] arweinydd ym mrwydr.[159]

> (Out of his gains he gave me ungrudgingly
> Firm-fleshed horses, honourable grace,
> And he knew me as eager to fight in the forefront.)[160]

Cynddelw Brydydd Mawr praised Madog ap Maredudd:

> Dosberthaist erioed tuag atom
> Feirch bychain hir eu llam o dan faner[161]

> (Often has he bestowed upon us
> High-stepping steeds with silken trappings.)[162]

From around the twelfth century in most of Europe there began a trend to commute traditional forms of reward to household members into money retainers. This was by no means universal, though, and other forms of retaining and reward continued to play a role. There is little evidence for commutation to cash in Wales where the amount of money in circulation was limited, but the later law texts suggest that an annual money retainer was starting to be paid to the *penteulu*.[163]

---

[158] *Law*, p. 11.
[159] *CBT*, I, 8.73–5.
[160] *Welsh Verse*, p. 144.
[161] *CBT*, III, 1.21–2.
[162] *Earliest*, p. 137. See also the praise of Gruffudd ap Cynan in Meilyr Brydydd's elegy: 'It was a generous king who used to distribute gifts in his sovereignty; He hoarded neither arms nor unused steeds'; J. E. Caerwyn Williams, 'Meilyr Brydydd and Gruffudd ap Cynan', in K. L. Maund (ed.), *Gruffudd ap Cynan: A Collaborative Biography* (Woodbridge, 1996), p. 185.
[163] *Law*, p. 9.

Possibly the most significant reward for members of the *teulu* throughout the period was the booty seized in raids. This could take the form of victuals, clothing, arms and armour, horses, cattle, slaves and hostages, precious objects and even land.[164] The laws make provision as to how the booty won on campaign should be divided. In the lives of Welsh saints, noble households tour the countryside demanding booty from its religious establishments.[165] In his early career, St Gwynllyw was said to be the ideal lord for a military household: 'He was a most famous conqueror in warfare, pacific after conquest, he was a victor never vanquished. His countrymen gloried in such a lord, frequently rewarded, they returned after every yearly circuit.'[166] The course of a typical raiding expedition is described in the *Brutiau* in 1110, when Owain ap Cadwgan was hiding as an outlaw with his men in Ceredigion:

> And his [Owain's] comrades went on forays to Dyfed and they plundered the land and seized the people and carried them off with them . . . On another occasion they summoned 'hotheads' [W. *ynfydion*] from Ceredigion to add to the numbers along with them, and by night they came to a township of Dyfed and slew all that they found, and despoiled others and carried others off with them as prisoners to the ships, and thence sold them to their folk. And after burning the houses and killing the animals and carrying others off with them, they returned to Ceredigion.[167]

Such were the spoils of war in the Middle Ages; they were prized by the *teulu* and did significant damage to the power of an enemy. Only in the taking of slaves did such spoils differ to those seized in warfare in contemporary England and France.

In addition to these irregular benefits of service, the laws list privileges to which *teulu* members were entitled. In certain instances they could take the dues from legal cases, but when they themselves, or those belonging to them, were judged it was for free.[168] *Teulu* members were entitled to free medical care

---

[164] Gwalchmai gloried in the victories of Owain Gwynedd: 'He [Owain] pours forth wealth and wealthy gifts': *Welsh Poems*, p. 35: (W. 'Tywallta gyfoeth, drudfawr roddion': *CBT*, I, 9.143).

[165] *Vitae*, pp. 11, 35, 59, 63, 73, 197–9.

[166] Ibid., p. 173.

[167] *Brut (Pen. 20)*, s.a. 1110.

[168] *Law*, pp. 16–17.

(barring specific injuries), a valuable privilege, given the hazards of their lives.[169] Life in the *teulu* offered a degree of security and support.

Apart from these material benefits, the *teulu* was motivated by more elusive forces arising from the martial nature of court life, the historical and family traditions in Wales, and the exhortations of the bards. These created a love of war and glorification of martial deeds, a sense of camaraderie, and codes of honour and duty. Perhaps the poetry of the court offers the best impression of this cultural ethos. The prince-poet Hywel ab Owain Gwynedd awaited the campaigning season:

> Caraf i, adeg haf, sathriad march,
> Eiddgar yw['r] fyddin o flaen arglwydd dewr.[170]
>
> (I love summer time and the thronging of horses;
> A warband is eager before a brave lord.)[171]

Hywel described his affection for Gwynedd:

> Caraf ei theulu a'i haml drigfan o'i mewn,
> Ac wrth fodd ei brenin reoli rhyfel.[172]
>
> (I love its warband and its strong buildings
> And at its lord's wish to go to war.)[173]

Such a prince shared the aspirations of his martial followers and earned their love and trust. The spirit created is reflected in the lament of one of Hywel's men, Peryf ap Cedifor, for the slaying of his lord:

> Tra buom yn saith, ni byddai tair gwaith saith yn ein herio,
> Ni pharent inni gilio cyn ein marwolaeth[174]

---

[169] Ibid., p. 24. See also M.E. Owen, 'Medics and medicine', in Charles-Edwards, Owen and Russell (eds), *The Welsh King and his Court*, pp. 116–41.
[170] *CBT*, II, 7.1–2.
[171] *Welsh Poems*, p. 39.
[172] *CBT*, II, 6.7–8.
[173] *WVIE*, p. 22.
[174] *CBT*, II, 19.1–2.

(While we were seven men alive, not three sevens
Challenged or routed us.)[175]

The Drinking Horn describes a raid made by Owain Cyfeiliog and his *teulu* through conscious imitation of the *Gododdin*, revealing the heroic milieu that transcended the centuries. Individual warriors are named and men would yearn for such recognition among their peers.[176] The poem describes how warriors 'went for the praise of glory' and delights in their comradeship in arms: 'Owain's cubs, brave men striking as one'.[177] As in the *Gododdin*, such comradeship could even transcend death if a glorious end were made; thus Cynddelw Brydydd Mawr in *The Fall of Powys*:

> Ym maes Bryn Actun can gŵr a fawrygais
> A'm cleddyf gwaedlyd ar fy nghlun,
> Mewn un enciliad yr oedd tri chan arweinydd mewn brwydr,
> Boed iddynt fynd i'r nef ynghyd![178]

> (At Maes Actun I hailed a hundred,
> My red blade at my side;
> In one ebb, three hundred lords:
> May they reach heaven as one.)[179]

Wales was a society in which men had defined duties to their lords. Babcock suggested that the arrival of the Anglo-Normans threatened these bonds, proving a dynamic for change in society.[180] The *Brutiau* described the followers of Gruffudd ap

---

[175] *Welsh Verse*, p. 148.
[176] Gwalchmai reveals similar values and also the desire to win female approval for his heroic actions, recorded in verse and sung to an admiring court: 'At the call of Môn's lord [Owain Gwynedd] I plunged into battle. / And to win favour of my pretty one, like snow on trees, / when they fought before the fort I shed blood': *Welsh Poems*, p. 33: (W. 'Er Iles brenin Môn ymosodais mewn brwydr, / Ac er ffafr [yr] un hardd o liw eira ar goed / Pam fu brwydr o flaen Caer, tywelltais waed.'): *CBT*, I, 9.40–2.
[177] *CBT*, II, 14.
[178] Ibid., III, 8.1–4. It was traditionally believed that Owain Cyfeiliog himself wrote this poem about his *teulu*, but the view is now favoured that Cynddelw Brydydd Mawr was the author.
[179] *Earliest*, p. 142.
[180] Babcock, 'Imbeciles', 1–8; also R. R. Davies, 'Henry I and Wales', in H. Mayr-Harting and R. I. Moore (eds), *Studies in Medieval History Presented to R. H. C. Davis* (London, 1985), pp. 133–47.

Rhys in 1116, and those of Owain ap Cadwgan in 1110, as *ynfydion* or 'imbeciles'/'hotheads', and Babcock suggested that this was because they had disregarded the traditional bonds of society. He said that some were members of the *teuluoedd* of other lords, but this cannot be established from the sources. What is certain is that men were drawn from regions not under the lordship of Gruffudd or Owain, thus breaking horizontal ties of lordship within Wales. It is likely that, as R. R. Davies suggested, these men were not taken from the *teuluoedd* of other lords, but that they represent the equivalent of the class of *juvenes* on the continent: young, restless, landless men of the military class. They were called 'imbeciles' because of the futility of their rebellion against Henry I.[181] Babcock's contention that they broke traditional loyalties to rally against the invading Normans under the 'patriotic' Gruffudd is a partial but insufficient explanation. These men represented an aristocratic surplus in Wales, possibly caused by a growing population, possibly by a shortage of land to sustain the native nobility following the conquests of the Normans. They were men desperate for a lord and desperate for patronage, in other words men without a *teulu*.

The chief motivation for being a member of a military household may have been the chance to win a lord's favour. Through loyal service and friendship a man could gain patronage and rise spectacularly, as in the case of William Marshal. The ultimate reward was land; such gifts were rare in Wales due to the shortage of land and the increasing inroads of the Anglo-Normans, but after his campaigns of 1136–7 Owain Gwynedd granted north Ceredigion to his brother Cadwaladr and following his conquests of 1256 Llywelyn ap Gruffudd was praised for keeping 'naught for himself'. These grants were at the highest levels of lordship in Wales. Further down the scale evidence is scarce and difficult, but there are suggestions that military service to a lord could be rewarded with land grants. The Llancarfan charters claim to record the grant of a township to Guengarth, the foster-son of King Morgan, after he saved the king from drowning.[182] If this

---

[181] For an examination of the class of *juvenes* on the continent, see G. Duby, 'Youth in aristocratic society', in his *The Chivalrous Society* (London, 1977), pp. 112–22. They were trained military men without land; thus they were wild, restless, in search of adventure and booty, 'the spearhead of feudal aggression'.

[182] *Vitae*, p. 131; there are many dangers in using this early charter material, but it at least seems that such a grant was considered plausible.

evidence is suspect, early thirteenth-century charters in the same area of Wales recorded grants made by Morgan ap Caradog to members of his *familia* in the fee of Newcastle, recently reconquered from the Anglo-Normans.[183] The *gwely* settlements seen in parts of Wales were land grants made to the free clans by royal licence from former bond townships. These used to be regarded as deliberate creations at strategic points and routeways in response to the Norman threat, but more recent scholarship indicates that the *gwely* was an ancient institution pre-dating the twelfth century.[184] This suggests that, though we lack early evidence, royal land grants to favoured men had a long history. In Welsh society a freeman of native descent was a noble (W. *bonheddig*), but to rise to the *uchelwyr* class he needed to be a landlord and head of a household;[185] successful service in the *teulu* would seem the most likely way to win such promotion. Over the years most kindreds needed additional land grants to maintain their status because of partible descent.[186] This, along with natural greed, helps to explain the pressure brought on a lord by his *teulu* to make new conquests. These developments have been examined in thirteenth-century Gwynedd, where the material exists for a more substantial study. Stephenson considered the rewards obtained by Ednyfed Fychan and his descendants for their service to the princes of Gwynedd. The family originated in Rhos, but over the years it gained extensive lands elsewhere, notably in Anglesey.[187]

Despite these examples, it was probably more usual for a successful member of the *teulu* to win a superior office in the court, or even simply to have the king's ear to ensure that personal disputes and legal cases would go his way. If the king's favour was maintained, a successful marriage to a wealthy heiress or a member of the royal dynasty could be arranged. Such was the currency of power and such was the ultimate motivation of a *teulu* member.

---

[183] *Handlist*, pp. 19 (59), 23 (72), 24 (75), 34 (110), 35 (112). Roger Cole was said to have received twenty acres, Rhys Goch and Einion ap Rhirid ten acres each. For a discussion of these men and others recorded in the Margam records, see M. Griffiths, 'Native society on the Anglo-Norman frontier: the evidence of the Margam charters', *WHR*, 14 (1988–9), 179–216.
[184] T. M. Charles-Edwards, *Early Irish and Welsh Kinship* (Oxford, 1993), pp. 252–3.
[185] Ibid., pp. 364–5.
[186] Ibid., p. 396.
[187] Stephenson, *Governance*, p. 97.

II
THE *LLU*

Although the *teulu* was the mainstay of the military power of a Welsh king, a larger force could be mustered for major campaigns. Such armies could take the character of a national levy intended to represent 'all the Britons', or, in the later period, 'all of Wales'; the *Triads* speak of Arthur assembling the army (W. *llu*) of the Island of Britain,[1] and in the *Mabinogi* Brân mustered 'all of Britain' for his expedition to Ireland, gathering 'the full complement of 154 districts [W. *gwledydd*]' and leaving only seven leaders to defend the land.[2] Some of the greatest lords in the period considered are associated with the leadership of national levies. Higham believes that Cadwallon of Gwynedd acted as an over-king with regard to the entire 'Irish Sea Province' and utilized the military resources therein to destroy Edwin and dominate Northumbria.[3] This stretches the evidence, but our sources support the idea that the lands of modern Wales stood together against Northumbria; forces from Powys subordinate to Gwynedd (or Mercia) played a role,[4] and the *Triads* tell of Cadwallon leading the force (W. *llu*) of the Welsh (W. *Cymry*) to Meigen.[5] At the earlier Welsh/Northumbrian battle of Chester (*c*.616) we have evidence of the involvement of Powys and Gwynedd and the *Triads* suggest the presence of Gwgon Red Sword, a leader connected with Ceredigion.[6]

After Cadwallon, in our sources we have no notice of a ruler leading a national host until the reign of Gruffudd ap Llywelyn.[7] In 1055 Gruffudd, at the height of his power and ranging over all of Wales, joined the exiled Ælfgar and his Irish mercenaries for

[1] *Triads*, p. 48.
[2] *Mabinogi*, p. 74; *PK*, p. 38.
[3] N. J. Higham, 'Medieval overkingship in Wales: the earliest evidence', *WHR*, 16 (1992–3), 145–59.
[4] See, for example, *Saga*, pp. 127–8.
[5] *Triads*, p. 182.
[6] Ibid., p. 163.
[7] Other rulers, notably Anarawd ap Rhodri, seem likely to have led hosts with some of the characteristics of a national force, but we lack supporting evidence.

an attack on Hereford. Gruffudd played the major role and John of Worcester tells us that the Welsh king 'at once assembled a large army from his whole realm [L. *Ille statim de toto regno suo copiosum exercitum congregans*]'.[8]

After Gruffudd we must wait until the thirteenth century and the two Llywelyns for more references to national levies. Gruffudd ab yr Ynad Coch wrote in praise of Llywelyn ap Gruffudd:

> Gwelais Lywelyn [a'i] luoedd fel [rhai] Merfyn
> A gwŷr Cymru [i'w] therfyn [i gyd] ymysg ei dyrfa.
> Gwelais benaethiaid Gwynedd a Deheubarth,
> Cynheiliaid byddinoedd [mewn] cynulliad ynghyd.[9]

> (I have seen Llywelyn like Merfyn in his hosts,
> And all of Wales trooped around him.
> I have seen chiefs of Gwynedd and the South,
> Columns of war assembled together.)[10]

The *Brutiau* described the force raised by Llywelyn ap Gruffudd to fight Gruffudd ap Gwenwynwyn in 1274 as the 'host [W. *llu*] of all Wales'.[11]

Large Welsh forces were not necessarily national in character. In *Math*, Pryderi is presented mustering the military force of 'South Wales' – drawn from 21 *cantrefi* – for an expedition against Gwynedd.[12] The coalition gathered to face Henry II in 1165 is described in the *Brutiau* as a series of individual hosts from the different regions of the country:

> And against him [Henry II] came Owain and Cadwaladr, sons of Gruffudd ap Cynan, and all the host of Gwynedd with them, and Rhys ap Gruffudd and with him the host of Deheubarth, and Owain Cyfeiliog and Iorwerth Goch ap Maredudd and the sons of Madog ap Maredudd and the host of all Powys with them, and the two sons of Madog ab Idnerth and their host.[13]

---

[8] JW, II, 1055.
[9] *CBT*, VII, 42.23–6.
[10] *Welsh Verse*, p. 158 (wrongly attributed to Elidir Sais in praise of Llywelyn ap Iorwerth).
[11] *Brut (Pen. 20)*, 1274.
[12] *Mabinogi*, p. 102; *PK*, p. 71.
[13] *Brut (Pen. 20)*, 1165. In a letter to Louis VII's court, Owain Gwynedd says that five armies (L. *exercitus*) came together on his side for the expedition; H. Pryce, 'Owain Gwynedd and Louis VII: the Franco-Welsh diplomacy of the first Prince of Wales', *WHR*, 19 (1998), 1–28; p. 7.

This still points to the larger units of lordship within Wales. At a more local level, *Math* tells of the muster of a single *cantref* to face a threat from seaborne pirates.[14] Carr's study of the Welsh military in the twelfth century suggests that the gathering of forces larger than the *teulu* was a development of the period to counter the Norman threat and that little is known about the earlier *llu*.[15] The evidence does not support this conclusion and an examination of the expanded Welsh military force is required.

Terminology

In considering the terminology employed to describe a large Welsh military force, it is dangerous to be too rigid and precise. The standard terms for 'army' are simple enough, *exercitus* in Latin and *byddin* in Welsh, but these are far from universal and other terms can be more ambiguous. Other common Latin terms include *copia*, *agmen* and *manus*, whilst the number of Welsh words are legion; *llu* is the most common, but others include *nifer*, *dygyfor*, *bragad*, *cyman*, *cadfiled*, *cordd*, *dull*, *miled*, *osb*, *lliwed*, *gwaedd* and *twrf*. It does not seem possible to draw any useful conclusions from these terms which can be translated generally as 'a military force'. The numbers and types of forces vary greatly and each term must be considered within its own context.

Numbers

All the problems in trying to assess the numbers in a *teulu* are multiplied when considering larger Welsh forces and conclusions remain highly speculative. In his assessment of Anglo-Norman warfare, Morillo emphasized that rulers never exhausted the available supplies of manpower; army sizes were limited by other factors including training, resources, communications and, most important of all, logistics.[16] Given the diverse nature of settlement and the low intensity of population that prevailed in Wales,

---

[14] *Mabinogi*, p. 110; *PK*, p. 82.
[15] See *Dulliau*, pp. 78ff.
[16] Morillo, *Warfare*, p. 58. See also the comments on logistics in *WW*, pp. 34–6.

a greater proportion of the adult male population was expected to perform military service than in the lowlands of England and France. However, the nature of Wales and its resources meant that there were limits to the size of a force that could be maintained; the potential pool of manpower for purely martial endeavours was not exhausted. Commanders would not muster a force that they could not supply or that was unable to live off the land.

Evidence of logistic support for Welsh forces is limited and, given the nature of the country, its climate and poor communications, little may be expected. However, there are references to the importance of pack-horses.[17] Lords were able to supply significant numbers of troops. Gerald of Wales described Rhys ap Gruffudd's resolve to take the Cross: 'The result was that for nearly a fortnight he applied himself with great energy to all the preparations necessary for so long a journey, collecting pack-animals and sumpter-saddles, persuading other men to go with him and raising funds.'[18] The thirteenth-century princes of Gwynedd applied themselves to the problems of supply. In 1217 Llywelyn ap Iorwerth lost significant numbers of sumpter horses when crossing the Black Mountain on an expedition to Gower.[19] Closer to home, the princes made efforts to organize Gwynedd into distinct upland military and lowland supply zones. Transportation of supplies between upland and lowland was organized, efforts were made to stimulate agriculture and vaccaries were established at strategic points to supply mobile sources of food for times of war.[20] Welsh leaders were capable of handling the provisioning of their forces and the scale of preparations suggests that they were able to muster significant numbers.[21]

Throughout the period considered the number of troops available in Wales seems high, although their mustering into

[17] *Law*, p. 41; *Triads*, pp. 107, 109.
[18] *Journey*, I, 1, p. 76. Rhys was concerned to maintain supplies to the castles he built to secure his realm; see R. Turvey, 'The defences of twelfth-century Deheubarth and the castle strategy of the Lord Rhys', *Arch. Camb.*, 154 (1995), 103–32.
[19] *Brut (Pen. 20)*, 1217.
[20] See *Defences*, p. 38; *Military*, pp. 105–17. J. B. Smith notes the military importance of the vaccaries, but also highlights the growing contribution of the marketing of cattle to Gwynedd's fiscal resources; see *LG*, pp. 230–1.
[21] In 1282 Edward I's officials were amazed at the amount of food and animals which Llywelyn ap Gruffudd had stockpiled, revealing an efficient system of production. Llywelyn was able to organize the distribution of these resources, even at long distance; see *LG*, pp. 246, 253.

large armies was restricted to rare occasions under the greater rulers. To analyse more specific figures, the previous chapter considered the evidence which numbers those in an early Anglo-Saxon or an early British army at around 300 and the fact that a force of 100 men could be considered an army.[22] Such numbers could realistically form a military elite from amongst the peoples of the day and they could be supplied through scouring the land whilst on campaign.

The *Triads* give some definite numbers regarding army size, purporting to refer to the earliest period of this study. Each of the 'Three Silver Hosts [W. *llu*] of the Island of Britain' was said to number 21,000 men.[23] This number is, however, simply a multiplication of the 2,100 men said to be in each of the 'Three Faithful *Teulu* of the Island of Britain'.[24] The figures are unrealistic with regard to the population of Britain at the time and the necessary logistic support for such a force. Perhaps a more realistic description is contained in *Branwen*; the army led to Britain by Matholwch, king of Ireland, came in thirteen ships.[25] Sawyer estimated that Viking ships in the early Middle Ages carried about forty men and if a similar figure is accepted here we can estimate a force of around 500.[26]

If we accept a figure of around 300 men for a typical army in the early British/Saxon period, there would seem to be a significant increase in numbers involved in the early seventh century. The conflict between Northumbria and the Welsh–Mercian alliance impressed our sources with its scale and the involvement of many of the peoples of Britain. Bede was horrified by the presence in Northumbria of Cadwallon 'and his vast forces [L. *copiis*], which he boasted were irresistible'.[27] Again numbers are nearly impossible to judge, but, given the scale and significance of the conflict, the combined Welsh–Mercian force

---

[22] One word for host in Welsh is *cant* or hundred, and when used in an early work like the *Gododdin* it is possible that it is meant to signify this number. There are references in the poetry to 'a hundred armies each with a hundred warriors'; *Saga*, pp. 480, 495.
[23] *Triads*, p. 78.
[24] Ibid., pp. 57–8.
[25] *Mabinogi*, p. 67; *PK*, p. 29.
[26] P. H. Sawyer, *The Age of the Vikings* (2nd edn, London, 1971). These figures should not be stressed as it is possible that the *Mabinogi* reflects earlier, pre-Viking traditions of Welsh or Irish boats that may have been smaller than Viking ships.
[27] Bede, III, 1, p. 213.

that fought at Hatfield Chase could have contained 2,500 fighting men.[28]

Cadwallon's defeat at Heavenfield by Oswald in 634 must have drained Welsh military reserves, but significant forces continued to be mustered by Cadafael and Cadwaladr of Gwynedd and by Powys. After the death of Cadwaladr in 681, though, armies of this size do not seem to have been gathered in Wales for many centuries; the more localized efforts of Welsh kings mean that army sizes of *c.*100–300 men may again be appropriate, although rulers like Rhodri Mawr and Anarawd were probably able to gather more.[29]

Gruffudd ap Llywelyn is the next Welsh leader about whom we have the evidence to base a discussion on army size and the evidence again suggests the exceptional nature of his reign. In 1039 Gruffudd was just starting to establish himself in Wales and may have enjoyed little military support outside his *teulu*, yet he was able to defeat a significant Anglo-Saxon force at Rhyd-y-groes. Gruffudd's opponents were led by an ealdorman named Edwin – the brother of Earl Leofric – who was slain along with other notable men.[30] Given Gruffudd's recent rise to power, his victory may be attributed to the leadership of the Welsh king rather than weight of numbers; John of Worcester suggests that Gruffudd caught his foe in an ambush.[31] On the strength of this victory, though, Gruffudd was able to increase his strength and by the 1050s his power was recognized throughout Wales. Militarily this meant that Gruffudd had significant forces at his disposal. Gruffudd's ability in 1047 to overcome the loss of an estimated 140 men from his *teulu* has been noted,[32] and in the

---

[28] Despite the chronological jump, Morillo's evaluation of the efficient Anglo-Norman military machine of later centuries has been taken into account. Problems of supply and distribution changed little in the pre-industrial age, but the Anglo-Norman state was far more efficient than Cadwallon's administrative back-up. Morillo regards 3,000 fighting men as the upper limit for an Anglo-Norman army, although this may have risen to around 6,000 for exceptional campaigns like Hastings; Morillo, *Warfare*, p. 58.

[29] A rare suggestion of numbers from this period is given by *HB*, p. 35, which says that at Badon 916 men were killed in one of Arthur's charges. The problems with this passage are legion, but given the legends that had built up around Badon as an epic battle it suggests that the ninth-century author of *HB* intended such numbers to be awe-inspiring.

[30] *ASC* (C), 1039; JW, II, 1039. The other Anglo-Saxon nobles recorded as being slain were Thorkil and Ælfgeat.

[31] JW, II, 1052.

[32] See above, p. 25.

1050s he was able to muster armies capable of troubling the Anglo-Saxon realm.[33]

In 1052 Gruffudd, whilst ravaging near Leominster, was challenged by a local levy – possibly the shire levy – led by Earl Ralf's Normans from the castle. Gruffudd's host slaughtered the enemy and carried away significant booty.[34] More impressive displays of his power were to follow. In 1055, Earl Ælfgar was forced into exile by the Godwine faction and, after gathering a fleet of eighteen ships in Ireland, he came to Gruffudd for help in regaining his position.[35] If we apply Sawyer's argument for the size of Viking ships, then Ælfgar's force numbered around 700 men, but these played a subordinate role to Gruffudd and the 'large army assembled from his whole realm'. After defeating Gruffudd ap Rhydderch in south-east Wales, the allies moved into Herefordshire. On 24 October, they were met two miles west of Hereford by an army comprising of the shire levy and the 'Normans and French' accompanying the leader of the force, Earl Ralf. In a brief, one-sided conflict Gruffudd and his men slew 400–500 of the enemy and wounded many others before sacking the town.

On hearing this news, Edward ordered the mustering at Gloucester of an army from 'all of England' to be led by Harold Godwinesson. Given the military resources available in late Anglo-Saxon England, Harold's army was undoubtedly large and impressive. Still, he was only able to advance a few miles along the Dore valley as Gruffudd withdrew towards the Black Mountains. The forces were at stalemate and as Harold began to refortify Hereford, a peace deal was negotiated. Ælfgar was accepted back into his earldom; Gruffudd had gained a valuable new ally and considerable plunder, and it is possible that at this point the lordship of Archenfield passed to him. To try to restore the situation on the border, Harold appointed his warlike priest Leofgar as the new bishop of Hereford. In 1056 Leofgar took the fight to Gruffudd, apparently relying on the strength of the shire levy:

[33] Parallels may be drawn in the period with Ireland where powerful over-kings had emerged, able to draw on superior economic and military resources compared to those of their predecessors and consequently able to wage more bloody and extended wars; see Ó'Cróinín, *Early Medieval*, p. 274.

[34] *ASC* (D), 1052; JW, II, 1052.

[35] *ASC*, 1055; JW, II, 1055; K. L. Maund, 'The Welsh alliances of Earl Ælfgar of Mercia and his family in the mid-eleventh century', *ANS*, 11 (1988), 181–90.

> He [Leofgar] gave up his chrism and his cross, and took his spear and his sword after his consecration as bishop, and so went campaigning against Gruffudd the Welsh king, and they killed him there and his priests with him, and Ælfnoth the sheriff and many good men with them; and the others fled. This was eight days before midsummer [16 June]. It is hard to describe the oppression and all the expeditions and the campaigning and the loss of men and horses that all the army of the English suffered, until Earl Leofric came there, and Earl Harold and Bishop Aldred, and made an agreement between them according to which Gruffudd swore oaths that he would be a loyal and faithful underking to King Edward.[36]

Again Gruffudd had forced the intervention of significant Anglo-Saxon forces. In the peace treaty he conceded nothing and won recognition of his position in Wales and his border conquests.[37]

Ælfgar was again exiled in 1058. We lack the details supplied by the chronicles in 1055, but know that the earl again sought help from Gruffudd and from a Norwegian fleet in the Irish Sea under Magnus, son of Harold Hardrada. With this aid, he recovered his position in England 'through force'.[38]

Gruffudd was outwitted by Harold and destroyed in 1063, but it is possibly a testament to the military strength that the Welsh king was able to gather that the earl had, by this point, given up on trying to overwhelm Wales by sheer force of numbers. Harold made a swift, surprise attack with a 'small troop of horsemen' on Gruffudd in his court at Rhuddlan soon after Christmas 1062.[39] In the depths of winter Gruffudd would have found it difficult to muster a *llu* and it is possible that even his *teulu* was absent.[40] Gruffudd's flight allowed his internal rivals to rise; with Harold fuelling dissent in Wales, Gruffudd was unable to recover his authority. In May, the earl and his brother, Tostig, finally

---

[36] *ASC* (C), 1056. The battle was in the Machawy valley above Glasbury; *HW*, II, p. 368.
[37] F. M. Stenton, *Anglo-Saxon England* (3rd edn, Oxford, 1971), pp. 565–6, suggests that this peace granted to Gruffudd the lands beyond Dee which he is said to have held in Domesday Book.
[38] *ASC* (D), 1058; JW, II, 1058.
[39] *ASC* (D), 1063; JW, II, 1063. It has been suggested that Ælfgar died at the king's Christmas court at Gloucester and that Harold struck from there to attack Gruffudd before the news of his ally's death arrived; I. W. Walker, *Harold the Last Anglo-Saxon King* (Stroud, 1997), p. 88.
[40] See above, p. 36, n. 110.

implemented a well-planned invasion and broke the power of Gruffudd.

In the period 1063–1200 no Welsh ruler of the stature of Gruffudd ap Llywelyn emerged and army numbers dropped correspondingly. In assessing numbers for this period *Gruffudd ap Cynan* is particularly useful; in contrast to the vast majority of sources from the Middle Ages it is conservative and realistic when dealing with army sizes. In his initial attempt to win Gwynedd in 1075, Gruffudd sent a force against Cynwrig of Powys consisting of eighty men from Anglesey, sixty of Robert of Rhuddlan's men from the lowland *cantref* of Tegeingl and 'the fighting men of the [three] sons of Merwydd [a *teulu*?] and other noblemen of their kin'.[41] These numbers are believable, although they are not intended to represent the entire military strength of Anglesey or Tegeingl. Gruffudd's men enjoyed some success and he proceeded to lead a *llu* against Trahaearn and then Robert of Rhuddlan,[42] but after this he lost the support of the sons of Merwydd and the men of Llŷn. They 'treacherously' killed fifty-two of Gruffudd's closest men and this was enough to turn the tide against him; Trahaearn and Cynwrig rallied and expelled Gruffudd at the battle of Bron-yr-erw (located above Clynnog Fawr).[43]

Back in Ireland, Gruffudd gathered a fleet of thirty ships for another attempt to gain Gwynedd.[44] Using Sawyer's ship-size reckoning, this would give an enormous force of over 1,000 men, but given the fact that the fleet merely plundered Anglesey before returning to Ireland, this should be dismissed as an attempt to whitewash what was little more than a ravaging raid by Gruffudd and a (probably small) force of 'pirates'. In 1081, however, Gruffudd received significant support from King Diarmait in Ireland; he gathered a 'royal fleet' and landed at Porth Clais near St Davids.[45] Here he met Rhys ap Tewdwr and the two joined forces to fight the alliance of Caradog ap Gruffudd, king of Gwent, Meilyr ap Rhiwallon, king of Powys,

---

[41] *Gruffudd ap Cynan*, p. 60.
[42] Ibid., pp. 61–2; the 'thousands' of men said to die on Trahaearn's side at the battle of Gwaed Erw should be dismissed as an exaggeration. It stands in stark contrast to the relatively small numbers elsewhere in the story which have significant effect on events.
[43] Ibid., pp. 62–3.
[44] Ibid., pp. 64–5.
[45] Ibid., pp. 66–7.

and Trahaearn, king of Arwystli. Rhys is portrayed as the junior partner, on the run and surrounded only by his *teulu* and a few of the men of Deheubarth. Although the author was stressing Gruffudd's contribution, the description fits with the picture in the *Brutiau* which, to this point, had barely noticed Rhys but recorded almost unbroken success for his rivals.[46]

Gruffudd's forces comprised his Danes and Irish along with 'many of the men of Gwynedd to the number of 160, with Cynddelw ap Conus of Anglesey at their head'. In the aftermath of the battle, Gruffudd's men ran amok in Wales before being betrayed to Hugh of Chester by Meirion Goch of Llŷn, one of Gruffudd's leading men. To break Gruffudd's power, Hugh proceeded to cut the right thumbs off each of his 'foreigners'. This would indicate that Gruffudd's 'foreigners' comprised the majority of his army and this caused tension with the men of Gwynedd. If the men of Gwynedd numbered 160, perhaps a figure of 500 'foreigners' (or about twelve ships) would be reasonable. If Rhys brought around 300 men to the battle, a total force of 1,000 men can be accepted.

Against this force came the three dominant kings in Wales, each bringing their *teulu* and the men of the regions under their control. In addition, Caradog brought a force of Normans. Such an army is likely to have outnumbered the forces of Gruffudd and Rhys and this could account for Rhys's reluctance to attack and Gruffudd's resolve to exploit the advantage of surprise and the confusion of a night attack.[47] At Mynydd Carn, then, it is possible that both sides numbered over 1,000 men. Although there were foreign mercenaries on both sides, significant military forces were available in Wales, if not available to a single ruler.

After his escape from Hugh of Chester's prison, Gruffudd was again a noble desperate for military support. At one stage he gained the help of the four sons of Gollwyn, noblemen connected to Harlech who may have been displaced by the Norman

---

[46] See R. S. Babcock, 'Rhys ap Tewdwr, king of Deheubarth', *ANS*, 16 (1993), 21–35; Babcock discusses the lack of support for Rhys in Deheubarth, but notes that he personally controlled extensive landholdings thanks to the recent deaths of many of his kin. It was probably from these lands that the *Deheuwyr* accompanying Rhys were drawn.

[47] The context of the text must be considered; the author was seeking to glorify Gwynedd and belittle the achievements of the south. Meilyr Brydydd wrote that the battle took place at midday; it seems that this description, too, could glorify Gruffudd's action and bravery; Meilyr, p. 185.

advance.[48] They lived as bandits in Gwynedd with 160 men, but their force proved insufficient to displace the Normans who enjoyed the support of at least some of the people of the land.

According to *Gruffudd ap Cynan*, Gruffudd was finally able to establish a more permanent position in Gwynedd in the course of the revolt against the Anglo-Normans in 1094–5.[49] Gruffudd again gathered support in Ireland, from Godred Crovan, king of Man and the Western Isles (*c*.1080–95). He is said to have obtained sixty ships,[50] but this would seem an exaggeration as the same troop is later numbered at 120 men and fourteen youths.[51] This force was repulsed from the castle of Aberlleiniog on Anglesey by 125 Normans in alliance with the 'men of the land'. Godred then recalled his troops, but Gruffudd gained the support of the men of five *cantrefi* – Llŷn, Eifionydd, Ardudwy, Rhos and Dyffryn Clwyd. These rich, populous lands provided a large *llu*, outnumbering the 134 earlier mentioned, and with this army Gruffudd destroyed Aberlleiniog and the remaining Norman castles in Gwynedd.

A passage in the *Brutiau* in 1162 deals with forces on a similar scale to those in *Gruffudd ap Cynan*. Owain Gwynedd had taken his *llu* to the *cantref* of Arwystli on a raid:

> And the men of Arwystli gathered together from all sides, about 300 men, along with Hywel ab Ieuaf, their lord. And they went after the spoil as far as Llanidloes. And when Owain saw his foes coming suddenly, he urged his men to fight manfully; and the foes were turned to flight and slain, so that scarcely a third escaped back.[52]

The defensive levy of a single *cantref* was therefore capable of raising 300 men. If a ruler controlled extensive domains, logistic considerations would stop him taking such numbers from every *cantref*, but the potential manpower is impressive.

On occasions, as at Mynydd Carn, large armies could be gathered under a coalition of leaders. The *Life of St Illtud* says that, in the revolt of 1094–5, a Welsh army of 3,000 horse and

---

[48] *Gruffudd ap Cynan*, p. 71.
[49] Gruffudd's role in the revolt may be questioned, but *Gruffudd ap Cynan* gives an idea of the numbers required for war.
[50] *Gruffudd ap Cynan*, p. 72.
[51] Ibid., p. 73.
[52] *Brut (Pen. 20)*, 1162.

foot gathered to attack Anglo-Norman-occupied Glamorgan;[53] this figure should be treated with caution, but it suggests the mustering of a large force in just one area of Wales when other Welsh leaders were concurrently engaging the enemy in Deheubarth, Powys and Gwynedd. Although the figures should again be treated with caution, all sources agree on the extensive forces gathered by the Welsh and their Anglo-Norman enemies in 1136. The *Brutiau* record that Owain and Cadwaladr of Gwynedd brought to the battle of Cardigan 6,000 footsoldiers, 2,000 'mailed horsemen' and, in alliance, Gruffudd ap Rhys, Hywel ap Maredudd, Madog ab Idnerth and the two sons of Hywel along with their forces.[54] Against them came an Anglo-Norman army, of which 3,000 were said to be killed whilst many more fled. The *Gesta Stephani* says that an Anglo-Norman army of 3,000 was defeated at Cardigan,[55] whilst John of Worcester claimed that 10,000 Anglo-Normans were killed and others captured.[56]

Anglo-Norman sources point to the number of Welsh available as mercenaries. It is not always clear where these mercenaries were being recruited. Many were taken from the conquered Marcher areas, notably Glamorgan. These were the richest and most populous parts of the country and the displacement of the native population had produced a landless class eager for the opportunities afforded by military service. Other mercenaries were drawn from the lands of native Wales. In the revolt against William Rufus in 1088, Robert Curthose's allies in the west of England gained the support of a 'large force' from Wales.[57] Robert of Gloucester used Welsh forces in England during the troubles of Stephen's reign and Henry II employed more for his continental campaigns against Louis VII, Philip II and his own rebellious sons.[58] Welsh troops followed the

[53] *Vitae*, p. 233.
[54] *Brut (Pen. 20)*, 1136.
[55] *GS*, p. 17.
[56] JW, III, 1136. Cynddelw Brydedd Mawr claims to have seen 300 dead on the battlefield, but this could be an attempt to echo the *Gododdin*; *CBT*, IV, 1.45.
[57] *ASC* (E), 1088.
[58] See, for example, Chrons., I, pp. 195–6; IV, p. 265; RH (T), pp. 87–8; RH, II, pp. 343–5. *The Deeds of King Henry II*, in D. C. Douglas (ed.), *English Historical Documents*, II (London, 1968), p. 377. Rhys ap Gruffudd sent his son Hywel Sais to aid Henry in Normandy in 1173 and the following year led 1,000 men to the siege of Tutbury. After the siege Henry took these men into his service and led them to Normandy; *PR* 20 Henry II, pp. 21, 77, 121. See also *PR* 34 Henry II, pp. 8, 107.

Anglo-Norman Marchers to Ireland in the 1170s.[59] Richard of Devizes suggested that John gathered 4,000 Welsh troops in his attempts to usurp power from Richard I.[60] The use of Welsh mercenaries was continued by Henry III,[61] and Edward I employed them in enormous numbers for his campaigns in Wales, Scotland and on the continent.[62]

Despite the reduction of native Wales by conquest and the manpower drain to English forces, the two Llywelyns were able to gather sizeable armies in the thirteenth century. Although their numbers are not to be trusted, the English chroniclers reported large armies. When William Marshal (II) fought a force led by Llywelyn ap Iorwerth's son Gruffudd in 1223, Wendover claims that 9,000 Welsh were killed or imprisoned.[63] Matthew Paris described a Welsh army of 10,000 cavalry and more footsoldiers in 1256 and another of 30,000 men in 1257.[64] The Westminster chronicler claimed that, in his clashes with the Welsh in 1262, Roger Mortimer regularly killed 300–500 of Llywelyn ap Gruffudd's men.[65] In his examination of the military organization of Gwynedd in the thirteenth century, G. R. J. Jones stressed the efforts made by the princes to maximize their manpower resources, efforts which, judging by reports of the king's ministers on the size of Llywelyn ap Gruffudd's forces, were successful.[66]

---

[59] Gerald of Wales says that Robert fitz Stephen initially took to Ireland a force of thirty knights, sixty other mailed troops and 300 Welsh foot archers; *Conquest*, I, 3, p. 31. This force is described in *Brut (Pen. 20)*, 1169, as 'a host of vast numbers'.

[60] *The Chronicle of Richard of Devizes of the Time of King Richard I*, ed. and trans. J. T. Appleby (London, 1963), p. 33. RH, III, p. 251, also mentions the presence of Welsh troops in Richard's crusading army. Both Richard and John made significant use of Welsh troops in England and on the continent; see *PR* 3 John, pp. 137, 264; *PR* 6 John, p. 146; *PR* 8, Richard I, pp. xvii, 41, 42, 88; *PR* 10, Richard I, p. 171.

[61] See RW, III, p. 93; MP, V, p. 442. Llywelyn and Owain were compelled by the treaty of Woodstock to serve Henry with twenty-four knights and 1,000 infantry in Wales and the Marches or 500 infantry in England when he desired; these numbers were drawn from Gwynedd uwch Conwy alone. See C. W. Lewis, 'The treaty of Woodstock 1247: its background and significance', *WHR*, 2 (1964–5), 37–65.

[62] See J. E. Morris, *The Welsh Wars of Edward I* (Stroud, 1996), pp. 95–6. Numbers include 9,000 Welsh infantry for the 1277 campaign and a remarkable 10,500 led to Newcastle for the Falkirk campaign of 1298.

[63] RW, II, p. 270.
[64] MP, V, pp. 597, 614.
[65] *FH*, II, pp. 476–7.
[66] *Defences*, pp. 39–41.

Early Welsh Armies, c.400–750

The traditional view of Welsh society has been that all freemen over the age of fourteen owed military service. Responsibility for this picture must be largely attributed to Gerald of Wales who portrayed Wales as populated by freemen of equal status, each of whom was required to fight for this privileged position: 'Not only the leaders but the entire nation [L. *totus populus*] are trained in war. Sound the trumpet for battle and the peasant will rush from his plough to pick up his weapons as quickly as the courtier from the court.'[67] In advising the Anglo-Normans how to conquer the Welsh, he wrote:

> All soldiers and all civilians, whatever their function, in short the entire population [L. *populo toto*], should be trained to bear arms. In this way freedom would be a match for freedom, and pride would be checked by pride. It must always be borne in mind that the Welsh are not being enervated by daily toil, they are not crushed and dispirited by slavery, they are not being maltreated by unjust taskmasters. They still carry their heads high and are prompt to avenge injuries. They are ready to take up arms and to rebel, and they will defend their country with the utmost courage. Nothing rejoices the hearts of men so much, nothing inspires them and encourages them to behave so nobly as the sheer joy of being free. On the other hand nothing dejects and dispirits them as much as oppression and slavery.[68]

The fundamental structure of Gerald's picture must be questioned. The availability of large numbers of Welsh troops for military service, both within the country and as mercenaries, may seem to support the idea of the universal nature of military duty. Other Anglo-Norman sources acknowledged the natural military prowess of all Welshmen; they were seen as a people 'accustomed to war'.[69] Modern scholars have endorsed this view, Huw Pryce suggesting that Wales was a society organized for war out of necessity as the country had meagre resources and lacked the wealth to recruit mercenaries.[70] Peter Edbury notes that Gerald of Wales's journey through the country was conducted

---

[67] *Description*, I, 8, p. 233.
[68] Ibid., II, 2, p. 270.
[69] *GS*, p. 17.
[70] H. Pryce, 'In search of a medieval society'.

because Henry II wanted soldiers from Wales for his crusade rather than the taxes he sought from his other lands.[71] It seems that the proportion of the Welsh population involved in military activity was higher than in western Europe generally in the Anglo-Norman period, but it would be an exaggeration to suggest that all free men were summoned to a king's host.

In his examination of early Merovingian Gaul, Bachrach stressed the composite nature of the military forces.[72] The invading barbarians relied on their household troops, Bachrach estimating that the warband of a chieftain like Clovis (481–511) contained 400–500 warriors. For larger campaigns, Clovis would summon the households of the other *reguli* in Gaul to produce a force of around 3,000 men. In addition to this, Clovis received support from surviving Roman military elements, including the private forces of Gallo-Roman magnates and units from the Roman army still remaining in some form.[73]

As a Merovingian army depended on combining the households of its chieftains rather than organizing a levy of the nation in arms, so Abels stressed that the early Anglo-Saxon *fyrd* comprised the combined warbands of its nobles.[74] It has been suggested that at a similar period the forces of Scottish Dal Riata were led by a high king who ruled over several sub-kings. Fighting men were organized by clans who would be summoned by the clan leader; these leaders joined forces when a larger force was required.[75] If similar conditions can be applied to the Britons in the fifth and sixth centuries, we may imagine the Roman *duces*, the leaders developing into the kings of our sources, each bringing their military followings to combine into a larger army under the greater rulers like Ambrosius. As in Gaul, a diverse

---

[71] P. W. Edbury, 'Preaching the crusade in Wales', in A. Haverkamp and H. Volbrath (eds), *England and Germany in the High Middle Ages* (Oxford, 1996), pp. 221–33.

[72] Bachrach, *Merovingian*, pp. 4–15.

[73] A suggestion of the survival of a professional Roman military class in Britain after the withdrawal of the legions can be found in Constantius' *Life of St Germanus of Auxerre*. Germanus cured the daughter of 'a man of high military rank' whilst in Britain; see F. R. Hoare (ed. and trans.), *The Western Fathers* (London, 1954), XV, pp. 298–9.

[74] Abels, *Lordship*, pp. 34–7. See, for example, the way Theobald's *exercitus* is separated from the rest of Æthelfrith's force at the battle of Degastan (s.a. 603); Bede, I, 34, p. 117. John France argued against the idea of universal militia service in early medieval Europe; see *WW*, pp. 5, 64–8.

[75] D. Nicolle, *Medieval Warfare Source Book: Vol. I, Warfare in Western Christendom* (London, 1995), p. 69. For the situation in Ireland, see Ó'Cróinín, *Early Medieval*, pp. 141–2; also D. A. Binchy, *Celtic and Anglo-Saxon Kingship* (Oxford, 1970).

system may be envisaged; in the militarized north, and possibly other areas like south-east Wales, old army officers would lead surviving elements of the Roman military as their warband, whilst in west and north Wales ancient territorial administration is likely to have provided each leader with his *teulu*.

Poetry concerning the 'Old North' describes the numerous lords involved and their fluctuating loyalties, rather than examining a two-sided conflict. The poem *Dwy Blaid*, for example, is concerned with the dealings of Dunawd, Pasgen, Gwallawg, Elffin, Brân fab Ymellyrn and Morgant.[76] Earlier in the *Canu Urien* cycle, the poet recalls 'the royal host, the army of Rheged [W. *rebyd uilet, reget dull*]';[77] the regal nature of the host is stressed as it is a force containing a number of men who, in Gaul, would be labelled *reguli*. Similarly, the *Triads* go to lengths to name several of the many lords brought to the battle of Arfderydd.[78] The *Gododdin* repeatedly refers to its 300 heroes, eighty-six of whom are named.

The forces raised by the kings of Gwynedd for their clashes with Northumbria in the early seventh century also seem to have been composed of the combined warbands of various lords or petty kings. In the *Triads*, one of the 'Three Noble Retinues [W. *gosgordd*]' was that of Belyn of Llŷn who was killed with his men when Edwin invaded Gwynedd in 628.[79] Cadwallon escaped to Ireland with the majority of his force and it may be speculated that Belyn's *gosgordd* was detached to delay Edwin and give Cadwallon time to get away. The battle-naming poem *Englynion Cadwallon* lists amongst Cadwallon's fourteen 'chief battles':

> The encampment of Cadwallon beyond Caer:
> A hundred armies [W. *bydin*] with a hundred ardent warriors,
> A hundred battles and the destroying of a hundred fortresses.[80]

This suggests the mustering of a host composed of the warbands of 100 lesser leaders. Although the figures should not be taken

---

[76] *Saga*, p. 480.
[77] Ibid., p. 479.
[78] *Triads*, p. 109.
[79] Ibid., p. 65. Belyn fought Edwin at Bryn Edwin in Rhos and at Erethlyn near Eglwysfach in the same region. Both are on likely invasion routes to north Wales from Northumbria; *HW*, I, p. 184.
[80] *Saga*, p. 495. 'Caer' is probably Chester.

literally, 100 men could be a reasonable number to suggest as the manpower strength of a *teulu* of a Welsh king in the period.

At the battle of Winwaed in 654, *Historia Brittonum* says that *all* the British kings with Penda were killed, except for Cadafael 'Battle Dodger' of Gwynedd who fled the night before.[81] The force led by Cynddylan to Winwaed was said to have been composed of 700 'lords', several of whom are named.[82] The twelfth-century *Life of St Wenefred*, set in the time of Cadfan of Gwynedd (d. 616), describes Wenefred's father, Teuyth ab Eylud, as 'a strenuous soldier [L. *miles*] who possessed three vills in Tegeingl'.[83] We lack information about Teuyth, but in most other saints's lives the holy person is closely related to a royal line. Another person who bears arms in the story, Caradog ab Alâog, is given royal blood in the genealogies;[84] Alâog appears as a minor king with connections to Hawarden (W. Penarlâg).

DEVELOPMENT IN THE EIGHTH CENTURY AND BEYOND

In post-Roman Wales, as in much of contemporary Europe, military obligation was personal rather than territorialized. As Europe changed, the numerous *reguli* ruling their small kingdoms declined in status and lost their royal nomenclature. As greater kings with more extensive domains emerged – and as kingdoms became increasingly territorialized – there was a need to find new ways of organizing forces and new guarantees of military service as opposed to the personal loyalties and coercions by which lesser rulers were formerly bound.[85] Bachrach considered the growth of local levies in Gaul which began to supplement the warbands of the great nobles,[86] and Abels discussed the

[81] *HB*, p. 38.
[82] *Saga*, p. 177.
[83] *Vitae*, p. 289.
[84] Ibid., p. 291.
[85] For the growth of duties imposed on the land and landholders in the period, see W. Davies, 'Adding insult to injury: power, property and immunities in early medieval Wales', in W. Davies and P. Fouracre (eds), *Property and Power in the Early Middle Ages* (Cambridge, 1995), pp. 137–64. A growth in demands from kings for tax, military service and other dues stimulated the development of counter-claims to protections and exemptions. These counter-claims were not seen in England or Europe generally and they reflect the problems Welsh kings had in imposing their powers.
[86] Bachrach, *Merovingian*, pp. 68–71.

imposition of common duties on the land in Anglo-Saxon England.[87] Parallels can be found in Ireland and Cornwall to suggest that the territorialized military system which emerged in Wales developed along a similar time-scale.[88] In Wales, Dark contended that the seventh and eighth centuries saw the emergence of new political centres and the concurrent abandonment of smaller sites, including many hill forts.[89] These new sites were the seats of the over-kings of Wales, notably in the emerging super-kingdoms of the country, Gwynedd, Deheubarth, Powys and Glywysing/Glamorgan. Smaller territorial units and kingdoms were absorbed and their kings reduced in status to become the leading men or *uchelwyr* of the land. Wendy Davies traced this process at a local level in south-east Wales, although she relied on the untrustworthy Llandaff charters.[90] In these circumstances there was a growing need for royal administration to impose authority on the land.[91]

The poem *Edmic Dinbych* or *In Praise of Tenby* (*c*.875) provides an insight into the changes that were taking place in Welsh military organization.[92] The bard wished to assert the rights of the kings of Dyfed against the expansion of the Merfyn Frych dynasty of Gwynedd. His lord at Tenby was capable of fielding a force more extensive than a household troop: 'There was a retinue in the court and a host besides' [W. *Bu goscor a bu kerd yn eil mehyn*]. But the host was of the traditional, royal kind, as, following a battle with the men of Gwynedd, the bard laments: 'With [my] nephew's son, a host [W. *llu*] of *kinsmen* fell' (my italics). In contrast, a deliberate jibe is aimed at the forces of Gwynedd: 'Than the yeomen [W. *eillon*] of Deudraeth [probably in Meirionnydd] better are the slaves [W. *kaeth*] of Dyfed.' The *eillon* (more often spelt *aillt* or *eilltion*) were a class in Welsh society between the *uchelwyr* and the *taeogion*, and their presence in the host of Gwynedd indicates the change of military personnel

---

[87] Abels, *Lordship*, pp. 56–9.
[88] See Ó'Cróinín, *Early Medieval*, p. 275; A. Preston-Jones and P. Rose, 'Medieval Cornwall', *Cornish Archaeology*, 25 (1986), 135–85.
[89] Dark, *Civitas*, pp. 220–3.
[90] W. Davies, *Patterns*, p. 34; see also her 'Land and power in early medieval Wales', *P&P*, 81 (1978), 3–23.
[91] For the possible emergence of the *cantref* and commote as administrative units in this period (and the reduction of minor kingdoms), see also R. Jones, 'The formation of the *cantref* and the commote in medieval Gwynedd', *Studia Celtica*, 32 (1998), 169–77.
[92] *Beginnings*, pp. 155–66.

being instituted by the kings there.[93] It is possible that we are seeing an expansion in the numbers required for service,[94] or a reduction in the status of the military class as royal power grew.[95]

On the continent in the late eighth century, the Carolingians drew up capitularies to regulate service in the royal host, providing an assurance that duties were performed as the overlord lost personal contact with the minor leaders who brought their forces to his muster; an administrative structure organized through laws and royal officers was replacing the earlier system of personal bonds. Carolingian administrative influences can be seen in Anglo-Saxon law and in the Welsh laws, whose initial codification is traditionally attributed to Hywel Dda (d. 950). By the time of Hywel, the process of reducing the status of the smallest kings and kingdoms of Wales was complete, new nomenclatures of power were emerging and it was possible that even the larger kingdoms could be moulded into units of 'north Wales' and 'south Wales', possibly leading to eventual unification of the whole country.[96] The codified laws outline the duties of the freemen of Wales to attend musters and impose other common duties on the land to keep it within royal control. Most of our evidence comes from the twelfth century and beyond, but there are suggestions that the military system applied to the earlier period. The Welsh laws say of the king's hostings:

> The king is not entitled to have from his country [W. *gwlad*] any hostings outside its limits [W. *ohoni ei hun*] save once in each year, and he is not entitled to be in that save for a fortnight and a month. In his own country it is free for him when he likes.[97]

The laws imposed defined military duties on the land and on the free status of its people, but only some codes demanded a levy of all free men and these add, 'if the king desires'. Laws can be

---

[93] The *aillt/eilltion* class was distinguishable from the unfree *bilain* and *taeog*. The original meaning of 'client' probably implies a position at the lower end of the scale of free men; see *Law*, pp. 310–11.

[94] Such developments could be linked to a growing density of settlement and changes from a majority-bond to a majority-free population; see G. R. J. Jones, 'The Dark Ages', in D. H. Owen (ed.), *Settlement and Society in Wales* (Cardiff, 1989), pp. 177–97; T. M. Charles-Edwards, *Early Irish and Welsh Kinship* (Oxford, 1993), pp. 226ff.

[95] For the tensions that could be raised by the growth of over-kingdoms, see Charles-Edwards, 'Early medieval kingships', pp. 28–39.

[96] See W. Davies, *Patterns*, pp. 42ff.

[97] *Law*, p. 124; see also p. 41.

inflexible and unrealistic and do not, in their entirety, relate to actual practice; it cannot have been practical to take every free man out of the country on a military expedition. Bachrach believes that the local levy of Merovingian Gaul involved selective recruitment that did not include all men, or even all free men. Poor free men could serve, but tended not to do so for economic reasons. The majority of the host was composed of small landholders with enough men and slaves to work the land in their absence and at least some of these men were mounted and well armed.[98] Scholars have long questioned whether all free men served in Anglo-Saxon forces as a legacy of their perceived past as free tribesmen, or whether the army was an aristocratic preserve. Abels concluded that the Anglo-Saxon *fyrd* never represented the nation in arms, that lords and their warbands were the key military institutions and that larger forces were organized by a select levy.[99]

Our evidence suggests that a similar system existed in Wales, organized through the framework of land administration based on the idealized legal model. Later medieval views of the early Middle Ages envisage select levies; in the *Life of St Cadog*, trumpets were used to mobilize only the 'warlike men' (L. *uiri bellatores*) of the community.[100] References to the 'Three Silver Hosts of Britain' in the *Triads*, despite their unrealistic sizes, describe select levies; all were said to be 'picked men'.[101] The story of the muster made by Yrp of the Hosts was based on a mathematical quirk that fascinated the story-teller; Yrp and his servant went to the thirty 'Chief Fortresses of Britain' in turn and asked that they should leave each with twice as many men as when they arrived. This would produce an army size running into fifteen figures, but the point is that Yrp *asked* that this form of muster be accepted, suggesting that the levy depended on a deal between the ruler and his subjects. In a later triad, Arthur is said to have left Britain for an expedition against Rome with 'the most select warriors of his kingdom'.[102] The muster was a selective process dependent on the nature of the campaign, the relation of a ruler to his

---

[98] Bachrach, *Merovingian*, pp. 68–71.
[99] Abels, *Lordship*.
[100] *Vitae*, p. 137.
[101] *Triads*, pp. 75–8.
[102] Ibid., p. 132.

uchelwyr and the value of the estate owned by an individual *uchelwr*. At the battle of Bron-yr-erw there fell on Gruffudd ap Cynan's side seventy 'of the foremost men [W. *oreuguyr*] of Anglesey', a phrase suggesting a select levy.[103] *The Dream of Rhonabwy* says that, in hunting for his brother Iorwerth, Madog ap Maredudd 'conferred with the men of Powys, and they decided to put 100 men in every three commotes to look for Iorwerth'.[104] If the author was basing his calculations on a model commote from the laws, it may be speculated that he envisaged one soldier being supported by every three townships. In 1118, the *Brutiau* state that Maredudd ap Bleddyn and the sons of Cadwgan ap Bleddyn went to the aid of Hywel ab Ithel after gathering 'about 400 kinsmen and comrades and a *teulu* of theirs'.[105] A passage from *Llyfr Colan* implies restricted access to arms to certain groups:

> If a person kills another with arms which are not his, it is right for him to whom the arms belong to pay a third of the *galanas*. If the owner of the arms set on the arms the protection of his lord and his goodmen, that no-one should do wrong with them, and that in the presence of the lord and his goodmen as he could prove by attestators, though persons should be killed with the arms after that, he should pay nothing in respect of the arms.[106]

Gerald of Wales's claims that the entire Welsh population performed military service can be related to his own motivations in writing, but also to real changes occurring in Welsh society in the twelfth and thirteenth centuries. Military service was the mark of a free man and in the early Middle Ages the bond population outnumbered the free;[107] this immediately gave a select military levy and it is likely that only a proportion of the free class served. From around the eleventh century social distinctions began to change; the free population grew rapidly, but their land was partitioned, meaning that their relative wealth

---

[103] *Gruffudd ap Cynan*, p. 63.
[104] *Mabinogi*, p. 178; *BR*, p. 1. These *llu* members would seem to be infantry; later in the tale, Rhonabwy and his companions are caught by a noble *marchog* (*Mabinogi*, p. 180; *BR*, p. 4).
[105] *Brut (Pen. 20)*, 1118.
[106] *Law*, p. 151.
[107] See Charles-Edwards, *Early Irish*, pp. 226ff.

and status declined. These developments were accompanied by the decline of slavery; this made the *taeogion* the near-equivalents of the old slave class, meaning that impoverished nobles would oppose any reduction in their status likely to move them into the *taeog* class.[108] Consequently, many free men eligible for military service in eleventh- and twelfth-century Wales are likely to have appeared little different from bondmen in the eyes of outsiders. Distinctions between the social classes were not as defined as elsewhere in Europe.[109] However, practical reasons mean a select levy of free men remained more feasible than a universal levy.

In the thirteenth century there were demands for larger armies. This is most apparent in Gwynedd where we have more evidence and where clashes between the princes and English kings assumed an increasingly national character. In these circumstances, a growing proportion of the free population were enlisted for military service, some of whom were poorly equipped.[110] The princes made land grants on privileged terms to leading free men in areas of strategic importance in return for guarantees of military service.[111] The demands were such that, in certain areas of Gwynedd, bond tenants were pressed into service, a policy that caused resentment and underlined the narrowing gap between free and unfree.[112] There are suggestions that boys under the age of fourteen were recruited for service, although their military value may be doubted.[113] Such measures were prompted by the increasingly desperate nature of the military position facing Gwynedd in the thirteenth century. The complaints from the people of the land and the erosion of support for Llywelyn ap Gruffudd show that a select levy was the usual expectation and that such a force was all that the land and economy could support over a protracted period.

---

[108] Ibid., p. 395. See also *Age*, p. 120.

[109] See J. Given, *State and Society in Medieval Europe: Gwynedd and Languedoc under Outside Rule* (New York, 1990).

[110] Clauses eight and seventeen of the *Gravamina* presented against Llywelyn ap Gruffudd by the people of Gwynedd relate that the military class was supported by revenues from non-combatants, but that Llywelyn took the dues and forced the payers to serve in his forces; L. B. Smith, '*Gravamina*', 158–76; *LG*, pp. 245, 254.

[111] *Defences*, p. 41; *Military*, p. 98; J. B. Smith, 'Land endowments of the period of Llywelyn ap Gruffudd', *BBCS*, 34 (1987), 150–64; *LG*, p. 264. Similar grants were also made in Deheubarth; see *Handlist*, p. 11 (28).

[112] *Age*, p. 121; Stephenson, *Governance*, pp. 92–3.

[113] *Defences*, p. 40; Stephenson, *Governance*, pp. 91–2. Stephenson suggests that the imposition of fines on those under fourteen not attending the muster is more likely.

Personnel of the *llu*

The laws provide clues as to the identity of the people targeted for a levy of the country. Amongst the officers of the king's court were the watchman, who had to be a *bonheddig* of the country, and the serjeant (W. *rhingyll*).[114] The latter officer, who enjoyed a number of privileges, was not in permanent attendance on the king as he was responsible for local law and order. He was required to possess a spear six feet in length. Given the nature of Welsh life, the tools used by the people of the land could be turned to military use; in the *Life of St Cadog*, a swineherd took up his spear to search for the robber troubling his pigs.[115]

When ably led by *teulu* members, such part-time forces could be effective. In 1147, Hywel ab Owain and his brother Cynan went against their uncle Cadwaladr in Meirionnydd. There they summoned 'the men of the land' and with this host (W. *byddin*) proceeded to besiege, storm and take Cadwaladr's castle of Cynfael.[116]

Although select levies were the norm, there are possible examples of universal service in a general levy when the country was faced with an emergency, notably an enemy invasion, and there was a desperate need to defend hearth and home. In the *Life of St Cadog*, King Brychan, faced with the invasion of King Gwynllyw, 'called to his aid all his friends and his subjects'.[117] *Y Drefwen* portrays the destruction of the town of that name (possibly Whittington near Oswestry) by the Anglo-Saxons.[118] In the fight, the 'people' (W. *gweri*) were all involved in the final attempt to beat back the invaders. *Gweri* has been translated as 'peasant population', but Rowlands believes it refers to those of

---

[114] *Law*, pp. 34–6. The serjeant fulfilled local peacekeeping duties covered in an earlier age by *teuluoedd*. Their numbers could be significant; twenty-four are recorded in Tegeingl in 1242, or eight to each commote. See Stephenson, *Governance*, pp. 46–50.

[115] *Vitae*, p. 41.

[116] *Brut (Pen. 20)*, 1147. An incident in *Math* suggests that, despite their effectiveness, *llu* members lacked the discipline and professionalism associated with the *teulu*. In a clash between the forces of north and south Wales a truce was agreed and respected, but with the armies in close proximity to each other it was the footsoldiers (W. *pedyt*) who could not be restrained from shooting (W. *ymsaethu*) at each other; *Mabinogi*, p. 103; *PK*, p. 72.

[117] *Vitae*, p. 27. Gwynllyw's opposing force was composed of '300 of his young men' who had been gathered quickly; this suggests that they were a *teulu*, although they are not actually named as such.

[118] *Saga*, p. 487.

sufficient status to bear arms, yet people who were basically farmers and not full-time warriors. It could be speculated that they were the men not usually called to a select levy of the land. The indulgence of the *gweri* in martial endeavours reflects the disruption to the traditional way of life caused by the enemy attack. Similarly, the outrage of the author of *Edmic Dinbych* at the presence of *eillon* in the hosts of Gwynedd has been considered. The *Brutiau* seem to refer to a general levy in 1110; Uchdryd ab Edwin was away from his land with its military force searching for Owain ap Cadwgan when Owain entered his territory of Meirionnydd. The sons of Uchdryd and their *teulu* 'bid *everyone* to assemble' to drive Owain out.[119] Similarly, in 1162 the men of Arwystli 'gathered together from all sides' under Hywel ab Ieuaf to meet a *llu* led by Owain Gwynedd which had gathered booty in their territory.[120] Of these general levies, that of Brychan was said to enjoy success, but all the others were heavily defeated; this would suggest that the troops were inexperienced and not of the calibre of those in a regular force.

Despite these findings, the value of irregular levies to a Welsh leader can be seen in 1157 at the battle of Tal-y-Moelfre, Anglesey.[121] Owain Gwynedd was engaged with Henry II's invasion force in Tegeingl when the king's fleet landed on Anglesey and ravaged the island.[122] Owain must have taken the cream of his military strength to face the king on the mainland as he dared to engage Henry in battle at Coleshill.[123] In this clash, two of Owain's sons, Dafydd and Cynan, led a detachment of his forces and it seems that another son, Hywel, had been left to organize the defence of Anglesey. Hywel was an experienced military leader,[124] and he may have had a *teulu* of his own to help organize his forces. However, the crisis had stretched Gwynedd's military resources; Hywel's own poem on the battle:

---

[119] *Brut (Pen. 20)*, 1110 (my italics).
[120] Ibid., 1162.
[121] This was probably on the east of the island; *HW*, II, p. 499 and n. 54.
[122] Gwalchmai ap Meilyr implies that Owain was at the battle, but this does not fit with the known chronology. The poet used the battle to reflect glory on Owain; see *CBT*, I, 8.
[123] For further discussion of this event, see below, pp. 129–30.
[124] See his description in *Brut (Pen. 20)*, 1147.

A mil o filwyr a'i gyrrai ar ffo,
Llwyr arfog [eto] heb un gŵr barfog ar Fenai.[125]

And a beardless warrior put to flight
A thousand leaders on Menai water.[126]

The reference to a 'beardless warrior' suggests that inexperienced troops, possibly boys under the usual military age of fourteen, were recruited for the emergency. This theory finds some support from *Brenhinedd y Saesson* which records that the 'youth of Anglesey' fought the invaders.[127] Despite the irregular nature of the Welsh levy, they inflicted a heavy defeat on the enemy that contributed to Henry's decision to make peace.[128]

The general assumption is that only Welsh free men served in the royal host, but the laws imposed non-combative duties on bondmen when the king was on campaign.[129] They state that 'the king is entitled to a man with an axe from every villein townland to make encampments for him in his hostings'. In addition, the bondmen were to supply pack-horses (and, presumably, supplies) for the host and to billet the king's 'aliens', possibly his foreign mercenaries. Despite social and economic hindrances, in certain circumstances it is possible that bondmen actually took part in fighting. The possibility that the *gweri* recorded as fighting in the poem *Y Drefwen* were the peasant population has been noted. The *Life of St Cadog* outlined a struggle between two 'unjust heirs' for possession of land in which the rival parties are likely to have trawled their net extensively for military support. In the succeeding battle there was a great slaughter in which 100 men of the 'rural army' (L. *rusticani agminis*) were killed and many others wounded.[130] Bondmen could be recruited in times of military emergency; problems arose in thirteenth-century Gwynedd because the princes were making this standard practice.

[125] *CBT*, II, 12.11–12.
[126] *Welsh Poems*, p. 44.
[127] *Bren.*, 1157. However, *Brut (Pen. 20)* and *Brut (RBH)* record that the 'men of Anglesey' fought.
[128] For further discussion of this battle and the suggestion that the Anglo-Norman force was caught whilst ravaging the island, see below, p. 131 and n. 192.
[129] *Law*, pp. 124–5; see also p. 41.
[130] *Vitae*, p. 35. However, in the *Life of St Illtud*, there is surprise that in 1094 an attack on a point fortified by the Anglo-Norman settlers in Glamorgan was repulsed with the aid of 'unarmed women' and 'weak boys'; ibid., p. 233.

If the presence of bondmen in Welsh armies is unusual and noteworthy, the service of mercenaries is comparatively common. Evidence is scarce in the early period, but the *Juvencus Englynion* has a line referring to the 'Frank' (taken here to mean 'foreign mercenary') of a Welsh lord.[131] The laws made provision for the king to billet armed 'aliens' (W. *alltud*) on his bondmen,[132] and the reliance placed by Gruffudd ap Cynan on his foreign mercenaries is clear. John of Worcester noted the effective use of Hiberno-Scandinavian mercenaries by Gruffudd ap Rhydderch and Gruffudd ap Llywelyn in raids against England.[133] A certain 'Ralph the crossbowman,' retained by Henry III in 1244, was said to have been in the service of Llywelyn ap Iorwerth.[134] The *Brutiau* give many examples of the use of both Hiberno-Scandinavian and Anglo-Norman troops in Welsh forces.[135] However, Welsh rulers lacked the resources to recruit large bodies of alien mercenaries for extended periods; forces from Ireland were recruited for short periods and paid with irregular methods, whilst Anglo-Norman forces fought alongside the Welsh under their own lords as political allies.[136]

THE *UCHELWYR*

Despite the legal obligations to military service imposed on the population, the only way for a king to rule and exploit his dues was to win the support of the powerful people in his realm. Similarities may be noted with the situation in the Carolingian lands where attempts to impose a royal administration faded under the weaker monarchies of the late ninth century. In the succeeding feudal age it was, as always, vital to win the personal support of the magnates of the land with their military households based in the private strongholds of the country.[137]

---

[131] *Saga*, p. 510; for discussion of this point, see above, pp. 29–30.
[132] *Law*, p. 124.
[133] JW, II, 1049, 1055.
[134] *Calendar of Liberate Rolls, 1240–5* (London, 1917).
[135] See, for example, *Brut (Pen. 20)*, 992, 1044, 1078, 1118.
[136] Caradog ap Gruffudd's use of Norman mercenaries in the 1070s and in 1081 would seem to be an exception to this general rule.
[137] See *WW*, pp. 4, 39–52. For examples of local powermongers, see the importance placed on the role of honorial barons in D. Crouch, *The Beaumont Twins: The Roots and Branches of Power in the Twelfth Century* (Cambridge, 1986); also J. C. Holt, *The Northerners* (Oxford, 1961).

Local rulers in Wales declined in status from being kings to leading men or *uchelwyr*, but it was still their loyalty and obedience that was needed. In 984, Einion ab Owain of Deheubarth was killed by the *uchelwyr* of Gwent whilst trying to impose himself on that region, and in 1047 Gruffudd ap Llywelyn met resistance from the *uchelwyr* of Ystrad Tywi. Militarily the *teulu* was the heart of a king's force, but to resist both outside enemies and internal challengers he needed the support of a wider base.[138] An examination of the career of Gruffudd ap Cynan is valuable in illustrating these points.

Gruffudd's initial success in 1075 came partly with the help of his Irish fleet, but mainly because he gained the support of 'the men of Anglesey and Arfon and the sons of Merwydd of Llŷn, Asser, Meirion and Gwgon, and other leading men'.[139] The named areas were the rich lowlands of Gwynedd which gave their ruler significant resources and military potential. On defeating Cynwrig, Gruffudd's priority was to tighten his grip on these areas and on 'the *cantrefi* bordering on England, to receive homage from their people'.[140] With control of this power base, Gruffudd led a host (W. *llu*) against Trahaearn and defeated his rival at Gwaed Erw (in Glyn Cyfring).[141] The 'leading men of the land' then urged (forced?) Gruffudd to attack his erstwhile ally, Robert of Rhuddlan.[142] Soon after the attack on Robert, the sons of Merwydd turned against Gruffudd, taking with them the men of Llŷn and Tudur and Gollwyn from Anglesey. They sided with Trahaearn and Gwrgenau of Powys and defeated Gruffudd at the battle of Bron-yr-erw.[143] Perhaps Gruffudd's rule was overbearing, perhaps his Irish allies were disliked, perhaps the attack on Robert had been a disaster, or perhaps there was another unknown reason, but the 'leading men' of Gwynedd had made it clear where true power in the land lay.

---

[138] Rhiwallon ap Tudfwlch, an *uchelwr* in south-east Wales in the early eleventh century, had his own *teulu* which he used to ravage a church; *LL*, pp. 264–5. Rhiwallon is thought to have been powerful enough to make his own reparation grant to Llandaff. An ambitious king would need to harness the support of such men in the localities of his domain.

[139] *Gruffudd ap Cynan*, p. 59. For a discussion of Gruffudd's reliance on a few local power bases, notably Anglesey, Llŷn and Arfon, see D. Moore, 'Gruffudd ap Cynan and the medieval Welsh polity', in *GC*, pp. 1–59.

[140] *Gruffudd ap Cynan*, p. 60.

[141] Ibid., p. 61.

[142] Ibid., p. 62.

[143] Ibid., pp. 62–3.

At Mynydd Carn in 1081, Gruffudd had the support of 160 men from Anglesey under Cynddelw ap Conus,[144] but the bulk of his force came from his foreign mercenaries. *Gruffudd ap Cynan* proclaims that after the battle Gruffudd returned to Gwynedd 'to his own proper possession and patrimony to rule and pacify it'.[145] This sounds impressive, but the next sentence reads 'and there was rest and peace in Gwynedd for a few days'. He was soon betrayed to Hugh of Chester by Meirion Goch of Llŷn, the same 'leading man' who had turned against Gruffudd in 1075. In 1081 Gruffudd enjoyed little support from the *uchelwyr* of the land and his rule amounted to little more than the ravaging of the country for a few weeks.

On his escape from prison, Gruffudd did enjoy, for a time, the support of the four sons of Gollwyn, another 'leading man'. They were hounded by both the Normans and 'the people of the land', indicating that, at this stage at least, some of the native population of Gwynedd accepted Norman rule and patronage.[146] When Gruffudd returned to Gwynedd with an Irish fleet in 1094 to fight the Normans in Aberlleiniog, it was initially 'the men of the land' who 'proved to be too much of an obstacle' to him.[147]

Gruffudd is said to have found success when his Irish fleet departed and he emerged as a leader of the people of the land. Gruffudd was fortuitously on the scene in 1094 when the Welsh revolt, which had at least some characteristics of a national rising against the Normans, erupted around him. Gruffudd harnessed himself to these forces and emerged as the leader of the men of Llŷn, Eifionydd, Ardudwy, Rhos and Dyffryn Clwyd. The leadership skills Gruffudd displayed during the revolt seem to have won a measure of loyalty from the men of the land, leaving him more secure within Gwynedd for the remainder of his reign, even if he had not yet achieved sole kingship in the land. *Gruffudd ap Cynan* considers that his youthful adventuring had ended at this point.

---

[144] For the importance of Cynddelw's family, see Charles-Edwards, *Early Irish*, pp. 206–11. It was imperative that the twelfth-century princes of Gwynedd flattered this family who themselves claimed royal descent.
[145] *Gruffudd ap Cynan*, p. 69.
[146] Ibid., p. 71.
[147] Ibid., p. 72.

Control of the *uchelwyr* was as important to a thirteenth-century prince of Gwynedd as to one of the eleventh century. In the thirteenth century, privileged land grants were made to the leading *uchelwyr* surrounding Llywelyn ap Iorwerth and Llywelyn ap Gruffudd.[148] Such grants were attempts to increase the military resources of the land, but they were also part of the traditional system of rewards used by a ruler to buy the favour of his leading men. Given the limited resources of the princes, the prodigality of Llywelyn ap Iorwerth could not be maintained.[149] Llywelyn ap Gruffudd began his reign with a grant of just half a township to one of his leading *uchelwyr*, but later rewards even at this level dried up. Many of the *uchelwyr* of Gwynedd were found on Edward's side in the wars of conquest; the grants did not ensure their loyalty as they transferred their allegiance to another lord with greater sources of patronage and reward.

The crucial requirement for a Welsh ruler, then, was to win and maintain the support of the *uchelwyr* of the land. These men, the petty kings of an earlier age who would bring their individual *teuluoedd* to the muster, now controlled the administration of the greater rulers at a local level. Babcock examined the law's treatment of the important local office of *pencenedl* ('chief of kindred'). This could only be held by an *uchelwr* of the country, not by one of the king's officers. The later law texts of thirteenth-century Gwynedd prohibit the *pencenedl* from holding offices of local administration controlling renders and the muster, suggesting that in an earlier age it was the local *uchelwyr* rather than the king who controlled these offices and effectively ruled in the localities.[150] In any case, it should be remembered that the king's officers were drawn from the ranks of the *uchelwyr*, meaning that these men regulated the behaviour of their friends, peers and kinsmen. This indicates the perennial problem faced by ambitious Welsh kings; rulers like Gruffudd ap Llywelyn and Llywelyn ap Gruffudd were able to control and direct the power

---

[148] See *Handlist*, pp. 43–4 (28), 46 (145), 47 (149), 49 (155); Stephenson, *Governance*, pp. 95–136.

[149] J. B. Smith, 'Land endowments', 150–64; *LG*, p. 264.

[150] Babcock, 'Rhys', p. 30. The office of *pencenedl* was held by powerful noble families, in many cases houses which had, or were believed to have, previously held kingship; see Charles-Edwards, *Early Irish*, pp. 205–6.

of the *uchelwyr*, but in doing so they threatened local autonomy and created tension amongst their subordinates. This created opportunities for rival dynasts and foreign powers to exploit.[151]

SERVICE FROM CHURCH LAND AND CHURCHMEN

In the early Middle Ages, significant amounts of land were granted to, and held by, the churches of Wales.[152] Given the meagre resources held by most rulers at the time, it is unlikely that they would be prepared to allow these lands to be free of military obligations, but the issue is clouded by later medieval claims to immunities made by the Church. We know little of the organization of the Church in early medieval Wales, but there are suggestions that the heads of large *clas* churches behaved little differently from lay rulers and would lead their own forces to battle. In the *Life of St Cadog*, the saint is portrayed as a lord who dominated his country, drove off invading armies, was surrounded by a *familia* including 100 *milites* and could be associated with a fort (L. *oppidum*).[153] Similarly, in Ireland churchmen adapted themselves to tribal society and warfare, and abbots could be laymen commanding significant military forces.[154] This might suggest that the 1,200 'monks' under the protection of Brochfael at the battle of Chester, and said by Bede to have been slaughtered by Æthelfrith, were a military detachment provided by the church of Bangor Iscoed.[155]

The nature of the early medieval *clas* church remains a mystery. In the twelfth century, lay rulers would use a royal *clas*

---

[151] The importance and power of the *uchelwyr* in Wales did not end with the Edwardian Conquest. R. R. Davies illustrated how in the Glyndŵr revolt their support in the localities remained the key to any sort of dominion in Wales. Particularly revealing is the case of Henry Don of Kidwelly. As the undoubted master of his locality, he initially opposed the revolt, then, as it grew, became one of its staunchest supporters. Following the collapse of Welsh resistance, he regained his old position under English rule and exacted fines from over 200 Welshmen who had refused to join him in the revolt! R. R. Davies, *The Revolt of Owain Glyn Dŵr* (Oxford, 1995), pp. 200–1.

[152] It has been contended that the entire *cantref* of Pebidiog owed render only to the head of St Davids in the early Middle Ages; *HW*, I, pp. 263–4.

[153] *Vitae*, pp. 63, 77.

[154] T. M. Charles-Edwards, 'Irish warfare before 1100', in T. Bartlett and K. Jeffery (eds), *A Military History of Ireland* (Cambridge, 1996), pp. 26–51; Ó'Cróinín, *Early Medieval*, p. 167.

[155] Bede, II, 2, p. 141.

to serve their secular and military interests.[156] In 1147, Morfran, head of the *clas* of Tywyn, acted as castellan of the nearby castle of Cynfael for Cadwaladr ap Gruffudd. Possibly aided by his household drawn from the *clas*, he put up a vigorous defence of the castle against Cadwaladr's nephews, Hywel and Cynan. The most vivid description of the *clas* is provided by Gerald of Wales. At Llanbadarn Fawr he claimed to be horrified that a layman was abbot and that the most powerful people of the locality had taken over the church. He claims that the abbot performed his church duties with a spear in his hand whilst surrounded by about twenty young men 'all armed and equipped according to the local custom'.[157] Gerald's opinions cannot always be trusted, particularly when he sought to describe the Church in Wales, but by contemporary Anglo-Norman standards the native Church does seem to have been secularized. It is likely that the Church was expected to provide troops for a king's army throughout this period. Whether these forces were always led by churchmen is debatable.

The question of exemptions from services on Church land is more problematic. The main purpose of many of the lives of Welsh saints would seem to be to stress exemptions from the dues (including military service) exacted by kings throughout their land.[158] These claims seem most likely to be forgeries of the twelfth century and beyond, made to substantiate claims to land and rights. However, Wendy Davies claims that a part of *Braint Teilo* – including a grant of land made by a Welsh king to Llandaff 'without hosting' – is genuine and dates from *c*.950–1090.[159] A complaint from Bede about the establishment of spurious monasteries to avoid military service from the land suggests that genuine exemption grants could be made by kings in Anglo-Saxon England, and possibly elsewhere in Britain.[160] However, such grants were far more limited and infrequent than the claims made in the later saints' lives and it seems that secularized *clas* churches drawn closely within the royal orbit were more common in Wales.

---

[156] For a discussion of the *clas* in this period, see *Age*, pp. 174–6.
[157] *Journey*, II, 5, p. 180.
[158] See, for example, *Vitae*, pp. 15, 81.
[159] W. Davies, 'Braint Teilo', *BBCS*, 26 (1974–6), 123–37.
[160] Bede, III, 24, p. 293.

THE *LLU*

The reform of the Church under Anglo-Norman influence led to the decline of the *clas* churches. Their replacements were more in line with the rest of the European Church; they were less overtly military and it became rare for churchmen to fight, but Church resources were utilized by rulers and men from Church land were an important military resource. Exemptions continued to be claimed, though these came under attack from lay rulers. In line with their exploitation of all military resources, the thirteenth-century princes of Gwynedd targeted such immunities. The *Iorwerth* law text states that:

> It is not right for any land to be kingless. If it is abbey land, if there are any laymen he [the king] is entitled to *dirwy* and *camlwrw* and *amobr* and *ebediw* and theft and hosting. If it is bishop's land he is entitled to hosting and theft. If it is hospital land he is entitled to theft and fighting. And accordingly there is no land without him.[161]

We are dealing with a flexible system, with service owed according to what a ruler was able to exact. Exemptions granted (or appropriated) under a weak or generous lord could be ignored under a domineering ruler. That military demands from Church land could be great can be seen from the exactions made by Llywelyn ap Gruffudd.[162]

RANGE AND DURATION OF CAMPAIGNS

The laws laid down definite rules regarding the period of time in which a king could lead his force on offensive operations; defensive services were unlimited, but outside the limits of his kingdom the restriction was forty days' unpaid service starting from the date of arrival at the muster, a likely borrowing from Anglo-Norman feudal practice. Again, the laws present an inflexible picture; strong rulers were able to demand a greater service from their subjects and for practical considerations such service would often have been a necessity. It is difficult to imagine the members of a host packing up and leaving in

---

[161] *Law*, p. 101.
[162] See *Defences*, p. 40; Stephenson, *Governance*, pp. 166ff.; *LG*, pp. 204ff.

the face of an enemy force because their allotted period of service had run out! Nor would a leader be prepared to discard the hard-won gains of a campaigning season for such considerations.

For a king to lead his army over great distances was a source of prestige; Urien Rheged is praised with the line 'his hosts were far-travelling'.[163] The men of Arfon were granted special privileges because of the extraordinary length of a campaign to northern Britain.[164] To look at some specific examples, Bede tells us that Cadwallon occupied Northumbria for an entire year with his forces drawn, it seems, largely from Wales.[165] Other seventh-century kings of Gwynedd led major expeditions, presumably over long periods of time, against their Northumbrian enemies. In the same period, Cynddylan was praised for leading his army 'beyond Tren', out of the borders of Old Powys, against the Anglo-Saxons.[166]

In the succeeding period, the emerging over-kings of Wales conducted wide-ranging campaigns throughout the country. The *teuluoedd* of such rulers were vital, but they would have needed to draw on military resources beyond this core. Gruffudd ap Llywelyn's 1055 campaign saw him mobilizing troops for an extended period. The date of the initial muster in the north is uncertain, but following this Gruffudd marched to meet Ælfgar and his Irish mercenaries. After joining forces, the army proceeded to Herefordshire where Earl Ralf's force was defeated and the town sacked on 24 October.[167] It was unusual for the host to be mobilized this late in the year, away from the summer campaigning season, but after the sack of Hereford Gruffudd's army remained with him throughout the time that it took to appoint Harold as the new commander on the border and for him to muster an army 'from the whole of England' to march into Wales against Gruffudd. The two forces were engaged in a stand-off for a time until Harold dismissed the majority of his force, possibly for logistical reasons or because of the time of year. The earl proceeded with extensive re-fortification of

---

[163] Rowland, *Saga*, p. 478. Compare Meilyr Brydydd's praise of Gruffudd ap Cynan: 'His far-roving confounded my mind'; Meilyr, p. 186.
[164] A. O. Owen, *Ancient Laws and Institutions of Wales*, 2 vols (London, 1841), I, p. 105.
[165] Bede, III, I, p. 213.
[166] *Saga*, p. 175.
[167] *ASC* (C), 1055; JW, II, 1055.

Hereford before peace was finally made with Gruffudd. After this point the Welsh king presumably disbanded his host.

In 1136, before the battle of Cardigan, Owain and Cadwaladr led their second campaign of the year from Gwynedd to Ceredigion, despite the fact that the laws only allowed for one such expedition.[168] After the conclusion of Rhys ap Gruffudd's protracted dispute with Henry II in 1159, Rhys 'gave his men leave to go to their own land'.[169] In 1215–16 Llywelyn ap Iorwerth led an expedition throughout the winter.[170] In 1233 he led large hosts on three separate occasions, the first besieging Brecon for over a month and the last besieging Carmarthen for three months.[171] The treaty of Woodstock, imposed on Gruffudd's sons Llywelyn and Owain in 1247, set no time-limit on the Welsh troops required to serve the king of England.[172] G. R. J. Jones suggested that the thirteenth-century princes of Gwynedd tried to meet new military demands by making privileged grants to free men in return for extended periods of service.[173] Stephenson refuted this theory, pointing out that none of the grants refer to extended military service; the forty-day limit reflects thirteenth-century reality, but the princes could always purchase service beyond this period.[174] When the occasion demanded, a Welsh ruler could request extended military service in distant lands from his subjects; if he was a powerful leader it seems unlikely that such a request could be denied, though it may have been purchased with rewards, privileges or cash.

ORGANIZATION OF THE MUSTER

The evidence for organization at a basic level is scarce and we must rely on supposition. The muster of a great leader involved many individual units which would eventually gather under his sole command, but at its most local level the commote seems

---

[168] *Brut (Pen. 20)*, 1136.
[169] Ibid., 1259.
[170] Ibid., 1215.
[171] Ibid., 1233.
[172] Lewis, 'Treaty of Woodstock', p. 63.
[173] *Defences*, p. 40. For further discussion of these grants, see above, pp. 48–9.
[174] Stephenson, *Governance*, pp. 89–91.

likely to have been the essential unit. With rulers of minimal power, it is possible that a single commote represented the full muster of a lord. Each bond commote had a *maerdref*, which was associated with some form of fortification, and this focal point would presumably be used to gather the forces of the area and the resources to supply the host. In *Math*, the army of north Wales musters in Math's chief court in Arfon, Caer Dathyl, before marching out to meet a *llu* coming from the south.[175] The involvement of the *teulu* in the process of recruitment has been speculated upon and these officers are likely to have relied upon the local *uchelwyr* for gathering the troops owing service in their areas of responsibility. Other royal officers were also involved; resentment at the authority of the *rhingyll* suggests that he had a role in enforcing the prince's commands. A number of references suggest the blowing of horns to muster the land and *The Life of St Gwynllyw* refers to 'watchers' on the Glamorgan coast to warn the people of a seaborne attack.[176]

In the *Triads*, 'Yrp of the Hosts' travelled to the 'Chief Fortresses of Britain' in order to assemble his levy, but, although the connection with fortifications is intriguing, in practical terms this seems unrealistic.[177] The muster of each commote would probably arrange to meet the other units at a *maerdref* convenient for the campaign to be undertaken.[178]

---

[175] *Mabinogi*, p. 102; *PK*, p. 71.
[176] *Mabinogi*, p. 110; *PK*, p. 82; *Vitae*, pp. 137, 185.
[177] *Triads*, pp. 75–7.
[178] In *Culhwch and Olwen*, Arthur summons Devon and Cornwall to muster before meeting him at the mouth of the Severn; *Mabinogi*, p. 173; *CaO*, p. 40.

III
CAMPAIGN STRATEGY AND TACTICS

In considering the campaign strategy and tactics adopted by Welsh leaders, it is important to recognize the essential continuity and similarity of all pre-industrial warfare. Cultural and technological factors produced differences in the nature of war in various areas, but certainly in post-Roman Europe the similarities far outweighed the differences. Perceptions of the differences between Welsh (and also Irish and Scottish) warfare and the practice of war in other parts of Europe, notably England and France, have been exaggerated, as has the impact of technological changes. In this aspect of the study, the long period of time considered does not present a major problem; as the nature of war remained constant, so good campaign strategy and tactics were unchanging. The impact of the arrival of the Normans on this aspect of Welsh history has been overestimated; the perceived differences made by their technological superiority and so-called professional attitude to war were not so great and did little to change the approach of Welsh leaders.

Whilst it is common to acknowledge the professional nature of warfare that prevailed in medieval Europe – warfare characterized by prudent generalship, a struggle for fortified points and occasional battles when great things were at stake – Welsh campaigns are usually dismissed as mere cattle raids. Powicke commented on the perpetual skirmishing in Wales in the thirteenth century:

> What seems to us an intolerable situation gave to the Welsh and probably to the Marchers ever fresh opportunities to play an exciting game. War, and especially guerrilla warfare, was the natural occupation of the Welsh free man, who spent little time on his pastoral pursuits and much on his roving exercises with bow or spear.[1]

---

[1] F. M. Powicke, *King Henry III and the Lord Edward*, 2 vols. (Oxford, 1947), II, p. 618.

The apparent lack of technical ability among the Welsh military was outlined by Nelson:

> As a consequence of frequent opportunities and mass participation, they [the Welsh] became expert in sudden raids and masterly ambushes. Pitched battles and protracted campaigns, on the other hand, were beyond their capabilities, and the intricacies of siege warfare were foreign to their experience. Within the limits of their training, however, and in the terrain in which they operated, there were no better warriors.[2]

A contrast has been perceived between this supposedly primitive warrior people and the Normans:

> The Norman military machine was composed of specialized, full-time mounted men ... The Welsh military machine was, accordingly, a loosely organized, part-time infantry force primarily designed to pursue feuds, and to engage in cattle raiding and looting expeditions ... the Welsh army was not the sort of organized field force which could be crushed in regular campaigns.[3]

Beeler noted Welsh ability in guerrilla warfare and stated: 'Although when they fought among themselves the Welsh frequently engaged in pitched battles, it became almost a national policy to avoid combat in the open with the better organized, far more heavily armed Anglo-Normans.'[4] He contended that after 1066 the Welsh began to adopt Norman military tactics whilst the Normans adopted Welsh ones.[5] Similarly, R. R. Davies wrote:

> There can be little doubt that the initial overwhelming impact of Anglo-Norman invaders in Wales and Ireland represented the victory of superior

---

[2] L. H. Nelson, *The Normans in South Wales, 1070–1171* (Austin, Texas, 1966), p. 12.
[3] Ibid., p. 115.
[4] J. Beeler, *Warfare in England, 1066–1189* (New York, 1966), p. 196.
[5] Ibid., p. 201.

military technology and tactics – notably, of course, heavily armed cavalry, carefully deployed bands of archers, and the rapidly built castle.[6]

This theme of the mixture and exchange of military cultures is explored by Suppe in a case study of the Shropshire March.[7] His revisionist theory questions Bartlett's belief in the progress of the Normans' more sophisticated military machine throughout Europe. In the field of strategy and tactics, however, it has not been acknowledged that the nature of war in Wales and Normandy was essentially very similar; in each area commanders were aware of a variety of strategies and tactics and chose those which were appropriate to the situation. With regard to technological changes, it is dangerous to argue that such developments led to inevitable success. DeVries contends that even advances like the tank and the machine gun have not proved decisive in modern wars and that to take such an approach when dealing with cavalry and bows is not sustainable.[8]

The dangers in classifying warfare in the ways outlined for Wales above have been considered by Nicolle's book on warfare in the Middle Ages:

> The medieval concept of a 'people' having a common ancestry, and thus forming a *gens* or race, was based on ancient Greek ideas of ethnic differences between such supposed 'races'. It also assumed that certain similarities within a *gens* were demonstrated by distinctive warlike capabilities. Apart from being unsound from an anthropological standpoint, and containing the seeds of later racist theories, this concept of

[6] R. R. Davies, *Domination and Conquest* (Cambridge, 1990), pp. 39–40; Davies refers to the thesis set out for Europe by R. Bartlett in 'Technique militaire et pouvoir politique, 900–1300', *Annales: Économies, Sociétés, Civilisations*, 41 (1986), 1138–59. Bartlett expanded his views in *The Making of Europe* (London, 1993), contending that *c*.950–1350 the nobility from the 'heartland' of Frankish and German Europe used their advanced military technology to make conquests on the 'fringes' of the continent. The three main components were missile weapons, castles and heavy cavalry. The theory has been applied to Welsh warfare, regarding Rhys ap Gruffudd's reign as the watershed when the Welsh began to put into practice Norman lessons; see *Dulliau*, 76–93. J. B. Smith says that the Welsh learnt from the Normans, but places more emphasis for their fight back from initial Norman onslaughts on the political recovery of dynasties rather than military lessons; *LG*, p. 4.
[7] F. C. Suppe, *Military Institutions on the Welsh Marches: Shropshire, AD 1066–1300* (Woodbridge, 1994); see also M. Strickland, 'Military technology and conquest: the anomaly of Anglo-Saxon England', *ANS*, 19 (1996), 353–82.
[8] K. DeVries, 'Catapults are not atomic bombs: towards a redefinition of effectiveness in premodern military technology', *War in History*, 4 (1997), 454–70.

distinct or separate early medieval ethnic groups is very misleading . . . Few if any of the larger barbarian 'nations' were drawn from a single ethnic background.⁹

Unfortunately, Nicolle applies all the usual stereotypes to Welsh, and even to so-called 'Celtic', warfare:

> Very little strategy, as such, seems discernible in the internal warfare of the Celtic lands themselves. In all areas it remained a case of minor skirmishing. Ireland was particularly noted for cattle rustling between rival chieftains; each striving to win both wealth and prestige in what sometimes seems to have been little more than a violent sport.
> The Normans could hardly have been more different in their attitudes to warfare. By the eleventh century Norman armies were noted for their discipline, while their commanders were noted for their remarkable patience as well as their caution. Norman warfare was, in fact, characterized by careful reconnaissance, prolonged sieges and blockades, occasional battles which were usually associated with such sieges, a preference for diplomacy whenever possible . . . A willingness to retreat when circumstances were unfavourable, and an ability to carry out winter campaigns were further characteristics of Norman warfare. Close attention to the security of supplies and supply lines, as well as considerable use of espionage and great effort to find traitors within an enemy's ranks were also typical of the Normans' realistic and unromantic attitude towards warfare.¹⁰

Nicolle highlights the characteristics of Norman warfare that have been stressed by modern commentators. These include an avoidance of battle whenever possible; the concentration on, and importance of, small-scale clashes; the value of supplies and of ravaging; recognition of the worth of surprise and cunning; appreciation of prudent generalship. Such values should be considered when reading Nicolle's argument on the distinct nature of war in Wales:

> During the twelfth and thirteenth centuries the main preoccupation of Welsh warfare was defence against English aggression. This resulted in the sort of prolonged guerrilla warfare that was otherwise rare in the Middle Ages. Welsh forces could attempt to harass and ambush the

⁹ Nicolle, *Medieval*, p. 13.
¹⁰ Ibid., pp. 75–6.

CAMPAIGN STRATEGY AND TACTICS 89

Anglo-Norman supply trains, particularly in wooded, marshy or confined mountainous terrain. But they rarely attempted to meet such heavier armed enemies in open battle. Above all the Welsh commanders tried to predict and then block an enemy's line of withdrawal, or force him down a specific route by blocking all others. In response the Anglo-Normans attempted to lure the Welsh into their own ambushes, often by pretending to retreat in disorder.[11]

Welsh and Norman commanders worked along similar, recognizable strategic and tactical principles. It must be asked why there was (and why there remains) a perceived difference and in the instances where principles did differ there is a need to seek an explanation.

RAVAGING, EVASION AND AMBUSH

To understand the central role of ravaging in medieval warfare, it is necessary to rid ourselves of the modern perception of the overriding importance of the decisive pitched battle. This emphasis has come since Napoleonic times and can be seen in the writings of Clausewitz. He felt that war had to be logical, directed towards complete victory:

> He who uses force unsparingly, without reference to the bloodshed involved, must obtain a superiority if his adversary uses less vigour in its application . . . to introduce into the philosophy of war itself a principle of moderation would be an absurdity.[12]

Such thinking owed much to Clausewitz's experiences of the Napoleonic Wars, the influence of Darwinism and the notion of the survival of the fittest. It describes a warfare run by the governments of the nation states of Clausewitz's day. The influence of such nineteenth-century thought on military historians has been traced by John Keegan.[13]

The standard view of warfare in the Middle Ages was, for many years, drawn from Charles Oman's work early in the

---

[11] Ibid., p. 125.
[12] Clausewitz, *On War*, ed. A. Rapoport (London, 1982), p. 101.
[13] J. Keegan, *The Face of Battle* (Harmondsworth, 1976), pp. 55–62; see also *WW*, p. 12.

twentieth century.¹⁴ The prevailing dogmas of military history at the time meant that war in the Middle Ages, with its continual small-scale skirmishes and feuds and relative shortage of battles, was seen as crude, amateur and unprofessional. Reaction to this view came through Smail's work on the crusades, which highlighted the professional attitude to war, with an emphasis on the importance of supplies and attrition.¹⁵ A more analytical approach to warfare within medieval Europe itself was adopted by John France who questioned the mastery of the armoured knight and the importance of the pitched battle.¹⁶ He stressed the importance of infantry, specialized troops, sieges and questions of logistics and supplies.¹⁷ Some felt that this military thinking could only be applied to Britain after 1066 when the Normans brought their 'new' approach to warfare to the isles, but Hooper and Strickland stressed the sophistication of the Anglo-Saxon military.¹⁸

The importance of ravaging is seen in the work of the late Roman writer Vegetius. He concentrated on the practical aspects of warfare and his *De Re Militari* was popular throughout the Middle Ages and beyond. 'The main and principal point in war is to secure plenty of provisions and to destroy the enemy by famine,' he wrote.¹⁹ Contact with enemy forces was not necessary. This theme has been taken up by modern writers:

> The ravaging of the enemy's countryside was the most common manifestation of medieval warfare and arguably the most fundamental of all its

---

[14] C. Oman, *History of the Art of War in the Middle Ages*, 2 vols. (London, 1924).

[15] R. C. Smail, *Crusading Warfare, 1097–1193* (Cambridge, 1956). See also J. France, *Victory in the East* (Cambridge, 1994).

[16] J. France, 'The military history of the Carolingian period', *Revue Belge d'Histoire Militaire*, 26 (1985), 81–100; see also his *WW*, pp. 1–15.

[17] This approach has been continued in other key works. See J. Bradbury, 'Battles in England and Normandy, 1066–1154', in *ANW*, pp. 182–93; J. Gillingham, 'William the bastard at war', in C. Harper-Bill (ed.), *Studies in Medieval History Presented to R. Allen Brown* (Woodbridge, 1989); also his 'Richard I and the science of war in the Middle Ages', in his *Richard Coeur de Lion: Kingship, Chivalry and War in the Twelfth Century* (London, 1994), pp. 211–26; and 'War and chivalry in the History of William the Marshal', in his *Richard Coeur de Lion*, pp. 243–56; M. Strickland, 'Securing the north: invasion and the strategy of defence in twelfth-century Anglo-Scottish warfare', in *ANW*, pp. 208–29; and his *War and Chivalry: The Conduct and Perception of War in England and Normandy, 1066–1217* (Cambridge, 1996).

[18] N. Hooper, 'The Anglo-Saxons at war', in Hawkes, *Weapons*, pp. 191–202; also his 'Anglo-Saxon warfare on the eve of the Norman conquest', *ANS*, 1 (1978), 84–93; Strickland, 'Military technology', 353–82.

[19] Vegetius, p. 67.

forms ... it consisted of an assault on the material and psychological basis of an opponent's lordship, achieved by the seizure or destruction of the central component of his landed wealth – his chattels, crops, livestock and peasantry.[20]

Armies often had little logistical support, and supplies for men and animals were vital. Ravaging weakened the enemy; the taking of plunder and tribute could lead to political subjection,[21] whilst booty was a primary aim. There was no feeling of shame attached to waging war on the peasants and their land. Cynan and Cadwaladr, the heroes of the *Armes Prydein*, are lauded as 'two generous lords, two noble raiders of a country's cattle'.[22]

If the defending force frustrated the attacker's ability to ravage, it could turn the course of a campaign. This could mean a scorched-earth policy, but the usual defensive tactic was to keep a force in the field without engaging the attacker. This would prevent the aggressor from splitting his forces as his ravaging parties would be exposed.[23] Meanwhile, goods and chattels would be moved away from the enemy, hidden, or placed in church sanctuary, and anything left behind would be destroyed.[24] Skirmishes and ambushes were common and could in themselves decide the campaign. Given this context, it can be seen that Welsh leaders followed standard military principles. War was directed at the structure of an enemy's lordship, the bondmen, animals, cultivated land and economic infrastructure that supported him.

The earliest account of post-Roman warfare in Britain is from Constantius's *Life of St Germanus*, where the saint is said to have taken command of a British force somewhere in the south in 429 to meet the invading Picts and Saxons. The invaders advanced hoping to surprise the British, but they were spotted by scouts. Armed with good intelligence, Germanus led his light troops forward to ambush the enemy. Although no blow was struck, the

---

[20] Strickland, *War*, p. 259.
[21] In Welsh law, a lord established possession of land by ruling over it for a year and a day 'without violence'; *Law*, p. 111.
[22] *AP*, p. 13. In the *Triads*, Arthur is lauded as the greatest of the three 'Red Ravagers' of Britain: 'for a year neither grass nor plants used to spring up where one of the three would walk; but where Arthur went, not for seven years'; *Triads*, p. 35.
[23] See *WW*, p. 10.
[24] For sanctuary, see below, pp. 255–8. Gerald of Wales says that in Ireland people hid provisions in underground vaults; *Conquest*, II, 19, p. 183.

enemy fled in panic and the event is proclaimed as a great victory.[25]

According to Gildas, the Anglo-Saxon conquest of Britain was characterized by ravaging rather than battles. We are told that fire spread from sea to sea, burning town and country and 'licking the western ocean with its fierce red tongue'.[26] The towns were assaulted, ravaged and left desolate. When the British responded: 'they kept fighting back basing themselves on the mountains, eaves, heaths and thorny thickets. Their enemies had been plundering their land for many years; now for the first time they inflicted a massacre on them, trusting not in man but in God.'[27] Alcock analysed the sources for British warfare in this period. Although the evidence is unreliable, it points to the mobility of forces and the concentration of clashes on major highways and fords.[28] Alcock contended that battles were fought in the vicinity of forts, but in the open rather than as sieges; people could shelter in fortifications, but the land and its wealth had to be defended in the field. If this was not done then claims to lordship over the land would pass to the invaders. The mobility of the forces suggests small numbers engaged in lightning raids. Defending forces would try to intercept these raiders on highways and river fords. If an army was shadowing its enemy then a ford was a spot where they could force them to fight. Also, an army crossing a ford could be exposed as a part became detached from the main body and left itself open to counter-attack.[29] Alcock uses the *Anglo-Saxon Chronicle* and *Historia Brittonum* to reveal the emphasis on fords, but this can also be seen in early poetry. Taliesin's *The Battle of Gwen Ystrad* describes a battle fought by Urien of Rheged at a ford;[30] in *Canu Llywarch*, Gwên's task was to watch the ford of Rhodwydd Forlas and keep the enemy from crossing;[31] the great battle envisaged in *Armes Prydein* is to be fought at a crossing of the Wye.[32]

[25] See Constantius, *The Life of St Germanus of Auxerre*, in F. R. Hoare (ed. and trans.), *The Western Fathers* (London, 1954), pp. 300–1.
[26] Gildas, p. 27.
[27] Ibid., p. 24.
[28] Alcock, *Economy*, pp. 285ff.
[29] Such a fate befell the French royal force at Varaville in 1057; see Gillingham, 'William', p. 153.
[30] *CT*, VI, p. 6.
[31] *Saga*, pp. 468ff.
[32] *AP*, p. 7.

The dykes in existence in much of Britain have been dated to the post-Roman period. They were used in the same way as river fords; defenders could challenge raiding forces at predetermined points.[33] An unburdened raiding party could cross a dyke at will, but when loaded with booty and driving cattle its options would have been restricted.

In the greatest campaigns of the day harrying remained the key element. Bede says that Cadwallon, after defeating Edwin at Hatfield Chase and destroying Osric's army, 'occupied the Northumbrian kingdoms for a whole year, not ruling them like a victorious king but ravaging them like a savage tyrant, tearing them to pieces with fearful bloodshed'.[34] Penda devastated Northumbria,[35] and before the battle of Winwaed Oswiu tried to buy off the Mercian king from further ravaging.[36] The fact that many of Penda's allies deserted him on the eve of the battle could indicate that, though happy to continue ravaging, they were not prepared to face the dangers of battle.

Surviving poetry reflects the importance of ravaging; it was a praiseworthy act of a lord. Taliesin hailed Urien of Rheged as 'a conquering prince, cattle raider':[37]

lloegrwys ae gwydant	pan ymadrodant.
agheu a gawssant	a mynych godyant.
llosci eu trefret	a dwyn eu tudet
ac eimwnc collet	a mawr aghyffret
heb gaffel gwaret.	rac vryen reget.[38]
(England's men know him	when they encounter:
Death is their portion	and pain in plenty,
their houses blazing,	their garments taken,
and heavy losses,	and grievous hardship,
no mercy granted	by Rheged's Urien.)[39]

---

[33] See Alcock, *Economy*, p. 310; Nicolle, *Medieval*, p. 28. Fox believed that Offa's Dyke and Wat's Dyke were built in later centuries in response to Welsh raids on Mercia; C. Fox, *Offa's Dyke* (Oxford, 1955), p. xxi.
[34] Bede, III, 1, p. 213.
[35] Ibid., III, 1, p. 263.
[36] Ibid., III, 24, p. 291.
[37] *CT*, II, p. 2; *Earliest*, p. 24.
[38] *CT*, III, p. 3.
[39] *Earliest*, p. 26.

The *Triads* hint at stories about the famous 'Red Ravagers' of Britain and of 'Unrestrained Ravagings' of the country.[40] In *Marwnad Cynddylan*, the lords Rhiau, Rhirid, Rhiadaf and Rhigyfarch are praised:

> They drove their flocks from the river meadows of the Taf,
> the captured ones complained, cattle bellowed and lowed . . .
> the greatness of swordplay – great booty –
> before Lichfield Morfael took it:
> fifteen hundred head of cattle and five
> eighty horses, and harnesses besides.[41]

To be able to protect one's lands from such ravaging was most praiseworthy. Urien scoffs at the intentions of his enemies:

> Brân fab Ymellyrn intended
> to exile me, to burn my homesteads . . .
> Morgant – he and his warriors – intended
> to exile me, to burn my land:
> a shrew who scratched at a crag.[42]

The *Canu Heledd* mourns the passing of lords capable of defending the lands of Old Powys:

> The cattle of Edeirnion were not wayfaring;
> they did not go with anyone's troop
> in the lifetime of Gorwynion, a wise warrior.[43]

Similar praise is seen in Cynddelw Brydydd Mawr's elegy for Madog ap Maredudd of Powys (d. 1160):

> Hael fu ei glod am bentyrru ysbail,
> nid yw'n osgoi pobl waedlyd ddifaol[44]

> Loaded his plunder made easy his praise,
> nor ever shunned he a pillaging host.[45]

[40] *Triads*, pp. 35, 147.
[41] *Saga*, p. 177.
[42] Ibid., p. 480.
[43] Ibid., p. 489.
[44] *CBT*, III, 7.18–19.
[45] *Welsh Verse*, p. 153.

Following his victory over Rhain at Abergwili in 1022, Llywelyn ap Seisyll took control of his conquered territory by 'ravaging the land and carrying off all the chattels'.[46] Walter Map saw Gruffudd ap Llywelyn's rise to prominence in these terms: 'he left his father, proclaimed war on his neighbours, and became a most crafty and formidable raider of others' goods'.[47] In 1052, Gruffudd's ravaging of Herefordshire provoked an Anglo-Saxon force to make a reckless attack,[48] and in 1055 his way of reinstating Ælfgar was to enter Herefordshire 'with the intention of laying waste the English border'.[49] If political motivations were Gruffudd's primary concern, the booty gained from the sack of Hereford was a major fillip: 'with vast spoil he returned home eminently worthy'.[50] It is generally considered that Gruffudd's power was broken immediately after Harold's raid on Rhuddlan in 1063, but the wording of the *Life of King Edward* deserves consideration:

> The English hastening under Harold joined
> Fast columns and platoons of Tostig's men
> They terrified the foe, till then so bold,
> With close attack in strength, with fire and sword.
> And though with many virtues he displayed
> Th'ancestral glory of his chivalry,
> Gruffudd, unequal to this fight, did fear
> T'engage with these, and sought remote retreats.
> Inured to lurk in distant dikes, from which
> He can with safety fly upon the foe,
> Exploiting barren lands with woods and rocks,
> He galls the brother earls with drawn out war.
> And these, resourceful in a doubtful case,
> Throw down the country in one general ruin.
> The enemy's house is sacked, the girded chests
> Are broached, and royal pomp exposed to loot.[51]

Gruffudd was weakened by the attack on Rhuddlan and by political intrigue within Wales, but this passage suggests that he

---

[46] *Brut (Pen. 20)*, s.a. 1022.
[47] Map, p. 191.
[48] *ASC* (D), 1052; JW, II, 1052.
[49] JW, II, 1055.
[50] *Brut (Pen. 20)*, s.a. 1056.
[51] *Life of King Edward*, p. 87.

was able to rally. In 'fearing to engage and seeking remote retreats', Gruffudd was following accepted strategic principles; he would not engage a stronger force in battle, but chose to shadow it and, when the chance arose, 'fly with safety upon the foe'.[52] This seems to have caused problems for the Godwinessons, but their determination and superior resources, and Gruffudd's internal problems, meant that resistance was overcome.

After 1066, Anglo-Norman writers describe the strategy of shadowing an enemy and avoiding battle as a characteristic of the Welsh whose armies were incapable of facing the Anglo-Normans in a fair fight. Henry of Huntingdon says that Rufus's 1097 expedition failed only because the Welsh were better defended by their rugged country than their prowess in arms.[53] He describes the Welsh at the battle of Lincoln in 1141 as 'rash, ill-armed and ignorant of the art of war'.[54] William of Newburgh described Welsh resistance to Henry II: 'The Welsh assembled their forces and stood guard on their frontiers; their light-armed levies warily refrained from advancing into the plain to engage the mailed knights in pitched battle and they lay hidden in the woods keeping watch on the narrow passes.'[55] This passage is more ambiguous than Huntingdon's; it could be seen as criticism of the Welsh, but it could equally praise their prudence. Certainly in 1173 Newburgh appreciated the military skills of the Welsh; at the siege of Rouen, Henry II used his Welsh troops, 'nimble and skilled in woodcraft', to work behind French lines, destroy their supply columns and end the siege.[56] Roger of Howden noted the ravaging skills of the Welsh in Henry's army in France in 1188.[57] Orderic says that William fitz Osbern was put on the border by the Conqueror 'with Walter de Lacy and other proved warriors to fight the bellicose Welsh'.[58] The *Gesta*

---

[52] This reading of the passage rejects the argument put forward by Hudson that it refers to Harold's 1055 campaign on the border; B. T. Hudson, 'The destruction of Gruffudd ap Llywelyn', *WHR*, 15 (1990–1), 331–50.

[53] HH, VII, 19, p. 445.

[54] Ibid., X, 17, p. 735; this is part of a speech given by Baldwin fitz Gilbert de Clare to the royalist army condemning all of Stephen's opponents, Anglo-Norman as well as Welsh.

[55] WN, p. 325; Chrons., I, p. 106.

[56] WN, p. 355; Chrons., I, pp. 195–6.

[57] RH, II, p. 345. Warren described Welsh troops as 'the Gurkhas of the twelfth century'; W. L. Warren, *Henry II* (London, 1977), p. 158.

[58] OV, II, 4, p. 261.

Stephani states that Wales 'breeds men of an animal type, naturally swift-footed, accustomed to war',[59] and Walter Map called the Welsh 'warlike and skilled in arms'.[60]

That the Normans could identify with warfare in Wales dominated by ravaging, ambush and evasion can be seen by the epitaph to one of their earliest settlers in the country, Robert of Rhuddlan:

> With a few men he ambushed great King Bleddyn
> And made him fly abandoning rich booty.[61]

When Robert of Bellême faced Henry I's superior forces in 1102 he adopted the strategy of ravaging and evasion and employed the Welsh to help him: 'He himself [Robert] then made a treaty with the Welsh, and formed an alliance with their kings, Cadwgan and Iorwerth, the sons of Rhys [*sic*], whom he sent on frequent forays to harass the king's army with their forces.'[62] Iorwerth's force was bought off by Henry and sent to plunder Robert's land: 'And the warband, cruelly and hostilely executing their lord's behest, gathered vast plunder and ravaged the land and pillaged it: for the earl had before that ordered his men to take their flocks and herds and all their chattels into the lands of the Britons.'[63] This prompted Robert to come to terms with the king. Matilda and Robert of Gloucester allied with the Welsh in their struggle against Stephen and sent their allies to ravage the lands of their opponents:

> Trouble spread far and wide. For more than 10,000 wild men (as they are called) were let loose over England, and they spared neither hallowed place nor men of religion, but gave themselves up to pillage and burning and massacre. I cannot relate in detail what sufferings the Church of God endured in her sons, who were daily slaughtered like cattle by the swords of the Welsh.[64]

---

[59] *GS*, p. 15.
[60] Map, p. 183.
[61] OV, IV, 8, p. 145.
[62] OV, VI, 11, p. 25. Read Bleddyn for Rhys.
[63] *Brut (Pen. 20)*, s.a. 1102.
[64] OV, VI, 13, p. 537.

Gruffudd ap Cynan is a rich source for strategy and tactics. In the 1070s, Gruffudd tried to reclaim his position in Gwynedd with an Irish fleet.[65] We are told that he failed because he would not allow his men to ravage and consequently they carried him back to Ireland, but this could be the source trying to hide how Gruffudd had been outwitted. Before his arrival, Gruffudd's opponent Trahaearn ap Caradog had moved the men and goods of the coastal provinces of Llŷn and Ardudwy to Meirionnydd, closer to the heartland of Trahaearn's power and more easily defensible against Gruffudd's attack. Trahaearn's actions left the invaders with nothing to ravage and they were forced to withdraw. The Welsh ability to transport their possessions quickly served them well in the face of invasion. In 1109, a force seeking to attack Cadwgan of Powys delayed their move overnight: 'On the following day they came into the land. And after seeing it deserted, they reproached themselves and accused Uchdryd . . . And they foraged about and obtained nothing save Cadwgan's stud.'[66] The common practice of transhumance facilitated this ability to empty threatened land.

The fighting amongst Welsh leaders in the 1070s gave the Normans the chance to move into the north of the country. They made their presence felt by ravaging, allying with Gwrgenau ap Seisyll and marching on Llŷn:

> In that *cantref* they encamped for a week, causing destruction there daily and ravaging it and inflicting a great slaughter of corpses which they left behind. The land then remained desolate for eight years, and the people of that land were scattered over the world, despised and destitute.[67]

Following his victory at Mynydd Carn, Gruffudd sought to impose his power on Gwynedd and Powys:

> [he] marched towards Arwystli and destroyed and killed its people; he burned its houses and took its women and maidens captive. Thus did he pay like for like to Trahaearn. Then he proceeded to Powys, where he straightaway displayed his cruelty to his adversaries according to the

---

[65] *Gruffudd ap Cynan*, pp. 64–5.
[66] *Brut (Pen. 20)*, s.a. 1109. Such movements of population were not undertaken lightly, however. They caused upheaval, disruption and suffering and invaders were still able to inflict damage on the vacated land.
[67] *Gruffudd ap Cynan*, p. 65.

manner of a victor; and he spared not even the churches. After he had thus killed his enemies and destroyed their land completely, he returned to his own proper possession and patrimony to rule and pacify it.[68]

This passage reveals the treatment a land could expect when its lord had been defeated and there was no force to shadow the enemy. In 1124, we see Gruffudd using the same strategy to project his power; his sons were sent to Meirionnydd to 'carry away all its men and chattels to Llŷn'.[69] To ravage with impunity was the sign of a powerful lord; Walter Map told the story of a king of north Wales who boasted that there was no land which he could not plunder before returning home *without* having to face battle.[70]

In the Welsh rising of 1094, the *Brutiau* refer to the ravaging of Ceredigion and Dyfed,[71] whilst John of Worcester noted incursions across the border into Chester, Shrewsbury and Hereford where townships were burnt.[72] In response Rufus gathered an army:

> [Rufus] marched into Wales after Michaelmas and dispersed his army and traversed all the country so that all the army came together at All Saints at Snowdon. But the Welsh went ahead into mountains and moors so that they could not be reached; and the king then turned homewards because he saw that he could do nothing more there that winter.[73]

The king must have led a large army to have been able to split it into effective units in the face of an enemy force. However, the Anglo-Normans were able to do little damage, presumably because Welsh forces shadowed and harassed the invaders. As winter drew in, Rufus was unable to keep his army supplied and, although he had advanced deep into Wales, was forced to retreat with nothing to show for his efforts. The description in *Gruffudd ap Cynan* cannot be relied upon as it places Gruffudd at the forefront of the revolt when we know, from the *Anglo-Saxon*

---

[68] Ibid., p. 69. Gruffudd had previously ravaged the land of his erstwhile ally, Rhys ap Tewdwr.
[69] *Brut (Pen. 20)*, s.a. 1124.
[70] Map, p. 151.
[71] *Brut (Pen. 20)*, s.a. 1094; *Brut (RBH)*, s.a. 1094.
[72] JW, III, 1094.
[73] *ASC* (E), 1095.

Chronicle and the *Brutiau*, that Cadwgan ap Bleddyn of Powys led the Welsh resistance; but the passage is illuminating nevertheless. Rufus was said to have gathered a large force:

> Prepared to exterminate and destroy all the people completely that there would not be left alive as much as a dog. He had also intended to cut down all the woods and groves, so that there would not be shelter or protection for the people of Gwynedd from then on. And he, therefore, set up camp and pitched his tents first in Mur Castell, with some of the Welsh as his guides. When Gruffudd heard that, he also mustered the host of all his kingdom, and marched against him, in order to prepare ambushes for him, in narrow places when he should come down the mountain. And he became frightened of that, and took his host back through the middle of the land till he came to Chester, without inflicting any kind of loss to the people of the land. He did not obtain any kind of profit or gain, except for one cow, and he lost a great part of his horsemen and esquires and servants and horses, and many other possessions. Thus did he completely avenge the presumption of the French.
>
> Throughout that time, Gruffudd constantly engaged them, sometimes in front, sometimes behind, sometimes to the right, sometimes to the left of them, lest they should cause any kind of loss in the territory. And had Gruffudd allowed his men to mingle with them in the woods, that would have been the last day for the king of England and his Frenchmen.[74]

In our terms the Welsh were 'avoiding battle', but the contemporary view was that Gruffudd 'marched against' Rufus and was 'constantly engaging' his forces; it was not a passive strategy.

Having failed to quell the revolt in the north, in 1096 the Anglo-Normans turned their attention to the south. They were foiled by the same strategy of evasion and then ambush as their disheartened troops retreated:

> And then the Britons of Brycheiniog and Gwent and Gwynllwg threw off the rule of the French. And the French moved a host to Gwent; but they returned empty-handed having gained naught. And as they were returning they were slain by the Britons at the place called Celli Carnant. After that the French moved a host to Brycheiniog and thought to ravage the whole land, but, having failed to accomplish their thoughts, as they were

[74] *Gruffudd ap Cynan*, pp. 74–5.

returning they were slain by the sons of Idnerth ap Cadwgan, Gruffudd and Ifor, in the place called Aber-Llech.[75]

Rufus led an expedition to the south in 1097, taking a large army and staying from midsummer until August, but 'achieving nothing but the loss of men and horses and goods'.[76] The *Brutiau* praise the strategy of evasion, saying that the 'Britons',

> avoided the assault of the French: for the French, not daring to invade the woods or the wilderness against the Britons, but foraging about and encompassing the open fields, returned home dejected and empty-handed. And so the Britons defended their land fearlessly.[77]

The expedition led into north Wales by Hugh of Shrewsbury and Hugh of Chester in 1098 was far more successful than previous Anglo-Norman efforts.[78] At first, Cadwgan and Gruffudd followed the usual strategy: 'and the men of Gwynedd, as was their custom, retreated to the strongest and wildest places they had'.[79] However, it seems that the earls were successful in flushing the Welsh out as they eventually retreated to Anglesey. On the flat terrain of the island the Welsh leaders could not face their powerful enemy, so a reason for the retreat must be sought. It is possible that they were outmanoeuvred by their enemy who were familiar with the terrain and whose army contained Welsh troops.[80] However, there is no mention of any previous action on the campaign and it seems more likely that the Welsh placed too much faith in the ability of their Irish allies to keep their enemies

---

[75] *Brut (RBH)*, s.a. 1096. A. G. Williams suggested that the battle of Celli Carnant took place on the Great Heath, north of Cardiff; 'The Norman lordship of Glamorgan: an examination of its establishment and development' (unpublished M.Phil. thesis, University of Wales, Cardiff, 1991), 127–8. Aberllech is three miles north-east of Ystradgynlais; *HW*, II, p. 407. In the same year a number of Welsh lords besieged the castle of Pembroke, held by Gerald of Wales's grandfather Gerald of Windsor. In the *Journey through Wales* we are told of the castellan's defence of Pembroke that forced the Welsh to turn away; *Journey*, I, 12, pp. 148–9. The fact that Gerald managed to hold the castle is significant, but the native chroniclers were more impressed with the fact that the land was ravaged and plundered of its cattle and that the Welsh returned home with 'vast spoil'; *Brut (RBH)*, 1096.
[76] *ASC* (E), s.a. 1097.
[77] *Brut (Pen. 20)*, s.a. 1097.
[78] Our sources were impressed with the scale of preparation; *Gruffudd ap Cynan*, p. 75, records 'a fleet and a mighty wondrous host'.
[79] *Brut (Pen. 20)*, s.a. 1098.
[80] Their guides were Owain and Uchdryd ab Edwin, probably tenants of Hugh of Chester in Tegeingl; *HW*, II, p. 408.

out of the island. Thus Cadwgan and Gruffudd deliberately departed from the strategy of shadowing the enemy and hiding chattels in the wilds and chose to defend Anglesey 'as a fortress'.[81] The strategy was exposed when the earls bought off the Irish fleet, leaving the Welsh outnumbered and unable to face the enemy in the field. Total defeat was averted by the unexpected appearance of Magnus Barefoot who challenged and defeated the earls, killing Hugh of Montgomery, but the Anglo-Norman victory over the Welsh was crushing. *Gruffudd ap Cynan* claims that Hugh of Chester:

> took with him the people of Gwynedd and all their possessions entirely as far as the *cantref* of Rhos, for fear of the arrival of Gruffudd at any time. And then were counted the cattle and plunder of every owner, which were divided in half, and with the one half he proceeded to Chester.[82]

The statement that Hugh 'feared the arrival of Gruffudd' can be ignored; the earl had routed his enemy's forces and seized the chattels taken to Anglesey for safe-keeping. In future campaigns Welsh leaders would know that Anglesey was no refuge; Anglo-Norman naval superiority meant that the island was a strategic weakness for Gwynedd. In preparation for John's invasion of 1211, Llywelyn ap Iorwerth 'moved Anglesey and all its chattels to Snowdon'.[83]

The dominance enjoyed by Henry I in Wales meant that there were few examples of large-scale opposition during his reign. On a more local level, the strategy of Owain ap Cadwgan can be analysed as he sought to win back the land of which Henry had deprived him in 1109. In 1110, Owain and his fellow exile Madog ap Rhiddid 'were committing mischief on the lands of the French and the Saxons. And whatever they carried off, either by violence or by stealth, they carried it into Iorwerth [ap Bleddyn's] territory.'[84] Henry forced Iorwerth to drive the outlaws away and they entered Meirionnydd where they routed a *llu* mustered to defend the land. After this, Owain's and Madog's men 'ravaged the land, burning the houses and the

---

[81] *Gruffudd ap Cynan*, p. 76.
[82] Ibid., p. 78.
[83] *Brut (Pen. 20)*, s.a. 1211.
[84] Ibid., s.a. 1110.

crops and killing the stock – as much as they found, but carrying nothing off thence'.[85] They were unable to carry off booty because they were on the run, but the ravaging created problems for Henry who, as an overlord, had failed to defend his vassals. Owain moved on to his father's land in Ceredigion whence he:

> went on forays to Dyfed and they plundered the land and seized the people and carried them off with them bound to the ships which Owain had brought with him from Ireland . . . On another occasion they summoned 'hotheads' from Ceredigion to add to the numbers along with them, and by night they came to a township of Dyfed and slew all that they found, and despoiled others and carried others off with them as prisoners to the ships, and thence sold them to their folk. And after burning the houses and killing the animals and carrying others off with them, they returned to Ceredigion.[86]

Because of his failure to control his son, Cadwgan was deprived of his lands by Henry, and Gilbert fitz Richard was sent to restore order. Owain remained a menace in Wales, though, and eventually he seems to have won Henry's respect. In 1111, after disposing of his Welsh rivals, Owain recovered land in Wales with Henry's blessing. Through his harrying of the land, Owain had achieved his political objective.

Gruffudd ap Rhys tried a similar strategy to recover his position in 1116. His revolt focused on the burning and looting of castles and lordships in the south. He is treated harshly by our sources, partly because, unlike Owain, he ultimately failed. In 1172 Iorwerth ab Owain, frustrated by the treacherous murder of his son and the refusal of the Anglo-Normans to recognize his claims to Caerleon, 'placing no trust in the king ravaged the lands around Gloucester and Hereford, pillaging and burning and slaying without mercy'.[87] Political outcasts in England tried the same strategy to gain the king's attention; in his revolt of 1233–4, Richard Marshal allied with Llywelyn ap Iorwerth before 'collecting all the forces they could muster, and

---

[85] Ibid.
[86] Ibid.
[87] Ibid., s.a. 1172.

penetrating a good distance into the king's territory, spreading fire wherever they went'.[88]

The continued presumption of Owain ap Cadwgan provoked Henry into leading an expedition against him in 1114. Owain allied with Gruffudd ap Cynan and Goronwy ab Owain and adopted the usual strategy: 'he [Owain] gathered his men and all their chattels along with them and moved into the mountains of Eryri; for that was the wildest and safest place in which to retreat.'[89] *Gruffudd ap Cynan* describes the positioning of a Welsh force to shadow Henry's army: 'he [Henry] thus came to Gruffudd's territory and encamped at Mur Castell. Gruffudd also, from his experience of warfare, encamped against him on the ridges of snow-clad Snowdon.'[90] Despite such claims, Gruffudd quickly submitted to the king, leaving Owain exposed so that he, too, requested terms. Henry was prepared to make concessions; he knew how difficult it would have been to overcome the Welsh.

In 1121 events followed a similar turn as Henry grew frustrated with continuing disorder in Wales. If we are to believe the *Anglo-Saxon Chronicle*, the king met little resistance. In the summer Henry 'went into Wales with an army; and the Welsh came to meet him, and they made an agreement with him according to the king's desires'.[91] The native sources tell a different story. *Gruffudd ap Cynan* says that Henry and his army again encamped at Mur Castell:

> with the intention of uprooting the territory of Gruffudd and destroying it, and killing and exterminating his people with the edge of the sword. When that was heard, after mustering a host, Gruffudd came against him according to his usual practice, and placed his abodes and villeins and the women and sons in the recesses of the mountains of Snowdon, where they did not suffer any danger. Therefore the king feared that he would fall into the hands of Gruffudd from the danger he was in, when he came down from the mountain, and having made peace with him he returned.[92]

---

[88] RW (T), II, p. 581; RW, III, p. 54.
[89] *Brut (Pen. 20)*, s.a. 1114.
[90] *Gruffudd ap Cynan*, p. 80.
[91] *ASC* (E), s.a. 1121.
[92] *Gruffudd ap Cynan*, p. 81.

CAMPAIGN STRATEGY AND TACTICS 105

Again the Welsh fighting host harassed its enemy and only the villeins, women and children, together with the booty, 'fled' from the foe. Gruffudd's success in protecting his land and goods is echoed in Meilyr's *Elegy* for Gruffudd (although this could equally apply to the 1114 expedition):

> The king of England came accompanied by hosts,
> Though he came he did not return with cattle:
> We in Eryri were rich,
> He did not break into [any] pasture land that contained herds.
> Gruffudd of renowned might – he was not hidden –
> Defended his men ferociously;
> He fought for his right with a thousand knights;
> His battling was heard as far as beyond Bannawg![93]

Although vivid and descriptive, these sources in praise of Gruffudd cannot be said accurately to reflect the events of 1121. The *Brutiau* indicate that Henry's might was mainly directed against Powys and that Gruffudd's resistance was minimal:

> As soon as summer came and the roads were dry and it was easy to find and to follow paths, the king moved a mighty host against the men of Powys, where Maredudd ap Bleddyn and the sons of Cadwgan ap Bleddyn, Einion and Madog and Morgan, were lords. And when they heard that, they sent messengers to Gruffudd ap Cynan, who held the island of Anglesey, to ask him whether he would unite with them against the king; and they told him that together they could hold the wild parts of their land against the king. But he had made peace with the king, and he informed them that, if they fled near his bounds, he would come against them and despoil them. And when Maredudd and the sons of Cadwgan learned that, they decided in council to keep themselves within their own bounds and to guard and defend them.
>
> And the king approached the bounds of Powys. And Maredudd sent young men to way-lay the king, to a certain counter-slope the way along which he was coming, in order to engage him with bows and arrows and to cause confusion among his host with missiles.[94]

---

[93] Meilyr, p. 184.
[94] *Brut (Pen. 20)*, s.a. 1121.

The king fell into this trap and became embroiled in a hot conflict in which a number of his people were killed and wounded and he was struck by an arrow. After the engagement, the Welsh came to terms and paid a hefty tribute to Henry. The triumphalism evident in the accounts of Gruffudd ap Cynan's actions could indicate that he was granted favourable terms by Henry thanks to his early submission. This left Powys exposed, but the strategy of evasion and ambush followed by its leaders still led to problems for Henry.

The Welsh met Henry II's expeditions with the usual strategy of ambush and evasion. In 1157 Owain Gwynedd tried a radical policy by electing to stand and face Henry's forces; this will be considered below,[95] but it was a unique strategy and after retreating from Coleshill, Owain followed the standard practice of falling back whilst continuing to 'harass the king by day and night'.[96]

When the Welsh sought to hide their chattels from an invading force, it was not only the mountains of mid- and north Wales that proved a suitable refuge. Gerald of Wales described Cantref Mawr as 'a safe refuge for the inhabitants of south Wales, because of its impenetrable forests',[97] and it was here that Gruffudd ap Rhys fled after his defeat at Aberystwyth in 1116, 'for it was a land wild with woods and difficult to approach, and easy for those acquainted with it to encounter their enemies'.[98] In 1158, when the other Welsh leaders had made peace with Henry, Rhys ap Gruffudd alone continued to resist: 'and he moved all Deheubarth and their wives and children and all their animals to the forest land of the Tywi'.[99]

Henry gathered a mighty force in 1165 and many of the significant leaders of native Wales united to oppose him.[100] These armies faced off each other, reluctant to engage in battle:

> And as they were on both sides staying in their tents, without the one daring to attack the other, at last the king of England was enraged; and he

---

[95] See below, pp. 129–30.
[96] *Brut (Pen. 20)*, s.a. 1157.
[97] *Journey*, I, 10, p. 139.
[98] *Brut (Pen. 20)*, s.a. 1116.
[99] Ibid., s.a. 1158.
[100] See above, p. 51.

moved his host into the wood of Dyffryn Ceiriog, and he had that wood cut down, and felled to the ground. And there a few picked Welshmen, in the absence of their leaders, manfully and valorously resisted them. And many of the bravest on either side were slain. And the king and his armies advanced, and he pitched his tents on the Berwyn mountain. And he stayed there a few days. And then there came upon them a mighty tempest of wind and bad weather and rains and lack of food; and then he moved his tents into England.[101]

Henry could not bring the main Welsh force to battle and probably did not wish to risk doing so. To advance in difficult terrain with the enemy in close attendance was dangerous. Henry was a cautious commander and he tried to clear a path through the forests of the Ceiriog valley to minimize the risk of ambush.[102] This signalled the king's intended line of advance, though, and a Welsh detachment made an attack. Such small-scale clashes could prove decisive and Henry's losses made him even more hesitant. It was finally the Welsh weather that forced Henry to turn back as he became bogged down on the high moors separating the Berwyn Mountains from the valley of the upper Dee, but Welsh strategy had robbed his campaign of dynamism and his superiority in numbers and resources could not be brought to bear.

The next major royal efforts in Wales were John's two campaigns of 1211. On the first occasion John moved to Chester: 'And then Llywelyn ap Iorwerth had Perfeddwlad and Anglesey and all their chattels moved to the wilderness of Eryri.'[103] John advanced to Degannwy, but supply problems made him retreat; by stripping the Perfeddwlad (possibly a scorched-earth policy) and using his warriors to harass John's foragers, Llywelyn forced the king to back down. John returned in August with a second force. Perhaps Llywelyn was caught by surprise or had exhausted his resources in the first expedition, but this time John brought enough supplies to cross the Conwy and penetrate into the heart of Snowdon, 'destroying all the

---

[101] *Brut (Pen. 20)*, s.a. 1165. Owain refers to this clash in a letter to Louis VII where he writes that 'more of his (Henry's) men fell than mine'; H. Pryce, 'Owain Gwynedd', p. 7.

[102] He also sought advice from local Welsh allies on his invasion route; F. C. Suppe, 'Roger of Powys, Henry II's Anglo-Welsh middleman, and his lineage', *WHR*, 21 (2002), 1–23.

[103] *Brut (Pen. 20)*, s.a. 1211.

places he came to'.[104] Llywelyn evaded battle but had lost strategic control and could not harass John's army or stop his ravagers; consequently he sent his wife to beg for peace and agree to humiliating terms.[105]

Henry III's expeditions to Wales met the same problems encountered by previous royal armies in the country. In 1228 he and his army camped at Ceri and the Welsh encamped nearby: 'and then by fierce attacks upon their enemies, they [the Welsh] caused great confusion amongst them'.[106] The king tried to clear the woods to flush the Welsh out, but his men suffered from ambushes.[107] Clashes followed a similar pattern in 1231 as the English army sat at Painscastle to guard work on a new castle whilst suffering raids and ambushes from the Welsh.[108]

Henry enjoyed more success after Llywelyn's demise and was helped in his 1241 expedition by unusually dry weather that hastened his advance along the north Wales coast.[109] The Welsh responded in 1244, their revolt following the typical pattern: 'during all this time the Welsh, swarming from their lurking-places, like bees, spread fire and slaughter, and unceasingly ravaged the countries adjoining their own'.[110] The English ability in this small-scale warfare was equally pronounced, as seen in 1245:

> Three hundred Welsh and more were slain at Montgomery by the English under the command of the castellan of the castle of that place, who had cunningly placed an ambuscade in their rear, and then, showing a semblance of alarm, retreated before the Welsh, when the English, who lay concealed, attacked them in the rear, and put them all to the sword.[111]

---

[104] RW (T), II, p. 255; RW, II, p. 58.
[105] J. B. Smith, 'Magna Carta', 344–62.
[106] Brut (Pen. 20), s.a. 1228.
[107] RW, II, pp. 349–50. In one such clash William de Braose (the Younger) was seized and imprisoned by the Welsh whilst he was taking part in a foraging raid.
[108] Ibid., III, pp. 11–12. For royal policy towards Wales in the period, see R. F. Walker, 'Hubert de Burgh and Wales, 1218–32', EHR, 87 (1972), 465–94; also his 'The Anglo-Welsh wars, 1217–67; with special reference to English military developments' (unpublished D.Phil. thesis, Oxford, 1954). The strategy of using royal expeditions to secure the construction of castles in Wales was limited but good for containment, important for future advances and a tribute to the strength of Llywelyn ap Iorwerth.
[109] MP, IV, p. 150.
[110] MP (T), II, p. 27; MP, IV, p. 385.
[111] MP (T), II, p. 45; MP, IV, p. 407.

It is revealing that the English are described as 'cunning' for planning this ambuscade, but that the tone used when dealing with the Welsh is rather different:

> In the same week, Dafydd, wishing to redeem his losses, harassed the English by continued nightly incursions, and vigilantly employed himself in slaughter and rapine. But when the brave English knights on the borders came to oppose them with the borderers subject to them, the Welsh, as was their custom, flew to the crags and inaccessible parts of the mountains, to lie in ambuscade for their passing enemies. From their summits of rocks they hurled stones and weapons, wounding many of the English.[112]

The importance of the motivation of our sources in the formation of our perceptions of warfare can be seen in the works of Matthew Paris. From the late 1240s, Paris's work becomes critical of Henry III's Poitevin friends and advisers, whom many believed to be running the country and taking advantage of royal favour to the detriment of native Englishmen. Paris described events in 1254:

> Some Welsh soldiers in the king's army in Gascony, according to their custom, made a foray on the lands of the king's enemies, and gave themselves up to pillage, for which they were made prisoners by the king's brothers, and by the bishop of Hereford, and were punished more severely than they deserved, for they that time did little or no harm.[113]

The Welsh are defended because they were punished by the Poitevins in the army when, it is claimed, this was not within their jurisdiction. Elsewhere, Paris denounced the Welsh for following this sort of tactic, but, given a different perception, their actions were supported and understood.

In the Welsh revolt of 1256–7 against Edward, Paris describes them ravaging enemy lands before retreating to the wild places: '[the Welsh] vented their fury incessantly and actively employed themselves in pillage, slaughter, and incendiarism.'[114] Paris is still hostile to Edward, and his tone when dealing with Welsh conduct is noticeably favourable:

[112] MP (T), II, p. 46; MP, IV, pp. 407–8.
[113] MP (T), III, p. 77; MP, V, p. 442.
[114] MP (T), III, p. 233; MP, V, p. 633.

> They were roving about at will, seizing the castles of the frontier nobles, and even those of the English with impunity, putting the garrisons to death, and spreading fire, slaughter, and incendiarism in all directions. The Welsh, thereon, learning that the king intended to take the field against them with his army, prudently sent away their wives, children and flocks into the interior of the country, about Snowdon and other mountainous places inaccessible to the English, ploughed up their fields, destroyed their mills in the road which the English would take, carried away all kinds of provisions, broke down the bridges, and rendered the fords impassable by digging holes, in order that, if the enemy attempted to cross, they might be drowned.[115]

Welsh tactics are acknowledged as 'prudent'. It is the English who are criticized for adopting a scorched-earth policy in the harvest season:

> The king, accompanied by a large army, approached Chester, and to prevent the Welsh from finding food thereabouts, his followers laid waste the rich and abundant crops of corn and other produce of the earth, to the injury of themselves as well as others.[116]

When the forces of the Marcher lords planned a surprise attack on the Welsh it was denounced as 'cowardly' and 'treacherous' and the eventual Welsh victory is explained in moral terms.[117] This section of Matthew Paris's work provides a rare example of a source written from 'mainstream' Europe that is in sympathy with the people on the 'fringe' of its culture.

Paris's continuation in the *Westminster Chronicle* loses this sympathetic view of Welsh tactics. In the years 1262–3 it describes raiding and ravaging in Wales and says that the Marcher forces were frequently able to trap and kill hundreds of the Welsh.[118] On one occasion, though, 300 infantry fighting for the Marcher lords were killed, 'treacherously slain by that people'. The *Brutiau* are more impartial, describing both sides ravaging, raiding, searching for booty and laying ambushes:

---

[115] MP (T), III, p. 238; MP, V, p. 639.
[116] MP (T), III, p. 245; MP, V, pp. 647–8.
[117] MP (T), III, p. 304; MP, V, pp. 717–8.
[118] *FH*, II, pp. 476–7.

CAMPAIGN STRATEGY AND TACTICS

> A little before Easter, John Lestrange the Younger, he being constable and bailiff over Baldwin's Castle, gathered a mighty host. And he came by night through Ceri upwards to Cydewain. And after he had gathered vast spoil he returned downwards along the way from Cydewain. And when the Welsh heard that they gathered in pursuit of them and slew 200 of the English, some in the field, others in the barn of Aber-miwl. And a little after that, John Lestrange had that barn burnt because of that slaughter. And a little after that, the Welsh were slain near the valley of the Clun. At that time Edward was moving in the March, and burning townships in Gwynedd.[119]

Edward's campaigns against Llywelyn ap Gruffudd are well known and will not be repeated, but it is important to stress that his success was brought about largely by ravaging the country to bring it to its knees whilst avoiding Welsh ambushes: 'Edward's Welsh wars, like most contemporary campaigns, were wars of manoeuvre and attrition in which the aim was not to bring the enemy to battle but to despoil his lands, terrorize his tenantry and methodically reduce his castles.'[120] Furthermore:

> The second war (1282–3), like the first (1276–7), had been won not by brilliant feats of generalship or decisive battles but by the efficient garnering and intelligent deployment of resources. Welsh resistance was ground down by the patient amassing of men and material: in one sense, Welsh independence did not as much perish in a clash of arms as suffocate in a welter of parchment.[121]

Battle

In addressing the rarity of pitched battles in Anglo-Norman warfare, Bradbury concluded that a battle was a departure from the standard military principles of ravaging, ambush and evasion.[122] Leaders fought battles when both were equally confident of victory, or alternatively when one side was supremely confident, saw a strong advantage in fighting and was able to draw his enemy into the field. Vegetius wrote that:

---

[119] *Brut (Pen. 20)*, 1263.
[120] I. Rowlands, 'The Edwardian conquest and its military consolidation', in T. Herbert and G. E. Jones (eds), *Edward I and Wales* (Cardiff, 1988), pp. 40–72, 41.
[121] Ibid., p. 48.
[122] Bradbury, 'Battles', pp. 182–93. His analysis is supported by the work of Strickland, France, Gillingham and others.

It is much better to overcome the enemy by famine, surprise or terror than by general action, for in the latter instance fortune has often a greater share than valour . . . Good officers never engage in general actions unless induced by opportunity or obliged by necessity.[123]

Bradbury claims that younger commanders often sought battle, whilst older, experienced campaigners would shy away. Battles were simply too dangerous: to the forces assembled, to the overall political position and to the life of the commander himself who was a major target in any engagement. Despite the danger, battles were not always decisive and better results could often be achieved by ravaging, diplomacy, or other forms of political pressure.

The perception that inferior Welsh strategy, tactics and technology left them incapable of facing their Anglo-Saxon and Anglo-Norman enemies in battle has been noted. This view was expressed by Bartlett and, despite revision of his work from Suppe and others, the thesis on battles remains largely unchallenged. The major influence on Bartlett's work seems to have been Gerald of Wales. Gerald's writings on Ireland stress that the Irish were unable to challenge their enemies in battle and the *Descriptio Cambriae* reaches the same conclusions about the Welsh.[124] In considering this view, we must take account of the motivations Gerald brought to his writing. The chapter is entitled 'Their Weakness in Battle: How Shamefully and Ignobly they Run away', and follows a discussion on Maximus leading a British army to the continent in the fourth century and Gildas's denunciation of the British leaders of his day; Gerald relates these ancient events to his argument for Welsh weakness in the twelfth century! Gerald was anxious to be perceived as a religious reformer. Gildas's tirade against the morals of British leaders was also primarily a religious work and Gerald seized its arguments to relate Welsh problems to failings of morality and character.[125]

---

[123] Vegetius, pp. 92–3.
[124] *Description*, II, 3, pp. 259–60. The passage is quoted above, pp. 4–5. Support for Gerald's description of the terrifying charge of Welsh troops can be found in the Margam chronicle's account of Richard Siward's raid on Devizes in 1233; see D. Crouch, 'The last adventure of Richard Siward', *Morgannwg*, 35 (1991), 7–30 (14).
[125] See above, pp. 8–9.

British/Welsh battles, c.450–1063

We should not place too much emphasis on Gildas's moral assessments of the military situation of his day, but it should be noted that he stated that the British were able to defeat their enemies in battle from the time of Ambrosius to the battle of Badon. Evidence from the *Anglo-Saxon Chronicle* suggests relatively high instances of battles in the fifth and sixth centuries. This can be explained by the fact that a war of conquest was being conducted. For the protagonists it was often a case of fight or die and there could be circumstances when both sides saw the advantage of forcing an engagement. Many of these battles would have been small-scale skirmishes or raids; in most cases we do not have the evidence to differentiate. With regard to British ability in battle, the *Anglo-Saxon Chronicle* gives few clues; it mostly records Anglo-Saxon victories, but several are listed without result and some British successes are noted.

It is possible to say a little more about certain battles. In the *Anglo-Saxon Chronicle*, s.a. 577, 'In this year Cuthwine and Ceawlin fought against the Britons and killed three kings, Conmail, Condidan and Farinmail, at the place which is called Dyrham; and they captured three of their cities, Gloucester, Cirencester, and Bath.'[126] This shows the decisive nature of battles that made them so dangerous; the leaders were killed and with their field force destroyed the Britons could not defend their cities, which fell to the Anglo-Saxons. The battle has been regarded as a significant turning-point in British history which allowed the Anglo-Saxons to cut off the Britons of Dumnonia from those of Wales and the Old North, but this point should not be exaggerated. Contacts between the Britons continued and our lack of sources simplifies the picture of complex political events.

The battle of Chester (*c.*616) has, like Dyrham, been considered a decisive engagement, one which split the Britons of Wales from those in the Old North and established a tradition of English overlordship in Wales. Æthelfrith of Bernicia was an ambitious king who had taken over Deira in 604 to create the kingdom of Northumbria. He fought against the Picts and in turning against Wales seemed to be seeking a position of overall

[126] *ASC*, 577.

dominance within Britain. The British decision to face Æthelfrith in battle reflects their rejection of his ambition. Chester was a devastating defeat for the Welsh; many were slaughtered, including one of their leaders, Selyf of Powys. Long-term repercussions were limited, however. The land link between Wales and the north was difficult and dangerous, and the sea routes, which remained open, were always more important. Moreover, in 617 Æthelfrith was killed by Edwin whom he had ousted from Deira, Edwin imposing himself as the new king of Northumbria; this scarcely gave Æthelfrith the chance to consolidate his victory over the Welsh. Perhaps the greatest long-term effect of Chester was to weaken Powys, allow Gwynedd a more powerful position within Wales and possibly to throw Mercia and the Welsh rulers into alliance.

The battle of Hatfield Chase in 633 was the culmination of a struggle for supremacy within Britain between two protagonists, Edwin of Northumbria and Cadwallon of Gwynedd. The desperate nature of the clash was shown as Cadwallon was driven to exile in Ireland, before fighting his way back at the head of an alliance including Penda of Mercia and Britons drawn from throughout Wales. The struggle involved much ravaging and numerous small skirmishes; these are hinted at in early Welsh poetry, but other sources only refer to the battle at Hatfield Chase.

Edwin was slain in the battle, allowing Cadwallon to occupy and ravage Northumbria, but the engagement cannot be called decisive. Cadwallon faced more fighting in Northumbria and at one point he was besieged within a city (probably York) by Osric of Northumbria.[127] Soon after, Oswald, Æthelfrith's son, fought Cadwallon at Heavenfield near Hexham, where the British leader was killed and his army scattered. Bede says that Cadwallon's army was immense and Oswald's tiny; this could be designed to glorify Oswald's victory, but if correct it emphasizes the danger and unpredictability of battle. It would suggest that Oswald chose to fight out of desperation, Cadwallon from overconfidence.[128]

---

[127] Bede, III, 1, p. 213.
[128] This view is supported by the possibility that Oswald chose to launch a night attack to surprise his foe. See Adomnán of Iona, *Life of St Columba*, ed. and trans. R. Sharpe (London, 1995), I, 1, p. 111; discussed below, pp. 140–2.

Heavenfield was not decisive and did not end the struggle. Penda now led the resistance to Northumbria, which included the kings of Wales, and in 643 he defeated and killed Oswald at Maserfelth (probably Oswestry). Further ravaging and skirmishing followed before Oswiu of Northumbria defeated and killed Penda at the battle of Winwaed (654). Oswiu was reluctant to engage in this battle; beforehand he tried to buy Penda off from further ravaging. The Mercian king was overconfident and anxious to score a decisive blow in the struggle and consequently chose to fight. Cadafael ap Cynfedw of Gwynedd was part of Penda's alliance, but was unwilling to follow such a dangerous strategy; he withdrew with his forces on the eve of the battle, immortalizing his name in literature as 'Cadafael Battle Dodger'. Given the numbers of kings killed in this series of seventh-century battles, his actions could be considered prudent. They could also be considered orthodox; in the struggle for supremacy in Britain in the period 616–54 we can identify five major battles, an average of one every eight years.[129] This is a high instance, reflecting the significance of the issues at stake. But the emphasis of our sources on battles should not hide the importance of the almost continuous ravaging and skirmishing; battles merely marked the ebb and flow of the conflict.

In the eighth and ninth centuries, evidence of battles involving Welsh forces is scarce. This reflects our lack of sources, but also the fact that campaigns had reverted to the regular pattern of raid and ravaging. *Annales Cambriae* (A), s.a. 722, record that the Britons fought and won three battles against the Anglo-Saxons, one in Cornwall, the others in Wales. Another clash is recorded in *Annales Cambriae* (A), s.a. 760. Immediately after the death of Offa of Mercia in 796, the Welsh fought a battle against the Mercians at Rhuddlan. There had been unrest on the border in Offa's later years and it seems that the Welsh seized the chance to try to break Mercian influence after the king's death. The early ninth century saw a series of internal battles in Gwynedd; it was a time of political unrest with competing nobles striving for power.[130] This succession of battles ended with the accession of a

---

[129] This figure hides the many minor clashes that occurred. One encounter at Lichfield, for example, was hailed as a great victory for Cynddylan (though whether against the Northumbrians or Mercians is debatable); see *Saga*, pp. 132–5.

[130] The Welsh annals record dynastic battles in 813, 814 and 817.

new dynasty. Merfyn Frych ap Gwriad reigned from 825 to 844 and in this period no further battles are recorded. In the year of his death, however, *Annales Cambriae* (A) refer to the battle of Cedyll. In the latter half of the ninth century, *Annales Cambriae* (A) record a battle between the men of Gwent and Brecon (s.a. 848), the battle of Bryn Onnen (s.a. 870) and the battles of Banolau and Ynegydd in Anglesey (s.a. 873); no further details are available.

Battles against peoples from outside Wales were rare in this period, but the Welsh had not become too insular militarily. In the late ninth century, the states of western Europe were troubled by Viking raiders and received humiliating defeats at their hands. In 855 Rhodri Mawr met a Danish fleet in Anglesey led by Gormr, a warrior who had worried Charles the Bald's kingdom. Rhodri defeated and killed Gormr; the news was greeted with relief when it became known in Charles's court in Liège.[131] The threat posed by the Vikings, who could quickly escape on their ships, was difficult to counter and it was necessary to adopt an unusual, battle-seeking strategy to hurt the raiders when the chance was presented. Rhodri was successful in 855, and in 893 the *Anglo-Saxon Chronicle* records that Welsh forces joined with the Anglo-Saxons to defeat a Viking force encamped near the Severn. In 906 a Welsh force engaged the Norse at the battle of Dinmeir, but on this occasion the natives were defeated and 'Mynyw [St Davids] was broken'.[132]

In 877 Rhodri Mawr was forced to flee to Ireland by an alliance of the Vikings and the men of Ceolwulf of Mercia. He returned the following year and defeated the Vikings in battle on Anglesey. Later in 878, Rhodri and his son Gwriad were slain by the Mercians, who were seeking to extend their influence in Gwynedd. Their ambitions would meet strong resistance; *Annales Cambriae* (A) s.a. 880 record: 'The battle of Conwy. Vengeance for Rhodri at God's hands.' Anglo-Saxon advances into north Wales continued and in 921 Edward built a fortified burh at Rhuddlan (Cledemutha). Around this time, *Annales Cambriae* (A) record the battle of Dinas Newydd ('new fortress'); this might suggest that the Welsh were drawn into another battle by

---

[131] The victory was also celebrated in Irish annals and poetry; see Ó'Cróinín, *Early Medieval*, p. 248.
[132] *AC* (A), s.a. 906.

Anglo-Saxon advances. The power of the Anglo-Saxon state at this time is suggested by Athelstan's victories in battle over two Welsh kings in 926.[133]

The latter half of the tenth century after the death of Hywel Dda (950) saw more dynastic strife in Wales. In such circumstances we may not expect to find Welsh kings leading armies to battle against either the Anglo-Saxons or the Vikings.[134] However, the power of rulers like Hywel ab Ieuaf and Maredudd ab Owain has probably been underestimated and Anglo-Saxon and Hiberno-Scandinavian forces were significant elements in the civil disputes. In periods of comparative political chaos throughout medieval Europe, we see increases in the numbers of battles; civil warfare meant that rivals for a patrimony sought to wipe out their foes. In Wales, the numbers of political murders are high and numerous battles between native rivals are recorded after the removal of Hywel's stabilizing influence.[135]

From the eleventh century our sources are richer in number and detail. There is still no suggestion that the Welsh were incapable of meeting their Anglo-Saxon and Viking enemies in battle, and in 1016 Welsh troops fought alongside Edmund Ironside in the campaigns against Cnut.[136] B. G. Charles contended that the Welsh alone could not face the Anglo-Saxons or the Anglo-Normans in the field, but could do so with the help of the Vikings who were better armed and familiar with battle.[137] However, in 1022 Llywelyn ap Seisyll defeated Rhain (possibly an Irishman) in battle and in 1044 Hywel ab Edwin was defeated and killed at the mouth of the Tywi by Gruffudd ap Llywelyn, despite the presence in Hywel's ranks of forces from Ireland.[138] It is possible that Hywel only needed to hire these outsiders because Gruffudd had defeated him in battle in 1041, presumably weakening Hywel's military potential. At the battle of Pwlldyfach in 1042, Hywel had himself defeated a Viking force ravaging

[133] JW, II, 926.
[134] AC (B) and (C), s.a. 982, do record that the Anglo-Saxons ravaging St Davids were 'brought to battle' by the Welsh.
[135] For considerations of this period, see Maund, 'Dynastic', 155–67; D. E. Thornton, 'Maredudd ab Owain (d. 999): the most famous king of the Welsh', WHR, 18 (1997), 567–91.
[136] Stafford, Unification, p. 120; M. K. Lawson, Cnut (London, 1993), pp. 77–9.
[137] B. G. Charles, Old Norse Relations with Wales (Cardiff, 1934), pp. 49–50.
[138] Brut (Pen. 20), s.a. 1022, 1044. In 1144, Owain Gwynedd defeated an Irish force brought to Wales by his brother Cadwaladr; ibid., s.a. 1144.

Dyfed.[139] At the battle of Bron-yr-erw in 1075, there were Irish in Gruffudd ap Cynan's army when he was defeated by Trahaearn.[140] However, they showed their value on his side at Mynydd Carn in 1081 when Gruffudd was victorious,[141] and in 1088 Rhys ap Tewdwr employed an Irish force for a battle that helped return him to power in Deheubarth.[142]

Any notion that Welsh forces were incapable of meeting the late Anglo-Saxon army in battle should be dispelled by the evidence of the career of Gruffudd ap Llywelyn.[143] At times, Gruffudd did call on Viking and Mercian aid, but he was always the leader and his Welsh followers were the dominant force. Gruffudd came to prominence in 1039 following his victory at Rhyd-y-groes over an Anglo-Saxon army led by Ealdorman Edwin, the brother of Earl Leofric, a success significant enough for its exact date to be remembered in England thirteen years later.[144] It has been suggested that this victory may be attributed to surprise and astute leadership.[145] It raised Gruffudd's profile in Wales and beyond, and he may have chosen to face the dangers of battle for the military prestige he would gain, thereby promoting himself above the nobles competing for power within Wales. The victory consolidated Gruffudd's position in Powys and secured his flank, allowing him to descend on Deheubarth and pursue his ambitions in the south.[146]

To establish his position, Gruffudd still needed to fight a number of battles against Welsh rivals. As has been seen, Hywel ab Edwin was defeated in battle in 1041 and in 1044. In 1052, Gruffudd's ravaging around Leominster provoked Earl Ralf and his French knights to lead the shire levy against the Welsh king and challenge him in battle; they were badly routed.[147] In 1056

---

[139] Ibid., s.a. 1042. The battle site is five miles north-west of Carmarthen; *HW*, II, p. 360.
[140] *Gruffudd ap Cynan*, p. 63.
[141] Ibid., pp. 67–9.
[142] *Brut (Pen. 20)*, s.a. 1088.
[143] *Liber Landavensis* boasts that English, Irish, Danes and the inhabitants of the Orkneys all fled before Gruffudd's face in battle: 'unconquered Gruffudd, the powerful monarch of the Britons'; *LL*, p. 269.
[144] Lloyd says that the battle was fought at an unknown ford on the Severn near Welshpool; *HW*, II, p. 359. Buttington used to be regarded as the most likely location, but the battle site has been more positively identified, lying three miles east of Forden, close to the spot where the name Rhyd-y-groes was preserved in the name of a farm; T. M. Davies and S. Davies, *The Last King of Wales: Gruffudd ap Llywelyn, c.1013–1063* (Stroud, 2012), pp. 32–3.
[145] See above, p. 55.
[146] T. M. Davies, 'Gruffudd ap Llywelyn', 212–13.
[147] Anglo-Saxon sources blame the defeat on Ralf's incompetence; this may be true, but their biases must be considered.

Gruffudd again defeated the shire levy of Hereford in a battle near Glasbury. The events of 1055 and 1058 have been discussed, but the scale of Gruffudd's victory in 1055 is worth emphasizing. Although there were forces from Ireland and Mercia in Gruffudd's army, he was the leader and it is likely that the majority of the army was Welsh. There was a need to force battle to reinstate Ælfgar in England, a position that was crucial to Gruffudd's strategic position. The victory made clear that the border could not be secured without Ælfgar's restoration; even when Harold Godwinesson brought the national levy to Herefordshire, there was reluctance to engage Gruffudd's army.[148]

Gruffudd ap Llywelyn was not the only Welsh leader capable of defeating Anglo-Saxon forces in battle. In 1049 Gruffudd ap Rhydderch overcame an army gathered from Gloucestershire and Herefordshire in the Forest of Dean, although in this case a key role was played by those men from the thirty-six ships from Ireland with whom Gruffudd allied. It should also be noted that many of the regular Anglo-Saxon troops from the area are likely to have been with the king's fleet at Sandwich. Gruffudd may have enjoyed the advantages of a surprise attack; John of Worcester says that the Welsh in the Anglo-Saxon force sent secretly to Gruffudd in the night, prompting him to 'rush up' at dawn and secure an easy victory.[149]

Inter-Welsh battles, 1063–1277

The latter half of the eleventh century saw numerous battles between competing lords. In 1069:

> The battle of Mechain took place between Bleddyn and Rhiwallon, sons of Cynfyn, and Maredudd and Ithel [sic], sons of Gruffudd. And there the sons of Gruffudd fell, Ithel [sic] in the battle and Maredudd of cold in flight. And there Rhiwallon ap Cynfyn was slain. And Bleddyn ap Cynfyn ruled after his victory. And Maredudd ab Owain ab Edwin held the kingdom of the south.[150]

---

[148] The events of 1058 are barely mentioned in the *Anglo-Saxon Chronicle*, suggesting shame at the buying off of the enemy without any attempt at armed resistance; F. Barlow, *Edward the Confessor* (London, 1989), p. 209. Again a reluctance to engage the strength of Gruffudd and his allies may be inferred.
[149] *ASC* (D), s.a. 1049; JW, II, 1049.
[150] *Brut (Pen. 20)*, s.a. 1069 'Ithel' should read Idwal, as in *Annales Cambriae*.

Caradog ap Gruffudd used Norman help (although it was not necessarily the decisive factor) to kill Maredudd ab Owain in battle on the banks of the Rhymney in 1072, removing his chief rival for power in the south. In 1075 the *Brutiau* record a series of political killings throughout Wales followed by two battles, one in the south and the other in the north.[151] At the battle of Camddwr in the south, Goronwy and Llywelyn – the sons of Cadwgan – and Caradog ap Gruffudd united to face Rhys ab Owain and Rhydderch ap Caradog;[152] Rhys and Rhydderch won the battle but failed to kill their rivals. In the north, the battle of Bron-yr-erw took place between Gruffudd ap Cynan and Trahaearn.[153] Gruffudd had returned to Gwynedd from exile in Ireland and was desperate to establish his position. This meant facing his rivals with a policy of extermination. Before Bron-yr-erw, Gruffudd's men had killed Cynwrig ap Rhiwallon of Powys in an ambush, and whilst the tide was flowing his way he decided to risk all in battle against Trahaearn at Gwaed Erw in Glyn Cyfing.[154] Gruffudd won the day, but his strategy did not pay off as he failed to kill his rival or destroy his fighting power; Trahaearn rallied support and defeated Gruffudd at Bron-yr-erw.

The desperate nature of these struggles is clear, but none of the battles was truly decisive. In 1076 Rhydderch ap Caradog was slain 'through treachery', but his enemies in 1075, Goronwy and Llywelyn, were defeated at the battle of Gweunytwl in 1077 by Rhys ab Owain.[155] In 1078 there was another battle at Pwllgwdig near Fishguard and, for a short time, this looked to be the decisive event to settle Welsh politics.[156] In the clash, Trahaearn defeated Rhys ab Owain and slaughtered his *teulu*, leaving Rhys to flee for his life. Later in the year Trahaearn's ally, Caradog ap Gruffudd, cornered Rhys and his brother Hywel and killed them both. It seemed that order had come to

---

[151] Ibid., s.a. 1075; *Brut (RBH)*, s.a. 1075.
[152] Lloyd located this battle between Buellt and Ceredigion, but Remfry argues for the Camddwr in eastern Maelienydd which flows into the Eithon below Llanbister; P. M. Remfry, 'The native Welsh dynasties of Rhwng Gwy a Hafren, 1066–1282' (unpublished M.Phil. thesis, University of Wales, Aberystwyth, 1989), 28–9.
[153] *Gruffudd ap Cynan*, pp. 60–3.
[154] See *HW*, II, p. 381.
[155] The site is unidentified, though the 'bloody field' beneath Crug y Buddais north of Felindre has been suggested; see Remfry, 'Native,' 29.
[156] *Brut (Pen. 20)*, s.a. 1078.

Wales, with Trahaearn ruling in the north, Caradog in the south and Meilyr ap Rhiwallon in Powys; the three were prepared to co-operate and support each other within the country.[157]

This comparatively settled situation lasted until 1081; there were still Welsh nobles with pretensions to kingship. In 1081 two claimants, Rhys ap Tewdwr from the south and Gruffudd ap Cynan from the north, united to challenge the established order. It has been suggested that the two were in a desperate situation, with Rhys under pressure in the south-west and Gruffudd venturing to Wales on another hopeful jaunt from Ireland.[158] It is likely that they were outnumbered and there was hesitancy about engaging the enemy, but the unpredictability of battle was their only hope; at Mynydd Carn, Gruffudd and Rhys defied the odds, defeated their enemies and killed Trahaearn, Caradog and Meilyr. Given the advantages enjoyed by the latter three, they made a mistake in accepting the dangers of battle; *Gruffudd ap Cynan* says that Gruffudd and Rhys made a surprise attack at night.[159]

Mynydd Carn was decisive in all the wrong ways for Trahaearn, Caradog and Meilyr. Despite his victory, Gruffudd gained little from the battle; he enjoyed a brief rampage through Wales before being betrayed by the men of Gwynedd and thrown into jail in Chester. Rhys was the great winner as he went on to enjoy a twelve-year reign in the south, but all his success should not be attributed to the battle. The engagement removed Rhys's main rival Caradog, but possibly the greatest factor in stabilizing his control in the south was the alliance he made with William the Conqueror later in 1081. This helped to ensure that Rhys was granted the respect of the surviving nobles in the south and protected him from Anglo-Norman incursions. Only after the Conqueror's death in 1087 was Rhys again forced to face the dangers of battle. In 1088 he was driven into exile by the sons of Bleddyn from Powys, but returned with an Irish fleet to give battle at Llech-y-crau; Rhys was victorious and two of his rivals, Madog and Rhiddid, were slain.[160] Problems with the *uchelwyr* of

---

[157] K. L. Maund, 'Trahaearn ap Caradog: legitimate usurper?', *WHR*, 13 (1986–7), 468–76.
[158] See above, pp. 58–9.
[159] *Gruffudd ap Cynan*, pp. 66–7.
[160] *Brut (Pen. 20)*, s.a. 1088.

Dyfed forced Rhys to a battle at Llandudoch (St Dogmaels) in 1091; again Rhys was victorious and was able to kill Gruffudd ap Maredudd, a pretender drawn from his manors in Herefordshire.[161] Rhys was still not secure, despite these victories; William Rufus allowed the Normans free rein against him and it has been suggested that they played a part in the 1091 rising.[162] Their pressure increased and, in trying to defend his kingdom against them, Rhys was defeated and killed near Brecon in 1093.[163]

The political situation in Gwynedd after the death of Owain Gwynedd in 1170 did not settle until the 1190s; Dafydd was the best-positioned heir, but was unable to exert uncontested power over the other nobles of Gwynedd. In 1194, Llywelyn ap Iorwerth allied with Rhodri ab Owain and the two sons of Cynan ab Owain and, after beating Dafydd in battle at the mouth of the Conwy, they drove him from his land.[164] This battle was the start of Llywelyn's rise to dominance in Gwynedd, but his position was sealed by political machinations and his alliance with John.

The turmoil in Gwynedd returned after the death of Llywelyn's son Dafydd in 1246. The main contenders for power were three sons of Gruffudd ap Llywelyn – Owain, Llywelyn and Dafydd. At first Llywelyn and Owain worked together, but in 1255 the tensions in the arrangement boiled over as Dafydd sought to win a position for himself. Owain was supported by Dafydd and the two instigated the conflict, but Llywelyn was victorious in battle at Bryn Derwin and imprisoned his two brothers.[165] Llywelyn had emerged as the most able, popular and dominant ruler in Gwynedd before Bryn Derwin and it may be speculated that his brothers sought battle as a desperate attempt to break his control.[166]

If there was less at stake than a kingdom, there was more reluctance to engage in battle. In 1110, Owain ap Cadwgan and Madog ap Rhiddid entered Meirionnydd on a ravaging raid and

---

[161] Ibid., s.a. 1091.
[162] Maund, *Ireland*, p. 90.
[163] *Brut (Pen. 20)*, s.a. 1093; JW, III, 1093.
[164] *Brut (Pen. 20)*, s.a. 1194.
[165] Ibid., s.a. 1255. The site is Bwlch dau fynydd, a mountain pass from Arfon to Eifionydd, near the site of Bron-yr-erw, and the clash probably occurred in mid-June; *LG*, p. 73.
[166] For the political background, see *LG*, pp. 69–74.

were ambushed by the men of the land who put the front ranks of the invading force to flight. Owain and Madog were on the run from Henry and to flee and lose the confidence of their troops would have meant the end for them. They were not likely to give up easily, 'and when the men of Meirionnydd saw Owain ready to fight and coming on bravely, they took to flight'.[167] The men of the land had surprised the invaders, but they were prepared to allow their land to be ravaged rather than face the hazards of battle. The wills of the opposing sides were not equally matched, so battle was avoided.

In 1156 Owain Gwynedd led a *llu* to Ceredigion against Rhys ap Gruffudd, but Rhys gained knowledge of his plans: 'he [Rhys] vigorously gathered a host. And he came as far as Aberdyfi, and there he raised a ditch [W. *ffos*] to give battle. And soon after that he had a castle built there.'[168] We hear no more of Owain's expedition; presumably Rhys's resolve to fight was enough to deter him. This ended Owain's ambitions in Ceredigion, which he had been pursuing since the 1130s.

In 1162 Owain led a ravaging raid through Arwystli. On his return he was harassed by Hywel ab Ieuaf, but at Llanidloes Owain turned and 'urged his men to fight manfully'; his enemies took to flight.[169] Owain was too powerful for Hywel to face in battle and the event had a considerable effect. Earlier in the year Hywel had destroyed Owain's castle of Tafolwern in an attempt to keep him away from Arwystli. Tafolwern was near the border in Cyfeiliog, but soon after Hywel's flight at Llanidloes Owain was able to rebuild the castle; Hywel could not counter the political ambitions of Gwynedd.

A dispute arose in 1221 between Llywelyn ap Iorwerth and his son Gruffudd. Tensions were strained between the two, presumably because Llywelyn favoured Dafydd as his sole heir. The disagreement led Llywelyn to assemble a host to march against his son:

> And Gruffudd, having arrayed his troops ready to fight, boldly awaited the coming of his father. And when wise men on either side saw that there was excessive danger on either side, they urged Gruffudd to surrender himself

---

[167] *Brut (Pen. 20)*, s.a. 1110.
[168] Ibid., s.a. 1156.
[169] Ibid., s.a. 1162.

and all his possessions to his father's will. And also they urged Llywelyn to receive him peacefully and mercifully.[170]

Battle was avoided thanks to the advice of 'wise men'; this may be intended to contrast with the young, headstrong men likely to have been amongst Gruffudd's advisers. It is notable that the chronicler refers to the danger 'on either side'; Llywelyn's forces were considerably stronger, but the uncertainties of battle meant that he needed to be wary.

If the usual strategy was to avoid battle, the intrusive influence of the Anglo-Normans affected this pattern and increased the incidence rate of native engagements. When they offered their support to a Welsh leader he would use the temporary increase in his military strength to its best advantage by forcing an engagement. Tension between rival Welsh lords in Powys was high in Henry I's reign, and this was exacerbated by Anglo-Norman interference that gave ambitious minor lords the backing they needed to try their luck. In 1118 the sons of Owain ab Edwin, lords of Dyffryn Clwyd, and their uncle Uchdryd gained the support of the Anglo-Normans of Chester and sought to exert pressure on Hywel ab Ithel in Rhos and Rhufoniog. Hywel beseeched the aid of Maredudd ap Bleddyn and his nephews, Madog and Einion, 'for it was through their support and help that he held and maintained himself what land had fallen to his lot'.[171] Both sides drew up their forces and fought a 'bitter battle' at Maes Maen Cymro.[172] Maredudd and his allies won, but the victory was pyrrhic as Hywel died from his battle wounds and they did not dare to take possession of the lands belonging to Owain's sons 'because of the French' (although on this occasion it was Gwynedd rather than the Anglo-Normans that profited most). Similar Anglo-Norman interference is apparent in 1150, although the *Brutiau* give fewer details.[173] Madog ap Maredudd of Powys sought the help of Ranulf of Chester to counter the power of Owain Gwynedd. The help which Ranulf could offer must have been limited by his distraction with events in England,

[170] Ibid., s.a. 1221.
[171] Ibid., s.a. 1118.
[172] The location is a mile north-west of Ruthin on the border between Dyffryn Clwyd and Cinmeirch, a commote within the *cantref* of Rhufoniog; *HW*, II, p. 465.
[173] *Brut (Pen. 20)*, s.a. 1150.

but some troops were sent. In this instance Ranulf did not simply play the role of a meddler in Welsh affairs; Owain's conquests had taken him to the borders of the earl's land and Ranulf was concerned about the intentions of such a powerful enemy. Owain encountered his foes at Coleshill and put them to flight; the scale of the fighting is unclear, but it secured for Gwynedd the conquest of Iâl, Ystradalwn and Tegeingl.

In 1210 Gwenwynwyn was granted the return of his land by John. His restoration delighted Maelgwn ap Rhys, Gwenwynwyn's ally in Deheubarth, who was emboldened to turn against his nephews Rhys and Owain, the sons of Gruffudd. Rhys and Owain responded by making a night attack on Maelgwn and his army; the risky tactic paid a temporary dividend as their hand-picked force destroyed the enemy, but the following year they were defeated by the king's forces.[174]

In 1213 Rhys Ieuanc tried to claim a share of the land held by Rhys Fychan, but was refused. Again it was Anglo-Norman interference that allowed Ieuanc to pursue his claims and force his rival to battle. Ieuanc allied with John and gathered a force which he led from Brecon to Ystrad Tywi. There he was joined by a troop led by Falkes de Breauté, sheriff of Cardiff, and Rhys's brother Owain. Rhys Fychan tried to intercept this army but was driven to flight.[175]

Battles against the Anglo-Normans, 1063–1277

An examination of Welsh conflict with the Anglo-Normans indicates that battles were the exception, not the rule. Supposed Anglo-Norman superiority in the field does not account for their conquest of the country and, moreover, their superiority has been exaggerated. The Welsh almost invariably declined to face royal expeditions in battle, but this was common sense. As has been demonstrated, it was standard strategic procedure to avoid battle with the enemy. When faced with a royal expedition the Welsh could not hope to match overwhelming Anglo-Norman resources. To see their strategy in context, in the period 1215–17

---

[174] Ibid., s.a. 1210, 1211. For a discussion of night attacks, see below, pp. 140–2.
[175] *Brut (Pen. 20)*, s.a. 1213.

no Marcher army dared to face Llywelyn ap Iorwerth in the field; as the most powerful leader in Wales he could muster the greatest force and it was sensible for the Marcher leaders to evade battle. It was clear to the Welsh that a king of England would have many calls on his attention and that he was likely to have been engaging in an unusual, battle-seeking strategy in order to damage the enemy when he had his resources mobilized.[176]

The early Anglo-Norman conquests in Wales were not characterized by successful battles against the native leaders. Their advances were thanks to their skill at exploiting divisions within Wales's native polity, their ability at ravaging and skirmishing, and their effective use of fortifications. The first battle in Wales for which we have evidence of Anglo-Norman participation came in 1072; although they fought on the winning side in this encounter, the clash can be considered as a native Welsh affair and the 'French' in Caradog ap Gruffudd's army were not the dominant element.[177] Similarly, at Mynydd Carn in 1081 Caradog's Anglo-Normans were only a minor element in this essentially Welsh battle, and in any case they fought on the losing side. In 1118 at Maes Maen Cymro, the Anglo-Normans were in the minority and their side was defeated.

The first recorded battle between Anglo-Norman and Welsh forces was in 1093 when Rhys ap Tewdwr was defeated and killed near Brecon by Bernard de Neufmarché.[178] This clash had far-reaching consequences as it destroyed the hegemony which Rhys had defended in south-west Wales.[179] Soon after, Dyfed

[176] Such a strategy was a way to control the border and contain the Welsh. The increased incidence of battles in these circumstances can be seen in Edward the Confessor's reign. Only three military events under Edward's rule could be considered battles and two of these were against the Welsh (Hereford in 1055 and Glasbury in 1056); see Barlow, *Edward*, p. 175.

[177] See above, p. 31.

[178] D. Walker, 'The Norman settlement in Wales', *ANS*, 1 (1978), 131–43, locates the encounter at the village of Battle, two miles north-west of Brecon. R. R. Davies prefers a site closer to the town and the new priory of Battle Abbey, established in conscious imitation of Battle Abbey, Hastings; R. R. Davies, 'Brecon', in R. A. Griffiths (ed.), *Boroughs of Medieval Wales* (Cardiff, 1978), pp. 46–70.

[179] JW, III, 1093. *Brut (Pen. 20)*, 1093, records Rhys's death at 'French' hands but does not mention a battle. This and Rhys's weak political position at the time could suggest that the clash was not a battle but an ambush or skirmish in which Rhys and a small force were defeated. However, the pride taken in the establishment of the priory of Battle may suggest otherwise. *Journey*, I, 12, p. 148, claims uniquely that Rhys was betrayed by his own troops, whilst it has also been suggested that Rhys brought troops from Ireland to the clash; see Maund, *Ireland*, p. 169.

was ravaged by Cadwgan ap Bleddyn of Powys, but the Welsh weakness ultimately opened the way for Arnulf of Montgomery to overrun and settle much of Dyfed and Ceredigion. Rhys's death was disastrous for the position he had established, but it should be put in the context of the increasing difficulties he had faced since the Conqueror's death in 1087. His position had been steadily eroded, both internally and externally, and his death in 1093 simply opened the floodgates.

The Welsh revolt of 1094 prompted the Anglo-Normans in Wales to gather a force and march on Gwynedd to track down Cadwgan ap Bleddyn. A Welsh triumph was needed to inspire the revolt and break the stranglehold which the invaders held on the country. Cadwgan engaged the enemy at Coedysbys, where 'he defeated them and drove them to flight, inflicting great slaughter upon them'.[180]

After 1094 there was a notable period in which no battles between the Welsh and the Anglo-Normans are recorded. The Welsh revolt continued, but it was characterized by ravaging, ambush and evasion, and if Rufus wished to force a battle on his expeditions to Wales he was unsuccessful. When faced with the expedition of the earls in 1098, Cadwgan and Gruffudd ap Cynan retreated, first to the wilds of Snowdon and then to Anglesey. When the earls crossed to the island their success is recorded, but no source mentions a battle against the Welsh. The earls had gathered a powerful army including many Welshmen, and Cadwgan and Gruffudd did not enjoy enough support to challenge them. The defeat of Gruffudd ap Rhys's forces outside Aberystwyth castle in 1116 is often taken as a sign of Welsh inability and lack of professionalism in battle, but the clash seems more of a skirmish. The Welsh sources criticize the disorderliness of Gruffudd's irregular troop and it seems clear that they were surprised by the sortie made from the castle.[181]

In Henry I's reign there were no notable battles between the Anglo-Normans and the Welsh, but in the revolt that followed his death, Welsh ability in the field confounded the settlers and put them on the defensive. As in 1094, the Welsh were in need of a successful battle to light the spark of revolt. Also, the fact that

---

[180] *Brut (Pen. 20)*, s.a. 1094. The location of Coedysbys is unknown.
[181] Ibid., s.a. 1116.

there was no threat of a royal response meant that any gains won through enduring the dangers of battle could be kept; there was no all-powerful force to come to restore the Anglo-Norman position. We lack details of the battle in Gower in 1136, but it seems that significant forces were involved as total casualties are said to have amounted to 516 men.[182] The Welsh under Hywel ap Maredudd of Brycheiniog won a convincing victory before proceeding to terrorize the lands and possessions of the Marcher settlers in the area.

The second battle of 1136 was recorded only by Gerald of Wales. He told the story of the wife of Gruffudd ap Rhys, Gwenllian, who led an army against Maurice of London and Geoffrey, Roger of Salisbury's constable at Kidwelly, 'like some second Penthesilea, Queen of the Amazons'.[183] Gruffudd had gone to north Wales to seek support for the rising when this encounter took place near Kidwelly. The fact that no other source describes the battle could indicate that it was not a major clash; the Welsh are unlikely to have wished to force an issue at this time, with their lord away and about to return with reinforcements. Gerald says that Gwenllian was defeated and killed in the battle, and that one of her young sons, Morgan, was killed and another, Maelgwn, captured.

The third and final battle of 1136 was the major engagement. All our sources suggest the gathering of large forces by both sides at Cardigan for a clash to determine control of Ceredigion.[184] An army was brought from Gwynedd to join the forces of the native lords of the south, and the *Gesta Stephani* indicates that the Anglo-Normans had gathered all their available forces, drawing knights and footsoldiers from the surrounding towns and castles. These were war-hardened men, professionals used to fighting. The *Brutiau* support the evidence of the *Gesta Stephani*:

> And against them [the Welsh] came Stephen the constable and Robert fitz Martin and the sons of Gerald and William fitz Odo, and the Flemings and

---

[182] JW, III, 1136; *GS*, p. 17; *Journey*, I, 9, p. 136. The battle took place between Swansea and Loughor, possibly on the slopes of Mynydd Garn Goch.

[183] Gerald, *Journey*, I, 9, p. 137.

[184] *Brut (Pen. 20)*, s.a. 1136; *GS*, p. 17; JW, III, 1136; *Journey*, II, 3, p. 177. The battle was fought on Crug Mawr, a hill to the north-east of Cardigan; see R. A. Griffiths, 'The making of medieval Cardigan', in his *Conquerors and Conquered in Medieval Wales* (Stroud, 1994), pp. 277–302.

all the knights from the estuary of the Neath to the estuary of the Dyfi. And after fierce fighting, then the Flemings and the Normans, according to their usual custom, took to flight as their place of refuge. And with some slain and others burnt, and others trampled under horses' feet, and others carried off into captivity, and others drowned in rivers like fools, and having lost of their own men about 3,000, they returned home weak and despondent. But Owain and Cadwaladr, having honourably won the victory, returned to their land, and along with them a great abundance of captives and spoils and costly raiment and fair armour.[185]

Both sides had assembled their full strength and had been determined to engage in battle, and the Welsh had won a resounding success.[186]

The tale of Welsh military success continued. In 1145, Hywel ab Owain and his brother Cynan led a force south from Gwynedd and won a 'fierce battle' near Cardigan, although this clash was not on the same scale as that of 1136; the *Brutiau* refer to a battle but it may be better described as a skirmish. The battle at Coleshill in 1150 has been discussed; it is best considered as a native Welsh scrap, but the men sent by Ranulf of Chester were again on the losing side.[187]

In the course of Stephen's reign the Welsh leaders built their positions within the country so that they, and Owain Gwynedd in particular, became powerful, established lords. Owain had secured his position in Gwynedd, where he built a number of castles and had made his influence felt in Powys and the south. When Henry II came to the throne he was determined to reverse developments of the last twenty years and return Wales to its situation in Henry I's day. He would find that Owain was not prepared to submit without a fight as, in a unique post-1066 development, a Welsh leader chose to face a royal expedition from England in battle.

---

[185] *Brut (Pen. 20)*, s.a. 1136. *CBT*, IV, 1.45, suggests that 300 Anglo-Normans were killed, but this could be a conscious imitation of the *Gododdin*.

[186] Gerald of Wales says that the Welsh were able to win the battle 'at the very first encounter' only because the Anglo-Normans missed their murdered leader Richard de Clare; *Journey*, II, 3, p. 177. Cynddelw Brydydd Mawr seems to describe a Welsh charge (whether mounted or on foot is unclear) that broke an infantry line of spears:

Ym Mrwydr Aberteifi drylliai gwaywffyn cwympedig
Fel ym Mrwydr Baddon [a'i] mawr floeddio [mewn] ymgyrch (*CBT*, IV, 1.39–40)
'Gwelais bicellau gwaedlyd oherwydd ymosodiad Owain' (*CBT*, 1.52).

[187] In 1146, Ranulf's steward, Robert of Mold, inflicted a heavy defeat on a raiding party from Powys at Wich; *HW*, II, p. 491.

Henry mustered a large force in 1157 and encamped near Chester in preparation for an expedition against Owain. In response, Owain brought his forces east and encamped at Basingwerk. King has indicated the unusual nature of this strategy as, rather than retreating west to the wildest lands of Gwynedd, Owain moved out into less easily defensible lands.[188] He did this to defend his new frontier province of Tegeingl; the only way this could be achieved was to show a presence in the field and prevent Henry from entering and ravaging at will.[189]

If Henry was allowed to advance into Wales then the nature of the country in the north-east, less wild and mountainous than further west, would make it difficult for Owain to counter Henry's superior forces or lay ambushes for his ravagers. Consequently, Owain chose to block the king's route on a narrow coastal path at Coleshill, land with which Owain was familiar from his experience of 1150. The Welsh leader was encouraging Henry to make a frontal assault on his position. The fighting would be on Owain's terms and he had strengthened his position by making a field fortification in front of his line, but the Welsh leader was not afraid to expose his men in battle against a powerful royal force. Henry declined an assault on this prepared position and sought to outflank Owain.

The Welsh leader had chosen his location well because in order to outflank him, Henry had to negotiate a path through the dense wood of Hawarden. The king led a strong force through the wood, but Owain had anticipated the move and his sons, Cynan and Dafydd, lay in ambush. After a hard struggle Henry, having sustained heavy losses, was able to break out into open land behind Owain's position, forcing the Welsh to retreat. Having failed to stop Henry, Owain reverted to the traditional strategy of harrying and evading the royal force as it moved along the north Wales coast to Rhuddlan.[190]

---

[188] D. J. Cathcart King, 'Henry II and the fight at Coleshill', *WHR*, 2 (1964–5), 367–75.

[189] J. G. Edwards disagreed with King over where Owain chose to face the king, but he also stressed Owain's unusual strategy and his suggested location is even closer to the English border; J. G. Edwards, 'Henry II and the fight at Coleshill: some further reflections', *WHR*, 3 (1966–7), 251–63. Edwards's argument was rebutted in D. J. Cathcart King, 'The defences of Wales, 1067–1283; the other side of the hill', *Arch. Camb.*, 126 (1977), 1–16.

[190] For detailed accounts of the events of 1157, see especially *Brut (Pen. 20)*, s.a. 1157; *Brut (RBH)*, s.a. 1157. See also Chrons., I, pp. 105–9; *Journey*, II, 7, p. 189; II, 10, p. 197.

A second, related battle took place in 1157 on Anglesey. Henry anticipated problems on his coastal march and had sent a strong fleet to land behind Owain's position to trap the Welsh leader. Against his orders, the fleet landed on Anglesey and began to ravage the island. The Welsh force on the island is unlikely to have been at full strength and probably contained irregular recruits.[191] Their decision to engage in battle seems to have been determined by the ravaging of the island and the fact that if the fleet remained unchallenged it would have left Owain in a desperate situation. The invaders were routed at Tal-y-Moelfre and a number of nobles killed, the *Brutiau* recording that 'the French fled according to their usual custom'.[192] The defeat of his fleet, coupled with his own problems against Owain, persuaded Henry to come to terms with the Welsh prince.[193]

In 1182 'Ranulf de Poer was slain by young men from Gwent, and many knights along with him'.[194] This entry in the *Brutiau* could be dismissed as another ambush by the Welsh, but in this instance we are furnished with additional details by Gerald of Wales, who is likely to have had access to local sources. Ranulf was building a castle at Dingestow near Monmouth and had with him a squad of knights from Hereford. Gerald is at pains to stress that Ranulf's men were not caught by surprise as they had been earlier in the year at Abergavenny:

> This time Ranulf's troop were not caught off their guard and they were not taken unawares, for they were not without information of the imminent arrival of their enemies. On the contrary, they knew well what was planned, they were fully forewarned, they were armed and they were drawn up in battle array. They were forced to take refuge in the fortifications which they had built, and Ranulf Poer, nine of the leading captains from Herefordshire and quite a few other fighting men died after being run through the body with lances.[195]

---

[191] For discussion of this point, see above, pp. 73–4.
[192] *Brut (Pen. 20)*, s.a. 1157. It is possible that the invaders were caught whilst ravaging and were disorganized, but the *Brutiau* note that the battle occurred on the day after the ravaging of the island.
[193] At Basingwerk in 1166, Owain routed another royal force led by the earls of Leicester and Essex; *HW*, II, p. 519.
[194] *Brut (Pen. 20)*, s.a. 1182.
[195] *Journey*, I, 4, p. 111.

It is perhaps an exaggeration to call this encounter a battle, but again the Welsh proved themselves capable of defeating their enemies in a fair fight.

After the death of Henry II, Rhys ap Gruffudd returned to a policy of aggression against the Anglo-Normans. On campaign in 1196, he destroyed the town of Carmarthen and the castles of Colwyn and Radnor; the Marcher settlers could take no more and resolved to face the Welsh in the field. Rhys was keen to demonstrate his strength as he was faced with internal challenges from his sons, but his resort to battle may best be explained by the tactical situation; the Marcher force had got behind him and blocked his route home.[196] *Brut (Pen. 20)* describes the battle:

> And after it [Radnor] had been burnt, on that day Roger de Mortimer and Hugh de Sai arrayed a mighty host in the valley near that town, and they placed their forces armed with corselets and shields and helmets against the Welsh. And when Rhys perceived that, as he was a great-hearted man, he armed himself like a lion with a strong hand and daring heart, and attacked his enemies and drove them to flight; and after driving them he manfully pursued them and slew them. And then the Marchers, oppressed with excessive terror, lamented the slaughter.[197]

Following the death of Rhys ap Gruffudd, Gwenwynwyn sought to establish himself as the most prominent Welsh leader. He needed the prestige of a military victory over the Anglo-Normans and in 1198 he mustered a large host from Powys, Gwynedd and Deheubarth to besiege Painscastle. All our sources express surprise at the prolonged, badly directed conduct of the siege, which allowed an Anglo-Norman army to be gathered. They were handed the tactical advantage as the Welsh forces were static and disheartened; the Anglo-Norman host fell on Gwenwynwyn's army and a massacre resulted. The *Brutiau* acknowledge the scale of the defeat and are critical of Gwenwynwyn,[198] whilst the tone of Roger of Howden is triumphalist:

---

[196] See Remfry, 'Native', 140–1. His explanation accounts for the high casualties; with both sides denied an escape route, the loser faced destruction.
[197] *Brut (Pen. 20)*, s.a. 1196.
[198] Ibid., s.a. 1198.

Geoffrey fitz Peter, the justiciary of England, assembling a large army proceeded to Wales to succour the people of William de Braose, whom Gwenwynwyn, the brother of Cadwallon, had besieged in Painscastle, and on arriving there, he fought a pitched battle with the said Gwenwynwyn and his people, and, although the Welsh in arms were very numerous, still, not being able to make resistance to the forces of the English, they were put to flight, and throwing away their arms that, being less burdened, they might run more swiftly, there were then slain more than 3,700 of them, besides those who were captured, and those who being fatally wounded escaped from the field; while on the side of the English only one person was killed, being accidentally wounded by an arrow incautiously aimed by one of his companions.[199]

This was a devastating defeat, caused by Gwenwynwyn's bad generalship. It was the first recorded Welsh defeat in battle at Anglo-Norman hands since Gwenllian's death in 1136 or, if the latter is not considered a true battle, since 1093.

The battles of 1210 and 1213 have been considered in the context of inter-Welsh warfare and it can be seen that Anglo-Norman support was not necessarily the deciding influence. In 1210 Maelgwn enjoyed such support and was defeated; in 1213 Rhys Ieuanc fought alongside Falkes de Breauté and was victorious.[200]

Anglo-Welsh battles to this point had been rare; they were more so after the rise of Llywelyn ap Iorwerth and the principality of Gwynedd. This is an indication that the conquered areas of Wales were more settled and also that the power of the native principality made further conquests a daunting proposition. Few Marcher lords could contemplate facing the prince of Gwynedd in the field without the back-up of a royal expedition. In 1223 William Marshal (II), the most powerful Marcher lord of his day with significant Irish resources to draw upon, did risk such a battle. This was to recover family lands that had been recently appropriated by Llywelyn. There are indications that the inhabitants of the land favoured the Marshal as their lord and this support may have encouraged his venture. Llywelyn sent his son Gruffudd south at the head of a large host and the two sides

---

[199] RH (T), pp. 426–7; RH, IV, p. 53.
[200] Even in the latter case, Rhys Fychan is said to have been defeated in his encounter with the first troop of the enemy army which was composed of Rhys Ieuanc and his men, although it is possible that many of the men under Rhys Ieuanc were English.

met outside Carmarthen. Both leaders were anxious to force a decision and this led to battle. William was keen to recover his lost lands and, moreover, faced a difficult political situation in England and needed the prestige which a victory in Wales would give him at court; he was acting without royal approval and a climb-down or defeat could have broken him. Llywelyn knew that the lands which William sought to regain, notably the key castles of Cardigan and Carmarthen, were vital to his ambitions in south Wales; victory was essential to his credibility amongst the people of the south and to contain his most dangerous Marcher rival. In addition, Gruffudd's relations with his father were strained, and this young, headstrong commander may have seen the chance to impress Llywelyn and the nobles of Gwynedd. English and Welsh sources differ in their descriptions of the ensuing clash. Roger of Wendover, an apologist for the Marshal family who does little to suggest his accuracy by stating that Llywelyn led the Welsh force, wrote:

> He [Marshal] boldly attacked the enemy, and, after slaying numbers of the Welsh, put all the rest to flight, and hotly pursuing them slew them without mercy; 9,000 of them were computed to have been slain and made prisoner, only a very few having escaped by flight.[201]

The sympathies of the *Brutiau* are with the Welsh:

> And Gruffudd received him [Marshal] and gave him a hard battle. And after fighting for the most part of the day on either side, each of the two hosts withdrew from the other to their tents, many having been slain and wounded on either side. And then Gruffudd returned to Gwynedd because of lack of food.[202]

The Welsh suffered losses in the battle and it was a strategic victory for the Marshal; he recovered Cardigan and Carmarthen and Gruffudd returned to Gwynedd. However, the battle was not as one-sided as Wendover suggests; there were losses on both sides in a hard-fought engagement and there was no rout of the Welsh troops.

---

[201] RW (T), II, p. 444; RW, II, p. 270.
[202] *Brut (Pen. 20)*, s.a. 1223.

In 1257, Henry III set out to break the alliance between Llywelyn ap Gruffudd and Maredudd ap Rhys Gryg by targeting the latter in Deheubarth. Henry's commander, Stephen Baucan, gathered Welsh troops including Maredudd's rival Rhys Fychan, along with a 'host past telling of barons and knights from England' before setting out from Carmarthen.[203] The force was harassed on its march up the valley of the Tywi to Llandeilo and was soon in difficulty. A night ambush at Llandeilo prompted Rhys Fychan to defect to the Welsh side, leaving the army no chance of reaching Dinefwr. They tried to fight their way back to either Carmarthen or Cardigan (the evidence is inconclusive), but after a second day of prolonged attack they lost their baggage train at Coed Llathen, three miles from Llandeilo. The force was overwhelmed around midday at Cymerau (which cannot be precisely located). English and Welsh sources claim that around 3,000 were killed in the Marcher army – including Stephen Baucan – and the battle is hailed as a great Welsh victory.[204]

If the subject of battles between the Welsh and Anglo-Normans is considered numerically, it does not tell the story of a primitive people unable to face their sophisticated enemies in a straight fight. Of the clashes that can confidently be described as battles in the period 1066–1277, we can record six Welsh victories, three defeats (counting 1223 as a defeat for Gruffudd) and one draw (at Coleshill in 1157). If we add to these figures the clash at Aberystwyth in 1116, Gwenllian's defeat in 1136 and the encounters in 1145 and 1182, the results become eight victories, five defeats and one draw. To add the battles which have been considered as inter-Welsh but in which the Anglo-Normans were involved, we reach eleven victories, seven defeats and one draw. Such comparisons are crude and each campaign needs to be considered in its own context, but the figures indicate that the unusual strategy of battle was adopted as a desperate measure by Welsh leaders who saw no other way to halt the tide of conquest that was flowing against them. The Anglo-Norman conquest of Wales proceeded by means other than battle, and Welsh success in the field helped to delay ultimate subjugation.

---

[203] Ibid., s.a. 1257.
[204] See *LG*, pp. 97–9; Walker, 'Anglo-Welsh', 652–4. The fullest account in the sources is found in *AC* (B).

Welsh involvement in Anglo-Norman battles

Before 1066 we have little to suggest a tradition of Welsh involvement in Anglo-Saxon battles, although the presence of Welsh in Edmund Ironside's forces for his battles with Cnut suggests that the reason could be lack of sources.[205] It is possible that Welsh kings joined Athelstan for his expedition to Scotland in 934 and Edmund for his campaign against the Britons of Strathclyde in 945.[206] There were Welshmen in the shire levies of Herefordshire and Gloucestershire that fought against Gruffudd ap Rhydderch in 1049.[207] Edwin of Mercia took Welsh troops to Northumbria in 1065 to support his brother Morcar against Tostig.[208] It is unclear if these were mercenaries or contingents owed by Welsh leaders. It is possible that Edwin took Welsh troops north to Fulford Gate (and perhaps Stamford Bridge) in 1066, but we do not have the evidence to support this theory.

After 1066 the regular and effective use of Welshmen as light troops in Anglo-Norman armies has been highlighted, but their role in battle has not been discussed. Welsh soldiers were prominent in one of the first major engagements fought on English soil in the twelfth century, the battle of Lincoln in 1141. The Welsh, fighting on the side of Robert of Gloucester, were led by three nobles – Morgan ab Owain of Glamorgan, Madog ap Maredudd of Powys, and Cadwaladr ap Gruffudd of Gwynedd.[209] These would have been supported by their *teuluoedd*, each of which would have formed an effective fighting unit, experienced, well equipped and drilled to fight with its comrades. Cadwaladr's presence is likely to have been particularly valued; the rarity of battles meant that few present at Lincoln would have previously experienced such combat and Cadwaladr was a veteran of Cardigan in 1136.

Orderic stated that at Lincoln 'the king's column consisted mainly of knights, but the enemy were more powerful because of their numerous footsoldiers and the Welshmen'.[210] Later in the

---

[205] Lawson, *Cnut*, pp. 77–9.
[206] Stenton, *Anglo-Saxon*, pp. 337, 355.
[207] JW, II, 1049.
[208] *ASC* (D) and (E), 1065; JW, II, 1065.
[209] D. Crouch, 'The March and the Welsh kings', in E. King (ed.), *The Anarchy of King Stephen's Reign* (Oxford, 1994), pp. 255–89.
[210] OV, VI, 13, p. 543.

civil war Robert, on hearing that Stephen was besieging Tetbury, 'immediately collected a vast force of knights as he had a great many castles near by . . . and assembled a cruel and savage army of footmen from Wales and Bristol and other neighbouring towns, as though he intended to join battle with the king'. Stephen quickly retreated and avoided battle because his knights were:

> alarmed at the untamed savagery of the Welsh and likewise the Bristol irregulars, whom the Earl of Gloucester was leading for their confusion . . . it was ill considered and extremely hazardous to expose a much smaller body of his knights among such a mass of cut throats on foot.[211]

Modern commentators have dismissed the role played by the Welsh at Lincoln. Bradbury merely notes that 'the first clash destroyed the poorly armed Welsh on the rebel side'.[212] Such perceptions seem to be taken from Henry of Huntingdon's account of the battle. His statement that the Welsh were 'rash, ill-armed and ignorant of the art of war' has been discussed in the context of the speech made to encourage the royalist army before the battle by denigrating all of the rebel forces.[213] Huntingdon states that the Welsh were on the flanks of Robert's forces and that they were attacked at the start of the battle:

> The line commanded by the Count of Aumale and William of Ypres attacked the Welsh, who were advancing on the wing, and put them to flight. But the earl of Chester's line overturned the said count's troop and it was routed in a moment just like the first line. So they fled – all the king's knights and William of Ypres . . .[214]

---

[211] *GS*, p. 173.
[212] Bradbury, 'Battles', p. 192. Beeler claims that 'the men of Gwynedd and Powys were not archers but spearmen, and their usefulness on the battlefield hardly justified the efforts of the earl of Chester in marching them clear across England'; J. Beeler, *Warfare in England , 1066–1189* (New York, 1966), p. 119. Beeler's accompanying map of the battle (reprinted in Nicolle, *Medieval*) portrays each unit in a neatly ordered strategic formation, save the Welsh who are thrown somewhere between the two armies without shape or pattern! See also J. Bradbury, *Stephen and Matilda: The Civil War of 1139–53* (Stroud, 1996), pp. 83–98; *WW*, p. 163.
[213] See above, p. 96, n. 54. It is notable that Baldwin singles out the Welsh for special attention and urges his men not to fear their charge. The rest of the opposing force are dismissed as 'deserters and vagabonds', suggesting that the ferocity of the Welsh onslaught was expected to be the main danger.
[214] HH, X, 18, p. 737.

We have two other reports of the battle, from Orderic and the *Gesta Stephani*. The *Gesta Stephani* concentrates on the seizure of the ford across the Witham, suggesting that the defeat of a strong troop sent forward by Stephen to take it effectively decided the battle. This troop was the same one identified by Huntingdon as being led by Aumale and Ypres:

> When he [Stephen] had sent forward a very strong body of knights and footmen to stop them as they emerged from a ford, they on the other side prudently drew up their line of battle, furiously charged the king's men, and seized the ford, and when they had scattered them with great vigour and put them to flight then with one mind and dauntless spirit they joined battle with the king's army.[215]

The force sent forward by Stephen was routed after being caught in a disorganized state by a disciplined charge from the rebel army. Why were Stephen's men in such a disorganized state? Orderic states that the 'first squadron' was sent forward by Stephen against the Welsh and agrees with the other sources that the defeat of this force settled the battle: 'Count Waleran and his brother, William of Warenne, Gilbert of Clare and other distinguished Norman and English knights gave way to panic when they saw the first squadron in flight and themselves turned tail.'[216] It seems strange that Huntingdon is the only source to mention the initial success of Stephen's men, particularly as the *Gesta Stephani* is often notably hostile towards the Welsh. Another explanation could be that the mounted, disciplined *teuluoedd* of the Welsh leaders were sent forward to draw the enemy charge. What Huntingdon describes as the 'complete rout' of the Welsh may have been a feigned flight, a difficult manoeuvre that could only be performed by an experienced force. The manoeuvre drew Stephen's men into the trap set by Robert.

The effectiveness of Welsh troops serving under their native commanders has been noted in 1173–4.[217] Rhys ap Gruffudd's son, Hywel Sais, gave valuable service to Henry II in Normandy in 1173, and the following year Rhys himself led 1,000 men to the siege of Tutbury. Henry was anxious to use this force, which

[215] *GS*, p. 111.
[216] OV, VI, 13, p. 543.
[217] See above, p. 61.

he took to Normandy where their efforts persuaded Louis VII to abandon the siege of Rouen. After 1170 the Anglo-Normans in Wales began their conquest of Ireland. For this expedition they adopted a battle-seeking strategy as they sought to impress themselves on the populace of the country. They took with them significant numbers of Welsh troops who fought in numerous battles, usually successfully.[218] In October 1233, Richard Siward led a raid from Wales to Devizes, his force containing a number of his knights along with Welsh spearmen and archers. On the return journey he twice encountered and defeated a levy of the men of Bristol.[219]

The Angevin kings frequently employed Welsh soldiers in their continental wars and, as has been seen, they were most noted for their skills in ravaging. In 1234, Wendover describes a successful battle fought by a predominantly Welsh army against a French force led by Louis IX. Henry III had gathered a force of sixty knights and 2,000 Welshmen which was sent to Brittany. The French were besieging a castle whereupon:

> The knights of the English king and their Welsh followers met them and killed a number of their horses, thus changing horse soldiers into foot, seized their carts and vehicles containing their provisions and arms, carried off their horses and other booty, and, after inflicting all this harm on their enemies, returned to their own quarters without any loss to themselves.[220]

There were Welsh troops in Simon de Montfort's army when he defeated the royalist forces at Lewes in 1264. We have no information to suggest the role they played in the battle. By the time of Evesham in 1265, de Montfort had lost the full backing which Llywelyn ap Gruffudd had offered in 1264 and no Welsh leaders are recorded at the battle.[221] *De Bellis Lewes et Evesham* has this account: 'The Welsh who were with him [de Montfort] in great numbers, took to flight from the beginning, like sheep, and

---

[218] See *Conquest*, I, 3, p. 31; I, 10, p. 51; II, 3, p. 141.
[219] See D. Crouch, 'Last adventure', 14–15.
[220] RW (T), II, pp. 596–7; RW, III, p. 93.
[221] *LG*, pp. 171–2, notes that there is no evidence that Llywelyn aided de Montfort in his final conflict. It is suggested that the Welsh forces at the battle were brought from Humphrey de Bohun's lands and led by him.

hiding in cornfields and gardens, and fleeing through the country round about, were afterwards found and slain.'[222]

The Anglo-Normans made more use of the Welsh as ravagers and guerrilla fighters than as battle troops. We should consider the identity of the Welsh forces employed in England and on the continent. They are likely to have been Welshmen drawn from the conquered, Marcher areas of Wales, upland Glamorgan proving a particularly rich source of recruits. In these lands the Anglo-Normans were the lords and knights and held the best land; consequently they were the better-equipped men who formed the military elite of the fighting force. Disinherited sons of Welsh princes are found in royal service.[223] Some of these men do not seem like impoverished lords; Cadwallon ab Ifor led large numbers of troops and helped Gerald of Wales out of financial difficulties in Rouen;[224] Leisan ap Morgan of Afan served John in 1205 with 200 Welshmen.[225] However, the soldiers they led were from marginal lands and the military class of society was declining in wealth; the *uchelwyr* of Glamorgan could not afford the trappings of knighthood as they became little more than peasant farmers.[226] The Welsh from these areas were often poor and desperate mercenaries, only valuable as irregular troops. In contrast, when the Welsh were employed to fight under native lords from the unconquered areas of Wales, they were a very different sort of force. At times of political chaos in England, as in Stephen's reign, in the crisis of 1173–4 and possibly at Lewes, the Welsh were brought onto the English scene as strong units that proved effective in battle.[227]

NIGHT FIGHTING

Whereas surprise and ambush always offered advantages to a force, night attacks fall into a different category. Fighting at night

---

[222] Translation from M. Salmon, *A Source Book of Welsh History* (Oxford, 1927), p. 169.
[223] See *PR* 34 Henry II, pp. 8, 107; *PR* 4 John, p. 166; *PR* 5 John, p. 80.
[224] H. E. Butler (ed. and trans.), *The Autobiography of Giraldus Cambrensis* (London, 1937), VI, p. 325.
[225] *PR* 6 John, p. 146.
[226] See M. Griffiths, 'Native', 179–216. For further discussion of the changes under way in Welsh society, see above, pp. 70–1.
[227] In the treaty of Woodstock, Henry III tried to ensure that military contingents sent from Gwynedd uwch Conwy would be led by either Owain or Llywelyn. He hoped to be supplied with an effective, self-contained fighting force; C. W. Lewis, 'The Treaty of Woodstock 1247: its background and significance', *WHR*, 2 (1964–5), 37–65.

was difficult because maintaining order and communication was extremely problematic; the usual chaos of battle was increased. In such an engagement danger was greater and everyone was at risk. A force choosing to instigate a night attack may have held an initial advantage, but in the ensuing confusion anything could happen as a commander lost tactical control. Night attacks were often a gambler's throw, the act of a commander under pressure or facing oppressive odds.[228]

Not only battles but all military activities were restricted by nightfall. Ravaging was curtailed for practical reasons; a camp would be established for the night in preparation for the next day's ravaging.[229] At Aberlleiniog in 1094, Gruffudd ap Cynan engaged in a hard-fought clash that raged throughout the day but 'night halted the battle'.[230] The ninth-century poem *Llym awel* indicates that night attacks could be contemplated, although the situation seems exceptional:

> Under the shelter of a steed, on a spirited steed
> with brave, dauntless warriors
> the night is fine to attack the enemy.[231]

An incident in the *Life of St Illtud* reveals the danger of night attacks and how darkness could be a great leveller. An army from Gwynedd ravaged Glamorgan in 1094–5, prompting the clergy and people to flee to an old hill fort. The 'incautious foe' made a 'hurried night attack' which was thrown back with heavy losses. The defeat of this experienced force by the people of the land, aided even by the women and children, is given a semi-miraculous flavour, but it is acknowledged that 'if they had attacked by daylight they would have ascended most smoothly'.[232]

Before Mynydd Carn in 1081, Rhys ap Tewdwr and Gruffudd ap Cynan were in a desperate situation, facing a superior enemy army and with the political tide flowing against them. *Gruffudd ap*

---

[228] At Heavenfield in 634, Oswald was outnumbered and in a desperate position, and there is a suggestion that a night attack helped to bring him victory; see Adomnán of Iona, *Life of St Columba*, ed. and trans. R. Sharpe (London, 1995), I, 1, p. 111.
[229] See, for example, *Vitae*, p. 73.
[230] *Gruffudd ap Cynan*, p. 72.
[231] *Saga*, p. 502.
[232] *Vitae*, p. 233.

Cynan states that they were able to defeat their enemies through an unexpected night attack, with Gruffudd leading the 'rush' forward.[233] The decision to undertake this night attack is used to illustrate Gruffudd's boldness. Although Rhys's reluctance reflects the bias of the source, it is possible that his attitude was a reflection of the fears of a competent commander at the unpredictability of a night attack.[234]

In 1210 Rhys and Owain, the sons of Gruffudd, faced a desperate political situation. Gwenwynwyn had returned to royal favour and this allowed his ally, Maelgwn ap Rhys, to lead a force into Deheubarth. To counter this army, Rhys and Owain chose a force of picked men from loyal *teuluoedd* to shadow Maelgwn before falling upon him at night. Their experienced, manageable force (about 300 men) was able to spread panic in the larger army, inflict severe casualties and cause the survivors to flee in chaos.[235] Such tactics were also used by the Welsh to even the odds when fighting against royal expeditions.[236]

Wherever possible, night attacks were avoided because of their unpredictability. In 1113 Madog ap Rhiddid was secretly shadowed through the night by the *teulu* of Maredudd ap Bleddyn, but they waited until morning to attack and capture him.[237] In 1109 a strong Welsh force sought to attack Cadwgan ap Bleddyn and his son Owain. They considered a night attack to ravage Cadwgan's lands, but rejected the plan as too dangerous: 'better to array our host and go in broad daylight.'[238]

---

[233] *Gruffudd ap Cynan*, pp. 66–7.
[234] It should be noted that Meilyr, p. 185, claims that the battle took place at midday.
[235] *Brut (Pen. 20)*, s.a. 1210.
[236] MP, IV, pp. 407, 481.
[237] *Brut (Pen. 20)*, s.a. 1113.
[238] Ibid., s.a. 1109.

IV
EQUIPMENT AND TACTICAL DISPOSITIONS

Equipment

A definitive analysis of the equipment of a medieval army is impossible; there was never standardization because a wide range of implements could be used for war, many being handed down through the generations.[1] Technological breakthroughs were rare; a spear was as effective at the end of our period as at the beginning. Individual preference and wealth were of significance in the type and quality of equipment used by each warrior.[2] Having said that, it is possible to gain some insight into the military equipment used by the Welsh and to see how it changed and developed. In the *Life of St Cadog*, Rhun ap Maelgwn Gwynedd made reparation to the saint for the ravaging of his land. Amongst other things, he gave his best stallion with accoutrements and his 'three chief weapons', his shield, sword and spear.[3] Other equipment was important and these three items might vary in style and quality, but they were the standard arms of the military elite.[4]

Iron production

Davidson examined the problems which people in the Middle Ages faced in producing high-quality iron and steel.[5] Most early furnaces were made of clay and were destroyed after each operation, although there were some early stone furnaces. After

---

[1] The value of weapons can be seen in attempts in the law to control who owned arms and to keep them within the kin group; *Law*, pp. 11, 61.
[2] For a discussion of weapons in Europe in the period 1000–1300, see *WW*, pp. 16–38.
[3] *Vitae*, p. 79; see also the description of 'Morcant' in ibid., p. 131.
[4] In *Culhwch and Olwen*, Culhwch goes to Arthur's court armed as a warrior. He has a sword, shield, two spears and a battle axe: *Mabinogi*, p. 137; *CaO*, p. 3. After they meet, Arthur promises Culhwch anything he should ask save his sword, spear, shield, knife, ship and wife: *Mabinogi*, p. 140; *CaO*, p. 6.
[5] H. E. Davidson, *The Sword in Anglo-Saxon England* (Woodbridge, 1994).

the departure of the Romans from Britain there was no central control of mines in the country, which meant that smiths had to use surface ores and old workings which produced poor-quality, impure iron. The more settled political conditions in England from the ninth century onwards led to the establishment of new mines and smelting sites, but in Wales we have little archaeological evidence on which to base a comparable study.[6] At Dinas Powys, Alcock found evidence of a primitive furnace and smelting, but he discovered no built furnaces and concluded that the scale was meagre compared with the extensive Norman iron working in Glamorgan.[7] It seems likely that a shortage of high-quality iron and steel adversely affected the quality and quantity of equipment used by Welsh troops from the end of the Roman period until at least the twelfth century.

Arms production

In *Manawydan*, Manawydan and Pryderi went to England to take up the professions of saddle-making and shield-making, possibly suggesting that arms were sought in England.[8] This is inconclusive, however, as the lords only moved to England when their land had been left desolate by 'magic'. The value of craftsmen able to work with such weapons is revealed in *Culhwch and Olwen*; Cei tricked his way into a giant's fortress by proclaiming his skill at burnishing swords.[9] Specialized craftsmen were itinerant around the courts of the chieftains of Wales. This system continued in Wales into the thirteenth century, by which time

---

[6] The only evidence of primary exploitation of iron ore in Wales comes from the Forest of Dean and Ewloe, Flintshire, and both were mainly exploited for use in England. Smithing was a regular village industry in Wales; see L. A. S. Butler, 'Rural buildings in Wales', in H. E. Hallam (ed.), *The Agrarian History of England and Wales 1042–1350*, II (Cambridge, 1988), pp. 931–66 (962).

[7] Alcock, *Economy*, pp. 40–2. He cautions that evidence for more extensive metalworking may be hidden or destroyed.

[8] *Mabinogi*, pp. 87–8; *PK*, pp. 52–4.

[9] *Mabinogi*, pp. 162–3; *CaO*, pp. 28–30. Wrnach the giant says: 'I need such a man for I have spent some time looking for someone to burnish my sword without finding anyone.' Bedwyr is also allowed entrance after his skill at making spear-heads is proclaimed. In the tale it is said that only a king or a craftsman bringing his craft could enter Arthur's court after a meal had begun; *Mabinogi*, p. 137; *CaO*, p. 3. In *Manawydan* there are suggestions that an armourer's was an honourable trade and that the king, Caswallawn, implemented measures to protect armourers; *Mabinogi*, pp. 87–8; *PK*, pp. 52–4.

specialist centres for arms production had been established elsewhere in Europe. This helps to account for the fact that outside observers regarded Welsh arms as backward. In the Anglo-Norman period, Welsh military equipment was considered dated and sub-standard; at Lincoln, for example, Henry of Huntingdon called the Welsh ill-armed.[10]

Armour

The terminology for armour is open to a variety of interpretations. There are many references to armour in the *Gododdin*, with two terms used, *seirch* and, more regularly, *lluric*. The Latin term *lorica* was used for any form of protective device, but most popular was a leather cuirass, and this probably applies to *lluric* in the *Gododdin*.[11] In Latin, *lorica squamata* was used for scale armour and *lorica hamata* for a cuirass of mail, and the Celts and Germans were able to make mail before they came under Roman influence. From grave evidence it is clear that the greatest Anglo-Saxon nobles wore mail, and the same probably applied to British forces of the period. As the *Gododdin* was intended to reveal the glory of the host of Mynyddog, it is possible that references to armour are meant to describe mail, although leather is more likely. There are other references to armoured Welsh troops of the early Middle Ages. The *Triads* mention Lludd Llurigog (Lludd 'of the Breastplate'), which would suggest that the armour of this hero was remarkable.[12] *Canu Llywarch* refers to armour (W. *caen*)[13] and speaks of warriors arming (W. *wisc*) for battle.[14] The tenth–eleventh century penitential lyric, *Kyntaw Geir*, compares the protection offered by a prayer with that given by armour.[15]

The vast majority of Welsh armour in the early Middle Ages would have been padded leather and other perishable material. It is likely that some mail, laminar and leather with iron plates

---

[10] HH, X, 17, p. 735. For the growth of large-scale weapon production in Europe with specialist centres, see *WW*, p. 30.
[11] Alcock, *Economy*, p. 299.
[12] *Triads*, p. 31.
[13] *Saga*, p. 471.
[14] Ibid., p. 468.
[15] Ibid., p. 499.

146   EQUIPMENT AND TACTICAL DISPOSITIONS

attached existed, owned by the greatest men and passed on to their descendants or conquerors. Some such armour may have survived from Roman times and other pieces would have been plundered from defeated Anglo-Saxon and Viking foes. The extent of Viking influence on armour in Wales is unclear. Certainly in Ireland its impact was pronounced and Viking influence led to improvements in Anglo-Saxon armour.[16] The possibility that native Welsh armour was produced should not be discounted.

In the Anglo-Norman period, Gerald of Wales described the Welsh as wearing leather corselets[17] and argued that in certain conditions such protection was preferable to iron armour.[18] Gerald cannot be taken at face value, but the impression of superior Anglo-Norman armour seems to hold true. The native sources were impressed with the quality and scale of Norman armour. *Gruffudd ap Cynan* boasts of Gruffudd's bravery in fighting against the 'mailed and helmeted French' at Aberlleiniog in 1094.[19] The 'mailed knights' from Aberystwyth had an effect on the native chronicler in 1116 and it is recorded that Henry I was saved from an arrow by his 'corselet and armour' in 1121.[20]

The Welsh had armour before 1066 and after this date they began to copy, and plunder, Norman styles, but their poverty and deficiency in productive capacity always meant that Anglo-Norman armour was superior.[21] Anglo-Norman leaders had the best armour of the day and even their light troops are likely to have had some protection. The armour of Welsh leaders was considered backward by the Anglo-Normans, whilst the poorest troops in a Welsh army would have been pleased with a leather jerkin. Owain Gwynedd was said to have led 2,000 'mailed

[16] Ó'Cróinín, *Early Medieval*, p. 269; N. Brooks, 'Weapons and armour', in Scragg, *Battle*, pp. 208–19. D. Moore contended that Scandinavian military influence on Wales was greater than Norman influence; see his 'Gruffudd ap Cynan and the medieval Welsh polity', in *GC*, pp. 1–59; p. 30.
[17] *Description*, I, 9, p. 234.
[18] Ibid., II, 8, p. 269.
[19] *Gruffudd ap Cynan*, p. 72. The possession of armour was also used to praise Gruffudd. Meilyr Brydydd recorded that 'ambling steeds bore his armour'; Meilyr, p. 184.
[20] *Brut (Pen. 20)*, s.a. 1116, 1121.
[21] Norman armour also made an impression on the Irish; see Ó'Cróinín, *Early Medieval*, p. 289; B. Ó'Cuir, 'A poem composed for Cathal Croibhdearg ó Conchubair', *Eriu*, 34 (1983), 157–74.

horsemen' to the battle of Cardigan in 1136. After his victory, though, the 'costly raiment and fair armour' taken from his defeated enemies was greatly prized.[22] Welsh armour continued to improve throughout the twelfth century, but *Brut (Pen. 20)* was impressed that the Anglo-Norman force sent against Owain at Coleshill in 1157 was 'fully equipped',[23] and the Marcher force defeated by Rhys ap Gruffudd in 1196 was noted for its 'horses and corselets and helmets and shields'.[24]

References to armoured Welsh troops increase in the thirteenth century and change is reflected in the increased importance which is given to armour in the laws. The quality of Welsh armour improved, but its calibre and scale never reached the levels seen in Anglo-Norman forces. Furthermore, as Welsh leaders in the thirteenth century drew a greater proportion of the population into their forces it is possible that the poorest troops had no armour of any kind.

The helmet

Given the problems associated with the production and working of quality metal, it may be suspected that helmets, which were non-essential and difficult to make, were absent from Welsh forces. Elaborate Anglo-Saxon helmets have been found, though, and it is possible that the leading Welsh nobility wore them both for protection and as status symbols. Of the Irish warriors in *Branwen*, only one had 'armour on his head'; this suggests the rarity of the helmet's use.[25] Helmets and coifs are mentioned in the laws, although these seem to be later additions to the texts.[26] The Latin elegy to Rhys ap Gruffudd mentions his helmet which now lies idle and rusting.[27] The fact that Gerald of Wales says that the Welsh wore helmets is noteworthy because, in general, he sought to underestimate their military sophistication and the

---

[22] *Brut (Pen. 20)*, s.a. 1136; see also ibid., s.a. 1260, for the equipment seized after the capture of Builth by Llywelyn ap Gruffudd. The significance of these references should not be exaggerated, as armour was prized booty for any victorious force in the Middle Ages.
[23] Ibid., s.a. 1157.
[24] *Brut (RBH)*, s.a. 1196.
[25] *Mabinogi*, p. 78; *PK*, p. 43. The Welsh phrase is *arueu am benn*.
[26] *Law*, p. 193.
[27] *Brut (Pen. 20)*, s.a. 1197.

scale of their armament. Some form of leather headgear is probably to be imagined.[28] The Welsh prose romances have descriptions of helmets and coifs, suggesting that Welsh equipment was getting more elaborate under Anglo-Norman influence;[29] care should be taken, however, because literary patterns and conceits were also borrowed.

The sword

The sword in the Middle Ages was a precision weapon, made by craftsmen and designed to last a long time.[30] A sword could enhance the stature of its bearer; Culhwch's was decorated with a gold hilt and blade, Arthur's was given the name Caledfwlch, and Cei had a famous sword.[31] Given the investment of time and money that went into producing swords, it is not surprising that they were decorated elaborately and became ceremonial, even mystical, objects as well as weapons.[32] On Welsh seals of the Anglo-Norman period, mounted Welsh leaders are almost universally depicted with swords, showing their importance as trappings of power.[33]

Gerald of Wales suggests that the main Welsh weapons were the bow and spear and he barely mentions the sword. This supports his picture of a society of poor freemen, fighting as equals for their status. It has been seen that the picture is inaccurate and it is clear that the sword was an important weapon in Wales throughout the period.[34] Swords were a key armament in the *Gododdin* and were in the possession of nearly every named warrior. They were probably the long, slashing blades as used by Roman cavalry rather than short, stabbing

[28] *Description*, I, 8, p. 234.
[29] See, for example, *Mabinogi*, pp. 197, 201, 232, 288.
[30] See R. E. Oakeshott, *The Sword in the Age of Chivalry* (London, 1964). The finest decorated sword would have taken a skilled craftsmen a month to make and would have required a great deal of charcoal. A mail hauberk required a similar effort.
[31] *Mabinogi*, pp. 137, 140, 149; *CaO*, pp. 3, 6, 14.
[32] See J. Langer and B. Ager, 'Swords of the Anglo-Saxon and Viking periods in the British Museum: a radiographic study', in Hawkes, *Weapons*, pp. 85–122.
[33] See D. H. Williams, *Welsh History through Seals* (Cardiff, 1982).
[34] Other Anglo-Norman sources frequently mention that the Welsh ravaged with 'fire and sword'; this was a stock phrase, but they saw no reason not to apply it to the Welsh. See JW, III, 1136; OV, VI, 13, p. 537. Gerald himself records that a Norman killed by the Welsh had his throat cut with a sword; *Journey*, I, 4, p. 111.

infantry swords.[35] The blades were only part of the offensive equipment of the *Gododdin* warriors, each of whom also had a number of spears. The universal ownership of swords in the poem should be seen as a reflection of the image which the author wished to portray. Although the sword was an important weapon, it is unlikely that it was used by every member of a Welsh force, or even by a majority of them.

In considering other poetry, we again face the problem of dealing with panegyrics to the greatest Welsh leaders, but the evidence gives some idea of the value attached to swords.[36] In *Gwahodd Llywarch i Lanfawr* the horseman holds the sword of Echel, a legendary Welsh hero.[37] The implication is that high-quality swords were reused throughout the generations (as happened elsewhere in Europe) and that to possess the sword of a great figure of the past would confer honour on the present bearer. In the Lives of Welsh saints, swords are granted as gifts in reparation or in exchange for privileges and rights over land, and in each case the worth placed on the blade is high.[38] The value varies according to the quality and this suggests that attempts to regulate the price of a sword in the laws are unrealistic. The laws do make provision for the increased value of decorated swords.[39] Swords were kept in scabbards, which could themselves be prized and decorated.[40]

The spear

The spear was always the standard weapon for Welsh troops. It was cheap, easily made from readily available material, needed only a small amount of metal for the tip, was used by cavalry and infantry and could be thrown or kept in hand as a stabbing

---

[35] J. Rowland, 'Warfare', 24.
[36] See, for example, *Saga*, pp. 175–6; *Earliest*, p. 142. Compare also the use in the *Mabinogi*, pp. 50, 61; *PK*, pp. 6, 22; *Mabinogi*, p. 180; *BR*, p. 4. The most vivid description of the use of the sword is in *Gruffudd ap Cynan*, p. 63; pictured at the battle of Bron-yr-erw in 1075 is 'King Gruffudd seated on his horse in the midst of his army, with his flashing sword mowing down both his traitors and enemies'. At Mynydd Carn, Gruffudd is depicted 'scattering opponents with a flashing sword,' *Gruffudd ap Cynan*, p. 67.
[37] *Saga*, p. 474.
[38] *Vitae*, pp. 79, 125, 131, 133. In *Liber Landavensis* swords are used as payment for land; *LL*, pp. 185, 202, 203(a).
[39] *Law*, p. 194.
[40] See *Mabinogi*, p. 163; *CaO*, p. 30; *Mabinogi*, p. 180; *BR*, p. 4; Meilyr, p. 183.

weapon. The spear was a free man's weapon that it was honourable to use.[41] Panegyric sources exaggerate the use made of the sword, but even so the majority of references are to spears in combat. When a warrior had a sword he also had a spear, but it is likely that many more had spears but no swords. The laws record that a spear-head was one of three things for which the court smith was entitled to payment, his other services being given freely. This was a late change to the texts, suggesting that it was originally a free service.[42] It is possible that the increased size of Welsh armies in the twelfth and thirteenth centuries meant that an increased demand for this service led to the introduction of payment.

The *Gododdin* has over fifteen terms for spear and not all variations can be explained by the demands of poetic metre.[43] This diversity of terminology continues in later literature and it seems likely that there were specialist throwing javelins and other heavier spears kept in hand.[44] Gerald of Wales described the effectiveness of these weapons: 'a cuirass of mail offers no resistance to one of these lances when it is thrown a short distance as a javelin'.[45] Some of the spears had heads designed to stick in an opponent's shield, allowing it to be dragged down or forcing him to cast it aside.[46] Gerald claimed that the people of north Wales were renowned for their skill with the spear.[47] *Gruffudd ap Cynan* lists the troops who fought at Mynydd Carn and specifically refers to the men of Gwynedd 'armed with spears and shields'.[48] However, their speciality with the spear does not imply that they were the only Welsh to fight in this manner; the wide range of references to the spear establishes its universality

---

[41] In *Culhwch and Olwen*, at Arthur's court Cei is the expert with the sword and Bedwyr with the spear; no other weapons experts are named. *Mabinogi*, p. 149; *CaO*, p. 14.

[42] *Law*, pp. 37–8.

[43] There is a similar variety of terms in the *Battle of Maldon* poem, supported by diverse spear finds in Anglo-Saxon graves. Different spears had different functions; see N. Brooks, 'Weapons and armour', pp. 208–19.

[44] In *Culhwch and Olwen*, Culhwch possesses two silver spears. It may be speculated that one is for throwing, the other for stabbing; *Mabinogi*, p. 137; *CaO*, p. 3.

[45] *Journey*, II, 5, p. 182.

[46] This was a common tactic used by the Romans and infantry forces throughout medieval Europe. Robert of Rhuddlan was killed by the Welsh after his shield had been brought down with the weight of the javelins hurled against it; OV, IV, 8, p. 141.

[47] See *Journey*, II, 5, p. 182; *Description*, I, 6, pp. 230–1. The use of spears in battle on Anglesey is described in *Journey*, II, 7, pp. 189–90. Gerald also mentions the use of spears in battle by the men of Gwent; ibid., I, 4, p. 111.

[48] *Gruffudd ap Cynan*, pp. 66–7.

and Gerald himself did not claim that it was only used in Gwynedd.[49]

The laws place a value of four pence on a spear (W. *gwayw*)[50] and state that the spear of a serjeant should be 'three ells' (six feet) in length, 'two behind him and one before'.[51] This gives an idea of the sort of weapon carried by an infantryman; a six-foot spear could be used in the sort of infantry shield wall discussed below.[52] The throwing spears used by infantry and cavalry were probably smaller and lighter.

The bow

The bow, like the spear, is a cheap, simple, easily produced and effective weapon and one that played a major role in combat throughout the period. Less metal is required for the tip of an arrow than for a spear and even sharpened wooden arrows could be effective.[53] The bow was used in ambushes, open combat, defensive positions and for attack or defence during a siege. The laws value an arrow at a farthing and a bow with twelve arrows at four pence.[54] Unlike the spear, there are few references to the use of bows in combat, and this is complicated by the fact that *saethu* ('to shoot') can refer to arrows or to the throwing of spears. This situation is reflected in other societies. The Merovingians did not list the bow as part of their military equipment, yet descriptions of their battles have references to 'hails of arrows'. The bow was too valuable to be ignored by medieval forces and was always used, but it was not considered an honourable weapon.[55] Its cheapness and availability meant that it was generally the weapon of the lower classes and there was resentment

---

[49] Gerald claims that the 3,000 Welshmen he inspired to take the Cross were all skilled with spear and bow; *Journey*, II, 13, p. 204.
[50] *Law*, p. 194.
[51] Ibid., p. 34.
[52] See below, pp. 177–86.
[53] Iron-tipped arrows were introduced by the Romans as the Britons had previously used bone or horn. *Saeth* ('arrow') comes from a Latin loan word; *HW*, I, p. 85.
[54] *Law*, pp. 193–4.
[55] J. Bradbury, *The Medieval Archer* (Woodbridge, 1985).

that they might be able to kill their social superiors, particularly as they could do so at a distance.[56]

Whilst Welsh nobles used the bow for hunting,[57] there are no references to them as archers in battle. *Brut (Pen. 20)* has a rare reference to the use of the bow in combat when Henry I was ambushed by a Welsh force.[58] A number of Henry's men were killed and wounded and the king himself was only saved when an arrow recoiled from his 'corselet and armour'. It is notable that the Welsh force was composed of 'young men' sent by Maredudd ap Bleddyn; there is no suggestion that Maredudd or any nobleman was present. The chronicler goes to some length to explain that the king was struck by accident, suggesting that it would not have been right for so great a man to have been killed in this way. There is a description of the idealized bows of a noble household in *Owein*. They are made of elephant ivory with strings of deer sinew and arrows with shafts of walrus ivory. Even so, it is stressed that these were the weapons of noble boys, not men, and they were probably intended for hunting or play rather than for combat.[59] All the general rules established for the use of the bow in medieval Europe would seem to be applicable in Wales.[60]

The distaste felt by nobles for low-class archers often manifested itself in their slaughter on the field of battle. Welsh archers suffered this treatment when serving on the Anglo-Norman scene. In 1116 we may see a reversal of roles. The Anglo-Normans in Aberystwyth Castle sent archers out to 'annoy' Gruffudd ap Rhys's force and to tempt the Welsh into a rash attack. Gruffudd's men were so amazed at the 'boldness' and

---

[56] In *The Battle of Maldon*, Byrhtnoth is depicted striking down all his enemies before finally being killed by a 'dart' fired from a distance, suggesting that he could not be beaten in a fair fight; D. C. Scragg (ed.), *The Battle of Maldon, AD 991* (Oxford, 1991), p. 25. In the poem the only named English noble to fire arrows was the Northumbrian Æscferth. He was a hostage in Byrhtnoth's warband, not trusted with the usual free weapons of spear and sword; N. Brooks, 'Weapons and armour', pp. 208–19.
[57] See *Law*, p. 186.
[58] *Brut (Pen. 20)*, s.a. 1121.
[59] *Mabinogi*, p. 194; *Owein*, p. 2.
[60] In *Rhigyfarch's Lament*, the bow is listed as the main weapon to be used in the fighting against the Normans, with the sword, spear and shield also named; Lapidge, 'Welsh', p. 91. All sources, Welsh and others, describe Magnus Barefoot using a bow in 1098 to kill Hugh of Montgomery at the battle of Anglesey Sound; this is an extremely rare example of a noble portrayed in a favourable light fighting with a bow.

EQUIPMENT AND TACTICAL DISPOSITIONS 153

audacity of the archers that they attacked 'imprudently' and were defeated.[61]

The best-known descriptions of Welsh bows are given by Gerald of Wales.[62] He noted the skill of the bowmen of Gwent, although he did not discount the use of the bow in other areas of the country.[63] It was once maintained that Welsh archery skills were learnt by the Anglo-Normans and that this helped them develop the successful longbow tactics which were so effective in the Hundred Years War. This theory cannot be sustained; the distinction drawn between the Welsh 'shortbow' and the later English 'longbow' is artificial, and Anglo-Norman armies already used the bow before they encountered the Welsh.[64] Gerald stated that the 'rough, unpolished' Welsh bows made from dwarf elm-trees were effective but aesthetically inferior to other bows known to him, made of horn, sapwood and yew.[65]

Gerald's accounts of the power of Welsh bows are famous. He said that the iron heads of their arrows penetrated the oak door of Abergavenny Castle 'which was almost as thick as a man's palm'.[66] On another occasion, an Anglo-Norman man-at-arms was said to have been shot through the leg, the arrow piercing his iron cuishes and leather tunic on both sides, passing through his saddle and killing his horse. Gerald said that a crossbow would not have been more effective, and that although the bows could not shoot far they were effective at close range and able to pierce armour.

---

[61] *Brut (Pen. 20)*, s.a. 1116.
[62] His descriptions of Welsh archers are generally favourable, but he tells of evil Anglo-Norman archers from St Clears coming to a bad end; *Journey*, I, 10, p. 140. Similar stories are contained in his Irish works.
[63] Peter Edbury noted the frequent use made of Welsh archers by the Anglo-Normans and Gerald's recruitment of them for the crusade. The only reference to a Welshman on the Third Crusade was in a context designed to show his skill as an archer; Edbury, 'Preaching', p. 231. Robert fitz Stephen's advance party taken to Ireland in 1170 contained 300 Welsh archers and many additional bowmen, presumably Welsh, followed later; *Conquest*, I, 3, p. 31.
[64] See, for example, *WW*, pp. 68–9.
[65] *Journey*, I, 4, p. 113.
[66] Ibid.

The crossbow

The crossbow is a more complex weapon than the bow, more difficult and expensive to produce, harder to master and slower to fire. Its advantage is its power and range, which surpasses that of the ordinary bow. In Wales, however, its disadvantages outweighed its advantages and it was little used. It is possible that the Normans introduced the crossbow to Britain, but its effect was limited.[67] There are few references to it in Wales, although it may have been used more frequently at sieges and in hunting. Carr has suggested that arrow loops at Castell y Bere and Cricieth could have been intended for crossbowmen and cited the example of a crossbowman retained by Llywelyn ap Iorwerth.[68]

The sling

The sling is one of the simplest missile weapons known to humankind, easy to produce and use and only needing a stone for ammunition. Its lack of sophistication did not undermine its effectiveness and certainly in Ireland its use continued into the Anglo-Norman period. We have little evidence to suggest the use of the sling in Wales, but it is probable that its military potential was exploited.

The axe

The axe was a common tool and its military potential is obvious; whenever it was used as a weapon, it was formidable.[69] In Wales it was not the usual weapon of choice, but on occasion it was used in war. Possible Viking influence should be considered, and the fact that its production required less metal and work than did a sword. The most common sort of axe in Wales was the work axe,

---

[67] Norman crossbowmen (W. *albryswyr*) were on Caradog ap Gruffudd's (losing) side at Mynydd Carn; *Gruffudd ap Cynan*, p. 66.
[68] Carr, '*Teulu* and *penteulu*', 71.
[69] See, for example, its use by Stephen at Lincoln in 1141; OV, VI, 13, p. 545; HH, X, 18, pp. 737–9; *GS*, p. 113.

used by bondmen and peasants in their day-to-day lives. In the law texts, bondmen were required to bring axes to make the king's camp on his hostings, and a broad axe is valued at four pence, a fuel axe at two pence and a small axe at one penny.[70] There was nothing to stop such tools being turned to military purposes, but there is a suggestion that they were not regarded as honourable weapons; in the *Triads*, the 'Three Unfortunate Assassinations' were carried out with blows from wood hatchets.[71]

The laws value a battle axe at two pence.[72] It was not a standard weapon, but there was no shame attached to its use; amongst Culhwch's equipment when he left for Arthur's court was a battle axe, 'the length of a full-grown man's forearm from ridge to edge'.[73] In the *Gododdin*, there is a reference to axe-blows (W. *bwyellodan*), although this is greatly outnumbered by references to other weapons.[74] The axe was a weapon associated with outsiders, notably the Hiberno-Scandinavians. Given his links with Ireland, it is notable that Gruffudd ap Cynan is the only Welsh leader clearly described fighting with an axe; at Aberlleiniog he 'leaped forward in the front troop to cut down the mailed and helmeted French with his double-edged axe'.[75] At Mynydd Carn it was Gruffudd's 'men of Denmark' who fought with 'two-edged axes'[76] and in the *Life of St Gwynllyw* Gruffudd's Hiberno-Scandinavian 'pirates' fought with 'battle axes and spears'.[77]

The knife

Knives were almost universally owned by men in the Middle Ages. They had many uses and their military role is unlikely to

---

[70] *Law*, pp. 41, 125, 192.
[71] *Triads*, p. 71. However, in *Culhwch and Olwen*, 'Caw of Scotland' (notably a foreigner) killed 'Chief Boar Ysgithyrwyn' from horseback with a small axe or hatchet (W. *bwyellig*) and there was glory rather than shame attached to this deed; *Mabinogi*, p. 169; *CaO*, p. 36.
[72] *Law*, p. 194.
[73] The word used for battle axe, *gleif*, was a rare French borrowing; *CaO*, pp. 53–4. In *Brut (Pen. 20)*, s.a. 1205, Maelgwn ap Rhys got an Irishman 'treacherously and unjustly' to kill Cedifor ap Gruffudd and his four sons with a battle axe; shame was attached to this deed, but not to the particular choice of weapon.
[74] *Gododdin*, p. 52.
[75] *Gruffudd ap Cynan*, p. 72.
[76] Ibid., pp. 66–7.
[77] *Vitae*, p. 185.

have been the primary one. In the laws a draw-knife is valued at half a penny, a hook-knife and a larder knife at one penny, and a dagger at two pence.[78] The knife as a weapon was considered underhand because it could be easily concealed; Welsh sources long nurtured a hatred of the Anglo-Saxons for the treachery of the 'night of the long knives'.[79] It was seen as the weapon of the lower classes, and in Anglo-Norman sources distaste is expressed at Welsh foragers who would scour a battlefield and kill fallen, helpless nobles with their knives. The *Gesta Stephani* records that King Stephen did not wish to expose his knights to the Welsh and the men of Bristol in Robert of Gloucester's army, 'a mass of cut-throats on foot'.[80] Despite this, a knife could be part of the accepted equipment of a noble warrior. In the *Gododdin*, Heinif ap Nwython armed for battle with 'spear, shield, sword and knife'.[81] Llywarch Hen's son Maen Wyn is urged not to leave his knife behind as he departs for battle,[82] and in *Culhwch and Olwen* Arthur's knife, given the name Carnwennian, is one of the few things which he refuses to grant to Culhwch.[83] In the tale Arthur kills a witch by throwing his knife at her and in *Peredur* two boys practise throwing knives.[84]

The shield

The shield was the key defensive weapon of the Middle Ages and was always carried by warriors. There are repeated references to the use of the shield in Wales. The hunting scene on the tenth-century Conbelin stone (now at Margam) depicts cavalry carrying small round shields; as shields are redundant in hunting, they can only have been for the riders to practise their balance for warfare.[85] For a warrior to be described as the 'shield of the land' was a great honour.[86] Shields were small and round so that

[78] *Law*, pp. 192, 195.
[79] See *HB*, p. 32.
[80] *GS*, p. 171. Walter Map depicts Gruffudd ap Llywelyn using a knife to slay a relative or rival treacherously; *Map*, p. 193. See also ibid., p. 203.
[81] *Gododdin*, p. 62.
[82] *Saga*, p. 472.
[83] *Mabinogi*, p. 140; *CaO*, p. 6.
[84] *Mabinogi*, pp. 175, 236; *CaO*, p. 42.
[85] J. Rowland, 'Warfare', 23.
[86] *Saga*, p. 478.

soldiers found them easy to handle in a fight. They were large enough, however, to use as part of a shield wall.[87] They were made of wood, oak proving a popular material, although some metal was required for the central boss and possibly for the edge.[88] They were sometimes covered in leather. The Anglo-Saxons had pointed metal bosses in the centre of their shields which covered the hole for the handle and could be used as an offensive weapon and it seems likely that Welsh shields were similar. In the panegyric material, one of the greatest praises of a warrior was to state that he returned with a broken or shattered shield, a sign that he had fought ferociously, or, indeed, that he shattered the shields of many enemies. These references and numerous others to pierced shields may indicate that the shields were thin, thereby keeping them light and manoeuvrable. Shields could be decorated, thereby increasing their value and the prestige reflected on the owner. The laws value a shield at eight pence, and at twenty-four pence if it has gold or blue enamel.[89] In *Culhwch and Olwen*, Arthur has a named shield and Culhwch's is described as a 'gold-chased buckler with ivory boss'.[90] Gruffudd ap Cynan is praised as 'the golden shielded one'.[91]

CAVALRY

Views have arisen about the Welsh use of horses in war as a result of assumptions about the Norman conquest of England. The idea remains strong that this conquest was achieved because the Normans brought to England the tactic of fighting from horseback and that at Hastings they were able to defeat the Anglo-Saxons who still relied on their infantry. The works of Smail, France and others have challenged the theory of the dominance of the cavalry charge with couched lance.[92] The

---

[87] See below, pp. 177–86.
[88] In *Taliesin and Ugnach* the fine equipment of the warrior who has gold on his shield boss is praised; *Saga*, p. 508.
[89] *Law*, p. 194. These high prices suggest that significant amounts of metal were used for the boss and edging.
[90] *Mabinogi*, pp. 137, 140; *CaO*, pp. 3, 6. At the battle of Guinnion Fort, Arthur's shield carried the image of the Virgin; *HB*, p. 35.
[91] Meilyr, p. 184.
[92] See below, pp. 89–90.

development of the heavily armoured knight was a gradual process that was not complete by 1066, and at no point was the charge with couched lance an invincible tactic. Bradbury's examination of Anglo-Norman battles from Hastings to Lincoln (1141) concluded that they were all won by tactics involving mixed forces, dismounted knights to stiffen the infantry, reserve cavalry and archers.[93] Such tactics were not new; they had been used in previous centuries and would be used in later ones.

There is dispute as to whether the Anglo-Saxons fought from horseback before 1066. They used horses for supply and to transport men to battle, but many writers believe that they always dismounted to fight their battles. Others have argued against this, stating that the Anglo-Saxons fought from horseback when the occasion warranted.[94] However, the consensus of opinion favours the belief that they were *capable* of fighting from a horse but, unlike the Normans, that they did not have specific cavalry tactics and could not perform a close-order charge.[95]

The thesis on the influence of the Normans on Anglo-Saxon tactics has been extended to explain how the Welsh began to master the horse for military purposes in the late eleventh and twelfth centuries. Support has been found in the works of Gerald of Wales: 'the Welsh have gradually learnt from the English and the Normans how to manage their weapons and to use horses in battle, for they have frequented the court and been sent to England as hostages'.[96] Furthermore:

> Their leaders ride into battle on swift mettlesome horses which are bred locally. Most of the common people prefer to fight on foot in view of the marshy, uneven terrain. The horsemen will often dismount, as circumstances and occasion demand, ready to flee or to attack.[97]

These views have been developed by modern commentators: 'By the end of the twelfth century the upper classes [in Wales] had learned to fight on horseback in the Norman style but even then, whenever the situation warranted, they dismounted and fought

---

[93] Bradbury, 'Battles', pp. 182–93; see also *WW*, pp. 150–86.
[94] See, for example, R. H. C. Davis, *The Medieval Warhorse* (London, 1989), p. 76.
[95] Hooper, 'Anglo-Saxons', p. 199.
[96] *Description*, II, 7, p. 267.
[97] Ibid., I, 8, p. 234.

on foot with the general levy.'[98] Such readiness to dismount to fight when circumstances warranted was common in many theatres of war. Moreover, the belief that the Welsh learnt from the Normans how to fight from horseback can be disproved; from the earliest times there was a tradition of horsemanship, and even if it is held that the Anglo-Saxons learnt cavalry warfare from the Normans this does not necessarily affect the argument for Wales.

The horse was an important cultural symbol in pre-Roman Britain and there was a tradition of fighting from horseback. The Celts from the Iron Age, and their descendants throughout the Romano-Celtic period, worshipped horses, linked them to their gods and saw them as crucial to hunting, warfare and nobility.[99] Their importance is seen in the abundance of equine terms found in the insular Celtic languages.[100] Julius Caesar was impressed by the cavalry of the Britons and after the conquest native units served in the Roman army.[101] The Vindolanda Tablet 85/32 says that the Britons had 'very many cavalry. The cavalry do not use swords nor do the wretched Britons take up fixed positions in order to throw javelins.' The Romans added new blood-lines and breeding techniques to improve the native equine stock.[102] In Wales itself, a cavalry regiment of 500 Spanish Vettonians was based at Brecon from about AD 100.[103] In the west of the Roman Empire, light, manoeuvrable cavalry was the norm. Similar cavalry forces were typical in post-Roman Europe and the tactics can be seen in action in early medieval Britain.

The breakdown in order in Britain following the departure of the Romans would have disrupted stud farms and breeding programmes.[104] However, the decline in Britain should not be

---

[98] Beeler, *Warfare*, p. 167; see also Nelson, *Normans*, p. 115; R. R. Davies, *Age*, p. 104; also his *Domination*, pp. 39–40.
[99] M. A. Green, 'The symbolic horse in pagan Celtic Europe: an archaeological perspective', in *Horse*, pp. 1–22.
[100] P. Kelly, 'The earliest words for 'horse' in the Celtic languages', in *Horse*, pp. 43–63.
[101] See J. Rowland, 'Warfare', 22–3; also J. Ryan, 'A study of horses in early and medieval Welsh literature, c.600–1300' (unpublished M.Phil. thesis, University of Wales, Cardiff, 1993), 7–15.
[102] A. Hyland, *The Medieval Warhorse from Byzantium to the Crusades* (Stroud, 1994), p. 67.
[103] V. E. Nash-Williams, *The Roman Frontier in Wales* (Cardiff, 1954), p. 108.
[104] See Davis, *Warhorse*, pp. 8, 34.

exaggerated, and even native British ponies were large, strong and hardy.[105] Though unsuitable for use as heavy cavalry, such horses were appropriate for the tactics employed and could carry a lightly armoured man. The possibility that the Brittonic nobility continued to possess superior, bred horses is suggested by Taliesin's poem on the battle of Gwen Ystrad. Urien's Pictish enemies are mocked as they retreat because the 'waves washed the tails of their horses'. The word used for horse is *kaffon*, an unusual, disparaging description for their small, pony-like horses that stand comparison with the fine steeds of the Britons.[106]

The *Gododdin* supports this theory; whilst the horses described were small, there are references to stalling and grain feeding. Steeds are given different values and the war horses were trained for battle.[107] A ninth-century Welsh poem echoes the *Gododdin* in referring to horses 'nurtured with grain' and 'growing sturdy on grain'.[108] The Welsh laws deal at length with the differing values to be placed on horses. A section on the 'Values of wild and tame' indicates the presence of trained horses in Wales, and whilst the later texts use the word *gre* to refer to a stud, the *Triads* have the ancient word *allwest*; there was a long tradition of horse breeding.[109] The *Triads* refer to Meinlas, the horse of Caswallawn ap Beli, a steed given to Caswallawn by the Romans in return for permission to land in Britain.[110] The story cannot be accepted as historical, but it suggests the value placed on a horse by the contemporary audience. In *Branwen*, large numbers of 'tamed horses' were given to the Irish after their own steeds had been mutilated by Efnisien, although the full quota had to be made up with young, unbroken colts from the next commote.[111] This incident may relate to the trade of horses from Wales to

[105] Hyland, *Medieval*, p. 69; see also I. Hughson, 'Horses in the early historic period: evidence from the Pictish sculptured stones', in *Horse*, pp. 23–42.

[106] Kelly, 'Earliest', p. 48. The earliest attested use of *ceffyl* (the standard word for horse in modern Welsh) comes in the *Mabinogi*, where Peredur arrives at Arthur's court as a rustic youth on a farm horse. He is mocked by the great *marchogyon* of Arthur's *teulu*. In Irish a nag or work horse is known as a *capall*; ibid., p. 48.

[107] See N. A. Jones, 'The horses of the Gododdin', *Pictish Arts Journal*, 4 (1993), 8–9.

[108] *Saga*, p. 505; see also Ryan, 'Study', 97–9. Jenkins suggested that a reference in the *Triads* denying a villein the right to sell a destrier without his lord's permission indicates that the villein was expected to tend the horse on his low-lying ground, which was better suited to the growing of suitable fodder than the elevated residences where the nobility held their courts; D. Jenkins, 'The horse in the Welsh law texts', in *Horse*, pp. 64–81.

[109] Jenkins, 'Horse', p. 77.

[110] R. Bromwich, 'The triads of the horses', in *Horse*, pp. 102–20.

[111] *Mabinogi*, pp. 70–1; *PK*, pp. 33–4.

EQUIPMENT AND TACTICAL DISPOSITIONS

Ireland in the early Middle Ages;[112] Welsh steeds were regarded as superior to Irish horses.

The mobility of early campaigns between the Britons and Anglo-Saxons has been noted and this suggests that the forces were mounted. It does not prove that they engaged as cavalry, but it seems likely that British forces were capable of fighting from horseback. Taliesin's poem, *The Warband's Return*, suggests this:

ei pawb oe wyt	dyfynt ymplymnwyt.
Ae varch ydanaw	yg godeu gweith mynaw.
a chwanec anaw	bud am li am law.[113]
Each went on campaign,	eager in combat,
his steed beneath him,	set to raid Manaw
for the sake of wealth,	profit in plenty.[114]

In post-Roman Gaul, Clovis enjoyed success thanks to his 'heterogeneous' military force composed of infantry and cavalry that could undertake 'flexible, professional and effective' tactics.[115] In Britain forces were equally flexible. Cavalry could make sweeping attacks on enemies, throwing javelins, slashing with swords and possibly even shooting from bows and slings. The shock charge with couched lance was not a tactic at this time, but there are indications of cavalry charges against infantry lines. Possibly the most valuable source on the tactics of the Britons in this period is the *Gododdin*.[116] The battle-horsemen (W. *cadfarchog*) are intended as the heroes of the poem:

---

[112] Sioned Davies, 'Horses in the Mabinogion', in *Horse*, pp. 121–40.
[113] *CT*, V, p. 5.
[114] *Earliest*, p. 27.
[115] Bachrach, *Merovingian*, pp. 15–17.
[116] Higham criticized the idea of the British use of horses in battle, dismissing the *Gododdin* as an unreliable text. Cessford, Hooper and Rowland responded to Higham's argument and effectively rebutted his conclusions. See N. J. Higham, 'Cavalry in early Bernicia?', *Northern History*, 27 (1991), 236–41; C. Cessford, 'Cavalry in early Bernicia: a reply', *Northern History*, 29 (1993), 185–7; N. Hooper, 'The Aberlemno stone and cavalry in Anglo-Saxon England', *Northern History*, 29 (1993), 188–96; J. Rowland, 'Warfare', 13–40.

> Thou didst not see the surging fury of the horsemen:
> They slew, they gave no quarter to the Saxons . . .
> It was usual on a spirited horse to defend Gododdin . . .
> Long-striding horses galloped
> beneath the thighs of noble warriors,
> swift as the movement of the wild men
> over the grassy plain.[117]

The hurling of spears and javelins from horseback is described:

> No one's horses overtook Marchlew.
> He cast spears in battle
> from a bounding, wide-tracked charger.
> Although his rearing was not with burdens, with suffering,
> his sword-stroke was fierce in his battle-station.
> He threw spears from the grasp of his hand
> from his steaming slender bay horse.[118]

Riders were offered stability by their saddle and from their experience on horseback. Stirrups were not used, and were not essential; horsemen used spears, swords, javelins and bows 'as effectively without stirrups as later riders did with stirrups'.[119] To wheel quickly on an enemy force and hurl spears was a common Roman tactic. Such manoeuvres were effective, particularly against infantry who were at a physical and psychological disadvantage. The poetry of the period praised speed in a horse, the crucial element in such tactics.[120] Other peoples of the day employed similar methods. The third carving on the Aberlemno stone depicts King Ecgfrith of Northumbria opposing a Pictish cavalryman and both appear to be preparing to hurl spears;[121] Bede described the Northumbrian priest Coifi casting a spear from horseback.[122] The tactic was common elsewhere in Europe in the early Middle Ages: amongst the Bretons, with the Gascons and possibly with the continental Saxons.[123] The equipment of

---

[117] *Gododdin*, pp. 36, 64, 72.
[118] Ibid., p. 20; see also pp. 28, 60.
[119] Hughson, 'Horse', p. 37; see also Ryan, 'Study,' 15–16.
[120] Ryan, 'Study', 88–90.
[121] For a picture of the Aberlemno stone, see Hughson, 'Horse', p. 36.
[122] Bede, II, 13, p. 185.
[123] Hooper, 'Aberlemno', 188–96.

EQUIPMENT AND TACTICAL DISPOSITIONS

the cavalry in the *Gododdin* accords well with that used by the Romans and by cavalry throughout early medieval Europe:[124] long, slashing swords and a variety of spears. The *Gododdin* has over fifteen terms for spear; the diversity indicates that there were throwing spears and others more suited to stabbing or charging with spear in hand.

The *Gododdin* describes warriors slashing with their swords from horseback:

> With sharpened blade he struck,
> he slew both Athrwys and Affrai . . .
> In the forefront of the men of Gwynedd he charged.[125]

One lord, Marchlew, was depicted casting his spears from horseback, and when these were spent he turned to his sword:

> The most lovable one distributed his plentiful wine,
> he slew with a blade, blood-stained and savage,
> as a reaper strikes in unsettled weather
> so Marchlew would cause blood to flow.[126]

Apart from praise poetry, spears were more common than swords as the in-hand weapon and they, too, are described in the *Gododdin*. Eithinyn is presented as 'a spear-thrusting lord, laughing in war'.[127] The tenth–eleventh-century poem *Gwyn ap Nudd* describes a horseman:

> I come from battle and great hewing
> with shields in hand
> spear blows shattered heads.[128]

The question of whether British cavalry could hold a spear rigid to charge an enemy line is more problematic. Such tactics were used occasionally by the Romans, although the spear was held in

---

[124] J. Rowland, 'Warfare', 24–5.
[125] *Gododdin*, p. 16.
[126] Ibid., p. 20.
[127] Ibid., p. 28.
[128] *Saga*, p. 406. *Culhwch and Olwen* supports the literary reputation of Gwyn ap Nudd as a famous horseman. One of the tasks set for Culhwch was to procure for Gwyn Du, the horse of 'Moro Battle Leader'; *Mabinogi*, pp. 159–60; *CaO*, pp. 26–7.

both hands rather than being couched as in the later Middle Ages.[129] This did not make for the most effective use of cavalry; it was most potent against other cavalry units. A disciplined infantry line could hold the charge of cavalry which lacked the stability offered by the stirrup and the force offered by powerful horses, heavy armour and specialized lances.

Passages in the *Gododdin* suggest cavalry charges against organized infantry lines:

> Warriors went to Catraeth, embattled, with a cry,
> a host of horsemen in dark-blue armour, with shields,
> spear-shafts held aloft with sharp points,
> and shining mail-shirts and swords.
> He took the lead, he cut his way through armies,
> five fifties fell before his blades.[130]

Cynon is described leading a successful charge:

> Sharp-pointed were his spears,
> with shattered shield he tore through armies,
> his horses swift, racing forward
> in the day of battle his blades spelt destruction,
> when Cynon charged with the green dawn.[131]

There is a reference to the couching of a spear, suggesting that, when the others had been thrown, one was kept to hand:

> Couching his best spear before he was laid low . . .
> The possessor of horses and dark-blue armour and icy-hued shields
> with comrades fighting side by side, retreating, attacking.[132]

Traditions preserved in the *Historia Brittonum* express the belief that the battle of Badon was decided by a British charge that blew enemy resistance away: 'The twelfth battle was at Badon Hill and in it 916 men fell in one day from a single charge of

---

[129] J. Rowland, 'Warfare', 24–5.
[130] *Gododdin*, p. 24.
[131] Ibid., p. 26; see also p. 16.
[132] Ibid., p. 46.

Arthur's.'¹³³ The triad concerning the 'Three Bestowed Horses' includes Caradawg Strong Arm's horse Host Splitter (W. *Lluagor*); Bromwich has argued for the antiquity of this name.¹³⁴ *Geraint fab Erbin* describes the battle of Llongborth in Dumnonia:

> Before Geraint, the driver of the enemy,
> I saw bowed, bloodstained horses because of battle . . .
> In Llongborth I saw battle-fury,
> and uncountable biers,
> and bloodstained warriors because of the rush of Geraint.¹³⁵

Similar lines are repeated again and again and the structure of the poem seems designed to echo the fury of a cavalry charge. *Gwyn ap Nudd* gives a similar message:

> Gwyn ap Nudd, benefit of hosts, armies
> would fall before the hooves of your horse
> more quickly than severed reeds to the ground.¹³⁶

In the history of warfare, warriors able to fire a bow from horseback have proved formidable opponents. Such forces are able to wheel and circle opposing troops, subjecting them to fire whilst staying out of range. The Roman army had mounted units specializing in the use of slings and bows, but there is no evidence for their presence in Britain.¹³⁷ Our sources are reluctant to describe the use of the bow in battle,¹³⁸ but as far as we can tell the use of mounted archers does not seem to have been a common British or Welsh tactic. Spears were used as missiles against the enemy, and in confined and mountainous terrain mounted archers were not so influential; they were always most effective when deployed in large numbers on open plains. However, it would be wrong to state conclusively that the British and Welsh had no mounted archers. Hunting was the much-practised sport of the nobility and the ability to fire an

---

¹³³ *HB*, p. 35.
¹³⁴ Bromwich, 'Triads', pp. 113–14.
¹³⁵ *Saga*, p. 504.
¹³⁶ Ibid., p. 506.
¹³⁷ J. Rowland, 'Warfare', 24.
¹³⁸ See above, pp. 151–2.

arrow from the saddle would have been an invaluable skill. The Welsh laws refer to the hunting of deer with bow and arrow.[139]

The Welsh may have been capable of other skilled cavalry tactics, hidden from us by lack of evidence and the concentration of our panegyric material on bold assaults. It is often alleged that references to feigned flights by cavalry in the Middle Ages are actually descriptions of genuine retreats. A feigned flight requires each member of a cavalry troop to have knowledge of, and confidence in, his fellows. The military households of the day provided such intimate understanding. There are descriptions of feigned flights on the continent in this period, and in 684 Bede describes such a manoeuvre successfully performed by the Picts.[140]

The importance of horses in the *Gododdin* is reflected elsewhere. The Welsh laws record the entitlement of each of the twenty-four officers of court to possess a horse. The original court complement was twelve officers, one of whom, the 'groom of the rein', had to attend the king and his horse (other officers presumably tended their own horses). Later, as the powers of the king and the size of his retinue grew, the office of 'chief groom' was created and other grooms cared for the court horses.[141] The fact that these were quality horses is shown by special provisions in the law for their feeding.[142] The wealth of legal material stands in contrast to Irish and Germanic law codes of the period; Irish law has few references to horses and one of these concerns their importing from Wales.[143] Further laws regard differing prices for ornamented and adorned saddles and stirrups, and the values placed on girths, cloths, bridles and gilts.[144]

Literature reveals how closely the horse was connected with nobility and how, indeed, descriptions of the horse are designed to reflect the nobility of the rider.[145] The association between horses and nobility is clear in the tenth-century poetry of the *Canu Heledd* saga. Heledd mourns the fact that the horses and land of her brothers have passed to the Saxons:

[139] *Laws*, p. 186.
[140] Bede, IV, 26, p. 429.
[141] Jenkins, 'Horse', pp. 64–81.
[142] Ibid., p. 72.
[143] Ibid., p. 64.
[144] Ryan, 'Study', 37–8.
[145] Ibid., p. 83.

EQUIPMENT AND TACTICAL DISPOSITIONS

> I am called wandering Heledd.
> Oh God, to whom are given
> my brothers' horses and their land?
>
> Wandering Heledd greets me. Oh God,
> to whom are given the dark trappings
> of Cynddylan and his fourteen steeds?[146]

The *Mabinogi* further indicate the intimate links between horses and the nobility. The horse's role is to reflect the noble qualities of the hero. In *Culhwch and Olwen* the horse helps Culhwch cut a fabulous appearance on his way to Arthur's court; 'no details are given regarding Culhwch's own physical appearance – everything is implied through his trappings, his weapons, his dogs, and of course his horse'.[147] In *Math*, the noble hero Lleu is appropriately raised 'until he could ride every horse'.[148] In *Pwyll*, Teirnon Twrvliant, lord of Gwent Is Coed, is notable because he possesses 'the most handsome horse in the realm' and his fame makes him a suitable foster-father for Pwyll's son Pryderi.[149] Later in the tale, Pryderi is given the colt of this prized horse and arms to mark his ascension to manhood. In *Branwen*, the mutilation of the horses of the Irish nobility is the reason for war between Britain and Ireland;[150] insults of this kind are apparent in the literature of other cultures.[151] Jenkins noted the large compensation required in Welsh law if a horse's tail were cut, reflecting the insult of the deed, the destruction of the noble image and the symbolic sign of impotence.[152] The *Triads* deal with 'Three Battle-Horsemen of the Island of Britain', reflecting the use of steeds in war,[153] and a large section of the entire body of the *Triads* deals exclusively with horses.[154] High status is accorded to the mounts of the heroes of the *Triads*, with personal

---

[146] *Saga*, p. 490.
[147] Sioned Davies, 'Horses', p. 130.
[148] *Mabinogi*, p. 109; *PK*, p. 81.
[149] *Mabinogi*, p. 61; *PK*, p. 22.
[150] *Mabinogi*, pp. 69–70; *PK*, pp. 31–3.
[151] Sioned Davies, 'Horses', p. 135; in Wales a similar attack is said to occur on the horses of St Cadog by a disrespectful *dux*; *Vitae*, p. 59.
[152] Jenkins, 'Horse', pp. 73–5.
[153] *Triads*, p. 31.
[154] Ibid., pp. 97–121.

names bestowed upon them, as in *Culhwch and Olwen*.[155] On occasions the horses are treated as heroes and discussed in the same way as their masters.[156]

Hunting was often pursued from horseback and required much the same skills as mounted combat. Mounted and unmounted hunting is described in the *Mabinogi*, both in the earlier tales and the later romances:[157] in *Culhwch and Olwen*, Caw of Scotland killed the boar Ysgwithyrwyn from horseback with a blow from a *bwyellic*, a small axe or hatchet;[158] Culhwch procured the horse of Gweddw for Mabon ap Modron to ride whilst hunting;[159] the pursuit of the Twrch Trwyth is conducted from horseback;[160] in *Pwyll*, both Pwyll and Arawn hunt from their horses.[161] The tenth-century Conbelin stone depicts a hunting scene in which the horsemen carry small round shields. Shields are not needed for hunting and Rowland suggested that they were carried so that riders could practise for war.[162] Hunting was the 'classic high-status activity, rarely, if ever, undertaken to provide food'.[163] There were easier ways to trap game, but hunting gave the chance to practise and display martial qualities, boldness, daring, horsemanship, expertise with spear and bow, and a fine horse and gear.

Horses were prized as the booty of war; in *Marwnad Cynddylan*, lords are praised for an expedition in which eighty horses were amongst the booty;[164] the *Triads* make reference to the 'Three Plundered Horses of the Island of Britain';[165] Walter Map relates the tale of an expedition undertaken by a Welshman to steal a heavily defended mare from the *llys* of a rival lord at Gelligaer in Senghennydd.[166] In 1109 a plundering raid of Owain ap Cadwgan and Madog ap Rhiddid 'burned the homestead of a leading man. And whatever they could plunder, they did,

---

[155] Bromwich, 'Triads', p. 103.
[156] Ibid., p. 117.
[157] Ryan, 'Study', 176–7.
[158] *Mabinogi*, p. 169; *CaO*, p. 36.
[159] *Mabinogi*, p. 158; *CaO*, pp. 25–6.
[160] *Mabinogi*, pp. 170–5; *CaO*, pp. 37–41.
[161] *Mabinogi*, p. 47; *PK*, pp. 1–2.
[162] J. Rowland, 'Warfare', 23.
[163] Hughson, 'Horse', p. 35.
[164] *Saga*, p. 177.
[165] *Triads*, p. 101.
[166] Map, pp. 199–201.

whether horses or raiment or aught else.'[167] Horses given as a gift were received with honour. In the *Mabinogi*, Pwyll and Arawn sealed their friendship by sending presents of 'horses, hounds, hawks and other treasures'.[168]

Apart from their use as cavalry, horses served other military purposes. In the laws, villeins were required to bring pack-horses to help in the building of a king's fortifications.[169] Such horses are likely to have been used to carry the supplies of a mobile fighting force. The *Triads* mention the 'Three Pack Horses of the Island of Britain',[170] and also 'Three Horses Who Carried the Three Horse Burdens';[171] the latter refers to horses bearing forces to battles at Arfderydd and at Pendinas in Ceredigion.

The use of horses by the Welsh military throughout the early Middle Ages is clear. As the Norman era approached, two eleventh-century chronicle references confirm the presence of mounted troops in Wales before 1066. Anglo-Saxon sources sought to blame their defeat at the hands of Gruffudd ap Llywelyn in 1055 on the Norman Earl Ralf. According to John of Worcester,

> He [Ralf] ordered the English, contrary to custom, to fight on horseback, but when they were about to join battle, the earl with his French and Normans was the first to take flight. The English, seeing this, followed their commander in flight. Almost the whole of the enemy army pursued them, and slew 400–500 of them and wounded many.[172]

This passage has been used to show that the Anglo-Saxons never fought from horseback and that their defeat came because they were forced to fight against their custom. This can be disputed, but for the present purpose it is enough to state that this mounted Anglo-Saxon force fled. They were successfully pursued by 'almost the whole' of Gruffudd's force which, it follows, must have been mounted, or at least able quickly to remount

---

[167] *Brut (Pen. 20)*, s.a. 1109.
[168] *Mabinogi*, p. 51; *PK*, p. 8.
[169] *Law*, p. 41.
[170] *Triads*, p. 107.
[171] Ibid., p. 109.
[172] JW, II, 1055.

horses after the battle. This would also explain the fact that Gruffudd's men were able to rush through the gates of Hereford in the post-battle chaos before a defence of the town could be made; the battlefield was several miles west of the town. The Anglo-Saxons struck back in 1063 when both Harold and Tostig led mounted troops against Gruffudd.[173] On the eve of the coming of the Normans the sight of mounted military men throughout Wales was by no means unusual.

The comparable social structures that existed in Wales and France are revealed by the selection of Welsh words used for the rank of squire or valet, the attendants of the knights; *gwas*, *gwas ystafell* and *daryanogyon* were the men who attended the Welsh *uchelwyr* and *marchogyon*. These are native words, not French borrowings, reflecting a social system that existed before the coming of the Normans. Welsh seals start to appear in the Norman period and show mounted native lords; whilst the seals themselves are borrowings from the Normans, they reveal how easily Welsh lordship could adopt such iconography. The same intimate association between rider, horse and nobility may be seen in the carved figure of a horseman on the late tenth–early eleventh-century cross at St Dochdwy's churchyard, Llandough, Glamorgan.

The impact of knighthood in a military sense can also be disputed. The Welsh fought from horseback before 1066 and the military influence made by the heavy cavalry charge with couched lance was minimal; there are no recorded instances in Wales in the period 1066–1282 when such a tactic had a decisive influence on an engagement. As the Welsh already had their own word for squire or valet, so they already had their own word for knight, *marchog*. In the later literature of Wales, *marchog* took on all the connotations of knight seen in the chivalric literature of later medieval Europe, but before the coming of the Normans it described the mounted warrior nobility of Wales. Welsh terminology was able to interpret the knighthood brought by the Normans and there is little to suggest shock at the sight of these mounted warriors, or that they brought revolutionary new tactics.

---

[173] Ibid., 1063.

EQUIPMENT AND TACTICAL DISPOSITIONS

In Meilyr's elegy to Gruffudd ap Cynan, Gruffudd is described fighting with 1,000 *marchog* and the existence of horse-breeding programmes in Gwynedd is suggested:

> Owner of a glorious line of horses from the long-maned stud, leader of the Welsh, audacious *marchog*.[174]

Another line suggests the use of pack-horses: 'Ambling steeds bore his armour.'[175] The description of the battle of Mynydd Carn in *Gruffudd ap Cynan* relates that 'the earth resounded with the tumult of horses and footsoldiers' and states that at least twenty-five *marchog* from Trahaearn's *teulu* were killed.[176]

That the Welsh maintained horse-breeding programmes to produce war horses is suggested by the *Brutiau* in 1109. A force sent by Henry I ravaged the lands of Cadwgan ap Bleddyn, but he had moved his valuables; consequently 'they foraged about and obtained nothing save Cadwgan's stud'.[177] Lowland Powys is suited to the raising of quality horses; according to Gerald of Wales:

> There are some excellent stud-farms. A superb race of blood-stock is now bred there, tracing its descent from the Spanish horses which Robert de Bellême, Earl of Shrewsbury, had gone to some pains to have imported long ago. The horses which are sent out from Powys are greatly prized: they are extremely handsome and nature reproduces in them the same majestic proportions and incomparable speed.[178]

This passage is often cited in support of the idea that the Normans introduced the war horse to Wales. Robert was earl of Shrewsbury from 1098 to 1102; he is unlikely to have had time to oversee the establishment of new stud farms in Powys. This suggests that the earl introduced a new blood-line to improve the studs already in the area. The tradition of breeding horses in Wales continued, as reflected in references in the *Gogynfeirdd* poetry to studs, breeding and trained stallions. In 1171, Rhys ap Gruffudd promised Henry II 300 horses as part of a peace

---

[174] Meilyr, p. 184.
[175] Ibid.
[176] *Gruffudd ap Cynan*, p. 68.
[177] *Brut (Pen. 20)*, s.a. 1109.
[178] *Journey*, II, 12, p. 201.

treaty.[179] In 1211, part of the tribute imposed by King John on Llywelyn ap Iorwerth was forty horses.[180] The discrepancy in the numbers of horses offered in these two tributes may reflect differences between horse breeding in north and south Wales; Ryan suggested that the greater number of references to horses in the southern tales of the *Mabinogi* as opposed to the northern ones may be explained by the topography in the south being better suited to the breeding and use of the horse.[181]

The Normans influenced horse breeding in Wales. Their expertise and their possession of fine studs made their mark on every country with which the Normans came in contact. Jenkins traced their impact through the thirteenth-century texts of the tenth-century Welsh laws; there are many names of French origin used for specific types of horses.[182] Whilst common horses retain Welsh names, more highly regarded steeds have foreign titles. The influences were not simply Norman, however, as there were repeated influxes of new blood-lines throughout the ages. The introduction of new breeds is reflected in poetry. Cynddelw Brydydd Mawr described Madog ap Maredudd as a 'companion of Gascon horses' and Llywarch ap Llywelyn says that Llywelyn ap Iorwerth had Gascon horses.[183] That such blood-lines improved native stocks is suggested by the reputation which Welsh destriers held outside the country and by the increasing legal value which was placed on stallions.[184]

In relation to the battle tactics employed by the Welsh in the eleventh century and beyond, there were flexible options available that mirror the skills seen in the *Gododdin*. The idea of a cavalry charge directed against an enemy line is suggested in Meilyr's elegy to Gruffudd ap Cynan:

> Medrawd's peer in the forefront of the army used to make a breach
> like the honourable Urien and/with his onslaught.[185]

---

[179] *Brut (Pen. 20)*, s.a. 1171.
[180] Ibid., s.a. 1211.
[181] Ryan, 'Study', 191. It should be noted that Rhys ap Gruffudd never gave, or was expected to give, 300 horses in 1171. He gathered all those he had promised before making a selection of eighty-six. Henry eventually took just thirty-six of the best horses; *Brut (Pen. 20)*, s.a. 1171.
[182] Jenkins, 'Horse', p. 64.
[183] N. A. Jones, 'Horses in medieval Welsh court poetry', in *Horse*, pp. 82–101.
[184] Jenkins, 'Horse', pp. 77–8.
[185] Meilyr, p. 183.

EQUIPMENT AND TACTICAL DISPOSITIONS

Gruffudd is described as a 'hurler of spear in battle before the cataclysm of the host'.[186] In *Gruffudd ap Cynan*'s account of the battle of Bron-yr-erw, Gruffudd was described 'seated on his horse in the midst of his army, with his flashing sword mowing down both his traitors and enemies'.[187] The *Brutiau* claim that in 1136 Owain and Cadwaladr led an army of 6,000 footsoldiers (W. *pedit*) and 2,000 mailed horsemen (W. *marchogyon llurygawc*) to Ceredigion.[188] Poetry of the twelfth and thirteenth centuries is rich in reference to warfare from horseback. It was vital for a Welsh prince to have a war horse (W. *cadfarch*) or destrier (W. *amws*) and he was often described as a 'horseman in battle' (W. *cadfarchawg*) or a 'horseman on the battlefield' (W. *marchog midlan*). As such he would fight from horseback, often hurling spears at his enemy, and the swift, spirited horse was a symbol of his might.[189] Witness Cynddelw Brydydd Mawr in praise of Madog ap Maredudd:

Clodfawr ei law waedlyd ar y maes brwydro,
eryr [o arglwydd] ar arglwyddi er pan fu'n bennaeth,
[un sy'n trin] hyrddwaywffon ar flaen byddin ar feirch cymesur eu cam,
erlidiwr, blaenwr, blaidd [mewn] ffyrnigrwydd.[190]

(Famed his bloodstained hand in the field,
eagle of lords, our finest warrior,
spear-thrust in strife from white-breasted steeds,
Ferocious war-wolf leading the chase.)[191]

In *The Fall of Powys*:

Ym maes Didlystun yr oedd ein dewrion yn gytûn,
nid er mwyn llesteirio clod [iddynt],
pob gwr hael ar farch graenus, eiddgar,
pob arwr a chleddyf dewr ar [ei] glun.[192]

---

[186] Ibid.
[187] *Gruffudd ap Cynan*, p. 63.
[188] *Brut (Pen. 20)*, s.a. 1136.
[189] N. A. Jones, 'Horses', pp. 83–4. See also Ryan, 'Study', 237.
[190] *CBT*, III, 1.25–8.
[191] *Earliest*, p. 137.
[192] *CBT*, III, 8.5–8.

(At Maes Didlystun our lord was alert,
he did not begrudge praise,
each kind lord on a keen steed,
each lion, sword at his side.)[193]

Cynddelw also wrote in praise of Rhys ap Gruffudd of Deheubarth, whom he described as a *marchog* who commanded 1,000 *marchogyon*; Rhys is portrayed in battle at St Clears aiming swords and 'brilliant blades' at his enemies from 'above the rein'.[194]

Hywel ab Owain Gwynedd praised his homeland, suggesting the existence of horse breeding and of the tactic of the spear-thrust from horseback:

Caraf ei milwyr a'i meirch hydrin . . .
Gwneuthum frwydr [lawn] glewder â hyrddiad gwayw
rhwng byddin Powys a gwŷr Gwynedd deg,
ac ar [farch] llwydwyn [drwy] ormodedd ymdrech
boed imi ennill rhyddhad o alltudiaeth.[195]

(I love its soldiers, and its trained stallions . . .
With the thrust of a spear I did splendid work
between the host of Powys and lovely Gwynedd.
On a pale white horse, a rash adventure,
may I now win freedom from exile.)[196]

Bleddyn Fardd described Llywelyn ap Gruffudd as 'a man staunch in charging wide-spread troops'.[197]

The role played by Welsh cavalry at Lincoln in 1141 has been discussed.[198] The feigned-flight tactic was also employed in 1231. Llywelyn ap Iorwerth sent a small force to tempt the garrison of Montgomery out from behind the castle walls. His main army lay hidden in ambush in difficult, marshy ground, suggesting that it consisted of infantry, but the decoy troop must have been mounted in order to evade the garrison knights:

[193] *Earliest*, p. 142.
[194] N. A. Jones and H. Pryce (eds), *Yr Arglwydd Rhys* (Cardiff, 1996), pp. 197–203 (197).
[195] *CBT*, II, 6.13, 21–4.
[196] *WVIE*, p. 22.
[197] *Earliest*, p. 168. 'Gwron grymus yn ymosod ar lu['r] asgeu'; *CBT*, VII, 50.21.
[198] See above, pp. 136–8.

The Welsh, seeing them advancing impetuously, immediately feigned a flight to a wood that was near; the knights of the castle pursued them hotly till they were immersed in the before-mentioned river and marsh up to their horses' bellies, and especially the foremost of them; those behind were forewarned by the immersion of their companions, for whose misfortunes they sorrowed greatly. The Welsh, seeing the condition of their enemies, then rushed impetuously on them, and with their lances caused a cruel slaughter amongst them, as they rolled about in the mud. A severe conflict then ensued but at length, after much slaughter on both sides, the Welsh were victorious.[199]

If the Welsh use of light cavalry from the earliest times is clear, more problematic is the suggestion that the Normans were responsible for the introduction of heavy cavalry into Welsh forces and, specifically, for developing the tactic of the charge with couched lance. Evidence to support this is found in references to armoured horsemen in Welsh poetry of the period, the works of Gerald of Wales and in references from the *Brutiau* for 1136 and the *Life of St Illtud* for 1094/5. In the revolt of 1256, Paris says that the Welsh army was composed of 30,000 men of whom 500 were 'well-armed and mounted knights'.[200] The Norman influence on armour in Wales is considered above, but the argument for the development of the new tactic with couched lance must be questioned. Following the work of Lynne White, the adoption of the couched-lance tactic has been associated with the introduction of the stirrup in Europe; the greater stability offered was said to have allowed a rider to stay mounted after delivering his blow.[201] The stirrup was introduced to Wales by the Norse in the eighth–ninth centuries, not by the Normans.[202] There are references to stirrups (W. *gwarthafleu*) in the Welsh laws and also in *Culhwch and Olwen*. Ryan contends that the Normans revolutionized tactics in Wales by adding their larger, stronger horses and the use of the couched lance to the existing cavalry traditions.[203] Their influence is said to have affected horse breeding and developments in saddlery and to

[199] RW (T), II, p. 541; RW, III, p. 12.
[200] MP (T), III, p. 217; MP, IV, p. 614.
[201] L. White, *Medieval Technology and Social Change* (Oxford, 1962).
[202] Ryan, 'Study', 30ff.
[203] Ibid., 41–63, 112–3.

have introduced plate armour for man and horse. These conclusions are based on a discussion of the Welsh prose tales; the early stories emphasized the speed of a horse, and the later tales praised power, strength and staying ability.[204] Similar themes can be detected in poetry where the size and build of a horse gain in importance.[205] It seems certain that Norman expertise led to the breeding of larger, stronger horses in Wales and likely that the need to carry increased weight in armour and weapons was a motivating factor in such a development. Also important was style, the need for the Welsh nobility to keep up with the latest fashions and be seen in the best light. However, the weight of evidence suggests that swift, agile horses remained of primary importance in combat and evidence for the couched lance is at best flimsy.

References in poetry of the period to lords described as thrusting spears or lances (W. *ergyrwaew*) from horseback, delivering 'shattering blows' and working as concerted groups of cavalry could be cited in support of the couched lance theory.[206] This evidence is inconclusive, though, and could equally suggest that the Welsh continued to fight as light cavalry in the manner described in the *Hengerdd* poetry.[207] The prose tales repeatedly describe how a successful rider would shatter his opponent's shield and armour and throw him 'over his horse's crupper to the ground' (W. *dros bedrein y uarch y'r lawr*). There is one reference to this in the *Four Branches* (in *Pwyll*) and the stock phrase occurs repeatedly in the romances. It is a description of individual combat between knights in a sanitized form, more akin to the tournament field than the battleground. Ryan suggests that the reference in *Pwyll* represented a spear thrust, but that the romances reveal that the heavy cavalry charge had been brought to Wales.[208] Sioned Davies is more cautious, arguing that it is doubtful that Welsh fighting techniques are reflected in these accounts and that we are seeing Welsh authors integrating foreign literary practices and reproducing set formulae.[209]

---

[204] Sioned Davies, 'Horses', p. 126.
[205] Ryan, 'Study', 241–3.
[206] Ryan, 'Study', 257–8.
[207] N. A. Jones, 'Horses', pp. 89–90.
[208] Ibid., pp. 178–9.
[209] Sioned Davies, 'Horses', pp. 136–7.

EQUIPMENT AND TACTICAL DISPOSITIONS

INFANTRY

In any large Welsh force gathered throughout the period, the infantry would be in the majority. This accords with what is seen in the rest of Europe. However, our sources concentrate on the nobility at war and, as has been seen, they were nearly always depicted fighting from horseback.[210] The only clear reference to a Welsh noble fighting on foot relates to Gruffudd ap Cynan at Aberlleiniog in 1094. It is notable that it occurs at a siege and that Gruffudd was alongside a large Hiberno-Scandinavian force which would usually fight as infantry:

> Then there was a battle ferocious, cruel, intense from morning till afternoon, and many fell on both sides, the bravest men first. And in the midst of that Gruffudd leaped forward in the front troop to cut down the mailed and helmeted French with his double-edged axe, like David amidst the Philistines.[211]

After 1066 there are references to Welsh infantry in Anglo-Norman sources where it is generally perceived as a rabble. Such a cursory glance suggests that Welsh infantry was limited in number and ineffective. This could not provide the basis for an effective military system and does not accord with the ability that has been noted in Welsh forces.

The equipment used by Welsh cavalry – swords, stabbing and throwing spears or lances, axes, shields, light armour and possibly bows – could all serve as infantry weapons. It was common throughout Europe for cavalry to dismount and fight as infantry when the circumstance and occasion warranted. Such 'dismounted cavalry' could form the entire infantry force or – as the mounted warriors were generally the elite, professional fighters with the best equipment – could serve to stiffen a larger infantry levy. Many of the tactics of the period demanded that a warrior dismount; ravaging was better accomplished on foot, whilst sieges and some ambushes required the use of infantry. Differing weather and topography often made infantry more effective than cavalry and, of course, a man who had his horse

---

[210] See N. A. Jones, 'Horses', p. 85.
[211] *Gruffudd ap Cynan*, p. 72.

killed under him had little choice but to carry on the fight from foot. It is above all crucial to recognize the flexibility of the warriors of the day, a quality vital in the fluid situation of combat.

Given the reluctance of our sources to describe a nobleman fighting from foot, it is difficult to give examples of 'dismounted cavalry'. In *Pwyll*, we see an attack made by Pwyll and ninety-nine *marchog* ('horsemen') on Gwawl in his court; although they are described as *marchogyon*, the warriors would have had to dismount to assault a building.[212] On a small-scale raid the *teulu* would operate as cavalry, but where an infantry force was required such professional military men could dismount. The idea that larger armies in the early period were formed by combining *teuluoedd* under the leadership of the overall commander has been discussed.[213] It seems inconceivable that there were no infantry in the battles of this period, and in these clashes it must be imagined that *teulu* members dismounted and fought as infantry. It is possible that this was done on a social scale, with the junior members of a *teulu* fighting from foot whilst the greater men remained mounted. Given the limited means of lesser kings likely to be found in such alliances, it is possible that some *teulu* members were without a suitable cavalry horse to begin with. Some hostings would have drawn freemen not usually belonging to a *teulu* and possibly even bondmen.[214] Such part-time warriors are likely to have fought as infantry and it seems probable that *teulu* members would have been dismounted to stiffen their ranks.

As the power of the over-kings of Wales grew and the status of the lesser kings declined, the number of *teuluoedd* declined correspondingly. The *uchelwyr* remained as *marchogyon* and whilst some were part of the king's *teulu*, many retained their own military followers. Although the terminology had changed, the actual military organization is likely to have altered little;[215] the *uchelwyr* brought mounted and unmounted men from the localities to the king's hostings and these would be divided into cavalry and infantry according to immediate military requirements.

---

[212] *Mabinogi*, p. 56; *PK*, p. 14.
[213] See above, pp. 63–6.
[214] See above, pp. 72–5.
[215] For fuller discussion, see above, pp. 66–71.

EQUIPMENT AND TACTICAL DISPOSITIONS

In the post-Roman period in Britain, there remained a memory of the battle tactics and discipline of the legions. The infantry had been the foundation of Roman military success and the numbers were always greater than those of the cavalry. Dark contended that the Britons fought as ordered units in battle, arranging their forces with a main body and wings and following Roman strategy and tactics.[216] Gildas condemned the Britons of the immediate post-Roman period for fighting their enemies with 'no orderly square, no right wing or other apparatus of war'.[217] This indicates that such tactics *were* known in his day and were expected to be followed by competent commanders. Gildas also suggested that the Romans gave the Britons military manuals.[218]

A steady body of infantry would form the shield behind which light cavalry could regroup after making their harrying attacks on enemy lines. Such organization is suggested in *Armes Prydein*:

> Brave men in battle-tumult, mighty warriors,
> swift in attack, very stubborn in defence.[219]

The *Gododdin* eulogizes the *marchogyon* who fought at Catraeth and thereby highlights cavalry warfare above all else. A number of references suggest that some of the heroes fought on foot; this may be because their horses had been killed, but it seems likely that an infantry screen was used to protect the cavalry. There are references to suggest that the forces were drawn into tactical units and were not merely thrown at the enemy in a disorganized charge: 'We are called the wing and van of the host in battle.'[220] References to the dogged, determined holding of ground by warriors simply do not sound like descriptions of light cavalry: 'in close ranks, grimly, the war-hounds fought';[221] 'an unyielding anchor amid the battle-host';[222] 'in the front rank Gwarddur was a palisade';[223] 'amid scattered weapons, breaking ranks, standing steadfast, with great destruction, the champion overthrew the

---
[216] Dark, *Civitas*, pp. 198–9, 254.
[217] Gildas, p. 18.
[218] Ibid., pp. 22–3; it is interesting (but in vain) to speculate on whether Vegetius' works were amongst the manuals.
[219] *AP*, p. 3.
[220] *Gododdin*, p. 48.
[221] Ibid., p. 6.
[222] Ibid., p. 56.
[223] Ibid., p. 64.

180   EQUIPMENT AND TACTICAL DISPOSITIONS

host of the men of England.'[224] There are suggestions of an infantry screen as warriors are praised for their sheltering of the host, possibly as the cavalry regrouped: 'haven of an army, spear of the haven';[225] 'undaunted in the strife, he was a refuge for a timorous host';[226] 'on his land a stronghold of shields';[227] 'there was violence at the ford before the warrior, with his shield as a stronghold.'[228] The last references suggest that the infantry line would face the enemy with a shield wall. Other references to 'strongholds in the face of battle' raise the possibility of the use of field fortifications, which could strengthen an infantry line and serve as a rallying point for disorganized cavalry.[229]

References in other *Hengerdd* poetry lend support to these theories. Taliesin's *The Battle of Argoed Llwyfain* describes Urien of Rheged leading infantry into battle in close order behind a shield wall:

> Atorelwis vryen vd yr echwyd.
> O byd ymgyfaruot am gerenhyd.
> Dyrchafwn eidoed oduch mynyd.
> Ac am porthwn wyneb oduch emyl.
> A dyrchafwn peleidyr oduch pen gwyr.
> A chyrchwn fflamdwyn yn y luyd.
> A lladwn ac ef ae gyweithyd.[230]

> (And Urien, lord of Erechwydd, shouted,
> 'If they would meet us now for our kinsfolk,
> high on the hilltop let's raise our ramparts,
> carry our faces over the shield rims,
> raise up our spears, men, over our heads
> and set upon Fflamddwyn in the midst of his hosts
> and slaughter him, ay, and all that go with him!')[231]

In the *Canu Llywarch*, Gwên ap Llywarch resolves to hold the ford of Rhodwydd Forlas:

[224] Ibid., p. 18.
[225] Ibid., p. 52.
[226] Ibid., p. 26.
[227] Ibid., p. 10.
[228] Ibid., p. 12.
[229] See below, pp. 186–9.
[230] *CT*, VI, p. 6.
[231] *WVIE*, p. 1.

Waves spread out around the bank of a fortress [W. *caer*], and I intend that there will be a broken, shattered shield before I retreat.[232]

The notion of the 'shattering of shield' was a standard poetic device to indicate bravery and Gwên had already been depicted riding a horse to battle. However, Gwên's resolve to hold his position at the ford and the reference to a *caer* is suggestive of a defensive position held on foot from behind a shield wall. In the *Stanzas of the Grave*, Gwên is praised for having led a 'compact host';[233] this could refer to cavalry, but it seems more like a description of an organized body of infantry.

In its exhortation to Cynddylan to defend his land, the *Canu Heledd* urges him:

> Cynddylan, block the place
> where the English come through Tren.
> A single tree is not called a forest.[234]

Rowland contends that this differs from the majority of *Hengerdd* poetry as it does not describe heroic warfare; Cynddylan's individual efforts are valiant but insufficient. Successful war is waged by ordered units and the need to 'block' the place of English advance again suggests an infantry force.[235]

The description of battle in *Armes Prydein* reflects the rush, clamour and violence of combat:

> They [the Welsh] will rush into battle like a bear from the mountain
> to avenge the bloodshed of their fellows;
> there will be spear-thrusts in a ceaseless flood,
> no friend [of ours?] will have pity for [?] the body of his opponent.
> There will be heads split open without brains,
> women will be widowed, and horses riderless
> there will be terrible wailing before the rush of warriors,
> many wounded by hand; before the hosts separate

---

[232] *Saga*, p. 468.
[233] *Stanzas*, p. 121.
[234] *Saga*, pp. 484.
[235] The line 'a single tree is not a forest' could also be translated as 'a single post is not a defensive wall', which would lend further support to the theory of staunch defence on foot; ibid. Similar conclusions can be drawn with regard to the description of a warrior as a 'pillar of warfare' in *Enwev Meiben*, ibid., p. 473. In the *Stanzas of the Grave*, Môr ap Peredur of Penweddig is described as 'the majestic staunch chieftain, pillar in the swift-moving battle'; Jones, *Stanzas*, p. 123.

the messengers of death will meet
when corpses stand up, supporting each other.[236]

It is unclear whether this refers to infantry or cavalry combat; a mixture of the two seems most likely. The 'rush of warriors with spears' suggests an infantry charge, whilst the presence of 'riderless horses' indicates the probable presence of cavalry (certainly the Bretons are said to fight as cavalry). Within the ensuing chaos of the battle there is evidence of the order and tactical units which the author expected of the armies of his day:

> The supporters of the *Cymry* will form orderly ranks,
> their van to [their enemy's] rear, the 'palefaces' [Anglo-Saxons] will be hard pressed.[237]

A long, bloody battle was expected, not a clash that would be settled in the first charge and the belief that ordered ranks of infantry would decide the day is suggested by the image of 'corpses standing up supporting each other'. There are references to the banners of the armies and to the Welsh rallying to, and leading the Irish with, the 'standard of Dewi'; standards were used in the Middle Ages to marshal and reorganize troops in the heat of battle.[238] It also seems that the Welsh used horns to help arrange tactical dispositions.[239]

The *Triads* describe one of the 'Three Fettered War Bands': 'The *teulu* of Cadwallon Long-Arm, who each one put the fetters of their horses on their [own] feet when fighting with Serygei the Irishman at the Irishman's Rocks in Môn'.[240] The descriptive element is a later corruption; the idea of warriors tying themselves together is impractical and Bromwich argued that the 'fettered war bands' were those bearing the insignia of royal office or leadership, possibly torques. However, the passage

---

[236] *AP*, pp. 9–11.
[237] Ibid., p. 7.
[238] Ibid., pp. 7, 11.
[239] In *Gwên and Llywarch*, Llywarch advises his son:

> The horn which Urien gave you
> with its band of gold around its mouthpiece –
> blow on it if you come to have need. (*Saga*, p. 469)

[240] *Triads*, p. 167.

reveals that the scribe could envisage *teulu* members dismounting and fighting as a closely knit body of infantry. The Anglo-Saxon use of the shield wall, most famously at Hastings, is well known and it may be speculated that the Welsh used similar infantry tactics in battle.[241] Welsh poetry refers to warriors bearing shields worn thin on the left, suggesting fighting in ranks with a wall of shields held in the left hands of the troops, allowing blows to be struck from above the shield with the right hand.[242] It may be speculated that spears were planted in front of the shield wall on occasion to meet the charge of cavalry.[243]

From the eleventh century onwards, the *Brutiau* give evidence for Welsh infantry to set alongside the literary references. Battle descriptions of the forces of Llywelyn ap Seisyll – and, later, of his son Gruffudd – suggest the presence of steady ranks of infantry. In their clash with Rhain in 1022, Llywelyn and the men of Gwynedd awaited the approach of their enemy 'calmly, steadily' and fought 'steadily' in a bloody and, presumably, lengthy battle.[244] These were the qualities of an army that were admired by the native chronicler. Gruffudd ap Llywelyn's army at Hereford in 1055 seems likely to have been a mixed force of cavalry and infantry. We are told that Gruffudd 'arrayed' his host and met the enemy with a 'well-ordered' force.[245]

In the twelfth century our sources are richer. It has been inferred from Gerald of Wales's work that the men of north Wales fought only with spears whilst those from the south used only bows.[246] Such categorization is too rigid and unrealistic and does not accord with Gerald's words; he states that the men of the south (especially Gwent) were particularly noted for their skill

---

[241] Abels has given a vivid reconstruction of Anglo-Saxon infantry tactics with the shield wall in the late tenth century in D. C. Scragg (ed.), *The Battle of Maldon AD 991* (Oxford, 1991), pp. 143–55. The strength of a line depended on the cohesion and morale of the troops; it was vital that they did not flee.

[242] See *Saga*, pp. 468, 474.

[243] Dafydd Benfras refers to Llywelyn ap Gruffudd's forces at Swansea in 1257 presenting 'a fine shield-wall defence'; see Bosco, 'Dafydd Benfras', 103. That the shield wall was a familiar disposition may be inferred from the prose tale, *The Dream of Maxen*. The emperor's troops made a *castell* with their shields to protect him from the sun; *Mabinogi*, p. 119; *BM*, p. 1.

[244] *Brut (Pen. 20)*, s.a. 1022.

[245] *Brut (Pen. 20)*, s.a. 1056.

[246] H. Delbrück, *History of the Art of War*, III (London, 1982), p. 388; the difference in the south is attributed to Anglo-Norman influence and the introduction of new technology.

with the bow and likewise those of the north with the spear.[247] Forces used mixed weapons to great effect. Although swords were used, spears and bows were the most common weapons. Whilst the spear (and sword) can be used equally well by cavalry and infantry, the bow should primarily be considered as an infantry weapon. It is a weapon rarely mentioned in our panegyric sources,[248] but its profusion, as noted by Gerald and as seen with the Welsh soldiers recruited by the Anglo-Normans, suggests that Welsh forces would usually use archers to support spearmen and cavalry. Such mixed forces, capable of flexible tactics, accord with those fielded by the Anglo-Normans and other peoples throughout Europe.

The *Life of St Illtud* tells of an attack made on Glamorgan by 3,000 'armed horsemen and footsoldiers' from north Wales in 1094–5,[249] and *Gruffudd ap Cynan* says that at Mynydd Carn in 1081 'the earth resounded with the tumult of horses and footsoldiers'.[250] The *Brutiau* record large numbers of Welsh cavalry and infantry at Cardigan in 1136, and at Coleshill in 1157 mounted *teulu* members fought on foot. Matthew Paris and other English chroniclers mention mixed forces in the thirteenth century; Wendover describes Welsh cavalry and infantry working in unison near Montgomery in 1231.[251]

The *Brutiau* describe the deployment of organized Welsh forces in the twelfth and thirteenth centuries. In 1110 the sons of Uchdryd and their *teulu* were able to organize a *llu* raised for the defence of Meirionnydd into a 'well-ordered troop'.[252] The irregular forces drawn for this muster (Uchdryd himself and his *teulu* were not present) are likely to have contained inexperienced infantry, but they put up a stout fight before being defeated by Owain ap Cadwgan and Madog ap Rhiddid.

At the siege of Aberystwyth in 1116, the *Brutiau* criticize the leadership of Gruffudd ap Rhys and the behaviour of the *ynfydion*

---

[247] *Journey*, I, 4, p. 113; II, 5, p. 182; *Description*, I, 7, p. 231. Support for the idea that the men of Gwynedd were noted for their skill with the spear is found in A. Owen, *Ancient Laws and Institutions of Wales*, 2 vols. (London, 1841), I, p. 105. The men of Arfon, who led the van of the host of Gwynedd, are called 'the men of the black-headed shafts'. It is possible that the title, and the story behind it, has a history dating to the sixth century.
[248] See above, pp. 151–3.
[249] *Vitae*, p. 233.
[250] *Gruffudd ap Cynan*, p. 68.
[251] RW, III, p. 12; for a discussion see above, pp. 174–5.
[252] *Brut (Pen. 20)*, s.a. 1110.

in his forces. *Brut (Pen 20)* says that Gruffudd did not arrange his forces well 'save for placing the standards in the van', but even this seems to be an overgenerous reading of the (lost) Latin original. *Brut (RBH)* says that the forces were arranged 'without placing ensigns in their van' and *Bren.* describes the forces as 'disorderly'. The Welsh were a 'furious rabble' who attacked the enemy 'imprudently'. The chronicle indicates contemporary criticisms of poor commanders and demonstrates an awareness of the importance of ordered troops and sound tactical principles. It is possible that the failures at Aberystwyth may be attributed to an over-reliance on *ynfydion* rather than regular *teulu* members. The importance placed on standards is again revealing; their use in *Armes Prydein* has been noted and in *Gruffudd ap Cynan* we are told that Gruffudd 'prepared for battle and raised his ensigns' before clashing with Robert of Rhuddlan.[253] The raising of standards seems to have been an essential prelude to battle as they were vital to tactical organization.[254]

The significance of Owain Gwynedd's battle with Henry II at Coleshill in 1157 has been stressed. Owain had prepared defences on the coast road,[255] and it must be presumed that he therefore intended to fight on foot with the rest of the army. The main battle took place in densely wooded country where Owain had positioned his sons, Cynan and Dafydd, to ambush the king; in such conditions the Welsh must have fought on foot.

The second battle of 1157 on Anglesey (Tal-y-Moelfre) was won by a scratch Welsh force as the elite of the military was with Owain on the mainland. Gerald described the death of one of the Anglo-Norman leaders, Henry fitz Henry: 'Henry behaved far too rashly and, with no support from his troops, fell in the first line of battle, pierced by a number of spears, to the great grief of his soldiers.'[256] Whether or not poor Anglo-Norman tactics were to blame for the defeat, it seems that the battle was won by an organized body of Welsh infantry, armed with spears and able to present an unyielding front to their enemies. Literary references further support the notion of ordered Welsh military

---

[253] *Gruffudd ap Cynan*, p. 62. At Mynydd Carn, Gruffudd's enemies feared the approach of his 'ensigns'.
[254] In *The Dream of Rhonabwy*, Welsh forces in battle rallied round standards; *Mabinogi*, p. 187; *BR*, p. 15.
[255] See below, pp. 188–9.
[256] *Journey*, II, 7, pp. 189–90.

units. In the *Life of St Cadog*, Rhun ap Maelgwn's army was divided into a number of *falangibus* ('phalanxes').[257] In both *Owein* and *The Dream of Rhonabwy* Arthur's *llu* is divided into a number of *byddin*, and in the *Dream of Maxen* Elen's brothers led a *llu bychan* ('small host') within Maxen's *llu* that was capable of effective individual action.[258]

FIELD FORTIFICATIONS

Artificial fortifications constructed on the battlefield could strengthen an infantry line. The Romans made little use of such works in combat situations, preferring to rely on the discipline of their infantry behind their wall of shields. This approach offered tactical flexibility and a psychological edge; the infantry could not only attack but retreat as an ordered body according to the ebb and flow of battle. A retreat from a prepared defensive position was more likely to turn into a rout.

The Romans utilized field fortifications in the form of camps which their forces constructed whilst on campaign. These provided defensive shelter at night, a measure of security from surprise attack and a local base in enemy territory from which to operate. Such camps were used by the British and Welsh after the departure of the Romans. In the *Life of St Germanus*, a British army shelters in its camp whilst on campaign before battle.[259] The Welsh laws make provision for bondmen to build a camp (W. *lluest*) for the king during his hostings.[260] The *Life of St Cadog* refers to Welsh armies using camps whilst on distant ravaging campaigns; the historicity of the events should not be trusted, but there is no reason to doubt that the author saw his descriptions of armies on campaign as accurate. The first reference describes Maelgwn Gwynedd bringing an army south to Glamorgan and using a camp to protect his host in the night: 'They marked out a camp [L. *castra*] in the region of Gwynlliog . . . that on the following day they might plunder the whole country.'[261] Years

---

[257] *Vitae*, p. 76.
[258] *Mabinogi*, pp. 125–6, 182–4, 211; *BM*, pp. 10–12; *BR*, pp. 6–10; *Owein*, p. 24.
[259] *Life of St Germanus*, XVII, p. 300.
[260] *Law*, pp. 41, 125.
[261] *Vitae*, p. 73. The camp was situated 'by the spring Brittrou', suggesting that it was prepared and sited to resist a limited siege, if the occasion arose.

later Maelgwn's son, Rhun, brought an army south; his camp was used to protect the cattle and other plunder that had been seized, whilst his ravagers dispersed across the country.[262] Similarly a 'Maredudd, King of Rheinwg' is said to have brought an army to Glamorgan: 'After arrival he gave orders to gather loot and drive off oxen to the camp for food.'[263] It is likely that Iron Age hill forts and Roman camps were used by medieval armies whilst on campaign.[264]

Although the link is tenuous, it is possible that twelfth- and thirteenth-century references to Welsh military leaders 'pitching their tents' against their enemies are indications of the construction of camps whilst on campaign.[265] There are a number of references to encampments made by the thirteenth-century princes of Gwynedd on campaign and it has been suggested that these were constructed using the building duties imposed on bondmen.[266]

The question of the construction of fortifications on the field of battle is more problematic. Such works limited the tactical flexibility of a force and there were other practical problems: a commander would need to predict where an enemy intended to attack and would also need time to prepare his position. However, in specific circumstances such works could be useful, particularly if a commander was unsure of the standard of his infantry or if he was facing superior forces. There are problems in identifying field fortifications in our sources; for example, are heroes being metaphorically compared to fortifications, or are infantry shield walls regarded as fixed fortifications? Possible references in the *Gododdin* to warriors fighting behind a shield wall 'like palisades' have been discussed and it seems likely that all such references describe bodies of infantry rather than constructed field works.[267] Several references raise the possibility that field fortifications were used, however: 'his sword resounded

---

[262] Ibid., p. 77.
[263] Ibid., p. 113. Another king, 'Cynan Carwyn of Reinmuc', established a camp beside the river Neath whilst on campaign; ibid., p. 115.
[264] In 1114 and 1121, Henry I encamped at Mur Castell, the old Roman fort where a castle was later built; *Gruffudd ap Cynan*, p. 80. G.R.J. Jones suggested that in 1165 the Welsh force at Corwen encamped at Caer Drewyn hill fort; 'Military', 87, fn. 1.
[265] See, for example, *Gruffudd ap Cynan*, p. 74; *Brut (Pen. 20)*, s.a. 1165.
[266] *LG*, p. 252, fn. 290.
[267] The same conclusion should be reached for a passage from Taliesin's *Battle of Argoed Llwyfain*; see above, p. 180.

above the rampart';[268] 'a refuge [W. *dinas*] for a host on the furthest flank';[269] 'he set up a stronghold in the face of battle'.[270]

If these examples are not to be taken as descriptions of field fortifications, a stronger case can be made for Gwên's planned tactical disposition in the *Canu Lywarch*.[271] In this example, the ford where the Anglo-Saxons intended to attack was known and the implication that Gwên was outnumbered is clear. For his defensive action, a field fortification constructed at the ford would have been of value and this may explain the reference to a *caer*. It is possible that a work of this nature was used at the battle of Arfderydd. The *Triads* say that the *gosgordd* of 'Dreon the Brave' fought at the *rotwyd* of Arfderydd; a *rotwyd* was an earthen dyke usually built on the rising ground above a ford.[272]

The only clear references to the Welsh use of field fortifications occur in the *Brutiau* in the two years 1156–7. In 1156 Owain Gwynedd intended to march south to reimpose his hold on Ceredigion which had been broken by Rhys ap Gruffudd. Rhys was determined to oppose this and marched north to the mouth of the Dyfi where Owain would be expected to cross; Rhys's resolve to fight was enough to deter Owain and no battle occurred.[273] *Brut (Pen. 20)* and *Bren.* tell us that at Aberdyfi Rhys 'raised a ditch [W. *ffos*] to give battle' and that when the danger had passed a castle was built on the spot to ensure future security.[274] Rhys, knowing the route of Owain's advance and determined to face battle if need be, had constructed a field work on an already-difficult river crossing.[275]

In 1157 field fortifications were used in battle. Each version of the *Brut* agrees that Owain Gwynedd 'raised ditches and

---

[268] *Gododdin*, p. 26.
[269] Ibid. This seems to refer to a warrior as the 'refuge' rather than an actual fortification.
[270] Ibid., p. 50.
[271] See above, pp. 180–1.
[272] *Triads*, p. 65.
[273] See above, p. 123.
[274] *Brut (RBH)* describes Rhys's resolve to fight and the later building of the castle but fails to mention the ditch. However, the other versions are supported by *AC* (B) and (C) which refer to the *ffos*. The sole reason to doubt this evidence is that the only references in the Welsh annals to ditches being dug for battle occur in two consecutive years; this could represent the style of the writer in describing preparations for battle.
[275] Turvey, 'Defences', 106, says that the later castle was sited where the Dyfi could be forded and was well placed to defend access to Ceredigion. A hostile force from Gwynedd would need to besiege the castle or risk having its communications harassed during the campaign.

prepared for battle' on the main coast road of north Wales in order to block Henry II's advance from Chester;[276] it is possible that the site was the ancient earthwork of Hen Blâs, situated in the fork of a near-impassable ravine that ends just a few hundred yards from the shore.[277] Henry sent a diversionary troop of knights and infantry against this position whilst leading another force through the wood of Hawarden to outflank Owain. Owain knew Henry's force was greater in number and contained more well-armed knights who could give the king the advantage in open battle. Consequently Owain, possibly inspired by Rhys's defence of Deheubarth the previous year, prepared fortifications on a narrow stretch of the main road. The obstacle was formidable enough to deter Henry from making a full-scale frontal assault. The Welsh prince also recognized the danger of trying to hold a fixed defensive position and anticipated Henry's outflanking manoeuvre; he had chosen the land well and laid a trap for Henry in the thick woods. This negated the weakness of static defence and turned it to the Welsh prince's tactical advantage.[278]

---

[276] *Brut (Pen. 20)* translates ditches as *ffos*; *Brut (RBH)* and *Bren.* have *clodyeu*; *AC* (B) has *vallum*. John Keegan suggested that the defences were pointed stakes carried by archers and driven into the ground, as were used effectively at Agincourt in 1415, but a more formidable field fortification would seem to be indicated; see his *The Face of Battle* (Harmondsworth, 1976), p. 83.

[277] See King, 'Defences', 7.

[278] It may be similarly imagined that the Welsh force outside Brecon in 1136–7 intended to fight on foot against the 500 knights and archers sent by Stephen under Baldwin fitz Gilbert; the Welsh had blocked the road with felled trees. See *GS*, pp. 19–21.

V
FORTIFICATIONS

Fortification Strategy

The value of castles to the peoples of Europe is a central tenet of Bartlett's theory of the expansion of technologically superior forces throughout the continent. The association of Norman knights with castles is particularly strong, whence Bartlett's model has seemed well suited to Welsh history in the Middle Ages. R. R. Davies considered the Welsh attitude to castles:

> The Welsh may already have made some use of the ancient earthworks so common in their land; but it was not until the coming of the Normans that they began to learn the art of castle building. Initially they were reluctant or slow pupils, often destroying castles when they captured them. But, living cheek by jowl with the Normans and even occasionally acting as keepers of the castles, they soon began to imitate Norman practice.[1]

Crouch believes that the Welsh found such military technology 'exhilarating': 'They joyfully embraced the new technology on display in England and France. As early as 1110 the Welsh were assiduously copying the Normans in building castles of their own.'[2] Castles, and fortifications generally, served more than a military purpose; they were administrative sites, structures designed to overawe the subservient people of the land and to display the might of a lord to his peers and rivals. It is essential to consider how we may differentiate between a castle and other forms of fortification. It would be unreasonable to suggest that before 1066 the Welsh had no notion of the concept of fortification. To position a few stakes or rocks to defend a position is an obvious response to a perceived threat and even the most basic fortification could give a defending force a great advantage. Moreover, we have evidence of sophisticated fortifications in Wales before the coming of the Normans.

[1] R. R. Davies, *Age*, p. 67; see also his *Domination*, pp. 39–40.
[2] Crouch, *Image*, p. 156.

Fortification strategy, c.450–1066

The extent of Roman remains at sites like Pevensey indicated that the Britons had outstanding models of fortification available to them. In Wales itself, Gerald of Wales was impressed by the Roman walls of Carmarthen and Caerleon. That Roman forts were occupied by the Britons is indicated by the Anglo-Saxon attack on Pevensey in 491.[3] Gildas suggested the importance of fortified towns to the early Anglo-Saxon conquests when he claimed that the invaders of Britain 'laid low the towns and battered walls and towers'.[4] The Anglo-Saxon conquests destroyed town life in the Roman cities of the Britons, but fortifications continued to play an important role in warfare; after the destruction of the cities the Britons went 'to the high hills, steep, menacing and fortified'.[5] There was a high incidence of battles in the vicinity of fortifications, which were used to control communications and stop ravaging. They could shelter the population and served to demonstrate mastery of the land, but ultimately lordship had to be defended in the field. A siege would not continue if it were known that no force could challenge the besieging army. Archaeological findings have recorded the impressive scale of British hill forts, but surprise has been expressed at the relatively puny nature of their defences. They were not designed to withstand major sieges; the defences were enough to hold off surprise attacks and to protect the non-fighting population who worked the land, but campaigns were decided in the field.[6] After the Anglo-Saxons destroyed a British army at Biedcanford in 571, four towns fell almost immediately, and similarly after the battle of Dyrham in 577 the cities of Gloucester, Cirencester and Bath succumbed.

The archaeological record of the use of fortifications is supported by literary references. The *Gododdin* has shields and warriors being compared to 'strongholds' or 'fortresses' for the host.[7] This would suggest that the army was familiar with the

---

[3] *ASC*, 491.
[4] Gildas, p. 28.
[5] Ibid.
[6] Erosion of these defences over the centuries should also be considered. With deeper ditches and topped by wooden palisades, many of these forts would have presented a daunting prospect to an attacker.
[7] See *Gododdin*, pp. 10, 12, 18, 26, 50, 52, 64.

protection offered by more permanent fortifications. Taliesin's poem in praise of Cynan Garwyn of Powys refers to a successful attack on a hill fort in Brycheiniog.[8] Whilst fighting the Northumbrians, Cadwallon made use of York's walls to shelter from Osric's army before making a sortie and destroying the besieging force.[9]

The Welsh fortification tradition continued throughout the early Middle Ages, although there was a marked reluctance to rely on fortifications as military strongpoints, or to invest too much in such sites. This can be partially explained by the necessity of defending the land in the field, but the increasingly overwhelming strength of the Anglo-Saxon kingdoms was another reason. It was impossible to defend a stronghold indefinitely against a superior enemy force. In the later Middle Ages, it was customary that a garrison could honourably surrender to a besieging army if it saw no hope of relief.[10] This rule of war can be seen in Wales in 1210; Rhys Fychan sealed an alliance with King John and with an overwhelming force besieged Llandovery castle: 'And the garrison surrendered the castle, after they had despaired of any kind of support, upon their being given their lives and their safety and what was theirs and all their chattels free and sixteen steeds.'[11] Such an event was influenced by notions of feudal conduct arising from chivalry, but the basic military principles remained consistent throughout the period of study: it was impossible to hold a fortification indefinitely against a superior force. A Welsh lord who placed all his hopes in a fortified point would have presented a static target against which enemy forces could direct their strength. It was preferable to rely on a war of movement, to keep one's chattels away from the enemy whilst shadowing his army with the fighting force. The dangers of relying on static fortifications are suggested in 823; the Mercian kingdom had been increasing the pressure on Powys and under Ceolwulf they destroyed the fortress at Degannwy which allowed them to 'take the kingdom of Powys for their own'.[12] Gruffudd ap Llywelyn developed an

---

[8] *CT*, I, p. 1.
[9] Bede, III, 1, p. 213.
[10] See Strickland, *Conduct*, p. 50.
[11] *Brut (Pen. 20)*, 1210.
[12] Ibid., 823.

administrative centre at Rhuddlan and such a place would have had some form of fortification; it was here, though, that Harold Godwinesson surprised Gruffudd at Christmas 1062. The Welsh king barely escaped and the losses he suffered shook his authority in Wales.

Welsh fortification in the early Middle Ages developed from a long tradition and performed vital military and administrative roles in society.[13] Within the model he outlined, G. R. J. Jones saw a connection between strongholds and the *maerdref* in each commote; the resources of the bond settlements in the locality were needed to construct such sites.[14] The system may have made possible the creation of the hill forts of the Iron Age, and in the early Middle Ages many of these were reoccupied and refortified. The duty of the subservient population to build fortifications may have been ancient. Gildas mistakenly believed that the Antonine Wall was built by the Britons in the fifth century, but the way he imagined the construction is telling; he thought it was done by 'private and public subscription'.[15] The building of fortifications was one of the 'common duties' imposed on landowners under Anglo-Saxon law and it seems that this represents a continuation from the previous Romano-British occupation of the country. The Welsh laws insist on a king's right to a man with an axe from every villein townland to work on fortifications.[16] Forts were sited in the uplands and sustained by the resources of the lowlands; this made tactical sense and also made best use of the limited supply of arable land in Wales. Examples include Dinorben and Dinas Emrys. Jones noted that sites like Dinas Emrys had many of the features of Scottish forts of the early Middle Ages and saw this as evidence of related trends towards the development of 'proto-feudal' strongholds in the post-Roman European world.

---

[13] See G. R. J. Jones, 'Dark Ages', pp. 177–97; also his 'Tribal system', 111–32; and his 'Distribution', 19–36.

[14] Longley, 'Royal courts', p. 43, notes the 'striking correspondence' between the distribution of post-Norman earthwork castles in Wales and *maerdrefi* sites, although it is unclear whether this represents an intrusive Norman form or Welsh development. Lloyd believed that there was no major fortification at the *maerdref* but that security was not neglected. The wall of the *llys* had a gate guarded all night by a watchman whose house was behind it, and strong enough to hold prisoners; *HW*, I, p. 314.

[15] Gildas, p. 22.

[16] *Law*, p. 125.

Early Welsh poetry is replete with references to fortifications. In the *Canu Llywarch*, Gwên ap Llywarch resolves to see waves of Saxon attackers break against him as against the walls of a fortress (W. *caer*).[17] The Welsh name for Tenby (*Dinbych*) means 'small (W. *bych*) fortress (W. *din*)' and the site is referred to as a fort (W. *caer*) and stronghold (W. *dinas*) in the poem *The Praise of Tenby* (*c*.875).[18] No traces of the Welsh works survive because the area was refortified by the Vikings and the Normans. It is common for strategic sites to be reused by successive generations of military men and the original Welsh structure, likely to have consisted of earthwork, rough stone and wood, seems lost for ever. Other pre-Norman Welsh poems refer to *caerau* or fortifications; *Gwyn ap Nudd* (tenth–early eleventh century) speaks of battle 'before Caer Fandwy'[19] and another early eleventh-century poem refers to a fortress (W. *tewdor*) on Anglesey.[20] *Culhwch and Olwen* has a number of references to fortifications, including the *caer* of Wrnach the Giant built of 'finished stone'.[21]

Gruffudd ap Cynan refers to pre-1066 fortifications in Wales when considering Gruffudd's genealogy. Etill, the mother of Rhodri Mawr, is said to have come from the castle (W. *castell*) of Dindaethwy. The use of *castell* may reveal post-Norman influences, but it is noteworthy that the term can be applied to an earlier fortified site. Dindaethwy was a commote in south-east Anglesey and it has been speculated that, whilst *daethwy* was probably a tribal name, *din* refers to the fortified point of the commote.[22] The site was probably Dinas, near Plas Cadnant, in the parish of Llandysilio. *Gruffudd ap Cynan* relates the coming of Gruffudd's grandfather Olaf, king of Dublin, to Anglesey: 'Olaf built a strong castle [W. *castell cadarn*] whose mound [W. *dom*] and ditch [W. *ffos*] are still visible, and which was called the castle of King Olaf. In Welsh, however, it is called Bon-y-Dom.'[23] A fortification comprising a hastily built motte surrounded by a ditch is, of course, characteristic of the Normans.

---

[17] *Saga*, p. 468.
[18] *Beginnings*, pp. 155–76.
[19] *Saga*, p. 506.
[20] *Beginnings*, p. 177.
[21] *Mabinogi*, p. 161; *CaO*, p. 28. Such a reference may suggest awe at mighty stone buildings, possibly Roman survivals, that could be attributed to 'giants'.
[22] *Gruffudd ap Cynan*, p. 53.
[23] Ibid., p. 55.

The site in question actually dates to the Bronze Age, but it should be noted that a private fortification is referred to as a *castell* and that the author of *Gruffudd ap Cynan* associated it with an alien intrusion into Wales. The terminology suggests that an invader was expected to have a heavily defended private stronghold as opposed to the more lightly defended refuges and administrative centres of Welsh fortifications.

One of the clearest pre-1066 references to a Welsh fortified site relates to Degannwy. The Welsh chronicles reveal that in 823 the Mercians destroyed a stronghold at this location which allowed them to dominate Powys. Confusion has arisen because *Brut (Pen. 20)* misread the Latin *arcem* from *Annales Cambriae* (A) for *arcum* and translated that as the 'arch' of Degannwy being destroyed. The Latin term *arx* that should be read from *Annales Cambriae* (A) means 'fortress', 'castle' or 'stronghold'; *Brut (RBH)* translates *castell*.

The archaeological record provides the most valuable information about pre-Norman fortifications in Wales. Alcock's work at Dinas Powys revealed the defended court and hall of a minor king or chieftain, occupied from the fifth to the eighth century.[24] This was not an Iron Age site, but one developed by a lord emerging from the political break-up of post-Roman south-east Wales. It was later reoccupied by the Norman invaders of Glamorgan. Dinas Powys has formidable natural defences to the north and west, but to the south and east only a weak bank and ditch. The compact nature of the site reveals the political decentralization in Romanized south-east Wales following the fall of the Empire. Elsewhere in Wales, Roman influence was less marked and the native organization of society stronger; in these areas larger forts, probably in use since Iron Age times, were designed to serve as a refuge for the community and their goods, not just the lord and his household. The development of the over-kingdom of Glamorgan in the south-east may account for the abandonment of Dinas Powys in the eighth century; the

---

[24] Alcock, *Economy*, pp. 7ff.

over-king would not permit a client ruler to maintain a private fortification.[25]

A site comparable to Dinas Powys was excavated at Hen Gastell, Briton Ferry.[26] The fort was sited on a hill controlling a crossing of the river Neath. There is evidence of occupation by a minor but wealthy lord, in this case from the fifth or sixth century until the tenth. The site was reoccupied by the Welsh princes of Afan in the later twelfth century. There is evidence for the burning of buildings in the late ninth century and it has been speculated that Vikings were responsible. This may be the case, but it is equally possible that the over-king of Glamorgan sought to impose his power over the lord of the fort.

The crannog on Llangors lake in Brycheiniog was constructed in the period 860–906.[27] The defences were not formidable, but the surrounding water and wooden stakes would have hindered an attacking force. Its construction has been considered as an assertion of the rights of the kings of Brycheiniog when faced with the expansion of the over-kingdoms, notably Gwynedd. The crannog is not large and was only designed to shelter the king and his household. It was burnt and abandoned after an attack from Mercia in 916.

Excavations at the medium-sized hill fort of Dinas Emrys in Caernarfonshire show the development of a native site in an area barely touched by the Roman occupation.[28] The site was inhabited in the Iron Age and Roman periods, but the mid-fifth century saw the addition of new defences and the construction of a cistern, probably for the watering of sheep and cattle sheltered behind the fortifications. The name of Dinas Emrys is associated with Ambrosius Aurelianus, the hero of Gildas's work, and,

---

[25] This argument is supported by the probability that the place-name element Powys derives from the Latin *pagus* ('region', 'district'), revealing an emerging post-Roman territorial organization; G. O. Pierce, 'The evidence of place-names', in *Glamorgan County History*, III, pp. 456–92; p. 482. The name Dinas Powys was not recorded until the twelfth century. This suggests a diminished role for the site after the rise of an over-king.

[26] P. F. Wilkinson, 'Excavations at Hen Gastell, Briton Ferry, west Glamorgan, 1191–2', *Medieval Archaeology*, 39 (1995), 1–50. The place-name may be significant; see below, pp. 199–200. The site is now buried beneath a bridge for the M4.

[27] E. Campbell and A. Lane, 'Llangorse: a tenth-century royal crannog in Wales', *Antiquity*, 63 (1989), 675–81; E. Campbell, A. Lane and M. Redknap, 'Llangorse crannog', *Archaeology in Wales*, 30 (1990), 62–3.

[28] H. N. Savory, 'Excavations at Dinas Emrys, Beddgelert (Caern.), 1954–6', *Arch. Camb.*, 109 (1960), 13–77.

although this cannot be proved, such a connection may be linked to the fifth-century developments on the site.

The two hills at the northern end of the eastern bank of the river Conwy show the repeated use of natural strategic sites throughout the ages.[29] Degannwy is best known as the castle of Henry III which was started in 1241. It was developed into a stone castle enclosing the two hills, until it was destroyed by Llywelyn ap Gruffudd in 1257. The castle was built on the site of a previous Welsh castle, but there is a far longer history of fortification there. Alcock found no evidence of occupation between the seventh and eleventh centuries, but chronicle records mention a fortified Welsh site in 812, a construction important to the dynasty of Powys that was destroyed by the Mercians in 823. Degannwy has associations with Maelgwn of Gwynedd, and Alcock found imported Mediterranean pottery from the sixth century. There is a suggestion of Degannwy's use as a fortified site in the Roman period and possibly in the Iron Age.

Another extended fortification tradition can be traced at Rhuddlan, although different sites in the same locality were used. In 921, Edward the Elder built a burh at Rhuddlan as the Anglo-Saxons advanced along the north Wales coast. The Welsh had reclaimed a firm grip on this region by the time of Gruffudd ap Llywelyn, who developed Rhuddlan as an administrative centre. When the Normans arrived in north Wales, the adventurer Robert of Rhuddlan raised a motte and bailey castle in the area, possibly on the site of Gruffudd's old hall. For the next 200 years the area regularly changed hands until a new site in Rhuddlan became the location for an Edwardian stone castle.

The first literary references to Carew castle in Dyfed refer to the Norman castle on the site, but excavations have revealed a longer history.[30] The ancient Welsh name means either 'fort on a hill' (W. *caer rhiw*) or, more probably, 'the fortifications' (W. *caerau*). A defended enclosure has been unearthed with at least five parallel lines of rock-cut ditches, covering an area much larger than that of the later castle. The north and west were

---

[29] L. Alcock, 'Excavations at Degannwy Castle, Caernarfonshire, 1961–6', *Archaeological Journal*, 124 (1967), 190–201.
[30] D. Austin, *Carew Castle Archaeological Report*, 1992 Season Interim Report (Lampeter, 1993).

protected by the tidal inlet of the Carew river. The fortifications are pre-Norman, but could be dated to any time from the end of the Iron Age to 1066. The nearby Carew Cross has an inscription to Maredudd ab Edwin, king of Deheubarth (1033–5); the cross and fortifications almost certainly pre-date him, but they reveal links to the royal dynasty of the area. The Normans deliberately slighted the older defences, probably in an attempt to remove the memory of the Welsh dynasty.

The archaeological record reveals a strong native tradition of fortification, but work at Mathrafal in Powys must also be considered. There, and at other sites in Powys including Buttington, Plas-yn-Dinas and Cwrt Llechryd, Norman motte and bailey castles are surrounded by rectangular earthwork enclosures. It had been considered that these earthworks pre-dated the castles and represented traditional Welsh centres, the fortifications being influenced by Roman and Anglo-Saxon traditions.[31] However, the work at Mathrafal has revealed that the earthworks post-date the castle and represent the bounds of a medieval estate. No pre-Norman connections have been found at the site.[32]

Fortification strategy, 1066–1283

The arrival of the Normans saw a greatly increased emphasis in our sources on the role of fortifications and repeated references to the castles of the invaders and of native lords. However, there is no astonishment expressed at the supposedly striking new invention of the castle; there were Welsh and Latin terms quite appropriate for the phenomenon.[33] What the Normans brought to Wales was a different style of fortification, appropriate to their needs and suitable for the conquest of the country. The

---

[31] For this interpretation, see C. R. Musson and C. J. Spurgeon, 'Cwrt Llechryd, Llanelwedd: an unusual moated site in central Powys', *Medieval Archaeology*, 32 (1988), 97–109.

[32] C. J. Arnold, J. W. Huggett and H. Pryce, 'Excavations at Mathrafal, Powys, 1989', *The Montgomeryshire Collections*, 83 (1995), 59–74; also C. J. Arnold and J. W. Huggett, 'Pre-Norman rectangular earthworks in mid Wales', *Medieval Archaeology*, 39 (1995), 171–4.

[33] Stenton, *Anglo-Saxon*, p. 561, says that Earl Ralf introduced castle building to Wales in the 1050s in an attempt to reorganize the defence of the Herefordshire border. His efforts do not seem to have had a major impact; the period was characterized by some of the most devastating of all Welsh raids across the English border.

importance of castles cannot be seen only in military terms. Denmark, for example, had a long history of fortification, but only in the fourteenth century did castles begin to proliferate: 'It was only then that a sufficiently numerous class of squirearchy consolidated their landed interests and set up permanent homes on their estates, frequently adopting variants on the motte and bailey theme.'[34] In Wales, the Norman influx brought a wealthy class of lower nobility to the country; their native predecessors had lacked the resources to develop private fortifications and may have been held back from so doing by the kings. In any case, such wide-scale castle building was a phenomenon new to nearly all of Europe in the eleventh century.

Many early Norman castles were hastily built structures bearing little resemblance to the great stone buildings into which some were transformed in succeeding centuries.[35] A mound topped with a few stakes is unlikely to have overwhelmed the Welsh by its military sophistication. Gerald of Wales described the first Norman castle built by Arnulf of Montgomery on the naturally defensible site of Pembroke as made of 'wooden stakes and turf . . . it was not very strong and it offered little resistance'.[36] Gerald may have exaggerated the weakness of the castle in order to glorify its defence by his grandfather Gerald of Windsor, but his description gives a better idea of how the original fort would have appeared than does the mighty stone castle that stands today.

The Latin term *castrum* means in the singular a fortified post or settlement and in the plural a camp. Such terms are common in the pre-Norman Latin sources of Wales and Ireland. *Castellum*, or 'castle', is the diminutive form of *castrum* and this term, or the Welsh *castell*, was adopted to describe the specific types of fortresses built by the Norman invaders.[37] The adoption was possibly influenced by the Latin term *castro* to signify that they

---

[34] R. Higham and P. Barker, *Timber Castles* (London, 1992), p. 351.
[35] For the importance and strength of such timber castles, see ibid., pp. 17ff.
[36] *Journey*, I, 12, p. 148.
[37] Early Welsh law texts detailing duties to work on the king's camp (W. *castra*) were later changed to require work on the *castell*. This has been interpreted as a major imposition by the thirteenth-century princes to help them keep up with military advances, but the change in terminology is minor and is unlikely to indicate a serious change in the duties owed. See also *LG*, p. 252.

were places 'cut off' or entrenched.[38] The early Norman castles were smaller than native fortified sites, reflecting the nature of the conquest and settlement; the Normans were few in number and needed a secure refuge to which to retreat in times of need before superior forces could be gathered. In the previous centuries the over-kings of Wales had succeeded in destroying the private fortifications of minor lords, but the proliferation of small fortresses soon after 1066 reflected the reduction of the native leaders.

When the Normans entered Wales and erected their castles they were seeking to '*transform* the political balance of any area in which it [the castle] was planted'.[39] The value of the castle to the Anglo-Norman conquest of Ireland was described thus:

> In which manner, know ye all,
> was the country planted
> with castles and with cities,
> with keeps and with strongholds.
> thus *well rooted* were
> the noble renowned vassals.[40]

The connection between the Anglo-Normans building castles in Wales and taking possession of the land was made clear in the *Brutiau* in 1093 following the death of Rhys ap Tewdwr: the invaders overran Dyfed and Ceredigion 'and made castles in them. And then the French seized all the lands of the Britons.'[41] Castles had their limitations in war; they could be bypassed and ignored and they did little to stop the recurrent raiding of the Welsh.[42] Similarly in Scotland, although castles were the key to the border defence of England, they could not stop ravaging or invasion and even strongly garrisoned castles could be contained

---

[38] Pierce, 'Evidence', pp. 471–2, suggests that the term *castell* was used in pre-Norman times for a smaller stronghold than a traditional *caer* or *dinas* and that it may have been used to refer to the fortified residence of a tribal chieftain. See also D. Longley, 'The excavations of Castell, Porth Trefadog: a coastal promontory fort in north Wales', *Medieval Archaeology*, 35 (1991), 64–85.

[39] Crouch, *Image*, p. 259 (my italics).

[40] G. H. Orpen (ed. and trans.), *The Song of Dermot and the Earl* (Oxford, 1892), p. 233 (my italics).

[41] *Brut (Pen. 20)*, s.a. 1093; see also ibid., s.a. 1110, where Gilbert fitz Richard is said to have 'taken possession' of Ceredigion by his building of castles near Aberystwyth and at Cardigan.

[42] Suppe, *Military*, pp. 26–30.

by detachments of a Scottish army.[43] What the castles provided for the Anglo-Normans was a foothold; however devastating a Welsh raid, the settlers were usually secure in their fortresses and could sit out the storm because they knew that, eventually, they would be relieved by their fellows or, ultimately, by a royal expedition. This final resort was denied to native rulers, and this explains why the Welsh never relied on castles as their last line of defence.

The revolt of 1094 left the Anglo-Normans on the point of being thrown out of Wales. The Welsh roamed at will through much of the country and were able to take and destroy a number of castles, but elsewhere the invaders sat tight and waited for better days. In 1096 the Welsh ravaged extensively in Brycheiniog, but the invaders were 'unafraid' because 'the castles were still intact and the garrisons in them'.[44] The Welsh besieging Gerald of Windsor in Pembroke were undaunted by their inability to take the castle as they plundered the land successfully, but Gerald retained his foothold and would prosper in later years. In 1105 Hywel ap Goronwy fell out of favour with Henry I and began to ravage Ystrad Tywi and Rhyd-y-gors: 'he burned the houses and the crops and ravaged the greater part of the whole land; and he slew many of the French as they were returning home and he encompassed the land on all sides and occupied it *except for the castles and their garrisons.*'[45] Hywel's failure to take the castles meant that his revolt remained a desperate affair and the following year he was killed 'by the treachery of the French of Rhyd-y-gors'.[46] Similarly, in his rebellion of 1116 Gruffudd ap Rhys failed to take many of the castles which he assaulted; he succeeded in storming the outer works but failed to overcome the inner keeps, the final, strongest refuge of the Anglo-Normans.[47] Even after the overwhelming Welsh victory in battle at Cardigan in 1136, they were unable to take the town's castle or remove the Anglo-Normans from the land; Cardigan was invested but relieved later in the year by a force brought from England by Miles of Gloucester.[48]

[43] Strickland, 'Securing', pp. 208–29.
[44] *Brut (RBH)*, s.a. 1096.
[45] *Brut (Pen. 20)*, s.a. 1105 (my italics).
[46] Ibid., s.a. 1106.
[47] Ibid., s.a. 1116.
[48] *GS*, p. 17.

As the Anglo-Normans built castles to take possession of the land, so in order to free the country the Welsh needed to destroy these fortifications. The revolt of 1094 was characterized by attacks on the castles; this was particularly notable after the battle of Coedysbys had weakened the field force of the Anglo-Normans.[49] *Gruffudd ap Cynan* describes the attack on Aberlleiniog, Anglesey:

> After the castle had been burned and the enemies defeated, Gruffudd rejoiced and moved against the other castles which were at other places in his kingdom, fought with them, burned them, wrecked them, and killed their occupants everywhere. He freed Gwynedd of its castles, took his country for himself.[50]

Even if this description of events is inaccurate, it reflects the attitude of the Welsh towards the alien castles. Gruffudd ap Rhys targeted Anglo-Norman castles in 1116, and after their success in the battle of Gower in 1136 the Welsh were able to destroy a number of fortifications.[51] Again in 1136, Owain's and Cadwaladr's first expedition to Ceredigion saw them burn four castles.[52]

It was some time before the Welsh began to use castles themselves and this has been seen in terms of their being slow learners. R. R. Davies says that Gerald of Wales 'noted two lessons in particular which the Welsh had learnt from the Normans, the use of arms and the management of horses, and to them should certainly be added a third, the construction of castles'.[53] In fact, Gerald notes that the fact that the Welsh avoided an over-reliance on fortifications made the task of conquering them more difficult: 'He [a conquering English king] can never hope to conquer in one single battle a people which will never draw up its forces to engage an enemy army in the field, and will never allow itself to be besieged inside fortified strong-points.'[54] In Scotland, the natives chose to destroy rather than utilize conquered castles; they did not want to be drawn

---

[49] See *ASC* (E), s.a. 1094–5; JW, III, 1094; *Brut (Pen. 20)*, s.a. 1094.
[50] *Gruffudd ap Cynan*, p. 73.
[51] JW, III, 1136.
[52] *Brut (Pen. 20)*, s.a. 1136.
[53] *Age*, p. 104.
[54] *Description*, II, 8, p. 267.

from a war of mobility and knew that the English could muster overwhelming force against any fixed point they chose to defend.[55] Similarly in Wales, when William fitz Baldwin, the castellan of Rhyd-y-gors, died in 1096 the castle was left empty; there seems to have been no fear of the Welsh utilizing the fortification and there is no indication that it was slighted.[56] In the revolts of 1094–6, 1116 and 1136–7 the Welsh were intent on destroying castles, but, as they were unsure of the response from the king in England, there was no suggestion of their refortifying and holding captured sites. Rhys ap Gruffudd followed a castle-burning strategy in his early career; his campaigns opened with him targeting the strategically important Marcher castle of Llandovery.[57] In 1157–8, Rhys could get no satisfaction in his dealings with Henry II: 'when Rhys ap Gruffudd saw that he could get nothing willingly save what he won with his arms he made for the castles which the earls and barons had built all over Ceredigion and he burned them all'.[58] During Rhys's campaigns of 1159 and 1164 he was still at loggerheads with Henry and continued to rely on a policy of destruction. Similarly, in the chaotic years in Deheubarth after the death of Henry in 1189, Rhys's son Hywel Sais ordered the destruction of his own castle of Llawhaden 'after he had seen that all his castles could not be held unless one of them were demolished'.[59]

In inter-Welsh warfare the same motivations regarding the use of castles may be discerned. In 1208 Llywelyn ap Iorwerth strengthened his alliance with King John whereby he was to obtain all of Gwenwynwyn's lands and castles. Maelgwn ap Rhys, who had been contesting control of Ceredigion with Llywelyn, knew that he could not now hope to face his enemy in the field and hence could not rely on castles for defence. In contrast, Llywelyn could hold Ceredigion with a chain of castles:

---

[55] Strickland, 'Securing', pp. 208–29. Castles were rarely used for defence by the native lords of Ireland in the period; see T. McNeill, *Castles in Ireland: Feudal Power in a Gaelic World* (London, 1997).
[56] *Brut (RBH)*, s.a. 1096.
[57] R. K. Turvey, 'Llandovery Castle and the Pipe Rolls (1159–62)', *The Carmarthenshire Antiquary*, 26 (1990), 5–12.
[58] *Brut (Pen. 20)*, s.a. 1158.
[59] Ibid., s.a. 1193.

And when Maelgwn ap Rhys learned that for fear of Llywelyn ap Iorwerth he overthrew the castle of Ystrad Meurig to the ground and burned Dineirth and Aberystwyth [these were all Maelgwn's own castles]. But nevertheless Llywelyn did not desist from his design, but he came to Aberystwyth and built it and took the *cantref* of Penweddig for himself.[60]

When the Welsh came to use castles, it was not simply a case of copying the Anglo-Normans when they had mastered the art of fortress building. They chose to invest their power and wealth in holding a castle only when political circumstances were right, namely, when they enjoyed the backing of the king in England or when he was too weak to intervene and when they were confident they could hold a castle against potential Welsh or Marcher rivals. The first reference in the *Brutiau* to Welsh lords holding castles comes in 1109.[61] Those concerned were client rulers of Henry I in Powys who were seeking the fugitives Cadwgan ap Bleddyn and his son Owain on behalf of the king. There is also a reference to Cadwgan's own castle; he had been another of Henry's clients, but after earning the king's anger he chose to flee rather than try to defend his stronghold.

In Stephen's reign it became clear that the king and the most powerful English lords were too preoccupied in England and Normandy to interfere in Wales. After the Welsh military successes of 1136–7 they began to invest in new castles, as Owain Gwynedd in particular sought to develop his lordship and to exert a firmer grip on his lands. As the most powerful force in Wales, he was confident in his ability to maintain his castles and relieve them from any besieging force. This helps to explain why, in 1157, Owain chose the unique strategy of facing a royal expedition in the field; he wanted to protect the lordship he had built and to prevent a superior force from assaulting his castles. A key moment in the Welsh development of castles seems to have been Ranulf of Chester's isolation from court in 1146; this negated a powerful force on the border and from this point, notably in the period 1149–51, there was a burst of native castle building and of examples of the Welsh making use of captured castles rather than destroying them.[62]

[60] Ibid., s.a. 1208.
[61] *Bren.*, s.a. 1109.
[62] See *Brut (Pen. 20)*, s.a. 1146–51.

Rhys ap Gruffudd's career of castle-burning until 1164 has been noted. He had faced strong opposition from Henry II, but the failure of the king's expedition of 1165 altered the strategic situation. Henry changed his attitude towards Wales as he was too preoccupied elsewhere for continued confrontation with the Welsh princes. Rhys and Owain had shown that, by working together, they could secure their realms against Henry and thus they had the confidence to develop their lands further and invest in castles. In 1165 Rhys took and burnt Cardigan but also, in a tentative change of policy, took and occupied Cilgerran.[63] The decisive change of direction came in 1170–1. Henry was embroiled in the Becket affair and, more importantly, was anxious to deal with the English in Ireland. He decided to come to terms with Rhys and to balance the Welsh king against the English of south Wales whose increasing power was troubling him. After their agreement, Henry 'gave to the Lord Rhys Ceredigion and Ystrad Tywi and Efelffre. And in that summer the Lord Rhys had built with stone and mortar the castle of Cardigan, which he had before had demolished when he took it from the earl of Clare.'[64] This is the first reference in the *Brutiau* to the Welsh building a castle in stone and it shows the investment which Rhys was prepared to make with the security offered by the king's acknowledgement of his right to rule. Rhys would later develop other castles including Rhayader and Llandovery. Following Henry's death, and with Richard preoccupied with the crusade and his French lands, Rhys took the offensive against the English and seized a number of their castles. In 1196, however, he raided certain occupied Marcher areas that he could not hope to hold permanently and his campaign of that year was characterized by the destruction of castles.

The use of castles by Rhys ap Gruffudd and Llywelyn ap Iorwerth was connected with their dealings on the wider political scene and it is clear that they never saw their fortifications as defences against the power of the English king. This should be remembered when considering Gwynedd in the thirteenth century. The princes pursued an ambitious fortress-building policy which G. R. J. Jones saw as part of a grand strategy; he

---

[63] Ibid., s.a. 1165.
[64] *Brut (RBH)*, s.a. 1171.

believed that they planned to advance to the east, south and south-east, whilst controlling barrier zones to protect the heartland of Gwynedd – Arfon, Llŷn and Anglesey.[65] There were three concentric mountain ramparts which Gwynedd would seek to hold, aided principally by the precipitous ground, thick woods and dangerous rivers that covered their approaches. Jones claimed that the princes tried to strengthen these natural defences by building stone castles at strategic points.

The argument is convincing and the castles seem to have been built according to a plan of strategic defence, but this interpretation needs qualification. The princes of Gwynedd had been increasingly drawn into the wider European world and their fortification policy was designed to raise their standing and prestige. Llywelyn ap Gruffudd's castles should be considered in the context of his struggles with Powys and the lords of the March, notably the Mortimers and Gilbert de Clare. At this level, castles were militarily crucial; the *Brutiau* refer to them as the 'bolts and stays' of a ruler's domain.[66] Fortification strategies at this level have been considered at length.[67] However, Welsh rulers never intended their castles to serve as defences against an attack by the English king; their situation on strategic points meant they could serve as local campaign bases from which mobile forces could harass an invading force, but they were not held to the last.

After the treaty of Montgomery (1267), Llywelyn ap Gruffudd felt that he had the security to develop his principality, as his position was accepted by the English monarchy. Llywelyn knew he could never hold his castles against a royal expedition and that if faced with such an eventuality he would have to rely on

[65] *Defences*, pp. 29–43; *Military*, pp. 94–104. J. B. Smith says that Llywelyn ap Iorwerth was the major investor in stone castles and that his grandson's building programme was less prominent; *LG*, p. 252. Longley notes that Gwynedd's native stone castles were built for military not administrative purposes as they were situated away from known *maerdref* sites. In this they contrast with the earlier earthwork fortifications built by the princes of Gwynedd; Longley, 'Royal courts', p. 52.

[66] See the description of Cardigan in *Brut (Pen. 20)*, s.a. 1200, and of Dinefwr and Llandovery in ibid., s.a. 1204

[67] In addition to G. R. J. Jones, see R. K. Turvey's work on Rhys ap Gruffudd's fortification strategy, 'The defences of Deheubarth and the castle strategy of the Lord Rhys', *Arch. Camb.*, 154 (1995), 103–32. Rhys built strong, new castles, many in stone, to define, consolidate and defend his principality. Turvey notes the importance of boroughs to the development of stone castles; Anglo-Norman skills, materials, finance and mercantile connections from the conquered boroughs made Rhys's building programme possible.

the traditional strategies of shadowing and evasion. In 1277 and 1282 no serious attempt was made by Llywelyn to defend any of his castles. With the exception of that at Dolforwyn, all his garrisons were small. Llywelyn made efforts to ensure mobile supplies for his troops; cattle farms were established at strategic points in the mountains to supply his field forces, whereas little was stockpiled so that the garrisons could sit out a siege.

Similar attitudes to fortifications can be perceived in south Wales in the thirteenth century.[68] Excavations at Dryslwyn Castle reveal that almost all major developments on the site can be traced to its period of Welsh occupation.[69] The initial phase came in the period *c.*1220–40 after Llywelyn ap Iorwerth settled the political situation in the south by the treaty of Aberdyfi. The greatest period of development came after 1282. Rhys ap Maredudd, the last surviving native Welsh prince, felt secure in his position, having proven his loyalty to Edward I in the wars of conquest. Rhys had increased his power and wealth and sought to compete with his peers, the lords of the March. This is revealed by the finds of exotic, imported foods on the site and by new fortifications dating from this period. When Rhys found himself disappointed by Edward and turned to revolt in 1287, the English siege of his castle lasted only three weeks. Rhys was almost caught at Dryslwyn, but he managed to flee and harry the English by using traditional, guerrilla tactics.

SIEGE TACTICS

From the end of Roman Britain to 1066 there is virtually no evidence of Welsh techniques used in siege warfare.[70] The

---

[68] Turvey's assessment of Rhys ap Gruffudd's castle strategy can be accepted without it being seen as a strategy for defence against the English king. Turvey claims that Rhys's decision to destroy Carmarthen in 1196 rather than utilize the captured castle is 'inexplicable'. He says that Carmarthen and Swansea would have provided Deheubarth with a complete 'defensive shield' against future aggression; see Turvey, 'Defences', 122. However, the other castles used by Rhys were captured from English lords whilst Carmarthen was a royal castle; Rhys could not hope to hold it against the king and a 'castle strategy' could not work at this level.

[69] C. Caple, 'The castle and lifestyle of a thirteenth-century independent Welsh lord; excavations at Dryslwyn Castle, 1980–8', *Château Gaillard*, 14 (1990), 47–59.

[70] An exception is the siege of Bamburgh. Oswiu was besieged by Penda, whose force contained a significant Welsh contingent. The siege and direct assault failed to take Bamburgh, so Penda tried to burn the town. This looked likely to succeed until Oswiu was saved by a change in wind direction; Bede, III, 16, p. 263.

external enemies of the Welsh – the Anglo-Saxons, Irish and Vikings – made little use of fortifications in their warfare in Wales and generally had the Welsh on the defensive so that sieges did not arise. In inter-Welsh warfare, chieftains needed to face their enemies to protect their land from being ravaged. It seems likely that assaults were, on occasions, made against the fortifications of rival Welsh leaders, however; Taliesin's poem in praise of Cynan Garwyn of Powys lauds the dominance of the king over contemporary Welsh rulers: 'kat ygwlat brachan/ katlan god aran'[71] (War in Brychan's land:/Hill fort a molehill!).[72] Further evidence of siege warfare is notably lacking. The only other pre-1066 reference of note is in 1055 when Gruffudd ap Llywelyn carried war towards the fortified settlements of England. After the battle outside Hereford, Gruffudd was able to breach the gates and wreak havoc in the walled town, but it seems that his entry was effected in the general post-battle panic as the English forces streamed back to the city.[73]

Given the lack of emphasis on siege warfare before 1066, it is not surprising that it is generally thought that the Normans introduced siege techniques to Wales.[74] However, the belief that siege tactics in the period required a significant military technology needs to be reconsidered. Studies of sieges in medieval Europe, even in the most advanced states like Byzantium, suggest that siege towers, catapults, bores and the like rarely forced the capitulation of strongholds.[75] Few new techniques emerged in siege warfare between the fall of Rome and the end of the Middle Ages. The human element – surprise, cunning and political machinations – might overcome a fortification, and such

---

[71] *CT*, I, p. 1

[72] Clancy, *Earliest*, p. 24. Urien of Rheged, a contemporary British leader in the north, 'blockaded' the Anglo-Saxons on the island of Lindisfarne for three days and nights; *HB*, p. 38.

[73] The fact that Harold Godwinesson later strengthened the city defences may indicate that the fortifications were also not maintained to the necessary standard. Equally, of course, there may have been a need for repair because of the damage caused by Gruffudd.

[74] See, for example, Nicolle, *Medieval*, p. 152; Nelson, *Normans*, p. 12; Warren, *Henry II*, p. 159; *Dulliau*, pp. 76–93.

[75] Bradbury, *The Medieval Siege* (Woodbridge, 1992); E. McGeer, 'Byzantine siege warfare in theory and practice', in I. A. Corfis and M. Wolfe (eds), *The Medieval City under Siege* (Woodbridge, 1995), pp. 123–9; *WW*, pp. 107–27.

techniques are reflected in practice and are emphasized in military manuals. Direct assault could be costly and success was far from assured due to the physical advantages gained by the defender of even the most modest fortification, but when attempted the simplest techniques were often the best; fire, scaling ladders, rams and bores were far more prominent than anything more sophisticated. In *The Dream of Maxen*, the elaborate assaults made by Maxen's army on Rome over the period of a year are described, but success was only achieved when his British troops tried a more cunning approach, by making one wooden ladder for every four of their men and scaling the walls whilst the enemy was at lunch.[76]

It could be argued that over the years the Welsh disadvantage in siege warfare became more pronounced as the English kings organized more elaborate siege trains against Welsh fortifications, and themselves built castles of increasing sophistication. However, even in the Glyndŵr revolt in the fifteenth century, Caernarfon castle was taken in a surprise assault by the Welsh. R. R. Davies emphasized the Welsh deficiency in siege equipment in the revolt and the superior English technology, noting the assembling of heavy guns by the English for the sieges of Aberystwyth and Harlech in 1407–9.[77] He acknowledged, however, that the guns had little effect and that both castles fell because of lack of supplies, the effect of hard winters, the exhausted Welsh war effort and the fact that there was no hope of eventual relief.

The siege tactics employed by the Welsh after 1066 will be examined with particular reference to the rich material contained in the *Brutiau*.[78] It is useful, however, to consider the contemporary techniques of Anglo-Norman warfare as described by Orderic Vitalis. It is notable how rarely assault succeeded, even when pressed closely by superior forces under effective commanders. To take one example: William the Conqueror failed to take the castle of Sainte-Suzanne from Hubert, *vicomte* of Le Mans. This was despite the fact that William pressed the

---

[76] *Mabinogi*, pp. 125–6; *BM*, pp. 10–12.
[77] R. R. Davies, *The Revolt of Owain Glyn Dŵr* (Oxford, 1995), p. 253.
[78] J. R. Kenyon's article 'Fluctuating frontiers: Normano-Welsh castle warfare, c.1075–1240', *Château Gaillard*, 17 (1996), 119–26, relies on the same sources used for this study, but the conclusions differ significantly.

siege vigorously for three years, tried numerous assaults and built a siege castle.[79] Robert of Bellême was acknowledged as an expert in the construction of siege equipment; the surrender of Bréval was attributed to his 'ingenious' machines, although the castle submitted and was not taken by force.[80] It was unusual for such techniques to enjoy much success; at Courcy, Bellême's forces suffered a torrid time, taking heavy losses and having their siege tower burnt by the garrison.[81] In contrast to these difficult sieges, the most common successes were won by surprise or cunning.[82] Other fortifications were taken because of disease amongst the garrison, shortage of supplies or fire.[83] In a world of shifting political alliances, garrisons might also surrender castles if they feared no backlash from an overlord, or felt that they would not be relieved.[84] In short, it was extremely difficult to take a castle held by an alert, determined and well-supplied garrison.

Given these factors, the level of success enjoyed by the Welsh in assaulting Anglo-Norman castles is remarkable. Of course, many of the fortifications were not of the standard seen in Normandy, but as a land of regular conflict the Welsh March contained well-supplied castles with experienced garrisons on a state of alert. More poignantly, the troops were determined; they knew they were fighting to maintain their foothold in a hostile land, fighting for their lives and homes, and that, if they held on, help would come from other lords of the March or the king. The Welsh could rarely afford to be drawn into sieges, which would leave their troops exposed to the superior resources which the Anglo-Normans were able to muster.

Carr contended that the Welsh learnt the art of siege warfare from the Normans by contrasting the failure of one of their earliest recorded sieges, at Pembroke in 1096, with the successes enjoyed by Rhys ap Gruffudd in the mid-twelfth century.[85]

[79] OV, IV, 7, p. 49.
[80] Ibid., IV, 8, p. 289.
[81] Ibid., IV, 8, pp. 233–7.
[82] Ibid., IV, 8, p. 295; VI, 11, pp. 33–5; VI, 12, p. 185.
[83] Ibid., IV, 8, p. 129; IV, 8, p. 209; IV, 8, p. 251.
[84] Ibid., V, 10, pp. 303–5; VI, 12, pp. 195–7.
[85] *Dulliau*, p. 83. Although the source is late and cannot be trusted, the earliest suggestion of a Welsh attack on a Norman castle was *c.*1075. Gruffudd ap Cynan attacked Robert of Rhuddlan's castle at Rhuddlan and burnt the bailey. As no mention is made of the keep and Robert continued to hold the land, it is presumed that this remained intact; *Gruffudd ap Cynan*, p. 62.

However, it was the Welsh successes in 1094–6 against all the Norman castles in Gwynedd, and all but two in Ceredigion and Dyfed, that were recorded by John of Worcester and the *Brutiau*, and these successes were remembered in *Gruffudd ap Cynan*.[86] Gerald of Wales's account of the siege of Pembroke sought to glorify the role of the castellan, his grandfather Gerald of Windsor, but even so it seems that the castle was in desperate straits and only the cunning of Gerald saved it from capture.[87] The threat of intervention from the king prevented the Welsh from taking the remaining strongholds and driving the invaders from the land.

We lack details of Welsh siege tactics in the revolt of 1094–6. The speed with which large numbers of castles fell suggests that they were carried by surprise or storm, although the protracted events at Pembroke indicate that the Welsh were capable of investing a castle. Accounts of the fall of strongholds in the *Brutiau* merely say that they were taken, giving no details of whether they were given up, easily overwhelmed, or taken after a hard fight. It is impossible to determine whether siege engines were used in 1094–6; *Gruffudd ap Cynan* refers to the 'quarrels, slings and mangonels' used at the siege of Aberlleiniog, but these may only have been used by the Normans and in any case the source is not contemporary.

Given the importance of siege warfare in Normandy, it is possible that the Anglo-Normans introduced siege engines to Wales. By 1116 such machines were an accepted element in Welsh tactical thinking; Gruffudd ap Rhys's army at Aberystwyth was criticized for wasting time deliberating whether to build engines and how best to assault the castle.[88] Catapults, slings, hooked ladders and engines were the siege machines used and, given the speed of their movement on campaign, those utilized by the Welsh were probably light and constructed on site.[89] The next reference to the use of siege engines does not

---

[86] *Gruffudd ap Cynan*, p. 73.
[87] *Journey*, I, 12, pp. 148–9.
[88] For the history of fortification at Aberystwyth, see R. A. Griffiths, 'The three castles at Aberystwyth', in his *Conquerors and Conquered in Medieval Wales* (Stroud, 1994), pp. 322–36.
[89] King, 'Defences', 14, says that the Welsh did not use siege towers, the trebuchet or the mangonel and that the perrière was probably their regular siege engine. The argument is reasonable but has no supporting evidence.

occur until 1193. In that year the *teulu* of Maelgwn ap Rhys took the castle of Ystrad Meurig 'with slings and catapults'.[90] *Teuluoedd* are frequently associated with successful sieges. Further references to the Welsh use of siege engines occur at Painscastle in 1196, Llandovery and Llangadog in 1203 and Dinefwr in 1213, where they were used by Welshmen in both the attacking and the defending forces. Llywelyn ap Iorwerth was noted for his use of machines and in 1231 a major siege using engines succeeded in forcing the submission of Cardigan after earlier attempts had failed. In 1233, however, the month-long siege of Brecon failed despite the presence of many engines. Given the number of sieges conducted and the amazement of the chroniclers that, in 1198, Gwenwynwyn continued the siege of Painscastle for three weeks 'without any recourse to catapults or slings', it seems likely that such machines were regularly employed by the Welsh.

It is possible that Anglo-Norman techniques remained more diverse. There were Welsh and Anglo-Normans involved in the siege of Welshpool in 1196 and word reached the native chronicler of the 'diverse engines and siege contrivances' employed. This suggests that some of the machines were, to the Welsh, out of the ordinary; they were similarly impressed by the 'wondrous ingenuity' by which the castle was eventually won, with sappers undermining the walls and forcing the garrison's surrender.[91] Mining was a common device employed in Anglo-Norman siege warfare. By the mid-thirteenth century at the latest it had been mastered by the Welsh; excavations of the south wall and gate built by Henry III at Degannwy (1250–2) revealed that it was destroyed by mining, having been under-propped with timber and fired. This accords with the chronicler's account of Llywelyn ap Gruffudd's destruction of the castle in 1263 after a seven-year siege.[92] Possible Welsh use of siege castles is more problematic. There is no documentary evidence of their use and it was usually to the tactical advantage of the Welsh to avoid such fixed

---

[90] *Brut (Pen. 20)*, s.a. 1193.
[91] Sappers were also employed at Dinefwr in 1213. It is possible that the Welsh had learnt from 1196 or the miners were directed by Anglo-Normans in Rhys Ieuanc's army.
[92] Alcock, 'Excavations at Degannwy', 192. 'Not less than 1,500 linear feet of walling was systematically thrown down, implying the labour of a large force of miners as well as the provision of an untold quantity of props. All this is a striking testimony to the authority, power and malice of Llywelyn ap Gruffudd.'

positions, but a number of unexplained mounds in Wales may have been siege works.[93]

Although the Welsh had knowledge of siege engines, other, simpler techniques were more common and often more effective. Many of the castles must have fallen to direct assault, with the attackers rushing forward and throwing ropes and ladders against the walls. This would be particularly effective against a heavily outnumbered garrison (the majority of garrisons are likely to have been small), although even then it was a dangerous tactic. At Llanstephan in 1146, the young Maredudd ap Gruffudd and a small force repulsed a determined Marcher assault with scaling ladders, inflicting heavy casualties. Examples of castles taken by direct assault include Cynfael (1147), Llanrhystud (1151) and Narberth (1220). Gerald of Wales describes how the Welsh hid in the overgrown ditches of Abergavenny Castle in 1182 before scaling the wall with ladders and burning the bailey,[94] and Ifor Bach entered the heavily defended Cardiff Castle using a ladder.[95] The attack on Dinefwr in 1213 saw the use of siege ladders in combination with engines, sappers and crossbowmen;[96] this combination of forces is likely to have characterized the usual conduct of a siege.

Fire was one of the greatest threats to buildings in the Middle Ages, and in siege warfare it was always an effective weapon. This particularly applies to the early timber castles, but plenty of flammable material was used in later stone fortifications.[97] There is a problem with the evidence supplied by the *Brutiau* in determining the use made of fire at sieges. At Narberth in 1116, Gruffudd ap Rhys burnt the castle 'in the first attack that he made'; it seems clear in this case that fire was used to achieve the taking of the stronghold. However, the usual formulae state that a Welsh leader 'took and burnt' a castle and it cannot be determined whether the castle was burnt after its capture or if

---

[93] Higham and Barker, *Timber*, p. 243, and Kenyon, 'Fluctuating', 125, suggest that a mound near Castell Cwm Aron, Radnorshire, may be a siege castle associated with attacks on the castle before one of its recorded rebuildings in 1144, 1179 and 1195. Another possibility is 'Lady's Mount' near Powis Castle; Higham and Barker, *Timber*, p. 242.
[94] *Journey*, I, 4, pp. 110–11; the keep remained intact.
[95] Ibid., I, 6, p. 122; this was an individual raid rather than a siege.
[96] *Brut (Pen. 20)*, s.a. 1213.
[97] Higham and Barker, *Timber*, p. 350, acknowledge the dangers of fire but note that there were ways to limit the threat.

fire was the key to the success of the siege. Almost a stock phrase to describe the actions of a Welsh leader in revolt was that he took the Norman castles 'and burned them all'. However, fire may only have been deployed if the attacking force was anxious for quick results, since the burning of a castle in the initial assault would mean the destruction of any booty kept within the walls.

The most economical way to take a castle, in terms of time, effort and lives, was by cunning, treachery or surprise.[98] Such tactics were employed by the Welsh and, as in the rest of Europe, they elicited no expressions of shame in the sources; rather the cunning of a successful commander would be commended.[99] Details of the methods employed are lacking, but we are told that Tafolwern (1162), Wizo's Castle (1193), Cilgerran (1199) and Cefn-llys (1262) were taken by 'treachery'. In 1202 Rhys Ieuanc took Llandovery by 'diligence and invention'.[100] Night was a great ally to surprise and the outer works of Carmarthen (1116) and Abergavenny (1182) were taken during night attacks; Tenby was taken in 1153 'by treachery at night'. We have more details concerning the fall of Builth in 1260. Llywelyn ap Gruffudd's initial siege was unsuccessful and he led his army away to ravage Deheubarth. He returned secretly to Builth and caught the garrison unawares:

> As men from the castle were opening the gates for the others who were without, behold Llywelyn's men leaping in by night and taking the castle. And so it was taken without so much as an arrow-shot, and such men and horses and arms and equipment as were in it; and it was destroyed to the ground.[101]

Dafydd Benfras was impressed with the ease of Llywelyn's victory: 'unimpeded brought to him Builth/without damage, with his flaming straw he sets fire'.[102]

---

[98] For the use of terror tactics to induce the surrender of garrisons, see below, p. 244.
[99] See the ruse employed by Richard I to take the 'impregnable' castle of Taillebourg, Aquitaine, in 1179; J. Gillingham, *Richard the Lionheart* (2nd edn, London, 1989), p. 81. See also Robert of Bellême's actions at Alençon in 1087; OV, IV, 8, p. 113.
[100] Gerald of Wales says that Rhys ap Gruffudd besieged Nevern with an armed force but that it was taken at the instigation of Rhys's son Gruffudd, 'a cunning, artful man'; *Journey*, II, 2, p. 170.
[101] *Brut (Pen. 20)*, s.a. 1260.
[102] Bosco, 'Dafydd Benfras', 103.

It was common for Welsh attacks to succeed in storming the outer bailey but to fail to take the inner keep. When we are told that a Welsh lord burnt an enemy castle, it is difficult to decide if the entire castle or just the bailey is meant. The revolt of 1094–6 virtually swept the Normans out of Gwynedd, Ceredigion and Dyfed. In the south-east, however, the hold of the invaders was firmer and, although the Welsh dominated the country, the castles remained intact. The Anglo-Norman hold on the south-east was never seriously shaken. In 1171 Iorwerth ab Owain revolted after shoddy treatment by Henry II; he attacked Caerleon which he destroyed 'to the tower'. Again in 1173 he took the bailey of Caerleon but not the keep, although this was later handed over to preserve the lives of those members of the garrison captured by Iorwerth in the initial assault. The revolt continued and Iorwerth's son Hywel was able to win all of Gwent Is-Coed 'except the castles'.[103]

Such limited success was mirrored elsewhere in Wales. Gruffudd ap Rhys's revolt of 1116 gives the impression of a rootless affair as he moved through the Marcher lands making a series of desperate assaults on castles. After initial success at Narberth, he attacked Llandovery and then Swansea; in both cases he was only able to take and burn the bailey and his force suffered heavy casualties. A successful night attack on the bailey (not the keep) of Carmarthen followed, before he moved against an unnamed castle in Gower which he 'burnt outright'. The host then moved to Ceredigion and the siege of Blaen-porth. There was a fierce assault on the keep with losses on both sides, but only the town and bailey were burnt. They proceeded to lay siege to, and completely overcome, Ystrad Peithyll, before reaching Aberystwyth. There, delay and hesitation before embarking on a siege allowed the Anglo-Normans to gather their forces and overwhelm Gruffudd.

If Gruffudd's revolt was a breathless affair, even the most powerful Welsh rulers sometimes succeeded only in taking the outer baileys of castles. In 1220, Llywelyn ap Iorwerth led an army against the Flemings of Rhos and Pembroke and managed to take Narberth and Wizo's Castle. At Haverford, he was only

---

[103] *Brut (Pen. 20)*, s.a. 1171, 1173.

able to burn the town 'to the gates of the castle'.[104] In 1233 he led a powerful force south to Brycheiniog, where he 'burnt all the towns and castles that were in that land'. He invested Brecon itself for a month, using siege engines to throw down the walls before burning the town. Eventually, he had to leave the castle intact and retreat 'for fear' – presumably of a relief army.[105] At Builth (1221) and Montgomery (1228), Llywelyn's men were forced to abandon sieges because of the approach of royal expeditions.

The course of a siege must be related to its political context. In 1116, Gruffudd ap Rhys was on the run and it would have been tactical suicide to settle his forces down for a prolonged siege. In 1147, his sons Cadell, Maredudd and Rhys faced a very different political situation and they reacted accordingly. There was no danger of royal intervention and the Anglo-Norman lords were themselves in dispute. Consequently, the sons of Gruffudd allied with William fitz Gerald, called Hywel ab Owain to their aid and laid siege to Wizo's Castle. As the strongest field force in the area, the allies had no fear of a long siege; we are told that the castle fell after 'great toil and conflict' and that 'at last' victory was attained.[106] Prolonged sieges were not beyond the capability of the Welsh; they were able to master the required organization and logistics.[107]

The importance of the political situation to the course of a siege may be seen in 1165. The castle of Cardigan had been besieged since late in 1164; it was the key to Ceredigion and, although the Welsh could ravage to its gate and dominate the countryside, the garrison held firm, secure in the expectancy of eventual relief and supply by sea. Soon after the failure of Henry II's 1165 expedition, however, Rhys ap Gruffudd was able to take and burn Cardigan Castle. Was this through successful assault, or was the garrison resigned to the fact that no relief force was coming? There is a suggestion that Rhys was aided by a Welsh cleric, Rhigyfarch, who had access to the castle, but it is possible that he merely brokered a deal between the rival parties.

[104] Ibid., s.a. 1220.
[105] Ibid., s.a. 1233.
[106] Ibid., s.a. 1147.
[107] At Swansea in 1192 the forces of Deheubarth mounted a ten-week siege of the castle. It failed because of Welsh disunity and a royal response that made the besiegers' position untenable; ibid., s.a. 1192.

With royal policy towards south Wales changing, and faced with an indefinite siege, the garrison was within its rights to submit. The repercussions of 1165 went further. In 1167 Owain Gwynedd allied with Rhys and moved to Rhuddlan, besieging the castle for three months before it eventually fell. The Welsh princes proceeded to besiege and take Prestatyn, allowing the recapture of Tegeingl after extended English rule.

In 1215, with the English king again unable to master the military situation in Wales, the native rulers achieved great success against the Anglo-Norman castles. Llywelyn ap Iorwerth led a coalition of Welsh princes and the garrisons knew that this was the most powerful force in Wales. Many castles submitted almost as soon as Llywelyn appeared before their gates. The lesser fortifications fell almost immediately, but even Carmarthen Castle capitulated after just five days and Cardigan and Cilgerran soon followed.[108] In 1159 and 1196 Carmarthen had resisted major Welsh sieges for extended periods. Even the greatest fortifications could not hold out when confronted by the dominant military and political force in the land.

---

[108] Carmarthen was besieged on 8 December and fell on 13 December. Cardigan and Cilgerran submitted on 26 December.

VI
CONDUCT IN WARFARE

The conduct of war in Wales, as often in Ireland and Scotland, tends to be seen as different, more brutal and primitive than that seen elsewhere in Europe in the Middle Ages. It is perceived that Anglo-Saxon conduct was in line with the rest of Britain, but that after 1066 new codes of behaviour were introduced to England related to the growth of chivalry.[1] This meant that, from the twelfth century, observers from England and continental Europe were horrified by the brutality of war in Wales, Ireland and Scotland. Part of the reason for the supposed total war seen in these lands is said to have been the inability of the native armies to compete with their enemies from England and France in terms of technology, numbers or military skill; they chose guerrilla warfare and terror tactics as a way of striking back.[2]

Guillaume le Breton described the activities of the Welsh in Richard I's service in Normandy in 1196: 'raiding our lands whose gates lay everywhere open to them, these savages slaughtered pitilessly young and old alike'.[3] By the time of Froissart, the Welsh, Irish and Highland Scots were decidedly outsiders of the tight-knit, chivalric world of western Europe as perceived by its chroniclers.[4] At Crécy in 1346, after the French cavalry charge had been broken by the English archers:

> Among the English there were pillagers and irregulars, Welsh and Cornishmen armed with long knives, who went out after the French (their

---

[1] See J. Gillingham, '1066 and the introduction of chivalry into England', in Garnett and Hudson, *Law*, pp. 44–55.

[2] Such notions are influenced by the perception of differences between so-called civilized warfare and the primitive warfare of non-state people seen in J. Keegan, *A History of Warfare* (London, 1993), p. 5. Even if such differentiation can be substantiated for cultures with different technologies and state structures, it is mistaken to imagine that such vast differences separated Wales and England in our period.

[3] M. Salmon, *A Source Book of Welsh History* (Oxford, 1927), p. 85. Such savagery was used to excuse the slaughter of the force when it was trapped by Philip's army.

[4] The chivalric values of prowess, loyalty, generosity, courtesy and 'franchise' were an ideal never approached in reality, but the ideal itself made an impact on society; see M. Keen, *Chivalry* (London, 1984).

own men-at-arms and archers making way for them) and, when they found any in difficulty, whether they were counts, barons, knights or squires, they killed them without mercy. Because of this, many were slaughtered that evening, regardless of their rank. It was a great misfortune and the king of England was afterwards very angry that none had been taken for ransom, for the number of dead lords was very great.[5]

In these examples the Welsh troops were recruited as the irregular units in the army and they acted under the direction of the commanding nobility.[6] It must be considered whether perceptions of excessive brutality in warfare in Wales have any basis in fact, how such perceptions may have arisen and whether any conventions controlled conduct. It has been suggested that warfare in Scotland differed from that seen in the post-1066 Anglo-French world in three specific areas: the indiscriminate killing of the population, ill-treatment or enslavement of prisoners, and disdain for the rights of the Church.[7] These areas of Welsh warfare will be considered. Evidence for the pre-1066 period is scarce, but where possible earlier traditions are discussed.

RAVAGING AND THE TREATMENT OF NON-COMBATANTS

Little further needs to be said about this subject; as is indicated above, no mercy was shown to the civilian population of the land.[8] Atrocities (in our perception) were commonplace and accepted by the chroniclers unless it served their purpose to condemn them. Although the blame for ravaging was often levelled at the troops on the ground, the commanding officers

---

[5] Froissart, *Chronicles*, ed. and trans. G. Brereton (London, 1968), p. 93.
[6] In Stephen's reign, Robert and Matilda employed numerous Welsh troops. They only started committing depravities after being 'let loose' by their commanders; OV, VI, 13, p. 537. Keegan argued that for centuries European commanders utilized the skills of irregular troops as essential to the functioning of their armies, whilst 'drawing a veil' over details of their conduct; Keegan, *History*, p. 5. At Agincourt (1415) French prisoners were taken in huge numbers, representing a danger to the English in the ongoing battle. Consequently Henry V ordered 200 archers to slaughter the captives; Keegan, *Face*, pp. 84, 110.
[7] Strickland, *War*, p. 304; and his 'Military technology', 381. Whilst acknowledging that the 'laws of war' in England and France were unwritten and frequently flouted, Strickland contends that they had the effect of limiting the brutality of conflict and that they produced a disparity with the conduct of warfare in the 'Celtic fringe' that was perceived by contemporaries.
[8] See above, pp. 89–111.

ordered the actions; it was the regular conduct of war. Conventions to control behaviour did not apply to the civilian population.[9] The Welsh reputation as savage and effective irregular troops has been noted. However, it is significant that they are rarely charged by sources from England with excessive, unacceptable ravaging. This contrasts with descriptions from England of the Scottish army at war; the Scots were labelled as animals who abused women and children, targeted the Church and clerics, and indulged in the drinking of blood and other inhuman acts. Such horror stories particularly relate to the raids made by the Scots into lowland England in the 1130s and 1170s; the English of these relatively sheltered communities were shocked as the reality of war was brought to their doorsteps. Independent Welsh forces were never powerful enough in the post-1066 period to pose a threat to the settled communities of lowland England.

In Wales, the closest comparable descriptions to the Scottish atrocity stories concern the revolt of 1136. After the battle in Gower, John of Worcester relates: 'thereupon the Welsh invaded in force, violently destroyed churches, townships, crops, and beasts far and wide, burnt down castles and other fortifications, slew, scattered, and sold into captivity abroad innumerable men, both rich and poor.'[10] The chronicler, familiar with warfare in Wales and capable of sympathy with the natives, betrays little sense of outrage. The author of the *Gesta Stephani* had access to similar sources of information regarding the events, but his treatment of the Welsh is hostile. After the battle in Gower it is recorded that the Welsh were 'addicted to every crime, ready for anything unlawful, they spared no age, showed no respect for any order, were not restrained from wickedness'.[11] John of Worcester and the Welsh chronicles agree that the battle of Cardigan in 1136 was bloody, but only the *Gesta Stephani* expands the story to include atrocity tales in the aftermath of the engagement:

---

[9] See Strickland, *Warfare*, pp. 258ff.
[10] JW, III, 1136. A sixteenth-century transcription by Sir John Stradling from the missing cartulary of Neath Abbey relates that after the battle *terra illa vastata fuit et depopulata*; F. R. Lewis, 'A history of the lordship of Gower from the missing cartulary of Neath Abbey', *BBCS*, 9 (1938), 149–54 (150).
[11] *GS*, p. 17.

with shouts and arrows they [the Welsh] pitifully slaughtered some, others they massacred by driving them violently into a river, a good number they put in houses and churches to which they set fire and burnt . . . old men they exposed to slaughter or mockery; the young of both sexes they delivered over to chains and captivity; women of any age they shamefully abandoned to public violation.[12]

In the 1136 revolt the Welsh descended on Anglo-Norman lowland communities in south-west Wales that had become established, and apparently secure, during Henry I's reign. This can account for the outrage in the *Gesta Stephani*; it was rare for the Welsh to strike into such settled areas. The nature of the colonization of south-west Wales also explains why the revolt was so bloody: in the preceding generation the land had been conquered from the Welsh, the native inhabitants displaced by force.[13] The most effective colonizers in south-west Wales were the Flemings. *Brut (Pen. 20)* records that they were brought into Rhos by Henry I in 1108 whereupon they 'drove away all the inhabitants from the land . . . And there they still remain, the inhabitants having lost the land.'[14] The bitterness, loss and anger felt at the methods of the Flemings created a lasting antipathy among the Welsh, fuelled by years of frontier conflict. After the victory at Cardigan the Welsh enjoyed the opportunity to strike back; in 1137 John of Worcester relates:

In the defence of their native land, the Welsh were hard pressed not only by the powerful Normans, but also by the Flemings. Many were killed on both sides, but in the end the Flemings were beaten, and the Welsh laid waste all around them, setting fire to townships and castles, killing all who resisted, whether innocent or not.[15]

---

[12] Ibid., pp. 17–19.
[13] Could this be why 'old men', the previous generation of conquerors, were singled out for special attention in 1136?
[14] *Brut (Pen. 20)*, s.a. 1108.
[15] JW, III, 1137. The hatred between the Welsh and Flemings was slow to dissipate; the praise of Maelgwn ap Rhys in *Brut (Pen. 20)*, s.a. 1187, includes the line 'the man who frequently slew the Flemings'. In 1258 Henry III heard that the Welsh 'had recommenced their sysytem of pillage, slaughter, and incendiarism, and had made incursions into the county of Pembroke, slaughtering great numbers of the inhabitants with great ferocity, and heaping insults and ill-treatment on those they allowed to escape with their lives'; MP (T), III, p. 268; MP, V, p. 676.

If there is need to search for reports of Welsh atrocities against the Anglo-Normans, there is an abundance of examples of mistreatment of the native population by the invaders. *Gruffudd ap Cynan* described the Norman advance into Gwynedd in the 1070s in biblical terms: 'they did so much damage as had never been done since the beginning of the world. And the cry of the people ascended unto the Lord.'[16] Rhigyfarch claims that their entrance into the south-west in the 1090s was equally bloody:

> Our limbs are cut off, we are lacerated, our necks condemned to death, and chains are put on our arms. The honest man's hand is branded by burning metals. A woman [now] lacks her nose, a man his genitals. [More] dire losses of our faculties follow, and prison shuts us in for many years. Serfdom is brought to the neck with a meat-hook, and learns that nothing can be had at will.[17]

In the early twelfth century, Welsh complaints even found support from English and continental sources concerned at the conquest of a Christian country. The ambivalent attitude of John of Worcester has been noted; in response to the 1094 revolt, he wrote that the Welsh were 'shaking off the yoke of slavery, which they had long endured, and holding their heads up high, sought to recover their liberty'.[18] Accounts in *Gruffudd ap Cynan* of Norman atrocities in Gwynedd are supported by Orderic Vitalis. Although he gives a favourable account of Robert of Rhuddlan, there is unease at the Marcher lord's activities in Wales:

> For fifteen years he [Robert] harried the Welsh mercilessly, invaded the lands of men who when they still enjoyed their original liberty had owed nothing to the Normans, pursued them through woods and marshes and over steep mountains and found different ways of securing their submission. Some he slaughtered mercilessly on the spot like cattle; others he kept for years in fetters, or forced into a harsh and unlawful slavery. It is

---

[16] *Gruffudd ap Cynan*, p. 70. The same source describes the invaders on Anglesey in 1098 'killing its people and breaking the limbs of others'; ibid., p. 77. John of Worcester supports this: '[they] killed many Welshmen taken prisoner there, blinding some, cutting off their hands and arms, and castrating them'; JW, III, 1098.

[17] M. Lapidge, 'The Welsh-Latin poetry of Sulien's family', *Studia Celtica*, 8–9 (1973–4), 68–106; 91.

[18] JW, III, 1094.

not right that Christians should so oppress their brothers, who have been reborn in the faith of Christ by holy baptism.[19]

The Normans showed no mercy to the people of the land in their campaigns in Wales after 1066. This is not to suggest that they introduced a more brutal form of warfare than was carried on by the Welsh; they were simply conducting the warfare with which they were familiar and which was practised throughout Europe. In 1116, a force containing Welsh and Anglo-Norman troops moved to Ystrad Tywi in an attempt to capture Gruffudd ap Rhys. Before entering this terrain they sent a declaration before them: 'And they pledged one another that not one of them would spare one person, neither man nor woman, neither boy nor girl, but that whomsoever they caught they would not let anyone go, but kill or hang him or cut off his members.'[20] Such terror tactics were used to clear the land and were accepted by Anglo-Norman and Welsh alike. Perhaps it was not standard practice to refuse mercy to any non-combatant and this total war was used in specific cases of conquest, revenge, danger or urgency, but it is clear that any grant of mercy was at the discretion of the warriors and their commander.

Slavery

The Vikings had been responsible for the establishment of a thriving slave market in the Irish Sea region, notably in the tenth and eleventh centuries, born of a demand for labour in Scandinavia and their new settlements in the north Atlantic.[21] The trade reached its peak in the eleventh century and by 1066 slavery in Anglo-Saxon England was a dying institution, but it took longer to disappear from Wales, Ireland and Scotland, and slave raiding continued while a market could be found in Ireland

---

[19] OV, IV, 8, p. 139. Gerald of Wales refers to Marcher men's atrocities when they invaded Cantref Mawr in 1136: 'my pen quivers in my hand as I think of the terrible vengeance exacted in our own times by the king's troops on the subject people of the commote of Caeo'; *Journey*, I, 10, p. 139.
[20] *Brut (Pen. 20)*, s.a. 1116.
[21] See P. Holm, 'The slave trade of Dublin: ninth–twelfth centuries', *Peritia*, 5 (1986), 317–45; also Ó'Cróinín, *Early Medieval*, p. 268; W. Davies, *Wales in the Early Middle Ages* (Leicester, 1982), p. 64; E. I. Bromberg, 'Wales and the mediaeval slave trade', *Speculum*, 17 (1942), 263–9.

and while lay power remained too weak to stop it.[22] Its importance in Wales is reflected in the many references to slavery in the native laws.

The acquisition of slaves was an important motivation for Hiberno-Scandinavian involvement in Wales. Opportunities to raid in England and Ireland had decreased under the powerful rulers who had emerged in these lands by the eleventh century.[23] Gruffudd ap Llywelyn was strong enough to stop external raiders plundering his land, but after his death Wales was an easy target. The significant Hiberno-Scandinavian support offered to Gruffudd ap Cynan may be related to the desire to keep the slave lanes open, and could help to explain Magnus Barefoot's decision to engage the earls of Shrewsbury and Chester in battle at Anglesey Sound in 1098.[24]

The Norman Conquest of England brought new ideas from the Church in Rome that condemned slavery as an institution and regarded its continued importance in Britain as barbaric. Anglo-French observers felt that the taking of slaves distinguished warfare in Wales, Ireland and Scotland from that elsewhere in Europe. Gerald of Wales described the former Irish policy of buying English slaves as a 'monstrous crime' and used this as a justification for the Anglo-Norman conquest of Ireland.[25] The difference was also one of perception. Elsewhere in Europe, non-combatants were routinely slaughtered and abused and their homes and livelihoods destroyed. Slavery was dying in Wales as in the rest of Europe and there are no known examples of Anglo-Norman nobles being enslaved. However, it was the delay in ending the institution that outraged Anglo-French commentators on the Welsh scene and made slavery one of the key differences between Welsh and Anglo-Norman conduct in war.[26]

---

[22] See, for example, ibid., 1110, 1124, 1136; *Gruffudd ap Cynan*, p. 65.

[23] In Ireland the slave trade was central to the growth of royal power as profits allowed the consolidation of resources and payment of large armies; see Holm, 'Slave trade'. It may be speculated that similar developments were seen in Wales and that Gruffudd ap Llywelyn used profits from selling slaves to Ireland to finance his ambitions.

[24] D. Wyatt, 'Gruffudd ap Cynan and the Hiberno-Norse world', *WHR*, 19 (1999), 595–617.

[25] *Conquest*, I, 18, p. 71.

[26] For the suggestion that it was rare for Welsh nobles to be enslaved, see below, p. 234, n. 71. For references to Welsh forces taking slaves from the Anglo-Saxons and Anglo-Normans, see *GS*, p. 17; JW, III, 1136; W. J. Millor and H. E. Butler (eds and trans.), *The Letters of John of Salisbury, Vol. I: The Early Letters (1153–61)* (Edinburgh, 1955), p. 135 (87); *Vitae*, p. 185; *Brut (Pen. 20)*, s.a. 1088, 1098, 1139, 1144. A charter from *Liber Landavensis* lists a Saxon woman as a part-payment for land; *LL*, p. 185.

Conduct towards the military elite

If the non-combatant population could expect little mercy in war in the Middle Ages, it is generally agreed that certain unwritten conventions were followed by the military elite in most of western Europe which went some way towards limiting the brutality of warfare.[27] These conventions only applied to the nobility and even then they were subject to qualifications and were often flouted, but it is held that they marked a delineation between warfare in the heart of Europe and that on the periphery. The section taken from Gerald of Wales's *Descriptio Cambriae* (which was repeated from his *Conquest of Ireland*), as quoted above, is crucial to this argument.[28] Gerald wrote that 'they [English and French troops] take prisoners, we [Welsh, Irish and Marcher troops] cut off their heads; they ransom their captives but we massacre them'.[29] The need to see this passage in its correct context has been stressed and we must consider all the available sources.

Early medieval Wales

We do not have the evidence to form a comprehensive study for this period. There are examples of political murders and of leaders being killed in battle, but we cannot determine whether such events were a matter of course or whether conventions governed the treatment of nobles.[30] Charter evidence may suggest that unwarranted attacks on laymen required some form of reparation to the Church, as did attacks on the Church itself, but the evidence is problematical.[31] References to poisoned weapons suggest that their use was dishonourable.[32]

---

[27] See Strickland, *War*, p. 335.
[28] See above, pp. 5–6.
[29] *Description*, II, 8, p. 269. Gerald does not suggest that captured combatants were sold into slavery.
[30] Two examples of the taking of noble hostages in Wales rather than their slaughter are provided by *ASC*, s.a. 916 and *ASC* (C), s.a. 1046.
[31] See, for example, *LL*, pp. 255–7; *Vitae*, p. 127. For discussion of the use of such evidence, see below, pp. 250–1.
[32] In *Culhwch and Olwen*, Ysbadadden treacherously casts poisoned spears; *Mabinogi*, pp. 152–4; *CaO*, pp. 19–21. In *Branwen*, Brân is wounded with a poisoned spear; *Mabinogi*, p. 79; *PK*, p. 44. Bede tells of an attempt to assassinate Edwin with a poisoned sword; Bede, II, 9, p. 165.

Literature of the early medieval period depicts a brutal society. This seems most clear in *Culhwch and Olwen*.[33] At the end of the tale the defeated giant is shown no mercy as an honoured opponent; he is dragged by his hair from his court, decapitated and has his head stuck on a stake.[34] Nobles from the *llu* of Gwythr ap Greidyawl are taken prisoner following a battle with Gwyn ap Nudd; Gwyn kills one and makes another eat his father's heart, thereby driving him mad.[35] It is difficult to use such passages as evidence of conduct in war. Gwyn ap Nudd, for example, was a supernatural character, and many interpretations of the extract are possible. In the tenth- or eleventh-century poem *Gwyn ap Nudd*, Gwyn defeats Gwyddno Garanhir and when the latter sues for protection it is granted; the two acknowledge each other as fellow nobles and show respect for the descent and arms of the other.[36] Examples of nobles resolving to fight to the death are rare in Welsh literature of the period and need to be explained.[37] *Math* tells of the taking of noble hostages during a conflict between the forces of north and south Wales;[38] although the combat itself was bloody, the hostages were treated honourably and were later allowed to go free. In *Branwen*, Brân refuses to dispose of the trouble-maker Evnissyen because he is his half-brother and because 'it would not be easy for me to have him killed or destroyed'.[39] *Math* and *Branwen* are subject to more significant later influences than *Culhwch and Olwen*, but it should be emphasized that Welsh literature cannot provide conclusive evidence for conduct in warfare in Wales in the early Middle Ages.

Late tenth-century Gwynedd does provide evidence of the sparing of nobility captured in warfare. In 969, Ieuaf ab Idwal was imprisoned by his brother Iago after a battle for control of Gwynedd and he remained a prisoner until 988. In 974, Iago

[33] For discussion, see Bromwich and Simon Evans, *Culhwch and Olwen*, p. lxxvii.
[34] *Mabinogi*, pp. 175–6; *CaO*, pp. 41–2. In *Pwyll*, Gwawl ap Clud is beaten and humiliated after his capture by Pwyll, although he is later allowed to return to his own kingdom after leaving some of his men as surety; *Mabinogi*, pp. 57–9; *PK*, pp. 16–18.
[35] *Mabinogi*, p. 168; *CaO*, p. 35. In the tale King Kilydd, the father of the hero Culhwch, desired the wife of King Dogel. He simply fought and killed the unfortunate Dogel, seized his wife and appropriated his land; *Mabinogi*, p. 136; *CaO*, p. 2.
[36] *Saga*, p. 506.
[37] See Rowland, 'Warfare', p. 37; also her *Saga*, pp. 14–17. Examples from the *Gododdin* and the *Llywarch Hen* cycle are discussed.
[38] *Mabinogi*, pp. 102–4; *PK*, pp. 71–4.
[39] *Mabinogi*, p. 70; *PK*, p. 33.

was himself taken captive by Hywel, the son of his dispossessed brother who had also been made captive in 969. Iago was expelled from Gwynedd for a time and his brother Meurig was blinded, probably at Hywel's instigation. Iago returned, but disappears from the record after another defeat by Hywel in 979.[40] It is possible that these are isolated examples of the sparing of captured rivals, but it seems more likely that they represent a regular practice hidden by lack of evidence.

Conduct between the native Welsh nobility in the Anglo-Norman period

Better evidence for the conduct of warfare among the native nobility emerges for the period after 1066. There are plentiful examples of the feuding Welsh nobility slaughtering each other and this has been considered a reflection of their underdeveloped society; as there was little or no money in circulation in Wales and a lack of towns or developed fortifications, there was little for a defeated lord to bargain with and consequently ransom was not an option. Instead, the bloody events outlined in the *Brutiau* in 1069 for the battle of Mechain and its aftermath are seen as typical.[41]

Gruffudd ap Cynan glories in the brutality of such political strife; the end of Gruffudd's rival Trahaearn at Mynydd Carn is depicted thus: 'Amidst that [battle] Trahaearn was stabbed in his bowels, until he was on the ground breathing his last, chewing with his teeth the fresh herbs and groping on top of his arms: and Gwcharki the Irishman made bacon of him as of a pig.'[42] If the violence of the society is undoubted, it should be noted that each event can be related to specific political circumstances. The *Brutiau* do not regard the events of 1069 as normal and they contrast with the settled conditions of Gruffudd ap Llywelyn's

---

[40] See Maund, 'Dynastic', 159–62. Another rival of Hywel, Iago's son Custennin, was killed in battle in 980. Hywel was succeeded by his brother Cadwallon who immediately arranged the killing of his first cousin, Ionafal ap Meurig. Soon after, Cadwallon was killed at the instigation of Maredudd ab Owain of Deheubarth.
[41] For the full passage, see above, p. 119.
[42] *Gruffudd ap Cynan*, p. 68. The slaughter of Trahaearn's *teulu* is also glorified.

later years.[43] Such feuds are comparable to periods of private warfare in Normandy when ducal authority was weak. As described by Orderic Vitalis, such times also saw frequent political killings with little regard for ransom; when lordships or kingdoms were contested the stakes were high. Indeed, this was how Gruffudd ap Llywelyn had risen to power in his early career.[44]

Some examples of treachery and political murders in Wales were inspired by Anglo-Norman interference in politics and the consequent destabilizing of the native scene.[45] In 1112 Richard, bishop of London, was prepared to grant Madog ap Rhiddid land in Powys because he was aware 'that they were all killing one another'.[46] As seen in 1069 and 1081, many Welsh nobles fell in battle; in such circumstances little mercy was expected and the taking of prisoners may have been impractical.[47] We cannot always be sure whether men fell in battle or in the immediate aftermath. In 1091 Rhys ap Tewdwr defeated a dangerous rising under the leadership of Gruffudd ap Maredudd. After the battle Rhys 'drove him [Gruffudd] to flight and pursued him and captured him, and at last he slew him'.[48] Rhys, who was facing serious internal and external political problems, was unwilling to let a dangerous rival live.

There are examples of Welsh nobles capturing, imprisoning and ransoming their native rivals. It is difficult to determine whether this was a continuation of regular practice, whether it

---

[43] Madog ap Rhiddid embarked on a policy of extermination of his rivals in the early twelfth century, killing, amongst others, Cadwgan ap Bleddyn. This was noted by the *Brutiau* which delight in recording his capture in 1113 and presentation before Owain ap Cadwgan who, in revenge for Madog's deeds, gouged out his prisoner's eyes; *Brut (Pen. 20)*, s.a. 1113.

[44] Gruffudd killed Hywel ab Edwin in battle in 1041 and Gruffudd ap Rhydderch in 1055. Walter Map describes the Welsh king's early years as covered in blood:

> Whatever young man he saw of good and strong promise, by some craft he either murdered him or maimed him to prevent his attaining manly strength, ever mindful of his own safety; and very quickly he became supreme, and this was his saying: 'I kill no-one, but I blunt the horns of Wales, that they may not hurt their mother.' (Map, p. 191)

[45] See, for example, Powys in the early twelfth century and the deaths of Iorweth ap Bleddyn and Cadwgan ap Bleddyn in 1111, along with that of Madog ap Rhiddid in 1113.

[46] *Brut (Pen. 20)*, s.a. 1112.

[47] In warfare elsewhere, even under the laws of chivalry, the slaying of nobles in combat was not condemned.

[48] *Brut (Pen. 20)*, s.a. 1091.

occurred under Anglo-Norman influence, or whether changing political and social circumstances could be the explanation. The problem is the lack of pre-1066 evidence, although we have seen a series of examples of leniency from late tenth-century Gwynedd. *Gruffudd ap Cynan* claims that at the battle of Bron-yr-erw (1075) there was a 'great slaughter on both sides' including seventy of the 'foremost men of Anglesey', but also that 'many were captured'.[49] Two captured nobles are named, both of whom were Irishmen from Gruffudd's force. It could be assumed that they were enslaved, but we have no further details. There are no references to captured Welsh nobles being enslaved by their native rivals.

In 1102, Maredudd ap Bleddyn was seized by his brother Iorwerth and sent to one of Henry I's prisons.[50] The fact that he was sent to England could indicate a number of things: for example, that he was too dangerous to keep in Wales, or that adequate prison facilities were lacking in the country. The most likely explanation is that Iorwerth was trying to win the favour of Henry. Similarly, when Llywelyn ab Owain was seized by his uncle Maredudd ap Bleddyn he was given to Payn fitz John and imprisoned in Bridgnorth Castle.[51]

Mercy towards fellow nobles seems regular practice in Wales by the twelfth century. Madog ap Maredudd of Powys (d. 1160) was praised in his elegy by Cynddelw Brydydd Mawr as a 'good friend to hostages'.[52] In panegyric poetry political murders are described as outrages, although they continued to be relatively commonplace. Peryf ap Cedifor wrote in despair following the murder of his lord, Hywel ab Owain Gwynedd, by Hywel's brother Dafydd in 1170:

> Pryd y cynlluniwyd brad anghristnogol [yn erbyn y] Brython
> o ran Cristin a'i meibion,
> na foed dyn yn fyw ym Môn
> o blith disgynyddion brych a moel Brochfael.

---

[49] *Gruffudd ap Cynan*, p. 63.
[50] *Brut (Pen. 20)*, s.a. 1102.
[51] Ibid., s.a. 1128.
[52] *Welsh Verse*, p. 153. '[Un] cyson [ei] rodd, hebryngwr gwystlon'; *CBT*, III, 7.20.

> Er yr hyn a ddêl o eiddo o ddal tir [yn] y byd presennol,
> anheddfan ansicr,
> gwae Ddafydd anghyfiawn! Â gwaywffon
> y bu gwanu gwalch rhyfel, [sef] Hywel dal[53]
>
> (Because of the treachery brewed, unchristian Briton,
> by Cristin and her sons,
> let there be left alive in Môn
> not one of her blotched kindred!
>
> Despite what good comes from holding land,
> world's a treacherous dwelling:
> woe to you, cruel Dafydd,
> to stab tall Hywel, hawk of war!)[54]

Political violence among the nobility in Gwynedd and in Deheubarth declined under the leadership of Owain Gwynedd and Rhys ap Gruffudd. There was a shift in attitudes, possibly caused by the influence of chivalric attitudes linked to a greater respect for the nobility in general, but also by changes in society. Lordships were becoming more settled, established territorial units and dependent vassals continued to reveal strong loyalties to their local overlords; it was difficult to kill powerful men without losing control of the localities. Such developments help to account for Owain Gwynedd's commitment to his brother Cadwaladr, despite numerous indiscretions by the latter. As lordships became more settled, Welsh leaders built castles and developed the economy of their lands; consequently, the ransoming of Welsh hostages was a worthwhile activity. Only in the late eleventh century did chivalric values begin to develop elsewhere; ducal Normandy, for example, was a very bloody land. In twelfth-century Wales we are seeing parallel, similar, if later, developments.

Changes in attitude in Deheubarth may have developed earlier than elsewhere in Wales. In the 1140s and 1150s the sons

---

[53] *CBT*, II, 19.17–24.
[54] *Welsh Verse*, p. 149. Perhaps criticism of this act led Dafydd to show more leniency in his attempts to establish himself in Gwynedd. In 1174 he seized and imprisoned his brother Maelgwn. In 1175 another brother, Rhodri, was captured and 'harshly imprisoned in shackles'. Such mercy was to cost Dafydd dear: 'before the end of the year Rhodri escaped from his brother's prison, and he drove Dafydd, his brother, from Anglesey and across the Conwy'; *Brut (Pen. 20)*, s.a. 1175.

of Gruffudd ap Rhys showed an ability to work together, and Rhys emerged as sole ruler by chance rather than by brutal design.[55] Such cooperation may have been due to the desperate position of native rule in Deheubarth. In the struggles of Rhys ap Gruffudd's later years the old lord and his feuding sons showed a marked reluctance to take each other's lives.[56] For Rhys to show mercy to his sons is understandable, but acts of leniency between noble brothers in Wales are notable (if not unprecedented). Indeed, the failure of one son to seize the initiative and destroy his brothers could be said to have contributed to the weakening and disintegration of the kingdom of Deheubarth. In 1189, Maelgwn ap Rhys was imprisoned by his father and brothers and in 1194 Rhys was himself imprisoned by his sons in Nevern Castle.[57] Rhys was succeeded in 1197 by his son Gruffudd; soon afterwards, he was attacked in Aberystwyth by Maelgwn and Gwenwynwyn, 'and there they captured Gruffudd ap Rhys and slew some of his men and imprisoned others'.[58] It would seem that those killed fell in battle, whilst the survivors were spared.[59] Gruffudd himself was imprisoned by Gwenwynwyn before being handed to the 'Saxons', probably in an attempt to win John's favour. Gruffudd ap Rhys was later released by John to trouble Gwenwynwyn and Maelgwn. In the subsequent clash, Maelgwn promised to give Cardigan Castle to Gruffudd in return for hostages. The prisoners were handed over unharmed, but there is outrage in the chronicle that Maelgwn refused to fulfil his part of the bargain, despite having sworn 'upon many relics in the presence of monks and ecclesiastics'.[60]

---

[55] For other examples of brothers working together, see the activities of the sons of Idwal Foel against the sons of Hywel Dda in the mid-tenth century, in Maund, 'Dynastic', 157; see also the raids of Cadwallon and Owain, sons of Gruffudd ap Cynan, into Rhos, Rhufoniog and Dyffryn Clwyd in the 1120s; *HW*, II, pp. 466–7.

[56] *Journey*, I, 1, p. 179, refers to a man from Elfael chained up in Rhys's new castle of Rhayader; it may be speculated that he opposed Rhys's advance into Gwerthrynion, suggesting that external Welsh enemies could also be spared.

[57] *Brut (Pen. 20)*, s.a. 1189, 1194; *Journey*, II, 2 , p. 170.

[58] *Brut (Pen. 20)*, s.a. 1197.

[59] Similar conclusions can be drawn about the deaths in 1210 when Maelgwn and his 'French' allies were ambushed by his nephews Rhys and Owain: 'And in that battle Cynan ab Hywel, nephew of Maelgwn, and Gruffudd ap Cadwgan, Maelgwn's chief counsellor, were captured, and Einion ap Caradog and many others were slain. And Maelgwn, after many of his men had been slain and others had been captured, shamefully fled on foot by night and escaped'; *Brut (Pen. 20)*, s.a. 1210.

[60] Ibid., s.a. 1198.

Soon after Dafydd ap Llywelyn succeeded to Gwynedd in 1240, he incarcerated his brother Gruffudd. It would have been to Dafydd's advantage to dispose of his sibling, but this was not an acceptable course of action. Gruffudd was taken to England by Henry III after his 1241 expedition and he proved a useful pawn for the king to use against Dafydd.[61] Llywelyn ap Gruffudd kept his brothers Owain and Rhodri imprisoned for long periods, although there was opposition in Gwynedd even to this treatment and Rhodri's rights were recognized (under pressure) by the prince.[62] Dafydd was given power in Gwynedd despite his defeat and capture by Llywelyn in 1255 and it is likely that he was Llywelyn's preferred heir. All of his brothers caused Llywelyn repeated problems; in an earlier age it is unlikely that they would have survived his accession to power.

The later Welsh prose romances reflect the chivalric attitudes to honour, the notion of a brotherhood in arms and the ideals of correct noble behaviour seen in literature throughout Europe.[63] By the thirteenth century some of these ideals were being put into practice in Wales, but as elsewhere in Europe there were limitations on chivalric behaviour and it could be overridden in the interests of expediency. It would be wrong to attribute change to the copying of Anglo-Norman chivalry, however. The realities of the political situation and the transformations in Welsh society should be seen as the catalyst for adjustment in the conduct of war.

Anglo-Norman treatment of the Welsh nobility

It has been argued that after 1066 the Anglo-Normans found a style of warfare on the so-called 'Celtic fringe' of Britain that gave no quarter to the nobility, and that they accordingly adapted to it – and quickly! This notion requires closer examination. A key debate concerns a passage from Gerald of Wales's *Conquest of Ireland*, describing the aftermath of the defeat of the

---

[61] See *HW*, II, p. 770.
[62] For criticism of the imprisonment of Owain, see *LG*, pp. 74–6.
[63] In *The Dream of Rhonabwy*, for example, Rhonabwy and his companions, who were mere footsoldiers, were captured by a knight who regarded them as hostages for booty; *Mabinogi*, p. 180; *BR*, p. 4.

men of Waterford by an Anglo-Norman force at Baginbun in 1170. Many were killed in the battle, but around seventy 'influential citizens' were taken captive and the people of Waterford wanted to ransom them in return for money or the town. A disagreement followed between two of the Anglo-Norman commanders, Raymond le Gros and Hervey de Montmorency, over what to do with the captives. Raymond argued that it would be honourable to have killed them in battle, but that now they had 'reverted to being fellow human beings' and that to kill them would bring shame on the perpetrators; ransom was better, both for profit and to give an example of noble conduct:

> In the midst of martial conflict it is a soldier's duty, clad in his helmet, to thirst for blood, to concentrate on killing, to plead his case with the sword alone . . . But by the same token when the turmoil of battle is over and he has laid aside his arms, ferocity too should be laid aside, a humane code of behaviour should be once more adopted, and feelings of mercy and clemency should be revived in the spirit that is truly noble.[64]

Hervey argued that Ireland could only be conquered by 'fire and slaughter' and that 'while people are still proud and rebellious they must be subdued by all possible means and clemency must take a back seat'.[65] He stressed how badly outnumbered the Normans were and claimed that, if they had lost the battle, no mercy would have been shown to them. Hervey won the argument; the limbs of the prisoners were broken and they were thrown from a cliff. This passage has been used to contend that the Anglo-Norman world saw the so-called 'Celtic fringe' as beyond the bounds of chivalry, a place where normal conventions of warfare did not apply.[66] If this were true then it would seem to be the Anglo-Normans who established these codes of conduct on their entry to Ireland by failing to respect the native nobility. Did they impose similar ground rules for warfare on their entry to Wales a century earlier?

---

[64] *Conquest*, I, 14, p. 61.
[65] Ibid., I, 15, p. 63. Another passage describes the attempt to retake Dublin from the Anglo-Normans by the city's former leader Askuluw. He was captured and his life spared, but when he vowed to return and gain vengeance he was killed; ibid., I, 21, p. 79.
[66] J. Gillingham, 'Conquering the barbarians: war and chivalry in twelfth-century Britain', *The Haskins Society Journal*, 4 (1992), 67–84.

It does not seem that the Anglo-Normans acknowledged the Welsh (or Irish) nobility as equals, worthy of sharing their chivalric world or being judged according to the same rules. This relates to the perception of the Welsh as barbarians, and betrays a failure to acknowledge differences in culture and society.[67] Writers with connections to the Marches of Wales and Ireland promoted this picture of backward barbarians to help justify conquests.[68] It is possible that the poorer equipment of the Welsh military elite would not have brought them noble status in an Anglo-Norman force and consequently they were treated no differently from footsoldiers and mercenaries.[69] It is also possible that the cultural differences were less important than the expedient behaviour of the conquerors in wiping out their native rivals to remove resistance to their conquest of their land.[70]

The lack of respect of the Anglo-Normans for the Welsh nobility is perhaps the major complaint in *Rhigyfarch's Lament*. The abuse of every Welsh institution was bewailed as the traditional, hierarchical society was destroyed: 'each man ploughs the earth, for with curved foot the nobleman as well as the poor man turns over the soil.'[71] When defeated Welsh nobles were not slain, their treatment in captivity was little better; Orderic's description of Robert of Rhuddlan's handling of the Welsh is revealing.[72] The Anglo-Norman entry into Wales in the late

---

[67] See W. R. Jones, 'The image of the barbarian', 376–407; also his 'England against the Celtic fringe', 155–71; R. R. Davies, *Domination*, pp. 21–3; J. Gillingham, 'The context and purpose of Geoffrey of Monmouth's *History of the Kings of Britain*', *ANS*, 13 (1990), 99–118; also his 'The beginnings of English imperialism', *Journal of Historical Sociology*, 5 (1992), 392–409; and his 'Conquering the barbarians', 67–84; F. C. Suppe, 'The cultural significance of decapitation in high medieval Wales and the Marches', *BBCS*, 36 (1989), 147–60; R. Bartlett, *Gerald of Wales*, pp. 158ff.; *WW*, pp. 187–203.

[68] At the outset of the *Conquest of Ireland*, Gerald promises to describe 'the taming of the ferocity of a very barbarous nation'; *Conquest*, I, p. 23. At the conclusion of a battle where Dermot's Irish footsoldiers beheaded 200 of their fallen enemies, the king is depicted lifting the head of one and biting its nose and ears; ibid., I, 4, p. 37.

[69] This was not the case in 1088, however. A force was defeated outside Worcester and we are told that, whilst the footsoldiers were put to the sword, the mounted (L. *milites*) English, Normans and Welsh were taken prisoner; JW, III, 1088.

[70] Reactions to the Norman conquest of England betrayed unease: 'The continental contemporaries of William the Conqueror expressed at least as much condemnation of the arguments and violence used by the Normans as they expressed admiration for the military victory and the reform of the English church'; E. Van Houts, 'The Norman Conquest through European eyes', *EHR*, 10 (1995), 832–53 (852).

[71] Lapidge, 'Welsh', p. 91. This line suggests that it was not usual for a Welsh noble to be enslaved when defeated by a native rival.

[72] Robert captured Gruffudd ap Cynan, but the Welsh leader did not expect release, ransom or 'noble treatment'. He was 'shackled' in Chester, 'the worst of prisons', for many years before his escape; *Gruffudd ap Cynan*, p. 69. Hywel ab Ithel 'was bound with thongs [by Robert] and dragged away a captive'; OV, IV, 8, p. 145.

eleventh century was facilitated by the political turmoil in the country and this was developed by their removal of leading Welsh figures;[73] Rhys ap Tewdwr, Maredudd ab Owain and Owain ap Cadwgan were amongst those to fall at Anglo-Norman hands or instigation.

Brutality continued to characterize the Anglo-Norman experience in Wales. In 1151, Cadell ap Gruffudd was caught by the men of Tenby whilst out hunting and maimed so badly that he barely survived; he played no further role in politics.[74] In the mid-twelfth century, Cadwallon ap Madog established the kingdom of Cynllibiwg that enjoyed Henry II's support and blocked Mortimer ambitions in the middle March.[75] It fell apart after 1179 when he was murdered by the men of Roger Mortimer of Wigmore on his return from Henry's court. Mortimer was punished but he still achieved his wider aims; even royal protection was of limited value to the Welsh nobility.[76] When Rhys ap Gruffudd was at Henry's court in 1158, Walter Clifford took the opportunity to raid Rhys's lands and 'slay his men';[77] the king took no action against Clifford, leading Rhys to further rebellion. A century later, Llywelyn ap Gruffudd's men were ambushed at Newcastle Emlyn when conducting peace talks with Patrick de Chaworth, the king's seneschal, at Carmarthen; this was condemned even by English chroniclers.[78]

The treatment of hostages was a controversial issue between Anglo-Norman and native nobility. Welsh captives were often taken after royal expeditions as a way of guaranteeing future obedience. The Welsh felt that treaties made on such terms were coercive and were not binding, but the Anglo-Normans reacted

---

[73] See K. L. Maund, *Ireland, Wales and England in the Eleventh Century* (Woodbridge, 1991), p. 118. R. R. Davies saw Anglo-Norman 'brutality' as a major factor in their success in Wales. It was 'traumatic' and 'disrupted the ordered pattern of nature and society'; R. R. Davies, *Domination*, pp. 26–7.

[74] *Brut (Pen. 20)*, s.a. 1151. He died in 1175 'of a long infirmity' as a monk at Strata Florida; ibid., s.a. 1175.

[75] P. M. Remfry, 'Cadwallon ap Madog, Rex de Delvain, 1140–79, and the re-establishment of local autonomy in Cynllibiwg', *Transactions of the Radnorshire Society*, 65 (1995), 11–32.

[76] There is a reference in this period to thirteen Welshmen captured in battle and imprisoned rather than killed, although they were firmly fettered with iron; J. C. Dickinson and P. T. Ricketts, 'The Anglo-Norman chronicle of Wigmore Abbey', *TWNFC*, 39 (1967–9), 413–43; 437.

[77] *Brut (Pen. 20)*, s.a. 1158. Rhys suffered further in 1164 when the murder of his nephew and *penteulu* Einion was instigated by Roger de Clare; ibid., s.a. 1164.

[78] Ibid., s.a. 1258; MP, V, pp. 717–18.

with fury to Welsh 'oath-breakers', believing that they had forfeited the rights of their hostages. The contrasting reports of Henry II's killing and maiming of twenty-two hostages following the failure of his 1165 expedition to Wales are telling.[79] The inability of John's vassals to trust him with noble prisoners, in the Angevin as well as the Irish and Welsh political worlds, contributed to his overall failures as a king;[80] in 1212 he hanged twenty-eight Welsh nobles, including the seven-year-old Rhys ap Maelgwn.[81]

The ill-treatment of Welsh nobles bred a culture of recrimination, leading to long-running feuds that shocked observers. The most famous began in Gwent uwch Coed in the late twelfth century.[82] In 1172 Owain ap Iorwerth was murdered by the men of Henry, the heir of Earl Roger of Hereford, whilst on his way to the royal court. Henry was killed in 1175 by Owain's kinsman, Seisyll ap Dyfnwal. Soon afterwards William de Braose succeeded to his uncle's lands in Brycheiniog and Gwent; Seisyll gained the king's pardon, but William wanted revenge and summoned his Welsh vassal to Abergavenny:

> And immediately after that Seisyll ap Dyfnwal was slain through treachery in the castle of Abergavenny by the lord of Brycheiniog. And along with him Geoffrey, his son, and the best men of Gwent were slain. And the French made for Seisyll's court; and after slaying Gwladus, his wife, they slew Cadwaladr, his son [aged seven]. And on that day there befell a pitiful massacre in Gwent. And from that time forth, after that treachery, none of the Welsh dared place trust in the French.[83]

---

[79] *Brut (Pen. 20)*, s.a. 1165; *Journey*, II, 12, p. 201; WN, p. 233. In a letter to Louis VII, Owain says that Henry had 'wrongfully and harmfully mutilated my hostages, although he had not presented them previously for the keeping of the peace'; H. Pryce, 'Owain Gwynedd', 7.

[80] S. Duffy, 'King John's expedition to Ireland in 1210: the evidence reconsidered', *Irish Historical Studies*, 30 (1995), 1–24. See also W. L. Warren, *King John* (Harmondsworth, 1961), p. 97.

[81] *Brut (Pen. 20)*, s.a. 1212; RW, II, p. 61.

[82] We have extensive information on this feud thanks to the founding of the Cistercian house of Llantarnam in 1179. Details found their way to the abbey's mother house at Strata Florida and then into the *Brutiau*.

[83] *Brut (Pen. 20)*, s.a. 1175. Gerald of Wales was initially critical of this episode but, with his church at Llanddew and de Braose as lord of Brecon, he soon changed his tune. He still felt the need to go to elaborate lengths to excuse de Braose's part in the massacre; see *Journey*, I, 4, pp. 109–12, with accompanying footnotes.

Descendants of the slain took revenge on Ranulf Poer and his men at Dingestow in 1182 and so the feud continued.[84] William de Braose did not soften his treatment of the Welsh nobility; his 1175 trick was repeated in 1197 when Trahaearn Fychan of Brycheiniog was summoned to de Braose's court at Llangors:

> There he was seized and imprisoned. And as a pitiful example and with unusual cruelty he was bound by his feet to the tail of a strong horse, and was thus drawn along the streets of Brecon as far as the gallows; and there his head was struck off and he was hanged by his feet; and he was there for three days on the gallows.[85]

The fact that atrocities on both sides led to increased brutality can be seen as a recurring theme. Matthew Paris preserved a letter written by a knight in Henry III's army in north Wales in 1245. The correspondence describes a detachment of Henry's army, comprising dismounted knights, 300 Welsh and Marcher footsoldiers and some (non-Welsh) crossbowmen, crossing the Conwy to pursue Dafydd's men. They ravaged the country, pillaging the abbey at Aberconwy. On their return they were ambushed by a Welsh force:

> Some of our knights they took alive, to imprison them; but hearing that we had slain some of their nobles, and above all Naveth[?] son of Odo[?], a handsome and brave youth, they also hung these knights of ours, afterwards decapitating and mangling them dreadfully: finally they tore their miserable corpses limb from limb, and threw them into the water, in detestation of their wicked greediness in not sparing the church . . . there fell in this conflict on our side some knights of the retinue of Richard, earl of Cornwall; namely Alan Buscel, Adam de Moia, Lord Geoffrey Sturmy, and a fourth, Raymond, a Gascon crossbowman, of whom the king used to make sport; and about 100 retainers were killed, besides those drowned, and the same number of the Welsh, or more.[86]

In another raid Henry's men brought back 'in triumph to our camp the heads of nearly 100 decapitated Welsh'.[87] In a later

---

[84] Ibid., I, 4, pp. 110–11; *Brut (Pen. 20)*, s.a. 1182. The brutality of the feud in the area continued into the thirteenth century.
[85] *Brut (Pen. 20)*, s.a. 1197.
[86] MP (T), II, p. 111; MP, IV, p. 482.
[87] MP (T), II, p. 112; MP, IV, p. 483.

passage, where Paris has shifted his sympathies in favour of the Welsh, he details a speech supposedly delivered by Llywelyn ap Gruffudd to his men in the 1256 rising:

> But you must know that now and henceforth we are fighting for our lives; if we are taken prisoners, we shall obtain no mercy at all . . . [as the king of England mistreats his own subjects] how then would he spare us, who seek to injure him and provoke him to vengeance?[88]

Although cultural and social differences help to explain why the Welsh nobility could not be fully accepted into the Anglo-French world, the main reason was that Wales remained a land of conquest. War was more brutal here than in Anglo-French clashes because there was more to fight for. Major battles outside Wales, as at Hastings and Bouvines, might see heavy noble casualties and little notion of a brotherhood of arms. In Wales, many clashes were of this kind, if on a smaller scale. In the thirteenth century, the princes of Gwynedd (though not the lesser nobility) were beginning to be accepted into the chivalric world. In 1282–3, however, Llywelyn ap Gruffudd was killed in battle and Dafydd executed as a traitor after his capture.[89] They felt they were fighting for an independent principality whilst Edward had determined their downfall as treacherous vassals who refused to perform homage. On both sides the stakes were higher than was generally seen in warfare elsewhere in the Anglo-French world and the penalties for those defeated were correspondingly more severe.

Welsh treatment of the Anglo-Norman nobility

The majority of Anglo-Norman nobles killed in Wales fell in battle. Such deaths tended to be accepted by even the most anti-Welsh of chroniclers; it was a hazard of military life that no code

---

[88] MP (T), III, pp. 243–4; MP, V, pp. 646–7.
[89] For the brutal treatment of Llywelyn, Dafydd and their surviving family, see Carr, 'Last and weakest', 393–5.

of conduct could mitigate.⁹⁰ Thus, Orderic laments the fall of Robert of Rhuddlan, but his death is not seen as an atrocity.⁹¹ Anger at Robert's demise rather stemmed from the cultural issue represented by the beheading of a fallen foe.⁹² The Welsh chronicles, John of Worcester and the *Gesta Stephani* acknowledge the bloodiness of the battle at Cardigan in 1136, but there is no condemnation.⁹³ Similarly, in 1157, the deaths of Anglo-Norman nobles at Coleshill and on Anglesey are not labelled as Welsh atrocities; criticisms are rather levelled at Henry and his commanders for not being more circumspect.⁹⁴ The death of Ranulf Poer and nine knights at Dingestow in 1182 was part of the wider feud in Gwent, but even so their deaths came in combat.⁹⁵ In reporting Henry III's expeditions to Wales in 1228 and 1231, Roger of Wendover described clashes involving slaughter on both sides where no blame is attached.⁹⁶ Matthew Paris deals with certain noble deaths in a similar manner.⁹⁷

Away from actual combat, the number of Anglo-Norman nobles slain by the Welsh is limited. Specific feuds or vendettas

---

⁹⁰ See Keen, *Chivalry*, p. 222; Strickland, *War*, pp. 159ff. On the Welsh side, *Brut (Pen. 20)*, s.a. 1198, records that at Painscastle large numbers of the Welsh were killed 'like sheep' and the nobles Anarawd ab Einion, Owain ap Cadwallon, Rhiddid ab Iestyn and Rhobert ab Hywel were slain, but there is no criticism of the Anglo-Normans. Heavy Welsh casualties were also accepted in the battle with William Marshal (II) in 1223; see *Brut (Pen. 20)*, s.a. 1223; RW, II, p. 270.

⁹¹ OV, IV, 8, p. 137.

⁹² See Suppe, 'Cultural', 147–60.

⁹³ Criticisms of the Welsh in the *Gesta Stephani* relate to their activities after the battle, as discussed above, p. 221. As in inter-Welsh warfare, it is difficult to determine whether a noble was slain in combat or in the immediate aftermath. However, the lack of criticism of Welsh conduct from English sources would suggest that the Anglo-Norman deaths occurred in the fighting.

⁹⁴ See Chrons., I, p. 108; *Journey*, II, 7, pp. 189–90; II, 9, p. 196; *Brut (Pen. 20)*, s.a. 1157.

⁹⁵ *Journey*, I, 4, pp. 110–11; *Brut (Pen. 20)*, s.a. 1182.

⁹⁶ RW, II, pp. 349–50:

A knight, who had lately been belted by the king, had gone out with others to forage, and was with his companions cut off by the enemy, on which he boldly dashed into the midst of them; but, after slaying numbers who opposed him, he at length fell slain together with some one other of the king's army.

See also ibid., III, p. 12.

⁹⁷ In 1256 an English force was surrounded by the Welsh:

They were defeated and put to the rout or slain at the will of the enemy. In that most sanguinary conflict some illustrious knights in the service of the king of England fell; amongst others, Stephen Baucan, a dear friend of the king, Robert of Norham, and many others, whose names we do not recollect. (MP (T), III, p. 242; MP, V, pp. 645–6)

account for many of these deaths; again Gwent uwch Coed provides pertinent examples of mistrust and treachery.[98] Other examples may be attributed to specific circumstances. Richard de Clare was ambushed and killed near Abergavenny in 1136 by Morgan ab Owain of upland Glamorgan, but it was Richard's lack of caution that is condemned rather than the brutality of the Welsh.[99] William de Braose (the younger) was hanged while in the custody of Llywelyn ap Iorwerth in 1230, but this judgement was accepted by English and Welsh observers; he had slept with Llywelyn's wife Joan.[100] As a captive of war, William had been treated well and had been released by the Welsh prince; his indiscretion occurred on a return visit to the overly friendly court.

References may be found to the Welsh giving quarter, and capturing and ransoming their enemies. The twelfth century saw a growing number of instances of Welsh leaders treating their native rivals in a more humane fashion. It is ironic that similar examples can be found in Welsh treatment of their external enemies at exactly the time when Anglo-French observers were beginning to label the Welsh as barbaric. Such actions had advantages for the Welsh in terms of exacting money or concessions from the Anglo-Normans. It is notable that the examples tend to increase with time, dramatically so in the thirteenth century. This reflects the evidence but also the bitterness of the early years of conquest, the gradual acceptance of the March and developments in society.

The earliest evidence that Welsh forces regulated their conduct against Anglo-Norman foes relates to 1121.[101] Henry I was waylaid and struck by an arrow (which recoiled), but the native chronicler goes to some lengths to explain that it was an accident and that 'young men' sent by Maredudd ap Bleddyn were responsible.[102] It may be suggested that a certain awe,

---

[98] See above, pp. 236–7; also *The History of William Marshal*, p. 94.
[99] *Journey*, I, 4, p. 108. Other sources note his death without condemnation on either side; see JW, III, 1136; *GS*, p. 17.
[100] *Brut (Pen. 20)*, s.a. 1230; RW, II, p. 383.
[101] It is possible that the reference in *ASC*, s.a. 1081, to the Conqueror 'liberating' many men in Wales indicates that he freed Normans held captive by Rhys ap Tewdwr after the battle of Mynydd Carn. They may have been spared to increase Rhys's bargaining position or to obtain ransoms. See A. G. Williams, 'Norman lordship in south-east Wales during the reign of William I', *WHR*, 16 (1992–3), 445–66 (456).
[102] *Brut (Pen. 20)*, s.a. 1121. For further discussion of this incident, see above, p. 152. William of Malmesbury believed that Henry was shot by one of his own men in a plot against his life; WM, V, 401, pp. 727–9.

respect, or fear of the king of England had developed which caused hesitation in personal attacks. Perhaps at this time no similar quarter would be shown to other Anglo-Norman lords.[103] Evidence for Welsh treatment of Anglo-Norman nobles is scarce, but in 1165 Robert fitz Stephen was captured and imprisoned by Rhys ap Gruffudd, his first cousin.[104] No surprise at this action is registered by the chronicle. Rhys kept his dangerous rival alive and unharmed; and in 1169 Robert was released on condition that he left Wales for Ireland.[105]

In the thirteenth century, instances of the Welsh sparing defeated Anglo-Norman nobles are relatively common.[106] Although he would later meet an unfortunate end, William de Braose (the younger) was captured in 1228 after he had been wounded in a skirmish with the Welsh, and Llywelyn ap Iorwerth intended to demand a ransom for his return.[107] When Rhys Fychan and his English allies were defeated outside Carmarthen in 1257, the garrison 'captured the best barons and knights of them, and they slew of the others about 2,000 and more'.[108] Such a policy of sparing the military elite and slaughtering the rest was common, understood and accepted throughout Europe. In a letter preserved by Matthew Paris, a defeated force of Anglo-Norman knights was initially spared to be imprisoned (and, presumably, ransomed), but they were later killed in retaliation for mistreatment of Welsh nobles and churches.[109]

The anticipated conduct of warfare in Wales conformed to the standard elsewhere in Europe. In 1258 Matthew Paris expressed surprise that the Welsh who had raided the border 'cut off the heads of all the men found in the towns, without mercy and without allowing them to ransom themselves'.[110] However, racial, social and cultural differences between Welsh and

---

[103] For the hesitancy of Anglo-Norman forces to face their overlord in battle, see M. J. Strickland, 'Against the Lord's anointed: aspects of warfare and baronial rebellion in England and Normandy, 1075–1265', in Garnett and Hudon, *Law*, pp. 56–77.
[104] *Brut (Pen. 20)*, s.a. 1165. After taking Wizo's Castle in 1193, Hywel Sais took Philip fitz Wizo captive along with his wife and two sons; ibid., s.a. 1193.
[105] Ibid., s.a. 1169; *Conquest*, I, 2, pp. 29–31.
[106] See, for example, *Brut (Pen. 20)*, s.a. 1217; RW, III, p. 12.
[107] *Brut (Pen. 20)*, s.a. 1228; RW, II, p. 350.
[108] *Brut (Pen. 20)*, s.a. 1257.
[109] See above, p. 237.
[110] MP (T), III, p. 258; MP, V, p. 664.

Anglo-Norman, allied to the experience of bitter frontier warfare, meant that mistrust continued to exist between the two sides and they never enjoyed the mutual respect seen amongst the military elite in the Anglo-French world. The complexities and contradictions of the issue are revealed in Matthew Paris's account of the death of an English noble, Herbert fitz Matthew, in Wales in 1245. Paris initially says that Herbert was killed in an accident when he was struck by a rock; such a death would be acceptable, a hazard of war. However, he continues:

> Other persons state that the said Herbert fitz Matthew fell from his horse, and whilst still alive the Welsh came up and contended with one another as to whose captive he ought to be, for the sake of the ransom, and one of them, wishing to put an end to the strife, ran Herbert through his body from behind, saying, 'Now whoever chooses may take him'. On the morrow he was found with his body pierced through, and with his hand placed on the wound, and, being naked, was only recognized amongst the other dead by an emerald ring.[111]

The initial Welsh response was to capture and ransom the noble; the numerous 'other dead' were of no significance. However, Paris and his audience believed that the Welsh were capable of slaying their helpless noble victims. Similar incidents undoubtedly occurred in the wider Anglo-French world, but when allied to the social and cultural differences in Wales they were enough to alienate the native nobility from the chivalric world of their neighbours.

Welsh Conduct in Siege Warfare

Bradbury contends that in Europe – 'from Rome to the Reformation' – fortifications which surrendered on terms could expect those conditions to be honoured, but those taken against resistance lost all rights (although 'expectations of mercy probably increased gradually').[112] Wales was not an exception to

---

[111] MP (T), II, pp. 46–7; MP, IV, pp. 408–9.
[112] Bradbury, *Medieval Siege*, p. 333.

these principles.[113] It was rare for a siege to reach the stage where the fortification had to be stormed and the garrison defended it to the last. In this respect the Welsh rising against the Anglo-Normans in 1094–5, when the castles were a major target, was an exception. All sources refer to the bloodiness of the treatment of the defeated garrisons, and the slaughter of the Montgomery (Hen Domen) garrison in 1095 is suggested as the catalyst for Rufus's expedition to Wales in that year.[114] However, there is little sense of outrage in the reports; the castles were stormed and the garrisons thereby forfeited their lives. It was unlikely that either side would seek terms; a war of conquest was being conducted in which the Welsh had nothing to lose and the early Anglo-Norman settlers, who had gambled all on their stakes in Wales, had nowhere to turn.[115]

Gruffudd ap Rhys's position in 1116 was equally desperate. If he could quickly take a number of castles he might win support for his revolt, but garrisons resisted because they saw the precariousness of their opponent's situation. At Llandovery and Swansea, Gruffudd lost many men in determined, fruitless attacks on the strongholds, but when he was able to capture a castle in Gower and later Ystrad Peithyll, he slew the garrisons.[116] If the all-or-nothing nature of these revolts was unusual, the general rule that the garrison of a stormed fortification lost their rights can be observed repeatedly during the succeeding years.[117] Such slaughters were not only part of Welsh warfare against the Anglo-Normans. In 1151, the sons of Gruffudd ap Rhys fought Hywel ab Owain to determine whether Gwynedd or Deheubarth would rule Ceredigion. They took Llanrhystud from him, but Hywel returned and 'took that castle by force, and burned it after killing all the garrison of the

---

[113] It has been contended that, whilst deals were often made in inter-Welsh dynastic warfare, they would not apply when the Welsh fought the Anglo-Normans. In these cases the garrison would either flee or be slain; Kenyon, 'Fluctuating', 126. The evidence does not fully support this theory.

[114] *ASC* (E), 1094–5; JW, III, 1094–5; *Brut (Pen. 20)*, s.a. 1094–5.

[115] The siege of Aberlleiniog was savage with heavy losses on both sides. Here, and elsewhere in Gwynedd, the Welsh killed the occupants of the castles; *Gruffudd ap Cynan*, pp. 71–3.

[116] *Brut (Pen. 20)*, s.a. 1116.

[117] See the siege of Aberafan in ibid., s.a. 1153, and of Humfry's Castle in ibid., s.a. 1158. The latter example may have had an extra edge because of Rhys ap Gruffudd's feeling of injustice.

castle'.[118] In 1147, Hywel and his brother Cynan challenged the authority of their uncle Cadwaladr in Meirionnydd by besieging his castle of Cynfael. They demanded that the commander of the garrison, Morfran, head of the *clas* at Tywyn, give up the castle, but he refused, saying he would not earn shame by treachery to his lord. The castle was taken by force and 'it was with difficulty that the keeper of the castle escaped through friends, after some of his men had been slain and others had been wounded'.[119] In 1233, Owain ap Gruffudd, in alliance with Richard Marshal, took and burnt Monmouth 'after making a great slaughter therein of the king's men who were dwelling there to strengthen it'.[120]

The overwhelming and slaughter of a garrison did not only occur in desperate situations. Such measures could be employed as terror tactics, designed to persuade other garrisons to surrender. In 1215, Llywelyn ap Iorwerth was supreme in Wales and numerous castles fell to his forces. Tal-y-bont chose to resist Llywelyn's ally Rhys Ieuanc, though 'he [Rhys] took it by force and burned some of the garrison and slew others'.[121] The other castles in the area quickly capitulated. Such terror tactics were used in inter-Welsh warfare. In 1167, Owain Cyfeiliog was driven from his land by Owain Gwynedd and Rhys ap Gruffudd, who installed Owain ap Madog in his place at the castle of Caereinion. Owain Cyfeiliog's right to rule had been challenged, but he returned to Caereinion with Anglo-Norman allies 'and he took and destroyed and burned it and slew all the castle garrison'.[122]

The Welsh were not criticized by outside sources for the slaughter of Anglo-Norman garrisons because the actions conformed to conventions seen elsewhere.[123] On occasion, however, there was an extra edge to siege warfare in Wales. Llywelyn ap Iorwerth had taken William Marshal's castles of Cardigan and

---

[118] Ibid., s.a. 1151.
[119] Ibid., s.a. 1147.
[120] Ibid., s.a. 1233.
[121] Ibid., s.a. 1215.
[122] Ibid., s.a. 1167.
[123] See, for example, Robert Curthose's siege of Robert of Bellême's castle of Saint-Cenéri in OV, IV, pp. 155–7, where the castellan was blinded and a number of the garrison mutilated after putting up a 'stout defence'. Curthose's actions could be seen as terror tactics; on hearing the news Bellême's other castellans began to panic and consider submitting.

Carmarthen in 1215 and had, according to Wendover, 'beheaded all the people he found in them'.[124] In 1223 they were retaken by William's son (also named William Marshal) 'and, because all his followers who had been taken in these castles by Llywelyn had been beheaded by him, so William Marshal, in retaliation, now beheaded all the Welsh he took prisoners'.[125] In this instance the issue was not the fact that the garrison was killed, but the manner of their execution; the matter of beheading brought into play different cultural perceptions among Welsh and Anglo-Normans and increased friction.[126]

Despite racial tensions, the Welsh did make and honour deals with their Anglo-Norman enemies; everything depended on the nature of the individual siege. This may be seen in the differing conclusions to various sieges in 1146.[127] The Anglo-Normans lost the castles of Dinweiler (Cantref Mawr) and Carmarthen to Cadell ap Gruffudd and Hywel ab Owain respectively: 'and they granted their lives to the prisoners who were there'. No account of the storming of these castles is given; the March was more settled than in 1094–5, suggesting that garrisons did not need to fight to the death because they had other lands to fall back on. Also in 1146, the sons of Gruffudd took Llanstephan; a severe struggle took place and many of the garrison were slain or wounded.[128] In the same year, Owain Gwynedd took Mold by assault: 'many of the garrison were slain and others captured and others imprisoned'. The garrison had forfeited their lives but Owain chose to spare some, possibly out of mercy, but probably from expediency; he could secure a ransom or political gains from their release.

In 1173 Iorwerth ab Owain attacked Caerleon and secured the bailey, capturing its defenders: 'and for those the castle [keep] was surrendered on the following day'.[129] Despite the

---

[124] RW (T), II, p. 443; II, p. 270. This is open to question as the Welsh chronicles state that the castles were surrendered to Llywelyn without a struggle. In such cases a massacre of the garrison would not be expected and the chronicles tend to be specific if defenders were slaughtered, imprisoned or allowed to depart. Walker, 'Anglo-Welsh wars,' 152, says that Wendover confused the taking of the castles of Narberth and Wiston in 1220 with the earlier capture of Cardigan and Carmarthen.

[125] RW (T), II, p. 444; RW, II, p. 270.

[126] Suppe, 'Cultural', 147–60.

[127] See *Brut (Pen. 20)*, s.a. 1146.

[128] Llanstephan was the only significant holding of the Marmion family in the twelfth century, implying that they were more likely to make a determined defence.

[129] *Brut (Pen. 20)*, s.a. 1173.

bitter feeling between Anglo-Norman and Welsh in Gwent, both sides were able to show restraint and make deals to their mutual advantage. In the thirteenth century such deals (or their known details) become increasingly elaborate, as is seen with Rhys Fychan's siege of Llandovery in 1210. In 1213, Rhys Ieuanc attacked Dinefwr; the bailey was taken and after a fierce assault on the tower the garrison came to terms: 'And they gave three picked hostages that they would surrender the castle unless help came to them by the following day, upon their being allowed in safety their lives and their limbs and their arms. And so it happened.'[130] Rhys's army moved on to Llandovery: 'and before they encamped the garrison surrendered the castle on condition they should be granted their lives and their members'.[131] It was not only in inter-Welsh warfare that such deals were made; Anglo-Norman troops were involved in the sieges mentioned above and in 1231 Llywelyn ap Iorwerth battered the Mortimer castle of Builth 'till the garrison was forced to surrender the castle and to leave it'.[132]

At Builth, Llywelyn allowed the garrison to depart when he had it at his mercy, presumably in order to avoid loss of life amongst his own force. Similarly, at Welshpool in 1196 a mixed Anglo-Norman and Welsh force spared the garrison of Gwenwynwyn's castle. After a hard-fought siege, the walls were undermined and it would seem that before they were collapsed the workings were shown to the defenders: 'And thus the garrison was *forced* to surrender: but *nevertheless* they all escaped free with their armour and weapons, except one who was slain.'[133] This deal negated the need to make a final assault and meant that the attackers could reuse the castle. Later in the year, however, Gwenwynwyn returned and besieged the castle. He 'forced' its surrender, but the garrison was allowed to depart safely with 'raiment and arms'.[134] Could they have been spared by Gwenwynwyn in recognition of the mercy previously shown to his men? If this was an act of munificence then it was a rare example. It was more usual to show selective mercy with regard

[130] Ibid., s.a. 1213.
[131] Ibid.
[132] Ibid., s.a. 1231.
[133] *Brut (RBH)*, s.a. 1196 (my italics).
[134] Ibid.

CONDUCT IN WARFARE 247

to those who would make worthwhile hostages. Thus, in 1199 Gruffudd ap Rhys's castle of Dineirth was stormed by his brother Maelgwn: 'and of as many men as he found there some he slew and others he imprisoned'.[135] In 1262, Llywelyn ap Gruffudd's men took Roger Mortimer's castle of Cefn-llys; the constable, Hywel ap Meurig, was seized along with his wife, son and daughters, whilst the gate-keepers were killed.[136]

CONDUCT TOWARDS THE CHURCH

Despite the importance of Christianity to the very notion of chivalry, and regular attempts by the Church in Europe throughout the Middle Ages to regulate warfare and control its brutality, it is generally acknowledged that such attempts were unsuccessful and that the Church itself was plundered in war, its sanctuaries violated and its clerics attacked.[137] Rome idealized western Christendom as one united body, but everywhere clerical power was localized and partisan; it was a part of every power struggle because churches were important sources of land, power and wealth which were controlled by, and remained loyal to, local power-brokers. The Church was not neutral and could not expect neutrality in warfare.[138]

Leaving aside the question of partisanship, it was unrealistic for the Church to expect to be ignored in war because, with its wealth, it was too tempting a target. Its resources were vital to an army on campaign. The Church in Wales was poorer than in other areas of Europe, but it provided centres where wealth was stored, including garments, precious articles and provisions.[139]

Despite these qualifying points, the fact that respect for the Church and Christian ideals formed an important plank of

---

[135] *Brut (Pen. 20)*, s.a. 1199. See also the taking of Llangadog in ibid., s.a. 1209.
[136] Ibid., s.a. 1262. See also the taking of the castle of Llangynwyd, Glamorgan, in ibid., s.a. 1257.
[137] See Strickland, *War*, pp. 55–97.
[138] Gerald of Wales acknowledged the partisanship of the Church when he complained to Innocent III that English kings used the spiritual as well as the secular sword to subdue Wales; Gerald of Wales, *Autobiography*, III, 19, p. 180. Ecclesiastical partisanship also operated at a far more localized level.
[139] See J. R. Davies, 'Church, property and conflict in Wales, AD 600–1100', *WHR*, 18 (1997), 387–406; H. Pryce, 'Ecclesiastical wealth in early medieval Wales', in N. Edwards and A. Lane (eds), *The Early Church in Wales and the West* (Oxford, 1992), pp. 22–32.

chivalry shows that some impact was made on the military elite of Europe and their notion of honour. Knights might ravage churches in the course of war, but save their reputation among clerical chroniclers by making reparations.[140] *Liber Landavensis* records examples of reparations made in Wales to save honour or the soul.[141] Throughout the period of study, Welsh leaders, whose wealth was not great, patronized the Church and made land grants. Although they worked closely with the Church – and local leaders and families retained much of the real power in their own hands – at least part of the reason for the patronage was respect for the Church, for the power and support of God and out of a desire to save their souls and those of their families. The Church could have a powerful effect on the thoughts and actions of men in Wales. Could its ideals influence the conduct of war?

Attacks on the Welsh Church from outsiders

The post-Roman Church was subject to attacks from the pagan Anglo-Saxons. They had no reason to spare the Church and their attitude could be expressed in the words attributed by Bede to Æthelfrith. He justified the slaughter of an estimated 1,200 monks who had come to pray for the British army at Chester: 'If they are praying to their God against us, then, even if they do not bear arms, they are fighting against us, assailing us as they do with prayers for our defeat.'[142]

---

[140] Strickland, *War*, pp. 55–97. OV, VI, 12, p. 229, suggests that destruction of Church property in war was acceptable if suitable compensation was made afterwards.

[141] See *LL*, pp. 264–5; Rhiwallon ap Tudfwlch and his household plundered the church of Llanmoda (*c*.1025), but Rhiwallon was mortally injured. On his deathbed he made a grant to Llandaff. Although much of the charter material is desperately unreliable, Wendy Davies feels that this example has a genuine core. The fact that the twelfth-century Llandaff scribes felt it feasible that a Welsh lord could make such a reparation grant is of significance. For further discussion of *Liber Landavensis*, see below, pp. 250–1.

[142] Bede, II, 2, p. 141; Bede's description may obscure the fact that many churchmen led their own forces; it is possible that Brocmail commanded a military detachment at Chester.

Following the conversion of the Anglo-Saxons, attacks on Welsh churches did not cease.[143] However, there was a certain amount of cooperation against the pagan threat posed by the Vikings; in 914 the Welsh bishop of Archenfield was ransomed from Viking raiders by King Edward for £40.[144] Welsh sources, composed and maintained in the monasteries of the land, were struck by the onslaught of the Vikings and the plundering of Welsh churches.[145] The scale of the attack was the major reason, but it is possible that part of the outrage was due to the fact that the assault came from a pagan rather than a Christian enemy.[146] It could also be suggested that the Vikings did not adhere to Christian conventions regarding warfare which were followed by the Welsh and Anglo-Saxons. The Welsh chronicles label the battle in 877 in which the Vikings defeated Rhodri Mawr as the 'Sunday Battle', implying that it was unusual to fight on the Sabbath and possibly that this battle was instigated by the Vikings.

If Anglo-Saxon attacks on the Church were accepted with a minimum of outrage, a change came with the new Christian enemies of Wales, the Anglo-Normans. They made the wealth of the Welsh Church a target, but greater indignation was aroused by their mistreatment of Welsh clergy and a lack of respect for sanctuary and other native practices.[147] The Anglo-Normans, infused with the latest reforming ideas from the papacy, saw the Church in Wales as backward, corrupt, barely Christian. They were appalled at the secular inclinations of the clergy, whom they treated with the same disregard that they reserved for the Welsh nobility. Rhigyfarch complained that Welsh priests were 'despised'

---

[143] See *Brut (RBH)*, s.a. 978; *Vitae*, pp. 111–13, 229–31. The *Life of St Gwynllyw* has an account of an attack on the saint's church in Glamorgan by Harold Godwinesson. When his approach was imminent the community fled, depositing their valuables and provisions in the church for sanctuary. Harold's men broke in and seized the goods, but there was at least a hope that the sanctuary would be respected; ibid., p. 187.

[144] *ASC*, s.a. 914.

[145] *HW*, I, p. 91.

[146] The point should not be overemphasized, however. In Ireland 'before, during and after the Viking period more churches were plundered and burned and more clerics killed by the Irish than by the Norse'; Ó'Cróinín, *Early Medieval*, p. 261. See also D. Ó'Corráin, 'Ireland, Wales, Man and the Hebrides', in P. Sawyer (ed.), *The Oxford Illustrated History of the Vikings* (Oxford, 1997), pp. 83–109; J. L. Nelson, 'The Frankish Empire', in Sawyer, *Oxford*, pp. 19–47; P. Sawyer, 'The Viking legacy', in his *Oxford*, pp. 250–61.

[147] *Brut (Pen. 20)*, describes the appointment of the Anglo-Norman Bernard as bishop of St Davids in 1115 as 'in contempt of the clerics of the Britons'.

by the invaders,[148] and the Anglo-Saxon monk John of Worcester was shocked by the activities of Anglo-Norman troops on Anglesey in 1098: 'They seized from his church a priest of advanced years, Cenred by name, to whom the Welsh turned to advise with their plans, castrated him, putting out one eye and cutting off his tongue.'[149] John cited this attack as the reason for their later defeat by Magnus Barefoot.[150] Such stories suggest that the Welsh clergy did not expect, and were not used to, such handling; some code of conduct evidently governed their treatment.[151] Familiarity with the Welsh Church did not lead to a lessening of Anglo-Norman attacks; in the thirteenth century sanctuary continued to be ignored[152] and Church property ravaged.[153] Attacks were directed against religious institutions which supported Welsh lords in opposition to the English king; after the conquest of 1282–3, compensation payments were made to Welsh churches.[154]

Welsh attacks on native churches

From Gildas's day Welsh rulers were criticized for abusing the Church. Throughout the early Middle Ages we lack evidence for attacks on churches by native rulers, but there are suggestions that they continued to take place and it would be unrealistic to expect anything else.[155] There are many possible interpretations

---

[148] Lapidge, 'Welsh', p. 91.

[149] JW, III, 1098. See also *Journey*, II, 8, p. 188.

[150] Anglo-Norman ravaging of Welsh churches was blamed likewise for their reversals in 1157 and 1165; *Brut (Pen. 20)*, s.a. 1157; *Journey*, II, 7, p. 189.

[151] The Welsh revolt of 1094 was described as 'the deliverance of Christendom'; Meilyr, p. 185.

[152] See *Brut (Pen. 20)*, s.a. 1211.

[153] See RW, II, pp. 349–50, III, p. 11; MP, IV, p. 482. For further examples of Anglo-Norman attacks on Welsh churches, see F. G. Cowley, *The Monastic Order in South Wales, 1066–1349* (Cardiff, 1977), p. 212.

[154] *Age*, p. 374.

[155] See, for example, *Brut (RBH)*, s.a. 978, where Hywel ab Ieuaf attacked Clynnog Fawr in alliance with an Anglo-Saxon force. This monastery had close connections with the Rhodri Mawr dynasty and may have been supporting Hywel's rival Iago ab Idwal; see Maund, 'Dynastic', 160, and compare Gruffudd ap Llywelyn's attack on Llanbadarn Fawr in 1039 (below). Asser recorded attacks on St Davids by Hyfaidd ap Bledri (d. 893), king of Dyfed, which J. R. Davies suggested were to secure resources to counter the threat posed by Gwynedd; J. R. Davies, 'Church', 398. A tenth-century penitential poem relates the penance of a clerk, Ysgolan, for 'the burning of a church'; *Saga*, p. 510. An inscribed stone of the mid-seventh century refers to a man who died defending Llanddewibrefi from spoliation, although we cannot identify the enemy; G. Gruffydd and H. P. Owen, 'The earliest mention of St David?', *BBCS*, 17 (1956–8), 185–93; also their 'The earliest mention of St David? An addendum', *BBCS*, 19 (1960–2), 231–2.

of the attacks made on the Welsh Church by native leaders as recorded in the charters and hagiographical works of *Liber Landavensis*.[156] Not only is the *Liber Landavensis* unreliable as evidence for the early Middle Ages, but it is also unwise to project the rights of the Church proclaimed by the Llandaff scribes of the twelfth century back to the earlier period. However, attacks on churches may be seen as indicative of the actions expected of Welsh nobles in the eleventh century and possibly earlier. The crimes recorded include the plundering of churches for their riches and provisions[157] and the killing of clergy and abuse of sanctuary.[158] It is difficult to decide whether such actions were regarded as acceptable by the rulers of early medieval Wales. In our sources the offenders are always made to show their contrition by grants of reparation or submission to the saints, but this was designed to prove the rights of Llandaff. It might be suggested that the seizure of goods and provisions by armies on campaign was common behaviour; in the majority of our examples, the warriors were forced to stop plundering by the power of a saint's miracle and fear of his wrath. By contrast, the killing of clergy seems more unusual, serious and morally unacceptable; large grants are said to be made after such deeds. Again, of course, such sensibilities may merely reflect twelfth-century attitudes, but when considered in the light of the horror felt at the treatment of the clergy by the Vikings and Normans, it could also suggest a code of conduct to be followed towards the Church.

In 1039 Gruffudd ap Llywelyn sought to dislodge Hywel ab Edwin from Ceredigion. Gruffudd invaded and during the campaign ravaged the lands of Llanbadarn Fawr.[159] This was early in Gruffudd's career as he sought to establish his power; the resources of Llanbadarn were a support to his rival Hywel and as

---

[156] For a summary of the views, see J. R. Davies, 'Church', 389–91. Wendy Davies's contention is that grants made to the Church in south-east Wales in a supposed period of social chaos in the eighth and ninth centuries made it a significant landowner and that the attacks show that it was a target of 'property-hungry aristocrats'. Patrick Sims-Williams says that the charter evidence is unreliable; it could be that there was less tolerance of such violence in the tenth and eleventh centuries, or the Llandaff scribes could have invented the stories. Kari Maund dismissed the charters as twelfth-century forgeries riddled with clichés.

[157] See *Vitae*, pp. 187, 219, 225, 299; *LL*, pp. 264–5, 272–3.

[158] See *LL*, pp. 125, 217–18, 249, 257, 259–60, 261–2, 267, 271–2.

[159] *Brut (Pen. 20)*, s.a. 1039. In Ireland, attacks on the monasteries of a rival were a standard part of an assault on his power; Ó'Cróinín, *Early Medieval*, p. 278.

such were an acceptable target. For the rest of Gruffudd's reign, however, there are no recorded attacks on the Welsh Church by native or alien forces.[160] Once he was established as lord of the land, Gruffudd became a patron and defender of the Church which, in its turn, supported him; favourable accounts of Gruffudd in the Welsh chronicles suggest that his 1039 attack was forgiven.[161] Gruffudd began to rule in south-east Wales after the defeat of Gruffudd ap Rhydderch in 1055 and *Liber Landavensis* preserves a charter of the former's from this period confirming the rights of Llandaff to Bishop Herewald.[162] Perhaps this should be seen as a reparation grant for damages done to Church land in the war, or an act to reconcile a leading power in the area after Gruffudd had killed the native king.

Chroniclers could be scathing of men who attacked churches, particularly if the ravagers made no later reparation. In 1109 the Welsh chronicles, now probably being compiled at Llanbadarn, recorded the attack of Welsh lords in the service of Henry I on the lands of Cadwgan ap Bleddyn and his son Owain in Ceredigion:

> And they destroyed some of those who had fled for sanctuary, others they did not kill. And then they heard that some had stayed in the place where there is a privilege or sanctuary of David the bishop and which is called Llanddewibrefi, along with the priests of the church. And they sent their accursed, evil-spirited company thither to violate the sanctuary of the church and to kill the inhabitants.[163]

---

[160] J. R. Davies, 'Church', 401.
[161] Such an attitude towards the Church, with all its inherent ambiguities, was far from unique. *Gruffudd ap Cynan* is unusual in glorifying its hero's ravaging of Powys in 1081 when 'he spared not even the churches'. But the same source delights in reporting that, in the settled later years of his reign, Gruffudd built churches so that 'Gwynedd glittered then with lime-washed churches, like the firmament with the stars' and that on his deathbed he made generous grants to the Church; *Gruffudd ap Cynan*, pp. 69, 81–3. The elegy to Gruffudd in *Brut (Pen. 20)*, s.a. 1137, says he died 'after building many churches and consecrating them to God and the saints'. The unusual nature of the account of the ravaging in 1081 is emphasized by a passage in the *Life of St Gwynllyw* recording an attack made by Gruffudd ap Cynan's men on the saint's church in Glamorgan. The source stresses that the assault was made by Gruffudd's Norse allies and that he and his Welsh followers opposed the attack; *Vitae*, p. 185. There was also a large Norse element in Gruffudd's force in 1081. The glory in the attack possibly reflects the tension between Gwynedd and Powys since 1075 as the latter's leaders ruled over the proud nobility of Gwynedd.
[162] *LL*, p. 269.
[163] *Brut (Pen. 20)*, s.a. 1109. The passage continues: 'and after that they returned after ravaging and plundering the whole land except the precincts of the saints themselves and David and Padarn'. The reading here is corrupt, however; *Brut (RBH)* makes it clear that the lands of David and Padarn were ravaged.

CONDUCT IN WARFARE 253

Part of the reason for the hostility of the native chronicle to Gruffudd ap Rhys in 1116 would seem to be that in the course of the revolt his men, whilst camped a mile from Llanbadarn, 'did wrong to the church: for they carried off cattle from the sanctuary for their dinner'.[164]

Welsh attacks on English and Marcher churches

Bede was scathing in his account of the ravaging of Northumbria by Cadwallon in 633–4:

> although a Christian by name and profession, [he] was nevertheless a barbarian in heart and spared neither women nor children . . . Nor did he pay any respect to the Christian religion which had sprung up amongst them. Indeed to this very day it is the habit of the Britons to despise the faith and religion of the English and not to cooperate with them in anything more than with the heathen.[165]

There are no details of the ravaging of churches and Bede's bias against the British, and Cadwallon in particular, makes it dangerous to rely on his work. Moreover, this single snapshot relates to an incident soon after the Northumbrian conversion to Christianity, at a time of tension with the Church elsewhere in Britain; it is possible that mutual recognition and respect had not yet developed.[166] We have no further accounts of Welsh attacks on English churches or clergy until the eleventh century,[167] when there are two references to them fighting against Anglo-Saxon bishops; in both examples the clerics were military men

---

[164] *Brut (Pen. 20)*, s.a. 1116.
[165] Bede, II, 20, pp. 203–5; see also the mention of Cadwallon's burning of a church in ibid., II, 14, p. 189.
[166] In relating a victory over the Anglo-Saxons near Lichfield, *Marwnad Cynddylan* glories in the fact that 'book-clutching monks did not protect them'; *Saga*, p. 177. Rowland assumes that the monks were Northumbrian priests with their army on campaign who were not attacked by the Welsh but whose prayers could not save their men; ibid., pp. 134–5. Brooks argued that Oswald installed Eowa as a client king in Mercia and that the monks had been brought from Northumbria or Iona to convert the pagans before they were slaughtered by the Welsh; N. Brooks, 'The formation of the Mercian kingdom', in Bassett, *Origin*, pp. 159–70.
[167] Æthelflaed's attack on Brycheiniog in 916 was in retaliation for the murder of a Mercian abbot by the Welsh; Stenton, *Anglo-Saxon*, p. 323.

responsible for leading levies against the Welsh.[168] In 1055, Gruffudd ap Llywelyn's sack of Hereford included the burning of the basilica after it had been looted of its relics and vestments. His force killed seven clerics who were guarding the church door.[169] It has been suggested that the Norse in Gruffudd's army were responsible for the attack on the church[170] and there was also a significant Anglo-Saxon element in his force, but Gruffudd as overall commander must bear the responsibility. The attack on the church is not mentioned in the account given by the Welsh chronicles; it is possible that a measure of shame was attached to the deed and so it was passed over. The singling out of the killing of the clergy could suggest that it was this act rather than the plundering of the church that was unusual and breached the accepted codes of conduct.

Condemnations from Anglo-Norman sources concerning Welsh attacks on Anglo-Norman religious institutions are rare. Unlike the treatment of the Scots in Anglo-Norman chronicles, such criticism is infrequently used to mark the Welsh as barbarians or to justify war against them.[171] Welsh attacks on lowland England were rare, but even references to assaults on churches in the March are limited in number.[172] An incident in 1231 may suggest that it was unusual for a church to be deliberately targeted. The garrison of Montgomery captured and decapitated a number of Welshmen, prompting an angry Llywelyn ap Iorwerth to ravage the March, 'sparing neither the churches nor ecclesiastics; and [he] burnt several churches, together with some noble women and girls who had fled there for safety'.[173] It seems to be suggested that Llywelyn's actions were extreme and unusual, prompted by the mistreatment of his men. His alleged burning of churches was then used by Henry as an

---

[168] *ASC* (D), s.a. 1049; JW, II, 1049; *ASC* (C), s.a. 1056.

[169] The killing of the clerics is mentioned by *ASC* (D), s.a. 1055, but not by the (C) version of the chronicle. JW, II, 1055 gives the number as seven.

[170] Charles, *Old Norse*, p. 46. Norse elements in mixed forces could be held specifically responsible for such attacks; see above, p. 252, n. 161.

[171] For treatment of some specific examples of Welsh attacks on churches, see M. Griffiths, 'Native society', 179–216; R. Turvey, 'The death of an excommunicate Prince: the Lord Rhys and the cathedral church at St Davids', *Journal of the Pembrokeshire Historical Society*, 7 (1996–7), 26–49.

[172] See Cowley, *Monastic*, pp. 212–13; also JW, III, 1136; *GS*, p. 19; MP, IV, p. 413. It could be suggested that attacks described in *The History of William the Marshal*, p. 95, and *Brut (Pen. 20)*, s.a. 1223, were fuelled by the on-running feud in Gwent.

[173] RW (T), II, p. 540; RW, III, p. 11.

CONDUCT IN WARFARE   255

excuse to excommunicate Llywelyn and lead an expedition into Wales.

Sparing the Church: restrictions on the brutality of warfare?

Little evidence exists to suggest that the Church was spared in the early Middle Ages, although horror at the ravaging of the Vikings might suggest that their conduct was more brutal.[174] In Ireland, abbots acted as peacemakers between lay powers, and it is possible that churchmen performed a similar role in Wales.[175] Following his death in 1127, Daniel ap Sulien, archdeacon of Powys, was described as 'the man who was mediator between Gwynedd and Powys', and churchmen helped to reconcile Llywelyn ap Iorwerth with Elise ap Madog and Gwenwynwyn in 1202.[176]

The subject of reparations to the Church in Wales is of significance here. The problems with the evidence have been considered, but it would seem that lords patronized and protected churches in their sphere of power which were seen as their own, or their family's, property. Any sparing of such institutions was in their own interests. Linked to the question of reparations is the evidence from *Liber Landavensis* suggesting that churches expected the sanctuary of their lands to be maintained.[177] This protection included not just the church itself but also all of its lands, potentially covering a wide area. Criminals and fugitives could not, in theory, be pursued into these areas. If secular rulers did trespass, compensation was due. Wendy Davies contended that the expansion and territorialization of these powers was a

---

[174] See above, p. 249. There is nothing in Wales in this period to compare with the *Law of Innocents* (697) promulgated by Adomnán of Iona. This sought to protect women, children and clergy from the horrors of war; it gained royal approval in Ireland, Northumbria, amongst the Scots and Picts and the Britons of Strathclyde, but had little practical effect.

[175] Ó'Cróinín, *Early Medieval*, p. 279. Welsh churchmen are seen performing this role in *LL*, p. 212. Lloyd believed that churches were granted lands on the borders of *cantrefi* and kingdoms to define the limits where war could take place; *HW*, I, p. 318.

[176] *Brut (Pen. 20)*, s.a. 1127, 1202. In *Culhwch and Olwen*, when Arthur led a force to Ireland in search of the Twrch Trwyth there was a great fear in the country until its saints sought, and were granted, protection; *Mabinogi*, p. 170.

[177] See W. Davies, 'Adding insult to injury: power, property and immunities in early medieval Wales', in W. Davies and P. Fouracre (eds), *Property and Power in the Early Middle Ages* (Cambridge, 1995), pp. 137–64.

late pre-1066 development, although the claims were elaborated in the Anglo-Norman period. Most rights remained purely theoretical and they cannot be substantiated in the early medieval period, but they might suggest an awareness of certain Church prerogatives.

Evidence for expected Church immunities is more readily available in the Anglo-Norman period and the outrage felt at the treatment of Welsh clergy has been noted; examples of similar conduct at the hands of native leaders cannot be found. An awareness of the sanctuary of Church land in war can be detected, although in practice it was not always respected. A twelfth-century poem written to promote the interests of St Davids boasts of similar privileges and sanctuaries to those claimed in *Liber Landavensis*;[178] in the mid-twelfth century, a grant of sanctuary and immunity was made to the church of Trefeglwys;[179] and Gruffudd ap Rhys's taking of the cattle of Llanbadarn in 1116 was considered a crime by the chronicler.[180] In 1109 there was criticism of the breaking of sanctuary and the killing of people under ecclesiastical protection; it is unclear if clergy or non-combatant laymen of the land were abused.[181] A clearer example is apparent in 1115, when Gruffudd ap Rhys sought sanctuary in the church of Aberdaron after being betrayed to Henry I by Gruffudd ap Cynan. The latter ordered that the southern prince be dragged from the church, but he was protected by the prelates and saved.[182] In 1075 the 'fighting men of the sons of Merwydd' found sanctuary from the men of Powys in the church of Clynnog Fawr; they proceeded to use the church as a place to rally before falling on their enemies.[183] The legal rights and immunities enjoyed by churches throughout

---

[178] M. E. Owen, 'Prolegomena to a study of the historical context of Gwynfardd Brycheiniog's poem to Dewi', *Studia Celtica*, 26 (1991), 51–79. The poem boasts of the privileges and sanctuary offered by David who protected his people from plunderers; war is said not to touch his churches or land, protected by powerful relics, and if plundering fleets approached from the Irish Sea their crews would be blinded.

[179] H. Pryce, 'The church of Trefeglwys and the end of the "Celtic" charter tradition in twelfth-century Wales', *CMCS*, 25 (1993), 15–54.

[180] *Brut (Pen. 20)*, s.a. 1116.

[181] Ibid., s.a. 1109.

[182] Ibid., s.a. 1115; of course, in this example Gruffudd ap Cynan would have gained no clear advantage in fulfilling Henry's request.

[183] *Gruffudd ap Cynan*, p. 60. As the men were Gruffudd's allies, there seems to be no shame attached to their use of sanctuary in this way. Gerald of Wales complained that some Welsh people abused the sanctuary offered by churches and used them as a base for raiding; *Journey*, I, 18, p. 254.

Wales were challenged in the later law texts composed under the influence of the thirteenth-century princes of Gwynedd. This suggests that in an earlier age, with weaker lay power, the rights were of some significance.[184]

In Anglo-Norman sources, the respect shown by the Welsh for the Church was used to shame the Anglo-Norman nobility into better behaviour. There was criticism of Henry II's attacks on the Welsh Church in 1157 and 1165; as in Gerald of Wales on the events of 1165:

> The leaders of the English army had burnt down certain Welsh churches, with their villages and churchyards. As a result the sons of Owain Gwynedd, supported by a band of young soldiers who were with them, bitterly harangued their father, and his fellow-princes, too, swearing that they would never in future spare any English churches.[185]

Most are said to have agreed until Owain argued that they should be glad because now God would be on their side and 'unless we have God on our side we are no match for the English'. Gerald said of the Welsh: 'they pay greater respect than any other people to their churches, to men in orders, the relics of the saints, bishops's crooks, bells, holy books and the Cross itself, for which they show great reverence.'[186] He also claimed that they showed greater respect for sanctuary than other people. Walter Map told a number of stories about a Welsh king 'Apollonides', a figure thought to represent Rhys ap Gruffudd. He described the king plundering 'immense wealth' from a neighbour's land but returning beasts accidentally taken from the clergy. Apollonides's respect for the clergy was shown by his allowing priests to cheat him without complaint.[187]

---

[184] See *Law*, pp. 81ff.; the passages are not found in earlier law texts. See also *LG*, pp. 208–15.

[185] *Journey*, II, 12, p. 202. This section was added to version II of the work, c.1199, and was not in the first edition.

[186] *Description*, I, 18, pp. 253–5. Support for Gerald's statement on respect for relics can be found in *Law*, p. 83; this acknowledged a person's right to protection if he were holding a relic, but stated that the protection would lapse if he was also holding a weapon! Gerald also claimed that oaths meant nothing to the Welsh, a common complaint levelled against them in Anglo-Norman sources; *Journey*, II, 1, p. 256. Maelgwn ap Rhys's breaking of an oath sworn on relics in the presence of religious men is treated with surprise and annoyance by the native chronicler; *Brut (Pen. 20)*, s.a. 1198.

[187] Map, pp. 409ff.

Such stories cannot be taken at face value. They were designed to make an impression on the Anglo-Norman world by describing supposedly primitive Christians displaying greater respect for the Church than did the decadent Anglo-Normans. It is notable that Gerald and Walter were able to use the Welsh in such examples; this would not have been possible if their attacks on churches were notorious. There may have been some truth in the stories. Rhys ap Gruffudd spared and patronized captured Marcher institutions, including towns and monasteries;[188] this was out of self-interest, but he was also prepared to accept alien religious institutions. In 1136 Owain and Cadwaladr spared Llanbadarn on their descent into Ceredigion.[189] Archaeological work in south-west Wales reveals that churches were separate from Anglo-Norman boroughs, set outside their defences;[190] does this suggest that they were not expected to be attacked in war? In 1212 Llywelyn ap Iorwerth sent a letter to his forces ordering them to protect and defend the lands, property and monks of Ratlinghope priory, out of respect for the canon Walter Corbet (Llywelyn's uncle).[191] This could be interpreted as an example of Welsh restraint towards the Church or as an exceptional case determined by Llywelyn's familial connection. In the Painscastle campaign of 1231, Llywelyn commanded the men of Maelienydd to uphold, protect and defend the monks and possessions of Leominster priory. This was prompted by a payment from the prior to obtain protection after Welsh harrying of his land.[192] Such examples at least indicate that commanders had control over their forces and could direct their ravaging.

---

[188] *HW*, I, p. 596.
[189] Ibid., II, p. 472; again self-interest was at work as they had many allies from Deheubarth and designs on rule in Ceredigion.
[190] K. Murphy, 'Small boroughs in south-west Wales: their planning, early development and defences', in N. Edwards (ed.), *Landscape and Settlement in Medieval Wales* (Oxford, 1997), pp. 139–56.
[191] *Handlist*, p. 100 (333).
[192] Ibid., p. 105 (352).

CONCLUSION

Throughout the period studied in this book, native Welsh military forces were comparable to those elsewhere in Europe. Whatever variations there were should be considered in relation to specific circumstances and the bias of our sources: it is unrealistic to apply ethnic or racial stereotyping to explain the make-up and activities of Welsh troops. The *teulu* was a key element in the organization, administration and implementation of a Welsh leader's military might. As such it may be compared with contemporary military households in Britain and throughout Europe. An understanding of the significance of the *teulu* establishes the presence in medieval Wales of a privileged, aristocratic military elite, supported by the labour and services of both bondmen and non-warriors of free status. It was vital for a leader to retain the loyalty of his household; this can help to explain the actions of lords and also the ambience of the court that is reflected in the surviving panegyric material. Many changes occurred in Welsh society between the seventh and the thirteenth centuries but, throughout, the power and needs of the *teulu* remained both the mainstay of a lord's power and a key influence on his actions.

A lord would often need to raise an extended military force beyond his regular *teulu*. Despite problems with logistics, resources and training, large forces could be raised in Wales under leaders with ability and power. These armies could be kept in the field for significant periods of time and they proved capable of competing with external enemies from Ireland and England. Many developments correspond with those seen elsewhere in Europe. Initially armies were composed of the combined *teuluoedd* of numerous independent leaders, but over time the rise of over-kingdoms saw the decline in status of lesser lords. The territorialization of over-kingdoms witnessed the imposition of duties on the land that would eventually be regularized in the law codes. Throughout the period, however, the key to military power lay in keeping the loyalty of the lesser nobility in the localities; without the support of the *uchelwyr*, theoretical duties could not be imposed. Similarly, service from churchmen and church land depended on winning the support of local religious leaders.

Despite the notably high numbers of troops available in Wales and the possibility that a higher percentage of the male population served than in other areas of Europe, the *llu* was always a select levy of the freemen of the country. Universal levies may have been called in emergency situations, but if so they were exceptional and their value is questionable. The thirteenth-century princes of Gwynedd were able to impose onerous military burdens on the population for lengthy periods, but this eroded their support and contributed to the downfall of Llywelyn ap Gruffudd.

The notion of the advance of superior military technology and techniques from the so-called 'heartlands' of Europe to the 'fringes', notably Wales, Ireland and Scotland, needs to be reconsidered. The central role played by ravaging, evasion, ambush and other small-scale clashes in the warfare of the day means that perceptions of the Welsh 'avoiding battle' and indulging in war for mere 'cattle raids' indicate that they were following standard strategic and tactical practices. They were highly skilled in such warfare. Perceptions of Welsh armies as ferocious but undisciplined and incapable of facing 'professional' armies must also be reassessed. Battles were the exception, not the rule, but throughout the period Welsh forces were capable of confronting their external enemies in such engagements. Battles were generally the product of political and dynastic turmoil, overconfidence or desperation, but they remained a tactical option for a Welsh commander, whether he was facing native, Anglo-Saxon or Hiberno-Scandinavian enemies. These trends continued in the Anglo-Norman period, where the number of battles increased when the Anglo-Normans added their destabilizing influence by supporting a native ruler. Battles between Welsh and Anglo-Norman forces were infrequent, but in contrast to the view that Anglo-Norman military discipline and skill led to the adoption of an unusual battle-seeking strategy, Welsh ability and success in engagements helped to delay the progress of the invaders. The value of Welsh troops in battle was shown by the use made of them in Anglo-Norman warfare. Distinctions must be drawn between Welsh forces serving as independent units under their native commanders and those recruited by Anglo-Norman lords from Marcher lands to act as ravagers and irregular infantry.

The effectiveness of the Welsh in medieval warfare implies the presence of mixed, flexible forces. An examination of Welsh cavalry suggests that they were an effective presence in Welsh forces from post-Roman times to 1283. Arguments for the neglect of cavalry in Anglo-Saxon forces do not apply to the situation in Wales, and the later impact of the heavily armed knight and the tactic of the shock charge with couched lance has been greatly exaggerated. Welsh cavalry fought as fast, effective raiders, capable of harassing an enemy force and also, it seems, charging at them in battle. Horses were greatly prized and there was a long tradition of breeding and training war horses of quality. However, the near-universal depiction in the panegyric sources of Welsh forces fighting from horseback exaggerates the importance of cavalry. Infantry was always vital and, when appropriate, many of the mounted military men would dismount to fight on foot, sometimes alongside a dedicated infantry force. There are indications of an awareness of tactical organization amongst infantry forces, of the value placed on disciplined troops and of the importance of the steadiness of a shield wall. Under specific circumstances it is possible that field fortifications were constructed to stiffen infantry lines and deter enemy attack. To complete the range of tactical options, Welsh cavalry and infantry were well supported by troops of archers whose reputation was renowned throughout Europe.

Fortification is an area where Anglo-Norman influence on Welsh military history has seemed most pronounced. Again, however, the idea of the impact of a more advanced military technology on Wales must be questioned. The relationship between private strongholds and political decentralization must be considered so that the history of fortifications in Wales can be seen within the context of wider movements in European society. In the Anglo-Norman period the Welsh use of castles was closely related to the wider political scene. Welsh rulers would only make considerable investment in castles and fortification strategies when they felt secure in their lordships. If they faced hostility from an overwhelmingly powerful native rival or an undistracted king of England, it made more sense to rely on a defensive policy that did not depend on fixed points. A fortification could not be held indefinitely against the politically dominant force in the land.

Castles provided the Anglo-Normans with their ultimate refuge in an often hostile country. From the beginning, however, the Welsh were adept at siege warfare and the importance of surprise, cunning, treachery and other apparently simple techniques should be stressed. Welsh forces were capable of more elaborate siege tactics, but these were often less effective and everything ultimately depended on the political situation.

It has been alleged that Anglo-Norman invaders found a more brutal form of warfare in Wales and adapted their behaviour accordingly. These claims have been exaggerated. Non-combatants could expect no mercy in Wales, but this aspect of warfare was customary in medieval Europe. Slavery did take longer to die out in Wales than in England and France and this was perhaps the major difference in behaviour in war. To assess conduct in warfare among the military elite is more problematic, but trends in Wales generally conform with those seen elsewhere in Europe. Over time, and certainly by the twelfth century, there are increasing instances of Welsh forces sparing and ransoming noble rivals. Whilst there are many references to the Anglo-Normans committing atrocities against the native nobility, there are few examples of the reverse, and most deaths occurred in the heat of battle. However, the continued bitterness of warfare in Wales – often involving conquest and the destruction of dynasties – coupled with social and cultural differences in relation to England, meant that war was perceived differently and hostile references to the Welsh were common.

With regard to the treatment of the Church in war, there are suggestions that restrictions applied to the conduct of Welsh forces. Outrage at the mistreatment of ecclesiastical property and, particularly, of churchmen at the hands of Viking and Anglo-Norman raiders suggests that there were some controls. The point should not be exaggerated as native attacks on Welsh churches were frequent, but evidence from *Liber Landavensis* and elsewhere suggests that reparation was expected in such cases and that churchmen were generally left unmolested. References to Welsh attacks on English and Marcher churches are limited and in this area there is a notable lack of criticism of Welsh conduct from English sources.

In conduct, disposition, tactics, strategy, organization and social composition, Welsh military forces from the seventh to the thirteenth century bear comparison with those throughout western Europe. The military history of Wales in this period, like the history of the country more generally, should be seen as an integral part of the development of post-Roman and medieval Europe.

BIBLIOGRAPHY

PRINTED PRIMARY SOURCES

A Mediaeval Prince of Wales: The Life of Gruffudd ap Cynan, ed. and trans. D. Simon Evans (Llanerch, 1990).
Adomnán of Iona, *Life of St Columba*, ed. and trans. R. Sharpe (London, 1995).
Aneirin, *Y Gododdin*, ed. and trans. A. O. H. Jarman (Llandysul, 1988).
—— *Y Gododdin*, ed. and trans. J. T. Koch (Cardiff, 1997).
Anglo-Saxon Chronicle, ed. and trans. D. Whitelock (London, 1961).
Annales Cambriae, ed. J. Williams ab Ithel (Rolls Series, London, 1860).
Annales Monastici, ed. H. R. Luard, 5 vols (Rolls Series, London, 1864–9).
Armes Prydein o Lyfr Taliesin, ed. I. Williams (Cardiff, 1955), Eng. vers. R. Bromwich (Dublin, 1972).
Asser, *Life of King Alfred*, in *Alfred the Great*, ed. and trans. S. Keynes and M. Lapidge (Harmondsworth, 1983).
Bede, *Ecclesiastical History of the English People*, ed. and trans. B. Colgrave and R. A. B. Mynors (Oxford, 1969).
Beginnings of Welsh Poetry, The, ed. I. Williams and R. Bromwich (2nd edn, Cardiff, 1980).
Black Book of Carmarthen, ed. and trans. M. Pennar (Llanerch, 1989).
Bosco, N., 'Dafydd Benfras and his *Red Book* poems', *Studia Celtica*, 22 (1987), 49–117.
Brenhinedd y Saesson or The Kings of the Saxons, ed. and trans. T. Jones (Cardiff, 1971).
Breuddwyd Maxen, ed. I. Williams (3rd edn, Bangor, 1928).
Breuddwyt Ronabwy, ed. G. M. Richards (Cardiff, 1948).
Brut y Tywysogyon, Peniarth Ms. 20 version, ed. T. Jones (Cardiff, 1941).
Brut y Tywysogyon or The Chronicle of the Princes. Peniarth Ms. 20 Version, ed. and trans. T. Jones (Cardiff, 1952).
Brut y Tywysogyon or the Chronicle of the Princes. Red Book of Hergest Version, ed. and trans. T. Jones (Cardiff, 1955).
Calendar of Ancient Correspondence Concerning Wales, ed. J. G. Edwards (Cardiff, 1935).
Calendar of Ancient Petitions Relating to Wales in the Public Record Office, ed. W. Rees (Cardiff, 1975).
Canu Aneirin, ed. I. Williams (Cardiff, 1938).
Canu Llywarch Hen, ed. I. Williams (Cardiff, 1935).
Canu Taliesin, ed. I. Williams (Cardiff, 1960), Eng. vers. J. E. Caerwyn Williams (Dublin, 1968).
Cartae et alia Munimenta quae pertinent de Glamorgancia, ed. and trans. G. T. Clark, 6 vols (Talygan, 1910).
Charters of the Abbey of Ystrad Marchell, The, ed. G. C. G. Thomas (Aberystwyth, 1997).
Chronicles of the Reigns of Stephen, Henry II, and Richard I, ed. R. Howlett, 4 vols (Rolls Series, London, 1884–9).
Clancy, J. P., *The Earliest Welsh Poetry* (London, 1970).
Clausewitz, K. von, *On War*, ed. A. Rapoport (London, 1982).
Constantius, *The Life of St Germanus of Auxerre*, in F. R. Hoare (ed. and trans.), *The Western Fathers* (London, 1954).
Cronica de Wallia, in T. Jones (ed.), '*Cronica de Wallia* and other documents from the Exeter Cathedral Library Ms. 3514', *BBCS*, 12 (1946–8), 27–44.

BIBLIOGRAPHY

Culhwch ac Olwen, ed. R. Bromwich and D. Simon Evans (Cardiff, 1992).
Cyfranc Lludd a Llefelys, ed. I. Williams (2nd edn, Bangor, 1922).
Cyfreithiau Hywel Dda o Lawysgrif Coleg y Iesu Rhydychen LVII, ed. M. Richards (Cardiff, 1990).
Cyfres Beirdd y Tywysogion, ed. R. G. Gruffydd, 7 vols (Cardiff, 1991–6).
Damweiniau Colan, ed. D. Jenkins (Aberystwyth, 1973).
Dickinson, J. C., and P. T. Ricketts, 'The Anglo-Norman chronicle of Wigmore Abbey', *TWNFC*, 39 (1969), 413–45.
Earldom of Gloucester Charters. The Charters and Scribes of the Earls and Countesses of Gloucester to AD 1217, ed. R. B. Patterson (Oxford, 1973).
English Historical Documents II, ed. and trans. D. C. Douglas and G. W. Greenway (2nd edn, London, 1981).
Facsimile of the Chirk Codex of the Welsh Laws, ed. J. Gwenogvryn Evans (Llanbedrog, 1908).
Flores Historiarum, ed. and trans. C. D. Yonge, 2 vols (London, 1853).
— ed. H. R. Luard, 3 vols (Rolls Series, London, 1890).
Froissart, *Chronicles*, ed. and trans. G. Brereton (London, 1968).
Geoffrey of Monmouth, *The History of the Kings of Britain*, ed. and trans. L. Thorpe (Harmondsworth, 1968).
Gerald of Wales, *Concerning the Instruction of Princes*, in J. Stevenson (ed. and trans.), *The Church Historians of England*, V, I (London, 1858).
— *Opera*, ed. J. S. Brewer, J. F. Dimock and G. F. Warner, 8 vols (Rolls Series, London, 1861–91).
— *Vita Ethelberti*, ed. M. R. James, *EHR*, 32 (1917), 214–44.
— *Invectiones*, ed. W. S. Davies, *Y Cymmrodor*, 30 (1920).
— *Autobiography of Giraldus Cambrensis*, ed. and trans. H. E. Butler (London, 1937).
— *Speculum Duorum / A Mirror of Two Men*, ed. M. Richter et al., trans. B. Dawson (Cardiff, 1974).
— *Journey through Wales, Description of Wales*, ed. and trans. L. Thorpe (Harmondsworth, 1978).
— *Expugnatio Hiberniae / The Conquest of Ireland*, ed. and trans. A. B. Scott and F. X. Martin (Dublin, 1978).
— *Gemma Ecclesiastica / The Jewel of the Church*, ed. and trans. J. J. Hagen (Leiden, 1979).
— *History and Topography of Ireland*, ed. and trans. J. J. O'Meara (Harmondsworth, 1982).
Gesta Stephani, ed. and trans. K. R. Potter and R. H. C. Davis (2nd edn, Oxford, 1976).
Gildas, *The Ruin of Britain and Other Works*, ed. and trans. M. Winterbottom (London, 1978).
Gruffydd, R. G., 'A poem in praise of Cuhelyn Fardd from the Black Book of Carmarthen', *Studia Celtica*, 10–11 (1975–6), 198–209.
Henry of Huntingdon, *Historia Anglorum*, ed. and trans. D. Greenway (Oxford, 1996).
Histoire de Guillaume le Maréchal, ed. P. Meyer, *Société de l'histoire de France*, 3 vols (Paris, 1891–1901).
Historia Brittonum' and the 'Vatican' Recension, The, ed. D. M. Dumville (Cambridge, 1985).
Historia Gruffud vab Kenan, ed. D. Simon Evans (Cardiff, 1977).
History of Fulk fitz Warine, ed. and trans. T. Wright (London, 1853).
John of Salisbury, *The Letters of John of Salisbury, Volume One: The Early Letters (1153–61)*, ed. and trans. W. J. Millor and H. E. Butler (Edinburgh, 1955).
— *Historia Pontificalis*, ed. M. Chibnall (Edinburgh, 1956).
— *The Letters of John of Salisbury, Volume Two: The Later Letters (1163–80)*, ed. and trans. W. J. Millor and C. N. L. Brooke (Oxford, 1979).
— *Policraticus*, ed. C. J. Nederman (Cambridge, 1990).
John of Worcester, *The Chronicle of John of Worcester*, ed. R. R. Darlington and P. McGurk, trans. J. Bray and P. McGurk, 3 vols (Oxford, 1995–).
Jones, G., *The Oxford Book of Welsh Verse in English* (Oxford, 1983).

Jones, T., 'The Black Book of Carmarthen *Stanzas of the Grave*', *PBA*, 53 (1967), 97–137.
Jordan Fantosme, *Jordan Fantosme's Chronicle*, ed. and trans. R. C. Johnston (Oxford, 1981).
Lapidge, M., 'The Welsh–Latin poetry of Sulien's family', *Studia Celtica*, 8–9 (1973–4), 68–106.
Latin Redaction 'A' of the Law of Hywel, ed. and trans. I. F. Fletcher (Aberystwyth, 1986).
Latin Texts of the Welsh Laws, ed. H. D. Emanuel (Cardiff, 1967).
Law of Hywel Dda, ed. and trans. D. Jenkins (Llandysul, 1986).
Laws of Hywel Dda, ed. and trans. M. Richards (Liverpool, 1954).
Liber Eliensis, ed. E. O. Blake (London, 1962).
Liber Landavensis, ed. and trans. W. J. Rees (Llandovery, 1840).
—— ed. J. G. Evans (Oxford, 1893).
Life of King Edward (who rests at Westminster, attributed to a monk of Saint Bertin), ed. and trans. F. Barlow (2nd edn, Oxford, 1992).
Llandaff Episcopal Acta, 1140–1287, ed. D. Crouch (Cardiff, 1988).
Lloyd, J. E., 'The text of manuscripts "B" and "C" of *Annales Cambriae* for the period 1035–93 in parallel columns', *THSC* (1899–1900), 165–79.
Llyfr Blegywryd, ed. S. J. Williams and J. E. Powell (3rd edn, Cardiff, 1961).
Llyfr Colan, ed. D. Jenkins (Cardiff, 1963).
Llyfr Iorwerth, ed. A. R. Williams (Cardiff, 1960).
Mabinogion, ed. and trans. J. Gantz (Harmondsworth, 1976).
Matthew Paris, *English History*, ed. and trans. J. A. Giles, 3 vols (London, 1852–4).
—— *Mattoei Parisiensis, Monachi Sancti Albani, Chronica Majora*, ed. H. R. Luard, 7 vols (Rolls Series, London, 1872–83).
—— *Chronicles of Matthew Paris*, ed. and trans. R. Vaughan (Gloucester, 1986).
New Translated Selections from the Welsh Medieval Law Books, ed. and trans. D. Jenkins (Aberystwyth, 1973).
Nennius: British History and the Welsh Annals, ed. and trans. J. Morris (London, 1980).
Orderic Vitalis, *Historia Ecclesiastica*, ed. and trans. M. Chibnall, 6 vols (Oxford, 1969–80).
'*Owein' or 'Chwedyl Iarlles y Ffynnawn*', ed. R. L. Thomson (Dublin, 1968).
Owen, A., *Ancient Laws and Institutions of Wales*, 2 vols (London, 1841).
Owen, M. E., 'Prolegomena to a study of the historical context of Gwynfardd Brycheiniog's poem to Dewi', *Studia Celtica*, 26 (1991), 51–79.
Patent Rolls, 1216–32 (London, 1901–3).
Pedeir Keinc y Mabinogi, ed. I. Williams (Cardiff, 1930).
Penguin Book of Welsh Verse, The, ed. and trans. T. Conran (Harmondsworth, 1967).
Pipe Roll 31 Henry I, ed. J. Hunter (London, 1833, reprinted 1929).
Pipe Rolls 2, 3 and 4 Henry II, ed. J. Hunter (London, 1844).
Pipe Rolls (published by the Pipe Roll Society, London, 1884–).
Poetry of Llywarch Hen, The, ed. and trans. P. K. Ford (London, 1974).
Rhigyfarch, *Life of St David*, ed. and trans. J. W. James (Cardiff, 1967).
Richard of Devizes, *The Chronicle of Richard of Devizes of the Time of King Richard I*, ed. and trans. J. T. Appleby (London, 1963).
Richter, M., 'A new edition of the so-called *Vita Davidis Secundi*', *BBCS*, 22 (1967), 245–9.
Roger of Howden, *Annals of Roger de Hoveden*, ed. and trans. H. T. Riley, 2 vols (London, 1853).
—— *Magistri Rogeri de Houedene*, ed. W. Stubbs, 4 vols (Rolls Series, London, 1868–71).
Roger of Wendover, *Flowers of History*, ed. and trans. J. A. Giles, 2 vols (London, 1849).
—— *Flores Historiarum*, ed. H. G. Hewlett, 3 vols (Rolls Series, London, 1886–9).
Rowland, J., *Early Welsh Saga Poetry* (Cambridge, 1990).
Salmon, M., *A Source Book of Welsh History* (Oxford, 1927).
Song of Dermot and the Earl, ed. and trans. G. H. Orpen (Oxford, 1892).
Taliesin, *The Poems of Taliesin*, ed. and trans. M. Pennar (Tern Press, 1989).

BIBLIOGRAPHY 267

Thomson, D. S., *Branwen Uerch Lyr* (Dublin, 1961).
Thomson, R. L., *Pwyll Pendeuic Dyvet* (Dublin, 1957).
Trioedd Ynys Prydein / The Welsh Triads, ed. and trans. R. Bromwich (2nd edn, Cardiff, 1978).
Vegetius, *De Re Militari*, ed. C. Lang (Leipzig, 1885), partial trans. in T. R. Phillips, *The Roots of Strategy* (London, 1943), trans. in full, N. P. Milner, *Vegetius: Epitome of Military Science* (Liverpool, 1993).
Vitae Sanctorum Britanniae et Genealogiae, ed. and trans. A. W. Wade-Evans (Cardiff, 1944).
Wade-Evans, A. W. (ed. and trans.), 'Hystoria o Uuched Beuno', *Arch. Camb.*, 85 (1930), 315–41.
Walter Map, *De Nugis Curialium / Courtiers' Trifles*, ed. and trans. M. R. James, C. N. L. Brooke and R. A. B. Mynors (Oxford, 1983).
Welsh Assize Roll, 1277–84. Assize Roll No.1147, ed. J. C. Davies (Cardiff, 1940).
Welsh Life of St David, The, ed. D. Simon Evans (Cardiff, 1988).
Welsh Poems, Sixth Century to 1600, ed. and trans. G. Williams (London, 1973).
Welsh Verse, ed. and trans. T. Conran (2nd edn, Southampton, 1986).
William of Malmesbury, *Historia Novella*, ed. and trans. K. R. Potter (Edinburgh, 1955).
— *Gesta Regum Anglorum / The History of the English Kings*, ed. and trans. R. A. B. Mynors, R. M. Thomson and M. Winterbottom (Oxford, 1998).
Williams, D. H., *Welsh History through Seals* (Cardiff, 1982).
Williams, J. E. Caerwyn, 'Meilyr Brydydd and Gruffudd ap Cynan', in *GC*, pp. 165–86.

SECONDARY WORKS

Abels, R. P., *Lordship and Military Obligation in Anglo-Saxon England* (London, 1988).
Alcock, L., *Dinas Powys* (Cardiff, 1963).
— 'Excavations at Degannwy Castle, Caernarfonshire, 1961–6', *Archaeological Journal*, 124 (1967), 190–201.
— 'Excavations at Castell Bryn Amlwg', *Montgomeryshire Collections*, 60 (1967–8), 8–27.
— *Economy, Society and Warfare among the Britons and Saxons* (Cardiff, 1987).
Alexander, L. M., 'The legal status of the native Britons in late seventh-century Wessex as reflected by the Law Code of Ine', *Haskins Society Journal*, 7 (1995), 31–8.
Arnold, C. J., J. W. Huggett, and H. Pryce, 'Excavations at Mathrafal, Powys, 1989', *The Montgomeryshire Collections*, 83 (1995), 59–74.
— and J.W. Huggett, 'Pre-Norman rectangular earthworks in mid Wales', *Medieval Archaeology*, 39 (1995), 171–4.
Austin, D., *Carew Castle Archaeological Report*, 1992 Season Interim Report (Lampeter, 1993).
Avent, R., *Castles of the Princes of Gwynedd* (Cardiff, 1983).
— 'Castles of the Welsh princes', *Château Gaillard*, 16 (1992), 11–20.
Babcock, R. S., 'Imbeciles and Normans: the *ynfydion* of Gruffudd ap Rhys reconsidered', *Haskins Society Journal*, 4 (1992), 1–10.
— 'Rhys ap Tewdwr, King of Deheubarth', *ANS*, 16 (1993), 21–35.
Bachrach, B. S., 'The feigned retreat at Hastings', *Mediaeval Studies*, 33 (1971), 264–7.
— *Merovingian Military Organisation, 481–751* (Minneapolis, 1972).
— 'The practical use of Vegetius' *De Re Militari* during the Middle Ages', *The Historian*, 27 (1985), 239–55.
— 'Some observations on the military administration of the Norman Conquest', *ANS*, 8 (1985), 1–26.
— *Armies and Politics in the Early Medieval West* (London, 1993).
Barlow, F., *William Rufus* (London, 1983).
— *Edward the Confessor* (London, 1989).

Barrow, G. W. S., 'Wales and Scotland in the Middle Ages', *WHR*, 10 (1980–1), 302–19.
Barry, T. B., R. Frame, and K. Simms (eds), *Colony and Frontier in Medieval Ireland* (London, 1995).
Bartlett, R., *Gerald of Wales, 1146–1223* (Oxford, 1982).
— 'Technique militaire et pouvoir politique, 900–1300', *Annales: Économies, Sociétés, Civilisations*, 41 (1986), 1135–59.
— *The Making of Europe* (London, 1993).
— and A. Mackay (eds), *Medieval Frontier Societies* (Oxford, 1989).
Bartlett, T., and K. Jeffery (eds), *A Military History of Ireland* (Cambridge, 1996).
Bassett, S. (ed.), *The Origins of Anglo-Saxon Kingdoms* (Leicester, 1989).
Bates, D., *Normandy before 1066* (Harlow, 1982).
— 'Normandy and England after 1066', *EHR*, 104 (1989), 851–76.
— *William the Conqueror* (London, 1989).
Beeler, J., *Warfare in England, 1066–1189* (New York, 1966).
— *Warfare in Feudal Europe, 730–1200* (New York, 1971).
Bennett, M., '*La Règle du Temple* as a military manual, or how to deliver a cavalry charge', in Harper-Bill, *Studies*, pp. 7–20.
— 'The medieval warhorse reconsidered', *Medieval Knighthood*, 5 (1994), 19–40.
Beresford, G., 'Goltho Manor, Lincolnshire: the building and surrounding defences, c.850–1150', *ANS*, 4 (1981), 13–36.
Binchy, D. A., *Celtic and Anglo-Saxon Kingship* (Oxford, 1970).
Blair, C., *European Armour* (London, 1958).
Bloch, M., *Feudal Society* (2nd edn, London, 1965).
Boussard, J., 'Les mercenaires au XIIe siècle', *Bibliothèque de l'École des Chartes*, 106 (1945–6), 189–224.
Bradbury, J., *The Medieval Archer* (Woodbridge, 1985).
— 'Battles in England and Normandy, 1066–1154', in *ANW*, pp. 182–93.
— *The Medieval Siege* (Woodbridge, 1992).
— *Stephen and Matilda: The Civil War of 1139–53* (Stroud, 1996).
Breeze, A., 'The *Anglo-Saxon Chronicle* for 1053 and the killing of Rhys ap Rhydderch', *Transactions of the Radnorshire Society*, 71 (2001), 168–9.
Bromberg, E. I., 'Wales and the mediaeval slave trade', *Speculum*, 17 (1942), 263–9.
Bromwich, R., and R. Brinley Jones, *Astudiaethau ar yr Hengerdd* (Cardiff, 1978).
— *Medieval Welsh Literature to c.1400 including Arthurian Studies* (Cardiff, 1996).
— A. O. H. Jarman and B. F. Roberts (eds), *The Arthur of the Welsh* (Cardiff, 1991).
Brooke, C. N. L., *The Church and the Welsh Border in the Central Middle Ages* (Woodbridge, 1986).
Brown, S. D. B., 'The mercenary and his master', *History*, 74 (1989), 20–38.
Burgess, E. M., 'The mail-maker's techniques and further research into the construction of mail garments', *Antiquaries Journal*, 33 (1953), 48–55, 193–202.
Campbell, E. et al., 'Excavations at Longbury Bank, Dyfed, and early medieval settlement in south Wales', *Medieval Archaeology*, 37 (1993), 15–77.
— and A. Lane, 'Llangorse: a tenth-century royal crannog in Wales', *Antiquity*, 63 (1989), 675–81.
— A. Lane and M. Redknap, 'Llangorse crannog', *Archaeology in Wales*, 30 (1990), 62–3.
Caple, C., 'The castle and lifestyle of a thirteenth-century independent Welsh lord: excavations at Dryslwyn Castle, 1980–8', *Château Gaillard*, 14 (1990), 47–59.
Carr, A. D., 'Welshmen and the Hundred Years War', *WHR*, 4 (1968–9), 21–46.
— 'The last and weakest of his line: Dafydd ap Gruffudd, the last Prince of Wales,' *WHR*, 19 (1999), 375–99.
Cessford, C., 'Cavalry in early Bernicia: a reply', *Northern History*, 29 (1993), 185–7.
Chadwick, N. K., et al. (eds), *Celt and Saxon: Studies in the Early British Border* (Cambridge, 1963).
Charles, B. G., *Old Norse Relations with Wales* (Cardiff, 1934).

Charles-Edwards, T. M., *The Welsh Laws* (Cardiff, 1989).
— *Early Irish and Welsh Kinship* (Oxford, 1993).
— M. E. Owen, and P. Russell (eds), *The Welsh King and his Court* (Cardiff, 2000).
— *Wales and the Britons, 350–1064* (Oxford, 2013).
Chibnall, M., 'Feudal society in Orderic Vitalis', *ANS*, 1 (1978), 35–48.
Church, S. D., 'The rewards of royal service in the household of King John: a dissenting opinion', *EHR*, 110 (1995), 277–302.
— 'The 1210 campaign in Ireland: evidence for a military revolution', *ANS*, 20 (1997), 45–57.
Contamine, P., *War in the Middle Ages* (London, 1984).
Conway-Davies, J., 'A grant by David ap Gruffudd', *NLWJ*, 3 (1943–4), 29–32, 158–62.
Coplestone-Crow, 'Robert de la Haye and the lordship of Gwynllwg: the Norman settlement of a Welsh *cantref*', *Gwent Local History*, 85 (1998), 3–46.
Corfis, I. A., and M. Wolfe (eds), *The Medieval City under Siege* (Woodbridge, 1995).
Coulson, C., 'Fortress policy in Capetian tradition and Angevin practice', *ANS*, 6 (1983), 13–38.
Cowley, F., *The Monastic Order in South Wales, 1066–1349* (Cardiff, 1977).
— *Gerald of Wales and Margam Abbey*, Friends of Margam Abbey Annual Lecture (1982).
Cox, D. C., 'The battle of Evesham in the Evesham chronicle', *BIHR*, 63 (1990), 337–45.
Crane, P., 'Iron Age promontory fort to medieval castle? Excavations at Great Castle Head, Dale, Pembrokeshire, 1999', *Arch. Camb.*, 148 (1999), 86–145.
Critchley, J. S., 'Military organisation in England, 1154–1254' (unpublished Ph.D. thesis, University of Nottingham, 1968).
Crouch, D., 'The slow death of kingship in Glamorgan', *Morgannwg*, 29 (1985), 20–41.
— *The Beaumont Twins* (Cambridge, 1986).
— 'The earliest original charter of a Welsh king', *BBCS*, 36 (1989), 125–31.
— *William Marshal* (London, 1990).
— 'The last adventure of Richard Siward', *Morgannwg*, 35 (1991), 7–30.
— *The Image of Aristocracy in Britain, 1000–1300* (London, 1992).
Curry, A., Review article: 'Medieval warfare, England and her continental neighbours, eleventh–fourteenth centuries', *Journal of Medieval History*, 24 (1998), 81–102.
Dalton, P., C. Insley and L. J. Wilkinson (eds), *Cathedrals, Communities and Conflict in the Anglo-Norman World* (Woodbridge, 2011).
Dark, K. R., *Civitas to Kingdom: British Political Continuity, 300–800* (Leicester, 1994).
Davidson, H. R. E., *The Sword in Anglo-Saxon England* (Oxford, 1962).
Davies, J. R., 'Church, property and conflict in Wales, AD 600–1100', *WHR*, 18 (1997), 387–406.
— *The Book of Llandaff and the Norman Church in Wales* (Woodbridge, 2003).
Davies, R. R., (ed.), *The British Isles 1100–1500: Comparisons, Contrasts and Connections* (Edinburgh, 1988).
— *Domination and Conquest* (Cambridge, 1990).
— *The Age of Conquest: Wales 1063–1415* (Oxford, 1991).
— 'The peoples of Britain and Ireland, 1100–1400', *TRHS*, 4–7 (1994–7).
— *The Revolt of Owain Glyn Dŵr* (Oxford, 1995).
Davies, Sean, 'Anglo-Welsh warfare and the works of Gerald of Wales' (unpublished MA thesis, University of Wales Swansea, 1996).
— 'The Battle of Chester and Warfare in Post-Roman Britain', *History*, 95 (2010), 143–58.
Davies, Sioned, *The Four Branches of the Mabinogi* (Llandysul, 1993).
— and Jones, N. A. (eds), *The Horse in Celtic Culture: Medieval Welsh Perspectives* (Cardiff, 1997).
Davies, T. M., 'Gruffudd ap Llywelyn, King of Wales,' *WHR*, 21 (2002), 207–48.
Davies, T. M. and S. Davies, *The Last King of Wales: Gruffudd ap Llywelyn, c.1013–1063* (Stroud, 2012).

Davies, W., 'Liber Landavensis: its construction and credibility', *EHR*, 88 (1973), 335–51.
— 'Braint Teilo', *BBCS*, 26 (1974–6), 123–37.
— 'Land and power in early medieval Wales', *P&P*, 81 (1978), 3–23.
— *The Llandaff Charters* (Aberystwyth, 1979).
— *Wales in the Early Middle Ages* (Leicester, 1982).
— *Patterns of Power in Early Wales* (Oxford, 1990).
— and P. Fouracre (eds), *Property and Power in the Early Middle Ages* (Cambridge, 1995).
Davis, P., *Castles of Dyfed* (Llandysul, 1987).
— *Castles of the Welsh Princes* (Swansea, 1988).
Davis, R. H. C., *The Normans and their Myth* (London, 1976).
— *The Medieval Warhorse* (London, 1989).
Delbrück, H., *History of the Art of War*, trans. W. J. Renfroe, 4 vols (London, 1982).
DeVries, K., 'Catapults are not atomic bombs: towards a redefinition of "effectiveness" in premodern military technology', *War in History*, 4 (1997), 454–70.
Douglas, D. C., *William the Conqueror* (London, 1964).
Duby, G., *Chivalrous Society* (London, 1977).
Duffy, S., 'King John's expedition to Ireland in 1210: the evidence reconsidered', *Irish Historical Studies*, 30 (1995), 1–24.
— 'Ostmen, Irish and Welsh in the eleventh century', *Peritia*, 9 (1995), 378–96.
Dumville, D. M., 'Nennius and the *Historia Brittonum*', *Studia Celtica*, 10–11 (1975–6), 78–95.
— 'Sub-Roman Britain: history and legend', *History*, 62 (1977), 173–92.
— Review of K. Hughes, *The Welsh Latin Chronicles*, *Studia Celtica*, 12–13 (1977–8), 461–7.
— *Celtic Britain in the Early Middle Ages* (Woodbridge, 1980).
— *Histories and Pseudo-Histories of the Insular Middle Ages* (Aldershot, 1990).
Edwards, J. G., 'Henry II and the fight at Coleshill: some further reflections', *WHR*, 3 (1965–6), 251–63.
Edwards, N. (ed.), *Landscape and Settlement in Medieval Wales* (Oxford, 1997).
— and A. Lane (eds), *Early Medieval Settlements in Wales, AD 400–1100* (Cardiff, 1988).
— and – (eds), *The Early Church in Wales and the West* (Oxford, 1992).
Ellis, T. P., *Welsh Tribal Law and Custom in the Middle Ages*, 2 vols (Oxford, 1926).
Evans, S. S., *The Lords of Battle: Image and Reality in the 'Comitatus' in Dark-Age Britain* (Woodbridge, 1997).
Fanning, S., 'Tacitus, *Beowulf* and the *comitatus*', *Haskins Society Journal*, 9 (1997), 17–38.
Finberg, H. P. R. (ed.), *The Agrarian History of England and Wales*, I (Cambridge, 1972).
Foster, I. Ll., and G. David (eds), *Prehistoric and Early Wales* (London, 1965).
Fox, C., *Offa's Dyke* (Oxford, 1955).
France, J., 'The military history of the Carolingian period', *Revue Belge d'Histoire Militaire*, 26 (1985), 81–99.
— *Victory in the East* (Cambridge, 1994).
— *Western Warfare in the Age of the Crusades, 1000–1300* (London, 1999).
— 'The Composition and Raising of the Armies of Charlemagne,' *Journal of Medieval Military History*, 1 (2002), 61–82.
Garnett, G., and Hudson, J. (eds), *Law and Government in Medieval England and Normandy: Essays in Honour of Sir James Holt* (Cambridge, 1994).
Gillingham, J., 'The context and purposes of Geoffrey of Monmouth's *History of the Kings of Britain*', *ANS*, 13 (1990), 99–118.
— 'Conquering the barbarians: war and chivalry in twelfth-century Britain', *Haskins Society Journal*, 4 (1992), 67–84.
— 'The beginnings of English imperialism', *Journal of Historical Sociology*, 5 (1992), 392–409.
— *Richard Coeur de Lion: Kingship, Chivalry and War in the Twelfth Century* (London, 1994).

—— 'The travels of Roger of Howden and his views of the Irish, Scots and Welsh', *ANS*, 20 (1997), 151–69.
—— and Holt, J. C. (eds), *War and Government in the Middle Ages: Essays in Honour of J.O. Prestwich* (Woodbridge, 1984).
Given, J., *State and Society in Medieval Europe: Gwynedd and Languedoc under Outside Rule* (New York, 1990).
Golding, B., 'Gerald of Wales and the monks', *Thirteenth-Century England*, 5 (1993), 53–64.
Grabowski, K., and D. M Dumville, *Chronicles and Annals of Medieval Ireland and Wales* (Woodbridge, 1984).
Green, J. A., *The Government of England under Henry I* (Cambridge, 1986).
—— 'Financing Stephen's war', *ANS*, 14 (1991), 91–114.
Gregson, N., 'The multiple estate model: some critical questions', *Journal of Historical Geography*, 11 (1985), 339–51.
Gresham, C. A., 'Aberconway charter', *BBCS*, 30 (1982–3), 311–47.
Griffiths, M., 'Native society on the Anglo-Norman frontier: the evidence of the Margam charters', *WHR*, 14 (1988–9), 179–216.
Griffiths, R. A. (ed.), *Boroughs of Medieval Wales* (Cardiff, 1978).
—— *Conquerors and Conquered in Medieval Wales* (Stroud, 1994).
Gruffydd, G., and H. P. Owen, 'The earliest mention of St David?', *BBCS*, 17 (1956–8), 185–93.
—— 'The earliest mention of St David? An addendum', *BBCS*, 19 (1960–2), 231–2.
Harper-Bill, C. (ed.), *Studies in History Presented to R. Allen-Brown* (Woodbridge, 1989).
Hawkes, S. C. (ed.), *Weapons and Warfare in Anglo-Saxon England* (Oxford, 1989).
Herbert, T., and G. E. Jones (eds), *Edward I and Wales* (Cardiff, 1988).
Higham, N. J., 'Cavalry in early Bernicia?', *Northern History*, 27 (1991), 236–41.
—— 'Medieval overkingship in Wales: the earliest evidence', *WHR*, 16 (1992–3), 145–59.
—— *An English Empire* (Manchester, 1995).
Higham, R., and P. Barker, *Timber Castles* (London, 1992).
Hill, D., 'The construction of Offa's Dyke', *Antiquaries Journal*, 65 (1985), 140–2.
Hill, J. W. F., *Medieval Lincoln* (Cambridge, 1948).
Hogg, A. H. A., and D. J. Cathcart King, 'Early castles in Wales and the Marches', *Arch. Camb.*, 112 (1963), 77–124.
Holden, B. W., 'The Making of the Middle March of Wales, 1066–1250', *WHR*, 20 (2000), 207–26.
Hollister, C. W., *Anglo-Saxon Military Institutions* (Oxford, 1962).
—— *The Military Organisation of Norman England* (Oxford, 1965).
Holm, P., 'The slave trade of Dublin, ninth–twelfth centuries', *Peritia*, 5 (1986), 317–45.
Holt, J. C., *The Northerners* (Oxford, 1961).
—— *Magna Carta* (Cambridge, 1965).
—— 'The end of the Anglo-Norman realm', *PBA*, 61 (1975), 223–66.
Hooper, N., 'Anglo-Saxon warfare on the eve of the Norman Conquest', *ANS*, 1 (1978), 84–93.
—— 'The Aberlemno stone and cavalry in Anglo-Saxon England', *Northern History*, 29 (1993), 188–96.
—— and M. Bennett (eds), *The Cambridge Illustrated Atlas of Warfare: The Middle Ages, 768–1487* (Cambridge, 1996).
Hopkinson, C., 'The Mortimers of Wigmore, 1086–1214', *TWNFC*, 46 (1989), 177–93.
—— 'The Mortimers of Wigmore, 1214–82', *TWNFC*, 47 (1993), 28–46.
Hudson, B. T., 'The destruction of Gruffudd ap Llywelyn', *WHR*, 15 (1990–1), 331–50.
Hughes, K., 'The Welsh-Latin chronicles: *Annales Cambriae* and related texts', *PBA*, 57 (1973), 233–58.
Hyland, A., *The Medieval Warhorse from Byzantium to the Crusades* (Stroud, 1994).
Jackson, K. H., *Language and History in Early Britain* (Edinburgh, 1953).

Jarman, A. O. H., and G. R. Hughes (eds), *A Guide to Welsh Literature* (Cardiff, 1992).
Jarrett, M. G., *Early Roman Campaigns in Wales*, Seventh Annual Caerleon Lecture (Cardiff, 1994).
Johnstone, N., '*Llys* and *Maerdref*: the royal courts of the princes of Gwynedd', *Studia Celtica*, 34 (2000), 167–210.
Jones, E.D., 'The locality of the battle of Mynydd Carn, AD 1081', *Arch. Camb.*, 77 (1922), 181–97.
—— N. G. Davies and R. F. Roberts, 'Five Strata Marcella charters', *NLWJ*, 5 (1947–8), 50–4.
Jones, G. R. J., 'The military geography of Gwynedd in the thirteenth century' (unpublished MA thesis, University of Wales Aberystwyth, 1949).
—— 'The pattern of settlement on the Welsh border', *Agricultural History Review*, 8 (1960), 66–81.
—— 'The tribal system in Wales', *WHR*, 1 (1960–3), 111–32.
—— 'The distribution of bond settlements in north-west Wales', *WHR*, 2 (1964–5), 19–36.
—— 'The defences of Gwynedd in the thirteenth century', *TCHS*, 30 (1969), 29–43.
—— 'Multiple estates perceived', *Journal of Historical Geography*, 11 (1985), 352–63.
—— 'The models for organisation in *Llyfr Iorwerth* and *Llyfr Cyfnerth*', *BBCS*, 39 (1992), 95–118.
Jones, N. A., and Pryce, H. (eds), *Yr Arglwydd Rhys* (Cardiff, 1996).
Jones, R., 'The formation of the *cantref* and the commote in medieval Gwynedd', *Studia Celtica*, 32 (1998), 169–77.
Jones, W. R., 'England against the Celtic fringe: a study in cultural stereotypes', *Journal of World History*, 13 (1971), 155–71.
—— 'The image of the barbarian in medieval Europe', *Comparative Studies in Society and History*, 13 (1971), 376–407.
Jones, W. R. D., 'The Welsh rulers of Senghennydd', *Caerphilly*, 3 (1971), 9–19.
Jones-Pierce, T., *Medieval Welsh Society*, ed. J. B. Smith (Cardiff, 1972).
Keegan, J., *The Face of Battle* (Harmondsworth, 1983).
—— *A History of Warfare* (London, 1993).
Keen, M., *Chivalry* (London, 1984).
Kenyon, J. R., and Avent, R. (eds), *Castles in Wales and the Marches* (Cardiff, 1987).
—— 'Fluctuating frontiers: Normano-Welsh castle warfare, c.1075–1240', *Château Gaillard*, 17 (1996), 119–26.
King, D. J. Cathcart, 'Henry II and the fight at Coleshill', *WHR*, 2 (1964–5), 367–75.
—— 'The defence of Wales, 1067–1283: the other side of the hill', *Arch. Camb.*, 126 (1977), 1–16.
Kirby, D. P., 'Hywel Dda: Anglophile?', *WHR*, 8 (1976–7), 1–13.
Knight, J., *South Wales from the Romans to the Normans: Christianity, Literacy and Lordship* (Stroud, 2013).
Knight, J. K., 'Welsh fortifications of the first millennium AD', *Château Gaillard*, 16 (1992), 277–84.
Koch, H. W., *Medieval Warfare* (London, 1978).
Lapidge, M., and Dumville, D. M. (eds), *Gildas: New Approaches* (Woodbridge, 1984).
Latimer, P., 'Henry II's campaign against the Welsh in 1165', *WHR*, 14 (1988–9), 523–52.
Lawson, M. K., *Cnut* (London, 1993).
Lewis, C. P., 'The Norman settlement of Herefordshire under William I', *ANS*, 7 (1984), 195–213.
—— 'English and Norman government and lordship in the Welsh borders, 1039–87' (unpublished D.Phil. thesis, Oxford University, 1985).
—— 'The French in England before the Norman Conquest', *ANS*, 17 (1994), 123–44.

Lewis, C. W., 'The treaty of Woodstock, 1247: its background and significance', *WHR*, 2 (1964–5), 37–65.
Lloyd, J. E., 'Wales and the coming of the Normans', *THSC* (1899–1900), 122–79.
— 'The Welsh chronicles', *PBA*, 14 (1928), 369–91.
— *A History of Wales from the Earliest Times to the Edwardian Conquest*, 2 vols (3rd edn, London, 1939).
Lloyd-Jones, J., 'The court poets of the Welsh princes', *PBA*, 34 (1948), 167–97.
Longley, D., 'The excavations of Castell, Porth Trefadog: a coastal promontory fort in north Wales', *Medieval Archaeology*, 35 (1991), 64–85.
Loyd, L. C., *The Origins of Some Anglo-Norman Families* (Leeds, 1951).
Loyn, H. R., *The Vikings in Wales* (London, 1976).
— 'Wales and England in the tenth century: the context of the Athelstan charters', *WHR*, 10 (1980–1), 283–301.
Ludlow, N., 'The Castle and Lordship of Narberth', *The Journal of the Pembrokeshire Historical Society*, 12 (2003), 5–43.
Mann, K. J., 'King John, Wales and the March' (unpublished Ph.D. thesis, University of Wales Swansea, 1991).
Marshall, G., 'The Norman occupation of the lands in the Golden Valley, Ewyas and Clifford and their motte and bailey castles', *TWNFC* (1936–8), 141–58.
Maund, K. L., 'Cynan ab Iago and the killing of Gruffudd ap Llywelyn', *CMCS*, 10 (1985), 57–65.
— 'Trahaearn ap Caradog: Legitimate usurper?', *WHR*, 13 (1986–7), 468–76.
— 'The Welsh alliances of Earl Ælfgar of Mercia and his family in the mid-eleventh century', *ANS*, 11 (1988), 181–90.
— *Ireland, Wales and England in the Eleventh Century* (Woodbridge, 1991).
— (ed.), *Gruffudd ap Cynan: A Collaborative Biography* (Woodbridge, 1996).
— *Handlist of the Acts of Native Welsh Rulers, 1132–1283* (Cardiff, 1996).
— 'Dynastic segmentation and Gwynedd *c*.950–*c*.1000', *Studia Celtica*, 32 (1998), 155–67.
— *The Welsh Kings: The Medieval Rulers of Wales* (Stroud, 2000).
Mayr-Harting, H., and R. I. Moore (eds), *Studies in Medieval History Presented to R. H. C. Davis* (London, 1985).
McCann, W. J., 'The Welsh view of the Normans', *THSC* (1991), 39–67.
McGeer, E., 'Byzantine siege warfare in theory and practice', in Corfis and Wolfe, *Medieval City*, 123–9.
McGlynn, S., 'The myths of medieval warfare', *History Today*, 44 (1994), 28–34.
McNeill, T., *Castles in Ireland: Feudal Power in a Gaelic World* (London, 1997).
Miller, M., 'Bede's use of Gildas', *EHR*, 90 (1975), 245–61.
Morillo, S., *Warfare Under the Anglo-Norman Kings, 1066–1135* (Woodbridge, 1994).
— 'Review of Suppe, *Military Institutions*', *Trans. Shropshire Arch. and Hist. Soc.*, 70 (1995), 218–19.
Morris, J. E., *The Welsh Wars of Edward I* (Oxford, 1901, new edn Stroud, 1996).
Musson, C. R., and C. J. Spurgeon, 'Cwrt Llechryd, Llanelwedd: an unusual moated site in central Powys', *Medieval Archaeology*, 32 (1988), 97–109.
Nash-Williams, V. E., *The Roman Frontier in Wales* (Cardiff, 1954).
Nelson, L. H., *The Normans in South Wales, 1070–1171* (Austin, Texas, 1966).
Nicolle, D., *Medieval Warfare Source Book: Vol. 1, Warfare in Western Christendom* (London, 1995).
Oakeshott, R. E., *The Sword in the Age of Chivalry* (London, 1964).
Ó'Cróinín, D., *Early Medieval Ireland, 400–1200* (Harlow, 1995).
Ó'Cuír, B., 'A poem composed for Cathal Croibdhearg Ó Conchubhair', *Eriu*, 34 (1983), 157–74.
Oman, C., *A History of the Art of War in the Middle Ages, 378–1485* (Oxford, 1991).

Owen, D. H. (ed.), *Settlement and Society in Wales* (Cardiff, 1989).
Parker, G., *The Cambridge Illustrated History of Warfare* (Cambridge, 1995).
Pierce, G. O., 'The evidence of place-names', in *Glamorgan County History*, III, (Cardiff, 1971), pp. 456–92.
Pierce, I., 'Arms, armour and warfare in the eleventh century', *ANS*, 10 (1987), 237–58.
—— 'The knight, his arms and armour in the eleventh century', *Medieval Knighthood*, I (1986), 157–64.
Power, R., 'Magnus Barelegs' expeditions to the west', *Scottish Historical Review*, 65 (1986), 107–32.
Powicke, M. R., *Military Obligations in Medieval England* (Oxford, 1962).
Preston-Jones, A., and P. Rose, 'Medieval Cornwall', *Cornish Archaeology*, 25 (1986), 135–85.
Prestwich, M., *Edward I* (London, 1988).
Pryce, H., 'In search of a medieval society: Deheubarth in the writings of Gerald of Wales', *WHR*, 13 (1986–7), 265–81.
—— 'Ecclesiastical wealth in early medieval Wales', in Edwards and Lane, *Early Church*, pp. 22–32.
—— 'The church of Trefeglwys and the end of the 'Celtic' charter tradition in twelfth-century Wales', *CMCS*, 25 (1993), 15–54.
—— 'Owain Gwynedd and Louis VII: the Franco-Welsh diplomacy of the first Prince of Wales', *WHR*, 19 (1998), 1–28.
Rees, S. E., and C. Caple, *Dinefwr Castle and Dryslwyn Castle* (Cardiff, 1996).
Rees, W., *A Historical Atlas of Wales from Early to Modern Times* (Cardiff, 1951).
Remfry, P. M., 'The native Welsh dynasties of Rhwng Gwy a Hafren, 1066–1282' (unpublished M.Phil. thesis, University of Wales, Aberystwyth, 1989).
—— 'Cadwallon ap Madog, Rex de Delvain, 1140–79, and the re-establishment of local autonomy in Cynllibiwg', *Trans. Radnorshire Soc.*, 65 (1995), 11–32.
Roderick, A. J., 'Feudal relations between the English Crown and the Welsh princes', *History*, 37 (1952), 201–12.
Rogers, R., 'Latin siege warfare in the twelfth century' (unpublished D.Phil. thesis, Oxford University, 1984).
Rowland, J., 'Old Welsh *franc*: an Old English borrowing?', *CMCS*, 26 (1993), 21–5.
—— 'Warfare and horses in the *Gododdin* and the problem of Catraeth', *CMCS*, 30 (1995), 13–40.
Rowlands, I. W., 'The making of the March: aspects of the Norman settlement in Dyfed', *ANS*, 3 (1980), 142–58.
—— 'William de Braose and the lordship of Brecon', *BBCS*, 30 (1982–3), 123–33.
—— 'The 1201 peace between King John and Llywelyn ap Iorwerth', *Studia Celtica*, 34 (2000), 149–66.
Ryan, J., 'A study of horses in early and medieval Welsh literature, *c*.600–1300 AD' (unpublished M.Phil. thesis, University of Wales, Cardiff, 1993).
Savory, H. N., 'Excavations at Dinas Emrys, Beddgelert, 1954–6', *Arch. Camb.*, 109 (1960), 13–78.
Sawyer, P. H. and P. Hayes (eds), *The Oxford Illustrated History of the Vikings* (Oxford, 1997).
Schenfeld, E. J., 'Anglo-Saxon *burhs* and continental *burgen*: early medieval fortifications in continental perspective', *Haskins Society Journal*, 6 (1994), 49–66.
Schubert, H. R., *History of the British Iron and Steel Industry* (London, 1957).
Scragg, D. C. (ed.), *The Battle of Maldon, AD 991* (Oxford, 1991).
Seebohm, F., *The Tribal System in Wales* (2nd edn, London, 1904).
Simms, K., *From Kings to Warlords* (Woodbridge, 1987).
Sims-Williams, P., 'Historical need and literary narrative: a caveat from ninth-century Wales', *WHR*, 17 (1994–5), 1–40.
Smail, R. C., *Crusading Warfare* (Cambridge, 1956).

Smith, J. B., 'The lordship of Glamorgan', *Morgannwg*, 9 (1965), 9–38.
— 'The middle March in the thirteenth century', *BBCS*, 24 (1970), 77–93.
— 'The kingdom of Morgannwg and the Norman conquest of Glamorgan', in *Glamorgan County History*, III (Cardiff, 1971), pp. 1–44.
— 'Owain Gwynedd', *TCHS*, 32 (1971), 8–17.
— 'Llywelyn ap Gruffudd and the March of Wales', *Brycheiniog*, 20 (1982–3), 9–22.
— 'Llywelyn ap Gruffudd, Prince of Wales and Lord of Snowdon', *TCHS*, 45 (1984), 7–36.
— 'Magna Carta and the charters of the Welsh princes', *EHR*, 99 (1984), 344–62.
— 'Land endowments of the period of Llywelyn ap Gruffudd', *BBCS*, 34 (1987), 150–64.
— *Llywelyn ap Gruffudd, Prince of Wales* (Cardiff, 1998).
— and T. B. Pugh, 'The lordship of Gower', in *Glamorgan County History*, III (Cardiff, 1971), pp. 205–83.
Smith, L. B., 'The *gravamina* of the community of Gwynedd against Llywelyn ap Gruffudd', *BBCS*, 31 (1984), 158–76.
Squatriti, P., 'Digging ditches in early medieval Europe,' *P&P*, 176 (2002), 11–65.
Stephenson, D., *The Governance of Gwynedd* (Cardiff, 1984).
— 'The politics of Powys Wenwynwyn in the thirteenth century', *CMCS*, 7 (1984), 39–61.
Strange, W. A., 'The Rise and Fall of a Saint's Community: Llandeilo Fawr, 600–1200', *The Journal of Welsh Religious History*, 2 (2002), 1–18.
Strickland, M. (ed.), *Anglo-Norman Warfare* (Woodbridge, 1992).
— 'Military technology and conquest: the anomaly of Anglo-Saxon England', *ANS*, 19 (1996), 353–82.
— *War and Chivalry: The Conduct and Perception of War in England and Normandy, 1066–1217* (Cambridge, 1996).
Suppe, F. C., 'The cultural significance of decapitation in high medieval Wales and the Marches', *BBCS*, 36 (1989), 147–60.
— *Military Institutions on the Welsh Marches: Shropshire, AD 1066–1300* (Woodbridge, 1994).
— 'Who was Rhys Sais? Some comments on Anglo-Welsh relations before 1066', *Haskins Society Journal*, 7 (1995), 63–73.
— 'Roger of Powys, Henry II's Anglo-Welsh middleman, and his lineage', *WHR*, 21 (2002), 1–23.
Thacker, A. and R. Sharpe (eds), *Local Saints and Local Churches in the Early Medieval West* (Oxford, 2002).
Thordemann, B., *Armour from the Battle of Wisby, 1361*, 2 vols (Stockholm, 1939).
Thornton, D. E., 'Maredudd ab Owain (d.999): the most famous king of the Welsh', *WHR*, 18 (1997), 567–91.
— 'Who was Rhain the Irishman?', *Studia Celtica*, 34 (2000), 131–48.
Toy, S., *A History of Fortification, 3000 BC–1700 AD* (2nd edn, London, 1966).
Treharne, R. F., 'The Franco-Welsh treaty of alliance in 1212', *BBCS*, 18 (1958–60), 60–75.
Turvey, R., 'Llandovery Castle and the Pipe Rolls (1159–62)', *The Carmarthenshire Antiquary*, 26 (1990), 5–12.
— 'The death and burial of an excommunicate prince: the Lord Rhys and the cathedral church of St Davids', *Journal Pembs. Hist. Soc.*, 7 (1996–7), 26–49.
— 'The defences of twelfth-century Deheubarth and the castle strategy of the Lord Rhys', *Arch. Camb.*, 144 (1995), 103–32.
— *Llywelyn the Great* (Llandysul, 2007).
— *Owain Gwynedd: Prince of the Welsh* (Talybont, 2013).
Van Houts, A. E., 'The Norman Conquest through European eyes', *EHR*, 110 (1995), 832–53.
Verbruggen, J. F., *The Art of Warfare in Western Europe in the Middle Ages* (New York, 1977).

Wainwright, F. T., 'Cledemutha', *EHR*, 65 (1950), 203–12.
Walker, D., 'A note on Gruffudd ap Llywelyn', *WHR*, 1 (1960–3), 83–94.
—— 'William fitz Osbern and the Norman settlement in Herefordshire', *TWNFC*, 39 (1967–9), 402–12.
Walker, I. W., *Harold, the Last Anglo-Saxon King* (Stroud, 1997).
Walker, R. F., 'The Anglo-Welsh wars, 1217–67; with special reference to English military developments' (unpublished D.Phil. thesis, Oxford University, 1954).
—— 'Hubert de Burgh and Wales, 1218–32', *EHR*, 87 (1972), 465–94.
—— 'The supporters of Richard Marshal, earl of Pembroke, in the rebellion of 1233–4', *WHR*, 17 (1994), 41–65.
—— 'William de Valence and the army of west Wales, 1282–3', *WHR*, 18 (1997), 407–29.
Warren, W. L., *Henry II* (London, 1973).
White, L., *Medieval Technology and Social Change* (Oxford, 1962).
White, S. D., 'Kinship and lordship in early medieval England: the story of Sigeberht, Cynewulf and Cyneheard', *Viator*, 20 (1989), 1–18.
Whitelock, D., et al. (eds), *The Norman Conquest* (London, 1966).
Wilkinson, P. F., 'Excavations at Hen Gastell, Briton Ferry, West Glamorgan, 1991–2', *Medieval Archaeology*, 39 (1995), 1–50.
Williams, A. G., 'The Norman lordship of Glamorgan: an examination of its establishment and development' (unpublished M.Phil. thesis, University of Wales, Cardiff, 1991).
—— 'Norman lordship in south-east Wales during the reign of William I', *WHR*, 16 (1992–3), 445–66.
Williams, A. R., 'Methods of manufacture of swords in medieval Europe', *Gladius*, 13 (1977), 75–101.
—— 'The manufacture of mail in medieval Europe: a technical note', *Gladius*, 15 (1980), 105–34.
—— 'The knight and the blast furnace', *Metals and Materials*, 2 (1986), 485–9.
Williams, J. E. Caerwyn, *The Poets of the Welsh Princes* (Cardiff, 1994).
Williams-Jones, K., 'Llywelyn's charter to Cymer Abbey in 1209', *Journal Merioneth History Society*, 3 (1957), 45–78.
Willoughby, R., 'The shock of the new', *History Today*, 49 (1999), 36–42.
Woolf, R., 'The ideal of men dying with their lords in the *Germania* and the *Battle of Maldon*', *Anglo-Saxon England*, 5 (1976), 69–81.
Wyatt, D., 'Gruffudd ap Cynan and the Hiberno-Norse world,' *WHR*, 19 (1999), 595–617.
Wyn Evans, J. and J. M. Wooding (eds), *St David of Wales: Cult, Church and Nation* (Woodbridge, 2007).

INDEX

Ælfgar (d. 1062), earl of Mercia, 50, 56–7, 82, 95, 119
Ælfnoth, sheriff of Hereford, 57
Æthelfrith, 64 n. 74, 79, 113–14, 248
Abbots, 79–80, 244, 255
Aberafan, castle of, 243 n. 117
Aberconwy, abbey of, 237
Aberdaron, church of, 256
Aberdyfi, 123, 188, 207
Abergavenny, 131, 240; castle of, 153, 213, 214, 236
Abergwili, battle of (1022), 95
Aber-llech, battle of (1096), 101
Aberlleiniog, 60, 77, 141, 146, 155, 177, 202, 211, 243 n. 115
Aberystwyth; battle of (1116), 106, 127, 135, 146, 152–3, 184–5, 211, 215; castle of, 127, 200 n. 41, 204, 209, 231
Afan, 196
Agincourt, battle of (1415), 189 n. 276, 219 n. 6
Aldred, bishop of Hereford, 57
Ambrosius Aurelianus, 64, 113, 196
Ambush, 41, 55, 86, 89–111, 120, 135, 151, 175, 237, 260
Anarawd (d. 916) ap Rhodri Mawr, 50 n. 7, 55
Anglesey, 42, 49, 58, 59, 70, 73–4, 76, 77, 101–2, 105, 107, 116, 127, 131, 150 n. 47, 185, 194, 202, 206, 222 n. 16, 229, 239, 250; Owain Môn, 30; *see also* Anglesey Sound, battle of; Tal-y-Moelfre, battle of
Anglesey Sound, battle of (1098), 102, 152 n. 60, 224
Anglo-Norman warfare, 15, 52, 64, 85–9, 97, 111
Anglo-Saxon Chronicle, The, 7, 24, 92, 99–100, 104, 113, 116
Anglo-Saxon warfare, 56, 67, 69, 147, 157–8, 169, 183 n. 241, 208, 218; army sizes, 23, 54; household forces, 15, 26, 39–40; *see also fyrd*, housecarls
Annales Cambriae, 11–12, 18, 115–16, 195
Antonine Wall, 193
antrustiones, 14
Archenfield, 56, 249
Archery, *see* bows
Ardudwy, 60, 77, 98
Arfderydd, battle of, 20, 32, 65, 169, 188
Arfon (Gwynedd), 76, 82, 84, 122 n. 165, 184 n. 247, 206
Armes Prydein, 91, 92, 179, 181, 185
armour, 45, 129, 145–7, 150, 175, 177, 246
arms production, 144–5; *see also* iron production
Arnulf of Montgomery, 127, 199
arrows, *see* bows
Arthur, 17, 20, 21, 34, 50, 55 n. 29, 69, 84 n. 178, 91 n. 22, 148, 155, 156, 157, 160 n. 106, 165, 167, 186, 255 n. 176
Arwystli, 59, 60, 73, 98, 123
Athelstan, king of England (d. 939), 117, 136
axes, 74, 154–5, 168, 177, 193

Badon, battle of, 55 n. 29, 113, 164
Bamburgh, 207 n. 70
Bangor Iscoed, 79
banners, *see* standards
Banolau, battle of (873), 116
bardd teulu, 35, 43
bards, 46–7; *see also bardd teulu*
Basingwerk, 25, 130, 131 n. 193
Bath, 113, 191
battle, 86, 111–40, 191, 260–1; battles

278 INDEX

c.450–1063, 113–19; battles against the Anglo-Normans 1063–1277, 125–35; inter-Welsh battles 1063–1277, 119–25; Welsh involvement in Anglo-Norman battles, 136–40
Bede, 7, 54, 79, 80, 82, 93, 114, 162, 166, 248, 253
beheading, *see* decapitation
Belyn of Llŷn, 23 n. 39, 65
Bernard de Neufmarché, 126
Bernicia, 113
Berwyn mountains, 106
Biedcanform, battle of (571), 191
Blaen-porth, castle of, 215
Bleddyn (d. 1075) ap Cynfyn, 97, 119, 121
Bleddyn Fardd, 174
Bondmen, 16, 26, 71, 74–5, 91, 155, 178, 186, 187, 259
Bond townships, 16, 49, 84, 193
bonheddig, 28, 49, 72
Booty, 35–6, 45, 56
Bourgthéroulde, battle of (1124), 15, 43 n. 150
Bouvines, battle of (1214), 238
bows, 105–6, 139, 146, 148, 151–3, 221; mounted archers, 161, 162, 165–6, 183–4, 240, 261; *see also* crossbows
Branwen, 11, 20, 22, 27, 54, 147, 160, 167, 226
Brecon, 83, 100, 116, 125, 128, 159, 189 n. 278, 192, 196, 201, 212, 216, 236–7, 253 n. 166; battle of (1093), 122, 126–7
Breintiau Gwŷr Powys, 41
Bridgnorth, castle of, 229
Bristol, 137, 139, 156
Brittany, 139, 162, 182
Brochfael, 79
Brocmail of Powys, 24, 248 n. 142
Bron-yr-erw, battle of (1075), 38, 58, 70, 76, 118, 120, 122 n. 165, 149 n. 36, 173, 229
Brut y Tywysogyon (Chronicle of the Princes), 11, 12, 21–2, 39, 41, 45, 51, 59, 60, 61, 70, 73, 75, 99, 100–1, 105, 110, 120, 124, 128–9, 131, 132, 134, 152, 171, 173, 175, 183, 184–5, 188–9, 195, 200, 204, 205, 206, 209, 211, 213, 227
Brycheiniog, *see* Brecon
Bryn Derwin, battle of (1255), 122
Bryn Onnen, battle of (870), 116
Builth, castle of, 147 n. 22, 214, 216, 246
Buttington, 118 n. 144, 198
byddin, 52, 65, 72, 186

Cadafael (d. 655) ap Cynfedw of Gwynedd, 55, 66, 115
Cadell (d. 1175) ap Gruffudd, 216, 235, 245
Cadfan (d. 616) ap Iago, king of Gwynedd, 28, 66
Cadwaladr (d. 681) ap Cadwallon, 55
Cadwaladr (d. 1172) ap Gruffudd, 48, 51, 61, 72, 80, 83, 117 n. 138, 129, 136–8, 173, 202, 230, 244, 258
Cadwallon ab Ieuaf, 227 n. 40
Cadwallon ab Ifor, 140
Cadwallon (d. 634) ap Cadfan, 39 n. 132, 50, 54–5, 65, 82, 93, 114, 192, 253
Cadwallon (d. 1132) ap Gruffudd, 231 n. 55
Cadwallon (d. 1179) ap Madog, 235
Cadwgan (d. 1111) ap Bleddyn, 37, 38, 70, 97, 98, 100–2, 103, 127, 142, 171, 204, 228 n. 43, 252
Caer Drewyn, 187 n. 264
Caereinion, castle of, 244
Caerleon, 103, 191, 215, 245; *see also* Iorwerth ab Owain
Caernarfon, castle of, 209
Camddwr, battle of (1075), 120
camps, 186–7
cantref, 16, 23 n. 39, 52, 58, 60, 67 n. 91, 98, 204, 255 n. 175
Cantref Mawr, 106, 223 n. 19, 245
Caradog (d. 1081) ap Gruffudd, 27–8, 31, 38, 58–9, 75 n. 136, 120–1, 126, 154 n. 67
Caradog ap Rhiwallon, 28
Cardiff, 125; castle of, 213

Cardigan, 135; battle of (1136), 61, 83, 128–9, 136, 147, 173, 184, 201, 220–1, 239; battle of (1145), 129; castle of, 134, 200 n. 41, 201, 205, 206 n. 66, 212, 216, 217, 231, 244–5
Carew, castle of, 197–8
Carmarthen, 83, 118 n. 139, 132, 135, 191, 235, 241; battle of (1223), 134, 135; castle of, 134, 207 n. 68, 214, 215, 217, 245
Carolingians, 68
castell, 183 n. 243, 194–5, 196 n. 26, 199–200 and n. 38; *see also* fortifications
Castell y Bere, 154
castles, *see* fortifications
cattle; as booty, 45, 91, 93, 253, 256, 257
cavalry, *see* horses
Cedyll, battle of (844), 116
Cefn-llys, castle of, 214, 247
Celli Carnant, battle of (1096), 100–1
Cenarth Bychan, 21
Ceolwulf of Mercia (d. 823), 116, 192
Ceredigion, 45, 48, 50, 83, 99, 103, 123, 127, 128, 169, 173, 188, 200, 202, 203, 205, 211, 215, 216, 243, 251, 252, 258
Ceri, 111
Charles the Bald, king of the west Franks (d. 877), 116
Chester, 21, 31, 59, 65 n. 80, 77, 100, 107, 110, 124, 130, 234 n. 72; battle of (*c*.616), 24, 50, 79, 99, 113–14, 121, 189, 248; *see also* Hugh of Chester; Ranulf of Chester
Church; attacks from Anglo-Normans, 241, 249–50; attacks from Anglo-Saxons, 248–50; attacks from Vikings, 248–50, 255; attacks from Welsh lords, 250–5; attitude to slavery, 224; *clas* churches, 79–81, 244; conduct towards, 247–58, 262–3; immunities, 79–81; land grants to, 79, 248; military service from the Church, 79–81, 260; oaths, 231; relics, 231, 257; reparations to, 225, 248, 251–2; sanctuary, 91, 247, 249, 251, 253, 255–6
Cilgerran, castle of, 205, 214, 217
Cirencester, 113, 191
Clausewitz, 89
Cledemutha, *see* Rhuddlan
clothing, 36, 43, 45
Clovis, Merovingian king (d. 511), 18, 64, 161
Clynnog Fawr, 58, 250 n. 155, 256
Cnut, king of England and Denmark (d. 1035), 117, 136
Coed Llathen, 135
Coedysbys, battle of (1094), 127, 202
Coleshill, battle of (1150), 125, 129; battle of (1157), 73, 106, 129–31, 135, 147, 184, 185, 189, 239
Colwyn, 132
commote, 16, 84, 193, 194
commutation, 44
Conwy, 107; battle of (880), 116; battle of (1194), 122; river, 197, 237
Cornwall, 17, 34, 67, 115, 218
Corwen, 187 n. 264
Crécy, battle of (1346), 218–19
Cricieth, 154
Cronica de Wallia, 11–12
crossbows, 75, 153, 154, 213, 237
Culhwch and Olwen, 11, 20, 21, 144, 148, 155, 156, 157, 167, 168, 175, 194, 226
Cwrt Llechryd, 198
Cyfeiliog, 123; *see also* Owain Cyfeiliog
cylch, 16, 17, 33, 36, 45
Cymerau, battle of (1257), 135
Cynan (d. 1174) ab Owain (Gwynedd), 72, 73, 80, 122, 129, 130, 185, 244
Cynan Garwyn of Powys, 192, 208
Cynddelw ap Conus, 59, 77
Cynddelw Brydydd Mawr, 39, 44, 47, 61 n. 56, 94, 129 n. 186, 172, 173–4, 229
Cynddylan, 20, 29, 43, 66, 82, 94, 115 n. 129, 167, 168, 181, 253 n. 166
Cynfael, castle of, 72, 80, 213, 244
Cynllibiwg, 235

Cynwrig (d. 1075) ap Rhiwallon, 58, 76, 120
Cynwrig (d. 1237) ap Rhys ap Gruffudd, 35

Dafydd (d. 1203) ab Owain (Gwynedd), 73, 122, 130, 185, 229, 230 n. 54
Dafydd (d. 1283) ap Gruffudd, 35, 122
Dafydd (d. 1246) ap Llywelyn, 109, 122, 123, 232, 237, 238
Dafydd Benfras, 32, 183 n. 243, 214
Dal Riata, 64
Daniel ap Sulien, 255
daryanogyon, 28, 170
De Bellis Lewes et Evesham, 139–140
decapitation, 225, 226, 237, 239, 241, 245, 254
Degannwy, 107, 192, 195, 197, 212
Deheubarth, 51, 59, 61, 67, 106, 118, 125, 132, 135, 142, 189, 198, 203, 214, 230–1, 243
Deira, 113–14
Description of Wales, *Descriptio Cambriae*, *see* Gerald of Wales
Dinas Emrys, 193, 196–7
Dinas Newydd, battle of, 116–17
Dinas Powys, 144, 195–196
Dindaethwy, 194
Dinefwr, 135, 206 n. 66, 212, 213, 246
Dineirth, castle of, 204, 247
Dingestow, battle of (1182), 131–2, 237, 239
Dinmeir, battle of (906), 116
Dinorben, 193
Dinweiler, castle of, 245
discipline, 36
distain, 33 n. 92, 35
Dolforwyn, castle of, 207
Dream of Maxen, The, 11, 43, 186, 209
Dream of Rhonabwy, The, 11, 34, 70, 186
Dryslwyn, castle of, 207
dux, 18, 64, 167 n. 151
Dyfed, 45, 67, 99, 103, 118, 122, 126–7, 197, 200, 211, 215
Dyffryn Ceiriog, 107
Dyffryn Clwyd, 60, 77, 124, 231 n. 55
dykes, 93, 188
Dyrham, battle of (577), 113, 191

ebediw, 33
Edmund I, king of England (d. 946), 136
Edmund Ironside, king of England (d. 1016), 117, 136
Ednyfed Fychan (d. 1246), 35, 49
Edward I, king of England (d. 1307), 53 n. 21, 62, 78, 109, 207, 238
Edward the Confessor, king of England (d. 1066), 56–7, 126 n. 176
Edward the Elder, king of England (d. 924), 116, 197, 249
Edwin, brother of Earl Leofric, 55, 118
Edwin of Mercia, 136
Edwin of Northumbria (d. 633), 50, 65, 93, 114, 225 n. 32
Efelffre, 205
Eifionydd, 60, 77, 122 n. 165
eilltion, 67, 68 n. 93, 73
Einion (d. 1163) ab Anarawd, 35, 235 n. 76
Einion (d. 984) ab Owain, 76
Einion (d. 1124) ap Cadwgan, 124
Elise ap Madog, 255
Eryri, *see* Snowdon
Evesham, battle of (1265), 139–40
exercitus, 51 n. 13, 52, 64 n. 74

Falkes de Breauté, 125, 133
familia, 18, 49, 79
feigned flight, 138, 166, 174
ffranc, 29–30, 75
field fortifications, 123, 130, 180, 185, 186–9, 261; *see also* shield walls
flags, *see* standards
Flemings, 128–9, 215, 221
footsoldiers, *see* infantry
fords, 92, 138, 180–1, 188
Forest of Dean, 119, 144 n. 6
fortifications, 69, 79, 84, 92, 116, 169, 190–217, 227, 261–2; fortification strategy *c*.450–1066, 191–8; fortification strategy 1066–1283, 198–207; *see also* camps; *castell*; field fortifications; hill camps; sieges
foster fathers, 30
Froissart, 218
Fulford Gate, battle of (1066), 136

furnaces, *see* iron production
fyrd, 15, 64, 69

garrisons, 110, 207, 210, 217, 243–7
Gascony, 162, 172
Gaul, 18, 64, 65, 66, 161
Gelligaer, 168
Geoffrey of Monmouth, 7
Gerald of Wales, Giraldus Cambrensis, 1, 3–6, 24, 40 n. 135, 43, 53, 62 n. 59, 63, 70, 80, 91 n. 24, 101 n. 75, 106, 112, 128, 131, 140, 146, 147–8, 150–1, 153, 158, 171, 175, 183–4, 191, 199, 202, 211, 213, 224, 225, 232–3, 257–8
Gerald of Windsor, 101 n. 75, 199, 201, 211
Gereint, 11
Gesta Stephani, 8, 61, 96–7, 128, 138, 156, 220–1, 239
Gilbert de Clare, 206
Gilbert fitz Richard, 103, 200 n. 41
Gildas, 7, 8–9, 17–18, 92, 112, 113, 179, 191, 193, 196, 250
Glamorgan, 61, 67, 84, 136, 140, 141, 144, 170, 184, 186–7, 195–6, 240
Glasbury, battle of (1056), 57 n. 36, 119, 126 n. 176
Gloucester, 103, 113, 191
Gododdin, 10, 19, 23–4, 27, 30, 33, 39, 40, 47, 65, 145, 148–9, 150, 155, 156, 160–6, 172, 178–9, 187–8, 191
Godred Crovan, 60
Gormr, 116
Goronwy ab Ednyfed, 33 n. 92
Goronwy ab Owain, 104
Goronwy (d. 1077) ap Cadwgan, 120
gosgordd, 19–20, 22, 23, 25, 27, 40, 65, 188
Gower, 53, 215, 243; battle in (1136), 128, 202, 220
Gregory of Tours, 18
Gruffudd ab yr Ynad Coch, 51
Gruffudd (d. 1135) ap Cynan, 12, 21, 22, 31, 38, 42, 51, 58–60, 70, 98–102, 104–6, 120–1, 127, 141–2, 149 n. 36, 157, 171, 172–3, 177, 210 n. 85, 227, 231 n. 55, 252 n. 161; Gruffudd's *teulu*, 27, 42; links to Ireland, 21, 31, 38, 58, 60, 76–7, 98, 101–2, 118, 120–1, 155, 224, 227, 229, 256; relations to *uchelwyr*, 76–7; use of mercenaries, 42, 75; *see also History of Gruffudd ap Cynan, The*
Gruffudd (d. 1286) ap Gwenwynwyn, 51
Gruffudd (d. 1063) ap Llywelyn, king of Wales, 25, 36 n. 110, 42, 50, 55–8, 75, 76, 78, 82–3, 95–6, 118–19, 156 n. 80, 169–70, 183, 192–3, 197, 208, 224, 227–8, 232, 250 n. 155, 251–2, 254
Gruffudd (d. 1244) ap Llywelyn, 62, 122, 123–4, 133–4, 135
Gruffudd (d. 1091) ap Maredudd, 122, 228
Gruffudd (d. 1055) ap Rhydderch, 56, 75, 119, 136, 228 n. 44, 252
Gruffudd (d. 1137) ap Rhys, 22, 33 n. 92, 47–8, 61, 103, 106, 127, 128, 152, 184–5, 201, 202, 211, 213, 215, 216, 223, 231, 243, 247, 253, 256
Gruffudd (d. 1201) ap Rhys ap Gruffudd, 35, 214 n. 100, 231
guerrilla warfare, 85–6, 140, 207
Gwaed Erw, battle of (1075), 21, 58 n. 42, 76, 120
Gwalchmai ap Meilyr, 44, 45 n. 164, 47 n. 176, 73 n. 122
Gwallawg of Elmet, 30
gwely, 49
Gwenllian, 33 n. 92, 128, 133, 135
Gwent, 58, 76, 100, 116, 131, 150 n. 47, 153, 167, 183, 215, 236–7, 239, 240, 246
Gwenwynwyn (d. 1216) ab Owain Cyfeiliog, 125, 132–3, 142, 203, 212, 231, 246, 255
Gwen Ystrad, battle of, 160
gweri, 72–3, 74
Gweunytwl, battle of (1077), 120
Gwrgenau ap Seisyll, 98
Gwriad (d. 878) ap Rhodri Mawr, 116

282 INDEX

Gwyn ap Nudd, 163, 165, 194, 226
Gwynedd, 38, 42, 43, 46, 49, 50, 51,
  53, 55, 58, 59, 60, 61, 62, 65, 66,
  67, 71, 73, 74, 76–8, 82, 83, 98,
  102, 111, 114–19, 120–5, 128–31,
  132, 133–5, 136, 141, 150–1, 163,
  174, 183, 187, 196, 202, 205–7,
  211, 215, 222, 226–7, 229, 230,
  232, 238, 243, 255, 257, 260
Gwynllwg, 100

Harlech, 59; castle of, 209
Harold Godwinesson, king of England
  (d. 1066), 22, 36 n. 110, 42, 56–7,
  82, 95–6, 119, 170, 193, 208 n. 73,
  249 n. 143
Harold Hardrada, king of Norway (d.
  1066), 57
Hastings, battle of (1066), 22, 55 n. 28,
  157–8, 183, 238
Hatfield Chase, battle of (633), 55, 93,
  114
Haverford, castle of, 215–16
Hawarden, 66, 130, 189
Heavenfield, battle of (634), 55, 114–15,
  141 n. 228
helmets, 147–8
Hen Gastell, Briton Ferry, 196
Henry I, king of England (d. 1135), 48,
  97, 102–6, 123, 124, 127–8, 129,
  146, 152, 171, 187 n. 264, 201,
  204, 221, 229, 240–1, 252, 256
Henry II, king of England (d. 1189), 7,
  51, 61, 64, 73, 83, 96, 106–7,
  129–31, 138–9, 171–2, 185, 189,
  203, 205, 215, 216, 235, 236, 239,
  257
Henry III, king of England (d. 1272),
  62, 75, 108–9, 135, 139, 197, 212,
  221 n. 15, 232, 237, 239, 254
Henry Don of Kidwelly, 79 n. 151
Henry (d. 1157) fitz Henry (II), 185
Henry of Huntingdon, 8, 96, 137–8,
  145
Hereford, 99, 103, 122, 131, 236; battle
  of (1055), 50–1, 56, 82–3, 95, 119,
  126 n. 176, 170, 183, 208, 254

Hexham, 114
hill forts, 67, 187, 191–2, 193
Historia Brittonum, 9, 66, 92, 164
History of Gruffudd ap Cynan, The, 12–13,
  18, 21, 22, 25, 58, 60, 77, 98,
  99–100, 102, 104, 141–2, 146,
  151, 171, 173, 184, 185, 194–5,
  202, 211, 222, 227, 229
horns, 84, 182
horses, 143; as booty, 44–5, 168–9;
  breeding, 98, 159–60, 171–2;
  mounted combat, 157–76, 261;
  pack-horses, 53, 74, 169, 171;
  saddles, 144, 162, 166, 175;
  see also feigned flights; *milites*;
  stirrups
hostages, 29, 45, 158, 229–32, 235–6,
  240–2
hostings, *see* muster
housecarls, 15, 22
Hugh of Chester, 31, 59, 77, 101–2,
  127, 224
Hugh of Shrewsbury, 101–2, 127, 152
  n. 60, 224
Humfry's Castle, 243 n. 117
hunting, 152, 156, 165–6, 168, 235
Hyfaidd (d. 893) ap Bledri, 250 n. 155
Hywel (d. 1044) ab Edwin, 117–18, 228
  n. 44, 251
Hywel (d. 985) ab Ieuaf, 117, 226, 250
  n. 155
Hywel (d. 1185) ab Ieuaf, 60, 73, 123
Hywel (d. 1118) ab Ithel, 70, 124, 234
  n. 72
Hywel (d. 1078) ab Owain, 38, 120
Hywel (d. 1170) ab Owain Gwynedd,
  24, 30 n. 84, 46–7, 72, 73–4, 80,
  129, 174, 216, 229, 243–4, 245
Hywel (d. 1106) ap Goronwy, 201
Hywel ap Iorwerth of Caerleon, 215
Hywel ap Maredudd, 128
Hywel ap Meurig, 247
Hywel Dda (d. 950) ap Cadell, 117, 231
  n. 55; connection to Welsh law
  texts, 13, 68
Hywel Sais (d. 1204) ap Rhys, 61 n. 58,
  138–9, 203, 241 n. 104

INDEX

Iago ab Idwal, 226, 250 n. 155
Iâl, 125
Idwal (d. 1069) ap Gruffudd, 119
Idwal Foel, 231 n. 55
Iestyn ap Gwrgant, 27
Ieuaf ab Idwal, 226
Ifor Bach, 213
Ine of Wessex, laws of, 23
infantry, 11, 62, 177–86, 261
Ionafal ap Meurig, 227 n. 40
Iorwerth ab Owain, 103, 215, 245
Iorwerth (d. 1111) ap Bleddyn, 97, 102, 229
Iorwerth Goch ap Maredudd, 34, 51, 70
Ireland, 8 n. 8, 11, 29, 50, 54, 56, 65, 67, 75, 82–3, 88, 98, 103, 112, 114, 117–19, 121, 146, 147, 154, 155 n. 73, 182, 208, 218, 223–4, 259, 260; Anglo-Normans in, 31–2, 62, 133, 139, 205, 224, 232–4, 236, 241; army sizes, 23; Church in war, 79, 251 n. 159, 255; horses, 160–1, 166, 167; *see also* Gerald of Wales, Gruffudd ap Cynan
iron production, 143–4

Joan (d. 1237), wife of Llywelyn ap Iorwerth, 240
John, king of England (d. 1216), 62, 102, 107–8, 122, 125, 140, 172, 192, 203, 231, 236
John of Hexham, 8
John of Worcester, 7, 50–1, 55, 61, 75, 99, 119, 169, 211, 220–1, 239, 250

Kidwelly, 79 n. 151; battle of (1136), 128; castle of, 128
knives, 155–6

lances, *see* spears
land grants, 45, 48–9, 71, 78, 83
law; law texts, 13, 70; military service, 68–9, 81–2, 169, 186–7; on horses, 160, 166, 172; on the *penceneдl*, 78; on the *penteulu*, 33, 35–6, 44; on the *teulu*, 26, 28, 37, 45–6; on weapons, 149, 150–1, 155, 156, 157, 175; social organization, 16, 75, 193; *see also* Hywel Dda
Leisan ap Morgan, 140
Leofgar, bishop of Hereford, 56–7
Leofric (earl of Mercia), 55, 57, 118
Leominster; battle of (1052), 56, 118; priory of, 258
Lewes, battle of (1264), 139–40
Liber Landavensis, 9, 18, 67, 248, 251–2, 255–6, 262
Lichfield, 115 n. 129, 253 n. 166; Lichfield Gospels, 17
Life of King Edward, 95
Lincoln, battle of (1141), 96, 136–8, 145, 154 n. 69, 158, 174
Llanbadarn Fawr, 80, 250 n. 155, 251–3, 256, 258
Llancarfan; charters, 28, 48
Llandaff, 9–10, 28, 76 n. 138, 80, 248 n. 141, 251–2; *see also Liber Landavensis*
Llanddewibrefi, 250 n. 155
Llandeilo, 135
Llandough, 170
Llandovery, castle of, 192, 203, 205, 206 n. 66, 212, 214, 215, 243, 246
Llandudoch, battle of (1091), 122
Llangadog, castle of, 212, 247 n. 135
Llangors, 25, 196, 237
Llangynwyd, castle of, 247 n. 136
Llanidloes, 60, 123
Llanrhystud, castle of, 213, 243
Llanstephan, castle of, 213, 245
Llantarnam, 236 n. 82
Llawhaden, castle of, 203
Llech-y-crau, battle of (1088), 121
Llongborth, battle of, 165
llu, 2, 39, 50–84, 102, 184, 186, 226, 260; duration and range of campaigns, 81–3; early Welsh armies, 63–6; later Welsh armies, 66–72; personnel, 72–5; role of *uchelwyr*, 75–9; service from the Church, 79–81; size of, 52–62; terminology, 52; *see also* muster
Lludd and Llevelys, 11
Llŷn, 58, 59, 60, 76–7, 98, 99, 206

Llywarch ap Llywelyn, 172
Llywarch Hen, 30, 40, 92, 145, 156, 180, 182 n. 239, 188, 194
Llywelyn ab Owain, 229
Llywelyn (d. 1077) ap Cadwgan, 120
Llywelyn (d. 1282) ap Gruffudd, 12, 24, 26, 32, 35, 38, 39 n. 126, 41, 43, 48, 51, 53 n. 21, 62, 71, 78, 81, 83, 111, 122, 135, 139, 140 n. 227, 147 n. 22, 174, 183 n. 243, 197, 206–7, 212, 214, 232, 235, 238, 247, 260
Llywelyn (d. 1240) ap Iorwerth, 33, 35, 43, 51, 53, 62, 75, 78, 83, 102, 103, 107–9, 122, 123–4, 126, 133–4, 154, 172, 174, 203–4, 205–6, 207, 212, 215–16, 217, 240, 241, 244–5, 246, 254–5, 258
Llywelyn (d. 1023) ap Seisyll, 95, 117, 183
logistics, 53, 74, 91, 107, 169, 171, 207, 216, 259
Louis VII, king of France (d. 1180), 51 n. 13, 61, 107 n. 101, 139, 236 n. 79
Louis IX, king of France (d. 1270), 139

Mabinogi, 11, 25, 50, 167, 168, 169, 172
mackwy, 29
Madog (d. 1140) ab Idnerth, 51, 61
Madog (d. 1236) ap Gruffudd Maelor, 33
Madog (d. 1160) ap Maredudd, 43 n. 154, 44, 51, 70, 94, 124–5, 136–8, 172, 173, 229
Madog ap Rhiddid, 102–3, 122–3, 124, 142, 168, 184, 228
Maelgwn ab Owain Gwynedd, 230 n. 54
Maelgwn ap Gruffudd (d. 1137) ap Rhys, 128
Maelgwn (d. 1231) ap Rhys, 35, 125, 133, 142, 155 n. 73, 203–4, 212, 221 n. 15, 231, 247, 257 n. 186
Maelgwn Gwynedd, 18, 30, 186–7, 197
Maelienydd, 258
maerdref, 84, 193, 206 n. 65

Maes Maen Cymro (battle of, 1118), 124, 126
Magnus Barefoot, king of Norway (d. 1103), 57, 102, 152 n. 60, 224, 250
mail, *see* armour
Maldon, battle of (991), 15, 150 n. 43, 152 n. 56
Man, Isle of, 60
Manawydan, 11, 20, 144
marchog, 160 n. 106, 170–1, 173–4, 178, 179
Maredudd (d. 1035), ab Edwin, 198
Maredudd (d. 999) ab Owain, 117, 227 n. 40
Maredudd (d. 1072) ab Owain ab Edwin, 119–20, 235
Maredudd (d. 1132) ap Bleddyn, 70, 105, 124, 152, 229, 240
Maredudd (d. 1212) ap Cynan, 43
Maredudd (d. 1069) ap Gruffudd, 119
Maredudd (d. 1155) ap Gruffudd, 213, 216
Maredudd (d. 1271) ap Rhys Gryg, 135
Maserfelth, battle of (643), 115
Math, 11, 33, 34, 40, 51, 52, 84, 167, 226
Mathrafal, 198
Matilda (d. 1167), 'Empress', daughter of Henry I, 97, 219 n. 6
Matthew Paris, 8, 62, 109–10, 175, 184, 237–8, 239, 241–2
Maximus, 9, 112
Mechain, battle of (1069), 119, 227
meddyg, 36
medical care, 35–6, 45–6; *see also meddyg*
Meigen, battle of (633), 50
Meilyr (d. 1081) ap Rhiwallon, 58, 121
Meirion Goch of Llŷn, 59, 77
Meirionnydd, 37, 67, 72, 73, 98, 99, 102, 122–3, 184, 244
mercenaries, 21, 29–32, 42, 50, 59, 61–2, 63, 74–5, 82–3, 101–2, 117–19, 121, 140; *see also ffranc*
Mercia, 25, 50, 54–5, 93, 114–17, 118–19, 192, 195, 196, 197, 253 n. 166
Merfyn Frych (d. 844) ap Gwriad, 67, 116

Merovingians, 18, 64, 69, 151; household forces, 14
Merwydd of Llŷn, 58, 76, 256
Meurig (d. 1055) ab Hywel, king of Glamorgan, 28
Meurig ab Idwal, 226
milites, 18, 24, 28, 66, 79
mines, 144, 212, 246
Mold, castle of, 245
Môn, *see* Anglesey
Monmouth, 131, 244; *see also* Geoffrey of Monmouth
Montgomery, 108, 174–5, 184, 216, 243, 254; treaty of (1267), 206
Morcar of Northumbria, 136
Morfran, 80, 244
Morgan (d. 1158) ab Owain, 136–8, 240
Morgan ap Caradog, 49
Morgan (d. 1136) ap Gruffudd, 128
Morgan (d. 1251) ap Rhys, 35
Mur Castell, 100, 104, 187 n. 264
muster, 36–7, 68–70, 83–4, 155, 178, 184
Mynydd Carn, battle of (1081), 25, 38–9, 59, 60, 77, 98, 118, 121, 126, 141–2, 149 n. 36, 151, 154 n. 67, 155, 171, 184, 185 n. 253, 227, 240 n. 101
Mynyddog Mwynfawr, 19, 23, 27, 30, 33, 40, 145

Narberth, castle of, 213, 215, 245 n. 124
Naval, 38, 54, 56, 58, 60, 101–2, 131; *see also* Vikings
Nest, 21, 24
Nevern, castle of, 214 n. 100, 231
Newcastle (Glamorgan), 49
Newcastle Emlyn, 235
nifer, 20–2, 31, 52
night fighting, 39, 114 n. 128, 125, 135, 140–2
Normans, *see* Anglo-Norman warfare
Northumbria, 50, 54–5, 65, 82, 93, 113–15, 136, 162, 192, 253, 255 n. 174

Offa of Mercia (d. 796), 93 n. 33, 115

Orderic Vitalis, 7–8, 96, 136–8, 209–10, 222–3, 228, 234, 239
Osric of Northumbria (d. 634), 93, 114, 192
Oswald of Northumbria (d. 643), 55, 114–15, 141 n. 228, 253 n. 166
Oswestry, 72, 115
Oswiu of Northumbria, 93, 115, 207 n. 70
Owain (d. 1105) ab Edwin, 101 n. 80, 124
Owain (d. 1116) ap Cadwgan, 21, 24, 37, 38, 45, 47–8, 73, 102–3, 104–6, 122–3, 142, 168, 184, 204, 228 n. 43, 235, 252
Owain (d. 1235) ap Gruffudd, 125, 142, 231 n. 59, 244
Owain (d. 1282) ap Gruffudd, 35, 62 n. 61, 83, 122, 140 n. 227, 232
Owain (d. 1172) ap Iorwerth, 236
Owain Cyfeiliog (d. 1197) ap Gruffudd, 30, 47, 51, 244
Owain Fychan (d. 1187) ap Madog, 40 n. 135, 244
Owain Glyndŵr, 79 n. 151, 209
Owain Gwynedd (d. 1170) ap Gruffudd, 44, 45 n. 164, 47 n. 176, 48, 51, 60, 61, 73, 83, 106–7, 117 n. 138, 122, 123, 124–5, 129–31, 146–7, 173, 185, 188–9, 202, 204–5, 217, 230, 231 n. 55, 244, 245, 257, 258
Owein, 11, 152, 186

Painscastle, 132–3, 212, 239 n. 90, 258
partible descent, 49
Patrick de Chaworth, 235
Pembroke, 215, 221 n. 15; castle of, 101 n. 75, 199, 201, 210–11
pencenedl, 78
Penda of Mercia (d. 654), 66, 93, 114–15, 207 n. 70
Pendinas, battle of, 169
Penllyn, 25, 40
penteulu, 32–7, 43, 44, 235 n. 76
Penweddig, 181 n. 235, 204
Peredur, 11, 156
Perfeddwlad, 107

Peryf ap Cedifor, 24, 46–7, 229
Pevensey, 191
Philip II, king of France (d. 1223), 61
Picts, 9, 91, 113, 160, 162, 166, 255 n. 174
Plas-yn-Dinas, 198
poisoned weapons, 225
Powys, 47, 50, 51, 55, 58, 61, 67, 70, 76, 82, 94, 98, 105–6, 114, 118, 120–1, 124, 127, 129, 132, 136, 171, 192, 195, 197, 198, 204, 206, 208, 228, 252 n. 161, 255, 256
Powys (place name), 196 n. 25
Prestatyn, castle of, 217
prison, 59, 77, 121, 228–9, 230 n. 54, 231, 234 n. 72, 235 n. 76
provisions, *see* logistics
Prydydd y Moch, 43
pueri, 14
Pwlldyfach, battle of (1042), 117
Pwllgwdig, battle of (1078), 38, 120
Pwyll, 11, 20, 25, 30, 41, 167, 168, 169, 176, 178

Radnor, 132
Ralf, earl of Hereford, 56, 82, 118, 169, 198 n. 33
ransom, *see* hostages
Ranulf de Poer, 131, 237, 239
Ranulf of Chester, 124–5, 129, 204
Ratlinghope, priory of, 258
ravaging, 45, 54, 89–111, 140, 141, 177, 191, 201, 219–23, 258, 260
Rhain, 95, 117, 183
Rhayader, castle of, 205, 231 n. 56
Rheged, 39, 65, 82, 92, 93, 180
Rhigyfarch, 152 n. 60, 216, 234, 249
rhingyll, 72, 84, 151
Rhiwallon (d. 1069) ap Cynfyn, 119
Rhodri (d. 1195) ab Owain Gwynedd, 24, 122, 230 n. 54
Rhodri (d. *c*.1315) ap Gruffudd, 232
Rhodri Mawr (d. 878) ap Merfyn, 55, 116, 194, 249, 250 n. 155
Rhos (Dyfed), 215, 221
Rhos (Gwynedd), 49, 60, 65 n. 59, 77, 102, 124, 231 n. 55
Rhuddlan, 57, 95, 116, 130, 193, 197, 210 n. 85, 217; battle of (796), 115; *see also* Robert of Rhuddlan
Rhufoniog, 124, 231 n. 55
Rhun ap Maelgwn Gwynedd, 143, 186, 187
Rhydderch (d. 1076) ap Caradog, 120
Rhyd-y-gors, 201, 203
Rhyd-y-groes, battle of (1039), 55, 118
Rhymney, river, battle of (1072), 120, 126
Rhys (d. 1078) ab Owain, 38, 120
Rhys (d. 1197) ap Gruffudd, the Lord Rhys of Deheubarth, 12, 35, 51, 53, 61 n. 58, 83, 87 n. 6, 106, 123, 132, 138, 147, 171–2, 174, 188, 203, 205, 206 n. 67, 207 n. 68, 210, 214 n. 100, 216–17, 230–1, 235, 241, 243 n. 117, 244, 257, 258
Rhys (d. 1212) ap Maelgwn, 236
Rhys (d. 1292) ap Maredudd, 207
Rhys (d. 1093) ap Tewdwr, 58–9, 99 n. 68, 118, 120–1, 126–7, 141–2, 200, 228, 235, 240 n. 101
Rhys Fychan (d. 1271) ap Rhys, 135, 192, 241, 246
Rhys Ieuanc (d. 1222) ap Gruffudd, 125, 133, 142, 212 n. 91, 214, 231 n. 59, 244, 246
Richard I, king of England (d. 1199), 62, 205, 214 n. 99, 218
Richard de Clare (d. 1136), 129 n. 186, 240
Richard Marshal, 103, 244
Richard of Devizes, 62
Richard Siward, 112 n. 124, 139
Robert Curthose, 61, 244 n. 123
Robert fitz Hamo, 27
Robert fitz Stephen, 62 n. 59, 153 n. 63, 241
Robert of Bellême, 97, 171, 210, 214 n. 99, 244 n. 123
Robert of Gloucester, 61, 97, 136–8, 156, 219 n. 6
Robert of Rhuddlan, 8, 58, 76, 97, 150 n. 46, 185, 197, 210 n. 85, 222–3, 234, 239
Roger de Clare, 235 n. 76

Roger Mortimer, 62, 132, 206, 235, 247
Roger of Howden, 8, 96, 132–3
Roger of Wendover, 8, 62, 134, 139, 184, 239, 245
Rome, 9, 64, 69, 145–6, 148, 159, 160, 163, 179, 186, 191, 209, 224, 247
Rouen, 96, 139, 140

St Cadog, 41, 167 n. 151; *Life of*, 9, 24, 25, 33, 69, 72, 74, 79, 143, 186
St Clears, 153 n. 62, 174
St Cybi, 34
St Davids, 11, 12, 58, 79 n. 152, 116, 117 n. 134, 249 n. 147, 250 n. 155, 256
St Dogmaels, *see* Llandudoch
St Germanus (of Auxerre), 18; *Life of*, 91, 186
St Gwynllyw, 27, 37, 41, 45, 72; *Life of*, 31, 84, 155
St Illtud, 27, 30, 33, 34; *Life of*, 60, 141, 175, 184
St Padarn, 34
St Tatheus, *Life of*, 24
St Wenefred, *Life of*, 28, 66
Sandwich, 119
Scotland, 11, 62, 155 n. 71, 168, 193, 200–1, 202–3, 218–19, 220, 223–4, 255 n. 174, 254, 260
seals, 148, 170
Seisyll (d. 1175) ap Dyfnwal, 236
Selyf of Powys, 114
Senghennydd, 168
serjeant, *see rhingyll*
shields, 143, 144, 150, 156–7, 168, 177, 191; *see also* shield walls
shield walls, 151, 156, 180–1, 183, 186–8, 261; *see also* field fortifications
ships, *see* naval
Shrewsbury, 7, 21, 99, 171; *see also* Hugh of Shrewsbury
siege warfare, 151, 177, 191, 207, 262; conduct, 242–7; mining, 212, 213, 246; siege castles, 210, 212–13; siege engines, 208, 210, 211–12, 213, 216; tactics, 207–17; *teulu* involvement, 39, 212; *see also* garrisons
Simon de Montfort, 139–40
slavery, 45, 71, 103, 222, 223–4, 262
slings, 154, 161, 165
smiths, 150; *see also* iron production
Snowdon, 99, 102, 104–5, 107, 110, 127
spears, 40, 72, 80, 139, 143, 148, 149–51, 155, 156, 161–5, 174, 176, 177, 180, 183–5
squires, 28–9, 170
Stamford Bridge, battle of (1066), 136
Standard, battle of (1138), 16
standards, 182, 185
Stephen Baucan, 135, 239 n. 97
Stephen, king of England (d. 1154), 61, 97, 129, 136–8, 140, 154 n. 69, 156, 189 n. 278, 204, 219 n. 6
stirrups, 162, 164, 166, 175
Strata Florida, 12, 235 n. 74, 236 n. 82
Strathclyde, 11, 136, 255 n. 174
supply, *see* logistics
Swansea, 128 n. 182, 183 n. 243; castle of, 207 n. 68, 215, 216 n. 107, 243
swords, 143, 144, 148–9, 150, 156, 161–5, 173, 174, 177, 184, 187

Tacitus, 14
taeog, 67, 68 n. 93, 71
Tafolwern, castle of, 123, 214
Taliesin, 39, 92, 93, 160, 161, 180, 192, 208
Tal-y-bont, castle of, 244
Tal-y-Moelfre, battle of (1157), 73–4, 131, 185, 239
Tegeingl, 28, 58, 66, 73, 101 n. 80, 125, 130, 217
Tenby, 19, 67, 73, 194, 214, 235
tents, 37, 106, 187
teulu, 2, 14–49, 50, 52, 55, 58, 59, 64, 66, 70, 72, 73, 74, 76, 78, 82, 84, 120–1, 136, 138, 142, 160 n. 106, 171, 178, 182–3, 184–5, 259; composition, 26–32 ; size of, 22–6, 52, 54, 57; special force operations,

39, 142, 212; terminology, 18–22; *see also penteulu*
Tinchebrai, battle of (1106), 15
torques, 39, 182
Tostig, 57, 95–6, 136, 170
Trahaearn (d. 1081) ap Caradog, 21, 25, 38–9, 58, 59, 76, 98, 120, 171, 227
Trahaearn Fychan (d. 1197), 237
tref, 16, 17, 35
Trefeglwys, church of, 256
triads, 10, 19–20, 32, 34, 39, 40, 50, 54, 65, 69, 84, 94, 145, 155, 160, 165, 167–8, 169, 182, 188
trumpets, *see* horns
tylwyth, 22, 31
Tywyn, 80, 244

Uchdryd ab Edwin, 21, 37, 38, 73, 98, 101 n. 80, 124, 184
uchelwyr, 16, 28, 49, 67, 70, 75–9, 84, 121, 140, 170, 178, 260
Urien of Rheged, 39, 82, 92, 93, 94, 160, 172, 180, 182 n. 239, 208 n. 72

Vegetius, 90, 111–12, 179 n. 218
Vikings, 31, 116, 146, 154–5, 194, 196, 208, 223–4, 249–50, 254, 255; ships, 54, 56–7, 59, 117, 119
villeins, *see* bondmen

Walter Clifford, 235
Walter Corbet, 258
Walter de Lacy, 96
Walter Map, 4, 7, 18, 37, 95, 97, 99, 168, 257–8

Welshpool, 118 n. 144, 212, 246
Whitland, 12
Wigmore, 235
William de Braose, 133, 236 n. 83, 237
William de Braose (the younger), 108 n. 107, 240, 241
William fitz Baldwin (d. 1096), 203
William fitz Gerald, 216
William fitz Osbern, 96
William Marshal (I), 15, 48, 244–5
William Marshal (II), 21, 62, 133–4, 239 n. 90, 245
William of Malmesbury, 8
William of Newburgh, 8, 96
William of Ypres, 137–8
William Rufus (II), king of England (d. 1100), 61, 96, 99–101, 122, 127, 243
William the Conqueror (I), king of England (d. 1087), 121, 127, 209, 234 n. 70, 240 n. 101
Winwaed, battle of (654), 66, 93, 115
Wiston, castle of, 245 n. 124
Wizo's castle, 214, 215, 216, 241 n. 104
Woodstock, treaty of (1247), 62 n. 61, 83, 140 n. 227

Ynegydd, battle of (873), 116
ynfydion, 45, 48, 103, 184–5
York, 114, 192
youths, 74, 131, 240
Ystradalwn, 125
Ystrad Meurig, castle of, 204, 212
Ystrad Peithyll, castle of, 215, 243
Ystrad Tywi, 25, 76, 125, 201, 205, 223